CORE PERL

ISBN 0-13-035181-4

90000

9 780130 351814

PRENTICE HALL PTR
CORE SERIES

Core MySQL, Atkinson

Core PHP Programming, 2/e, Atkinson

Core Python Programming, Chun

Core Java Media Framework, Decarmo

Core Jini, 2/e, * Edwards

Core Servlets and JavaServer Pages, * Hall

Core Web Programming, 2/e, * Hall/Brown

Core ColdFusion 5, Hewitt

Core Java 2, Vol I–Fundamentals, * Horstmann/Cornell

Core Java 2, Vol II–Advanced Features, * Horstmann/Cornell

Core JSP, Hougland & Tavistock

Core Perl, Lerner

Core CSS, Schengili-Roberts

Core C++: A Software Engineering Approach, Shtern

Core Java Web Server, Taylor & Kimmet

Core JFC, 2/e, Topley

Core Swing: Advanced Programming, Topley

Core Web3D, Walsh & Bourges-Sévenier

*Sun Microsystems Press titles

CORE PERL

Reuven Lerner

Prentice Hall PTR
Upper Saddle River, New Jersey 07458
www.phptr.com

Library of Congress Cataloging-in-Publication Data

Lerner, Reuven
  Core Perl / Reuven Lerner.
    p. cm.
  ISBN 0-13-035181-4
   1. Perl (Computer program language) I. Title.

QA76.73.P22 L47 2001
005.2′762--dc21   2001055192

Editorial/Production Supervision: Jan Schwartz
Acquisitions Editor: Greg Doench
Marketing Manager: Debby van Dijk
Manufacturing Manager: Alexis Heydt-Long
Buyer: Maura Zaldivar
Cover Design Director: Jerry Votta
Cover Design: Talar Boorujy
Art Director: Gail Cocker-Bogusz
Series Interior Design: Meg VanArsdale
Editorial Assistant: Brandt Kenna
Compositor: Lori Hughes

©2002 Prentice Hall PTR
Prentice-Hall, Inc.
Upper Saddle River, NJ 07458

Prentice Hall books are widely used by corporations and government agencies for training, marketing, and resale.

The publisher offers discounts on this book when ordered in bulk quantities.
For more information, contact: Corporate Sales Department, Phone: 800-382-3419;
Fax: 201-236-7141; Email: corpsales@prenhall.com; or write: Prentice Hall PTR,
Corp. Sales Dept., One Lake Street, Upper Saddle River, NJ 07458.

Printed in the United States of America
10 9 8 7 6 5 4 3 2 1

ISBN 0-13-035181-4

Pearson Education LTD.
Pearson Education Australia PTY, Limited
Pearson Education Singapore, Pte. Ltd.
Pearson Education North Asia Ltd.
Pearson Education Canada, Ltd.
Pearson Educación de Mexico, S.A. de C.V.
Pearson Education—Japan
Pearson Education Malaysia, Pte. Ltd.
Pearson Education, Upper Saddle River, New Jersey

To my parents

Contents

Preface

Perl has been my programming language of choice since early 1992, when I began work on my undergraduate thesis. Part of the work required that I put 10 years of campus newspaper archives on the Internet using a system known as WAIS (Wide Area Information System).

For this project, I bought two books: One described `sed` and `awk`, the traditional Unix text-processing languages. The second described Perl, which was then relatively new. It was obvious that Perl was more advanced than the other two options, and I began to write small- and medium-sized Perl programs to make the newspaper available online.

My affinity for Perl has increased significantly since my graduation from college. I depend on it for much of my consulting work, as well as many personal projects. The speed with which I can produce a working program, and the wealth of modules available on the Internet, makes Perl a great choice.

Perl has matured greatly since I first read about it. Modern versions support object-oriented programming, complex data structures, modular code, and excellent diagnostic error messages. Perl now runs on nearly every operating system and comes standard with many. Perl is particularly popular among Web site developers, but it can also be used to construct graphical user interfaces, database client programs, and network applications. The Perl community has grown along with the language, spawning scores of newsgroups, mailing lists, books, magazine articles, and Web sites.

If you are new to programming

Like other books in the Core series, *Core Perl* does not teach you how to program. It is meant to teach you enough about Perl syntax, functions, and idioms to begin writing intermediate and advanced programs. The numerous examples are often described in great detail so that you can incorporate them into your own programs. I have used drafts of this book in training my own employees, and have incorporated their feedback into the final product.

Structure of the book

This book is divided into three parts:

Perl basics. We examine Perl syntax, beginning with the different major data types (scalars, arrays, and hashes) and quickly moving onto references and complex data structures. We then discuss a number of built-in functions and variables, and how to use regular expressions to process text. This part of the book ends with chapters on subroutines, modules, and object-oriented syntax.

Using Perl. Perl has excellent facilities for working with files, networks, and relational databases. In this part of the book, we create programs that exercise all of these features, creating simple network clients and servers, parsing text, and using Perl's database interface (DBI). We also discuss ways to improve and fix our programs, including the "tainting" mechanism, various command-line flags and the built-in Perl debugger.

The World Wide Web. Perl is an excellent and popular choice for server-side Web programs. We begin by looking at CGI, an old but popular method for generating dynamic content. We also discuss HTTP cookies, HTML/Perl templates, and how to incorporate a relational database within a site. The final chapter describes the mod_perl module for Apache, ending with the Mason component-based Web publishing system.

What this book is not

Perl is a rich language, and it continues to grow daily. Consequently, no one book can hope to cover everything. Here are some topics that *Core Perl* does not discuss:

Tk and graphical user interfaces (GUIs). You can create GUIs with Perl using the cross-platform Tk toolkit. The programs in *Core Perl* use a command-line (text) interface, or are meant to be run as a server-side Web program.

Embedding Perl. It is possible to put Perl inside of a C or C++ program. This functionality is demonstrated best by mod_perl (see Chapter 17), but is also used by Oracle and other products. *Core Perl* does not discuss this subject, about which you can read in the perlembed manual page.

External linking with XS. XS allows Perl to use C-language libraries and forms the core of a number of important Perl modules, including DBI. We do not discuss XS in this book; see the standard perlxs and perlxstut manual pages if this subject interests you.

Compilation. Perl programs are traditionally compiled when they are invoked. The compiler turns a program into "opcodes," which are then interpreted and executed by Perl. Many programmers would like a true Perl compiler, which would produce standalone, precompiled programs. This goal is still somewhat far off, but the Perl compiler project continues at a steady pace. *Core Perl* does not discuss compilation, but you can read more on this subject in the documentation for the B module.

Threads. Perl grew up on Unix, which traditionally uses many processes. Modern operating systems allow for multiple threads of execution within a process, which is more efficient. Threading is still an experimental feature in Perl, and is not discussed in *Core Perl*. However, a tutorial on Perl threading is available in the online perlthrtut manual page.

Who am I?

Now that you know a bit about the book, let me tell you something about myself: I have been working as a networking and Internet consultant since 1995, when I moved from the United States to Israel. Since then, I have worked on a variety of projects, most of which involve server-side Web applications using a relational database. Since January 1996, I have written the monthly "At the Forge" column in *Linux Journal*, in which I explore Web-related technologies and programming techniques.

Before moving to Israel, I worked for Hewlett-Packard's Medical Products Group, connecting hospital devices to databases. I also worked for Time Inc.'s ill-fated Pathfinder Web site, helping such magazines as *Fortune*, *Money*, and *Sports Illustrated for Kids* produce their initial Web sites. At both jobs, I used Perl to solve a wide variety of problems, from analyzing error logs to storing personalization information in a database.

I also rely on Perl for personal projects. The GNU Emacs FAQ, which I edit, is maintained by a small set of Perl programs. The maintenance work that I do on a Web site and mailing list for residents of the Israeli city of Modi'in is largely done in Perl. And, of course, Perl played a major role in the production of this book, uploading new drafts to my editors and extracting program fragments from the manuscript.

Credits

My friends and family know that this book has taken a long time to write. Along the way, I have learned about writing and editing, about Perl and related technologies, and about programming languages in general. I have also learned much about the computer book publishing industry.

I would like to thank Greg Doench, the executive editor of the "Core" series at Prentice-Hall, for inviting me to write this book. Jim Markham, my development editor, provided useful advice and writing tips. Finally, Matt Wagner, my agent at Waterside Productions, taught me that it is always a good idea to have an agent when writing a book.

Most of *Core Perl* was written using free software, sometimes known as open-source software. I used the Linux operating system, the GNU Emacs editor (including its powerful "AUC-TeX" mode), the `ispell` spell checker, and the TeX and LaTeX formatters. The people who create, maintain, and document this software deserve our thanks for producing and distributing such high-quality products.

I would like to thank Larry Wall and the other people who spend so much of their time trying to improve Perl, its associated modules, and the volumes of free documentation that come with it.

I also want to thank the people who read over initial drafts of the book, noting mistakes, inconsistencies, poor examples, and other items that have (I hope!) disappeared over time. In particular, I want to extend my appreciation to Asaf Bartov, Stas Bekman, Ralph Birnbaum, Mark-Jason Dominus, Michael Faurot, D. Ben Gordon, Leonid Igolnik, Rouslan Krapkovsky, Gaal Yahas, and Omer Zak. I got particularly extensive comments from MySQL authors David Axmark and Michael "Monty" Widenius. Uri Guttman gave a good, methodical analysis of the book's first half, and Rob Kolstad commented on some of the middle chapters. And Kyle Hayes looked over every word of the rough draft, and gave extremely useful advice, even if I didn't always take it.

Simson L. Garfinkel, a friend whose work I greatly respect, deserves credit for convincing me not to give up, and for generally being supportive.

Thanks are due to my wife, Shira Friedman-Lerner. Her willingness to put up with the book during the entire time that we dated, got engaged, planned our wedding, bought an apartment, settled into our lives as a married couple, and planned for the birth of our daughter Atara Margalit testifies to the strength of the love between us. I appreciate her extreme patience, and look forward to being able to spend at least one day together without having to stress over the progress of "the book."

Finally, I would like to thank my parents, Rabbi Barry Dov and Barbara Lerner, my sister Shulamit, and my brother Avi, who have encouraged me at every step of the way. They might live thousands of miles away, but I feel their presence every day, and am grateful for the technologies that keep us close.

Corrections and updates

Despite my best efforts, there are undoubtedly still some errors in this book. Please send corrections to bugs@coreperl.com; I will post updates on the *Core Perl* Web site, at http://www.coreperl.com.

Typographical conventions

Like most computer books, *Core Perl* uses different typefaces to represent different types of information. This book was laid out using LaTeX, a system of macros based on Donald Knuth's TeXtypesetting system.

Aside from regular text, which is used in the majority of the book, *Core Perl* employs a number of typographical conventions:

- `Typewriter text` is used for code examples and other instances when characters must be typed literally. This font also represents variable and header values, text strings, and program names.

- San-serif text is used for the names of variables, methods, subroutines, packages, keywords, HTTP headers, and HTTP cookies.

- SMALL CAPS represent values that should not be typed literally, such as TRUE and FALSE, as well as keys on the keyboard, such as ENTER and ESC.

- *Italics* indicate a placeholder for a real value. For example, {*min*} means that you should enter a value in place of `min`, rather than the literal characters `min`.

One of the mantras of the Perl community is that programming should be fun. If this book makes it possible for you to work more efficiently and enjoyably, my mission will have been accomplished.

WHAT IS PERL?

Topics in This Chapter

- What is Perl?
- What are Perl's strengths and weaknesses?
- Perl's license and cost
- Getting support
- Retrieving and installing Perl
- CPAN and Perl modules

Chapter 1

Perl 1.000 was released by Larry Wall in December 1987. Since then, many thousands of people have programmed in Perl, writing everything from simple scripts for system administration to sophisticated end-user applications.

This chapter provides some background on Perl and tells you how to retrieve and install the latest version. By the end of this chapter, you should know Perl's history, understand the licenses under which it is distributed, and know how to get help if you need it. You will also know how to install and update Perl modules from CPAN, the Comprehensive Perl Archive Network.

1.1 What is Perl?

Perl is a high-level language, allowing programmers to concentrate on getting jobs done without getting bogged down with details. As Perl creator Larry Wall put it, "Easy things should be easy, and hard things should be possible." Many programmers prefer Perl because of the speed and ease with which they can write programs. Perl programs should never crash, and can be checked with the language's built-in debugger.

This book focuses on Unix versions of Perl, but most programs should run without modification on a variety of operating systems, including Apple Macintosh and Microsoft Windows. Read the `perlport` documentation (described in Section 1.6.2) for more information on this subject. The programs in this book were tested on a computer running Red Hat Linux 6.2.

It is theoretically possible to write any sort of program in Perl. However, the language has strengths that make it especially appropriate for certain applications:

Text. Perl handles text strings naturally and easily, thanks in part to powerful pattern-recognition features (see Chapter 5). Built-in operators for matching and substitution have made it into a favorite language of Unix system administrators (see Chapter 13) and people building text-processing systems. Perl is also popular among Web developers, who create and manipulate text files that are formatted in hypertext markup language (HTML) and extensible markup language (XML) every day.

Files. Perl makes it easy to open, read, and write files containing text and binary data (see Chapter 9). There are built-in functions for working with records containing fixed- and variable-length fields. Perl also supports many varieties of DBM files, such as Berkeley DB and GDBM (see Section 8.3.1).

Networks. Perl makes it easy to write clients and servers for TCP/IP networks (see Chapter 10). The IO::Socket module can create a client or server in just a few lines of code, and the libnet library contains even more functionality. In addition, Perl offers LWP (library for Web programming) for writing applications based on HTTP and FTP.

Memory management. Perl handles memory management issues, freeing you from worrying about memory leaks. As in Java and Lisp, unused memory is reclaimed automatically by Perl's garbage collector.

No pointers. Perl lacks pointers, removing many types of hard-to-trace crashes and problems. Perl does support references, allowing for complex data structures and the passing of subroutines as data (see Section 2.8).

Rapid application development. It usually takes less time to write a Perl program than a similar program in another language. This can be attributed to Perl's large function library, the number and variety of available modules, and the lack of type checking in Perl programs. Development takes less time, and the resulting code is often quite short.

Robustness. Perl programs should never crash. Moreover, Perl provides facilities for inspecting and trapping errors, including Unix signals.

The debugger. Perl includes a built-in debugger, which steps through programs and makes it possible to inspect them (see Section 13.4.2).

Learning Perl should not be difficult for someone with previous programming experience. Perl also lends itself to long-term study; you can begin writing practical Perl programs almost immediately, adding new functions to your vocabulary over time.

1.2   When not to use Perl

Perl is probably the wrong tool to use when program speed and size are the main concerns. Because Perl is written in C, a Perl program will never run faster than its C-language counterpart. At the same time, many projects unnecessarily stress execution speed, when programmer time and program maintainability are more serious issues. Consider your options before deciding that Perl is unsuitable for the job.

Perl lets programmers work quickly and efficiently. The trade-off, however, is that Perl can be a bit of a system hog. Then again, many of Perl's libraries and built-in functions have been finely tuned over the years, making them more efficient than most home-grown solutions.

Perl does not enforce type constraints, allowing you to use the same variable for strings, numbers, and objects. Moreover, Perl will never complain if you use a number instead of a string, or vice versa. If you want the safety of a strongly typed language, Perl is a poor choice.

Perl's objects are normally open, such that instance variables and methods can be inspected and modified by any other part of the program. This requires more programmer discipline than C++ and Java, which allow classes to hide data with `private` and `protected`.

Finally, Perl is not a good language for writing software with a source that must remain secret. Because programs are compiled at runtime, their source is also available. Intellectual property laws, rather than compiled binaries, prevent people from stealing Perl programs. There are ways to make Perl programs less easily accessible, but they are uncommon and clumsy.

1.3 The Perl license

Perl is distributed under both the GNU General Public License (GPL) and its own Artistic License. Both are open-source licenses, guaranteeing your freedom to inspect, modify, improve, and redistribute Perl. If you distribute a modified version of Perl, you may choose which of the two licenses applies to your redistributed version. Someone who pays for a copy of Perl is typically compensating the distributor for an Internet connection or CD manufacturing costs, rather than the language itself. Although it is theoretically possible to charge for Perl, its licenses and availability on the Internet make it an unlikely scenario.

The restrictions associated with the GNU GPL and the Artistic License apply to Perl itself, not to programs written in Perl. Your programs can be distributed under more restrictive or permissive licenses, as you see fit. Nevertheless, it is common for Perl programs to be released under one or both of Perl's licenses.

1.4 Perl versions and standardization

As of this writing, the latest production release of Perl is 5.6.1. If your computer runs an earlier version—and particularly if you're still using Perl 4—you should upgrade. Each new version of Perl fixes memory leaks, speed problems, and cross-platform incompatibilities, and adds new functionality. Perl's maintainers stress backward compatibility, so software written for earlier versions of Perl should continue to run unmodified even after you upgrade.

Larry Wall remains in charge of Perl development, although much of the work has been passed to members of the perl5-porters mailing list. The list serves as a central forum for bug reports and fixes, new feature requests, documentation updates, and future directions for Perl. One list member, designated the pumpking, coordinates the other developers' work, eventually deciding when to release a new version. There is no specified schedule for Perl releases; when enough functions and bug fixes have been bundled together, the release is announced and made available for download. There is currently an effort to specify and write Perl 6, but as of this writing that effort is still in its early stages.

There is no written Perl standard, other than Perl itself. That said, different versions are available for different platforms, and each may work slightly differently. If you find a problem of this sort, it is probably a bug, and you should report it with `perlbug` (see Section 1.6.2).

1.5 Perl support

Because Perl is developed and released by a loose confederation of developers, some companies and individuals refuse to use it. After all, where can they go for training and support? And who will get the blame if Perl stops working?

Perl's licenses disclaim any warranty in case anything should go wrong. But consider that Perl is maintained by the people who use it most heavily, giving them incentive to fix bugs quickly. Besides, Perl's open-source license means that you can fix bugs on your own, or hire someone to fix it for you. (If you have ever read software licenses, you know that commercial products similarly disclaim any responsibility, without giving you the freedom to fix bugs yourself.)

There is no central organization for Perl support. The notion of a "certified Perl programmer" is alien to the free-wheeling Perl community. However, many skilled consultants are available for hire to provide this sort of service. Such consultants train Perl programmers, answer questions, and fix bugs in the source code. It is not hard to find such consultants (indeed, the author of this book is one) by looking online, or through issues of *The Perl Journal*. Perl Mongers (http://www.pm.org) sponsors a "Perl jobs" mailing list, through which you may be able to find someone appropriate for your needs.

1.6 Retrieving and installing Perl

Perl is available from CPAN, a worldwide network of Web and FTP servers. If you have sufficient bandwidth and disk space, consider becoming a CPAN site, as described at http://www.cpan.org/. The following sections describe how to retrieve Perl from CPAN, compile it, and install it onto a Unix system from the source code.

If you are new to compiling large C programs, consider downloading a precompiled version of Perl from the Internet. For example, users of Red Hat Linux can install Perl from "RPMs." http://www.perl.com has pointers to binary versions of Perl for a number of platforms.

1.6.1   Compiling Perl for Unix

You can retrieve the current Perl distribution from any CPAN mirror, a list of which is at http://www.cpan.org. Perl is normally available as a file named `stable.tar.gz`, in the `src` directory.

CORE Note

Compiling and installing Perl from source means compiling C programs, which requires both make *and a C compiler. Be sure that you have both of these before starting.*

Much of Perl's build process is automatic, and should be relatively easy for even beginning programmers. However, it is more difficult to compile a program from source than to install a binary version, and Perl is no exception. You may want to consider getting help from an experienced system administrator before continuing.

After downloading `stable.tar.gz`, uncompress it with GNU `gunzip`, and open the resulting archive with `tar`:

```
gunzip --verbose stable.tar.gz
tar -xvf stable.tar
```

CORE Note

The Perl source code is quite large, and unpacking it will create many new files. Do not be surprised if the process takes several minutes.

You must now configure the source code for your particular platform. Enter the distribution directory (e.g., `perl-5.6.1`) with the `cd` command, and run `Configure`:

```
./Configure
```

`Configure` asks questions about your operating system and system configuration, preparing the source code accordingly. The defaults are usually right, so press ENTER if you are not sure.

An alternative to `Configure` is `configure.gnu`, the automatic configuration program. This program tries to guess the right answers to your system's configuration, and thus saves you from having to answer the questions yourself:

```
./configure.gnu
```

CORE Note

Configure *begins with a capital C, whereas* `configure.gnu` *begins with a lowercase* c.

When configuration is complete, compile Perl:

```
make
```

The compilation process can take up to 30 minutes on older computers, so don't be alarmed if you end up waiting a while. Once you have compiled Perl, test it using the included validation suite:

```
make test
```

If it passes the tests, you may install your new copy of Perl. On most Unix systems, you will need to be logged in as **root** to install it in the default directory.

```
make install
```

1.6.2   What comes with Perl?

Perl comes with many programs and files:

perl The Perl compiler, interpreter, and debugger is a program called `perl`. This book assumes that Perl is installed in `/usr/bin/perl`. By default, `Configure` installs Perl in `/usr/local/bin/perl`, with a symbolic link from `/usr/bin/perl`.

perlbug `perlbug` produces and sends bug reports about the main Perl distribution.

If you configured, compiled, and installed Perl on your own, and if you are confident that the behavior you saw was a bug, report it with `perlbug`. Your report will be sent to the perl5-porters, who will look into the problem. Don't be shy; without bug reports, problems may go unrepaired for a long time.

If you find a bug in a prepackaged (i.e., binary) Perl distribution, send a problem report to the maintainer of that distribution, rather than using `perlbug`.

perldoc `perldoc` is the Perl documentation reader, displaying text formatted in Perl's POD (plain old documentation) format (see Section 6.5). Perl comes with extensive online documentation, including many sample programs, tutorials, and caveats. The included documentation covers every part of Perl, including interprocess communication (`perlipc`), regular expressions (`perlre`), object-oriented programming techniques (`perlobj`), debugging (`perldebug`), and embedding Perl inside of other programs (`perlembed`). For a complete list, type `perldoc perl`. The documentation includes many example programs, as well.

For example, you can read about Perl's regular expressions (see Chapter 5) with:

```
perldoc perlre
```

`perldoc`'s -f flag displays documentation for a single built-in function. For example, you can read about the **split** function:

```
perldoc -f split
```

CORE Note

perldoc −f *only works with built-in functions, not with operators (such as* eq) *or anything defined in a module. If you don't find the documentation using* perldoc −f, *consider checking* perldoc perlop *or the documentation for the appropriate module.*

Perl FAQ The list of frequently asked questions (FAQ) about Perl has been distributed on Usenet for many years, and has grown considerably over time. The FAQ, which comes with extensive answers, is included in the Perl distribution, and can be read with `perldoc`:

```
perldoc perlfaq
```

Reading the FAQ is a good way to improve your Perl skills. Before posting a question to Usenet or a mailing list, look for your question in the FAQ.

Standard Perl modules One of Perl's greatest strengths is the large number of available modules. Modules are distributed via CPAN, but the Perl distribution comes with the "standard" modules that everyone should have. These include CGI (for writing CGI programs), IO::File (for working with files, as described in Section 9.3.6), and File::Copy (for copying files).

The central Perl maintainers try to keep the number of standard modules to a minimum, since so many are updated regularly. See Section 1.7 to learn how to install new modules and update existing ones.

Each Perl module comes with its own documentation. Such documentation is available via `perldoc`. For example, the following displays documentation about IO::Filehandle:

```
perldoc IO::Filehandle
```

Miscellaneous Perl comes with a number of files that defy categorization. It comes with `cperl.el`, an Emacs Lisp mode that makes it especially easy to write Perl using the GNU Emacs editor. It comes with some example programs that demonstrate basic operations, and it also comes with a set of utilities for creating modules and documentation.

1.7   Retrieving modules from CPAN

Much of Perl's power is in its modules. Thousands of modules, available at no cost from CPAN, implement a wide variety of functionality. Before beginning to write your own modules (see Chapter 6), you should understand how to install and upgrade modules from CPAN. Modules are updated on a regular basis, often between Perl version updates, and are a good way to add functionality to your system.

CORE Note

Users of ActiveState's ActivePerl package can install modules using the PPM program. Not everything that is available on CPAN is also availble via PPM.

1.7.1   *Manual installation of Perl modules*

The traditional way to install or update modules is to download a file via FTP from CPAN. Although `ftp.cpan.org` is almost always available, try to use a CPAN mirror closer to you. This reduces the load on `ftp.cpan.org` and will probably result in faster download times.

You can retrieve modules from CPAN by module name, by category, or by the author's unique ID. To try these different views of the module archive, look at the `modules` directory on a CPAN mirror. This directory contains three subdirectories, `by-authors`, `by-category`, and `by-module`. If you know exactly what you want, then `by-module` is probably the easiest way to retrieve it, since it places the modules in directories according to their names. If you are searching for a module for a particular task, then `by-category` might be the best approach.

CORE Note

Installing modules requires the make *command, and sometimes requires a C compiler. You can download both of these from the Free Software Foundation, at* http://www.gnu.org/.

After retrieving a module, you can normally install or update it in the following way:

Unpack the module If the module comes in a file called `Module-1.23.tar.gz`, unpack it using GNU `gzip` and `tar`:

```
gunzip Module-1.23.tar.gz     # Uncompress the module archive
tar -xvf Module-1.23.tar      # Extract file verbosely
```

Create the Makefile `tar` will unpack the module into an appropriately named directory, such as `Module-1.23`. `cd` into that directory name and configure the module for your system:

```
cd Module-1.23    # Switch into the module's directory
perl Makefile.PL  # Use Perl to create a Makefile
```

This step requires that Perl already be running on your system.

Build the module Now build the module and any files it might need:

```
make
```

CORE Note

Many modules use functionality in other modules, and thus will not install correctly unless the other module exists and is installed. Pay close attention to any error messages you see.

Test the module Check that the module works, using the included test suite:

```
make test
```

If the module fails one or more tests, check to see why this happened. Many modules come with a README file that describes the module and common installation pitfalls. If you cannot fix the problem even after consulting the documentation and searching the Web, contact the module's author. Describe the error as fully as possible, so that the author can fix the bug and help others.

Install the module If the module passed the test suite, install it. You will probably need to be logged in as root to perform this final step:

```
make install
```

If the installation is successful, the module will be available to any Perl program on the system.

1.7.2 Easier installation of Perl modules

The CPAN module, included with the standard Perl distribution, handles much of the download and installation process automatically. It also tracks module versions, only suggesting that you upgrade modules as needed.

To use CPAN, log in as a user (normally root) with permission to modify the Perl installation. Once you have done so, enter the following:

```
perl -MCPAN -e 'shell'
```

The first time that you use CPAN, you will be asked to describe your system's configuration. Perl often guesses the correct values for program locations, but double-check them before blindly pressing ENTER.

You will then have to choose a CPAN mirror close to you, selecting a continent, a country, and then a mirror within that country. If you choose more than one CPAN mirror, CPAN will try them in order until one succeeds.

Once CPAN is configured, you can install a module by typing `install` followed by the module's name:

```
cpan> install Module
```

This downloads the module from CPAN, unpacks it, and runs `make`, `make test`, and `make install`. The module does not get installed if it fails any test, although you can override this by typing `force install Module`.

The most useful feature of CPAN is its ability to search through the current list of available modules. To search for a text string in the list of module names, use the `i` command, which ignores case when searching. For instance, the following command displays all modules containing the string `real`:

```
cpan> i /real/
```

The `r` command (which takes no arguments) lists the modules that are currently installed on your system for which upgrades are available.

1.8   Conclusion

In this chapter, we briefly looked at Perl's history, its licenses, and its strengths and weaknesses. We also saw how to install Perl from the source code, and how to retrieve modules from CPAN.

In the next chapter, we will begin to write our own programs, and explore the different types of data structures Perl offers.

GETTING STARTED

Topics in This Chapter

- Turning a file of Perl code into a working Perl program

- Statements and blocks

- Variables: Scalars, arrays, and hashes

- References

- Creating complex data structures with references

- Lexical and global variables

Chapter 2

In this chapter, we begin to write short, working Perl programs, beginning with simple statements, blocks, and built-in functions. We spend a significant amount of time looking at Perl's different types of variables (scalars, arrays, and hashes).

The key to defining complex data structures in Perl is the reference, which is similar to a pointer. We look at references from a number of perspectives and explore how they can be used in programs.

Finally, we look at lexical and global variable scopes. The differences between these scopes are easy to understand, but can be tricky when put into practice.

By the end of this chapter, you should feel comfortable writing and executing small Perl programs, creating complex data structures, and thinking about things in the high-level way that Perl encourages.

2.1   Basic programs

Type the following at your computer's shell prompt and press ENTER:

```
perl -e 'print "The Eagle has landed!\n"'
```

The following should appear on your screen:

```
The Eagle has landed!
```

Congratulations! You have executed a simple program that demonstrates some of the basic concepts behind Perl.

If the above one-liner does not work, and if you have entered it exactly as written, check that Perl is installed (see Section 1.6). It is also possible that Perl was installed in a directory not mentioned in your PATH environment variable, which tells the operating system where to look for programs. You can always invoke `perl` with an explicit path name, as in:

```
/usr/bin/perl -e 'print "The Eagle has landed!\n"'
```

The -e command-line switch tells `perl` to execute the program between the ' marks. Your choice of shell (e.g., `csh` vs. `bash` vs. `zsh`) may well influence what types of quotation marks you use with -e.

The test program displays a message on the user's screen with `print`. The message concludes with a NEWLINE character, represented by \n.

If a program is longer than one line, it is usually easier to save it in a file. Create a file named `myprog.pl` consisting of our one-line program:

```
print "The Eagle has landed!\n";
```

You can now execute that program as follows:

```
perl myprog.pl
```

On Unix systems, a text file containing a program can invoke Perl by itself. To do this, begin the file with the hash-bang (or shebang) characters, # and !, followed by the full path name of `perl`. `myprog.pl` can thus be rewritten as:

```
#!/usr/bin/perl
print "The Eagle has landed!\n";
```

After making the program executable with `chmod u+x myprog.pl` (see Section 9.6), run `myprog.pl`:

```
./myprog.pl
```

CORE Note

Without the first (#!) line, most Unix systems will think that `myprog.pl`
*contains shell commands. In such a case, the system will display one or
more "command not found" errors, as the Unix shell tries to execute a
Unix program named* `print`.

2.2 Compiler or interpreter?

Beginning Perl programmers often ask whether Perl is a compiler or an
interpreter. The answer is that it's both.

`perl` first compiles your program into internal *opcodes*. During this compilation phase, Perl checks the program's basic syntax, performs a few sanity
tests, and produces warnings whenever it can. The Perl compiler also attempts to optimize your program as best as possible.

Once the program is compiled, the Perl interpreter takes over, executing
each of the opcodes. This is known as the *runtime* or *execution* stage. Any
errors that you might see at this point are thus considered runtime errors.

Perl's compilation phase normally takes place each time a program is
invoked. Luckily, the Perl compiler is extremely fast; you should not have
to wait long for your program to compile before it executes. Indeed, Perl's
compiler works so quickly that many beginning programmers think that the
language is only interpreted.

As we continue in our exploration of Perl, it is important to remember
the distinction between these two phases. Because Perl is so flexible, it is
possible to execute code during the compilation phase, or to compile and
execute new code during the runtime phase. This does not remove the
distinction, however. Rather, it means that we must pay close attention to
the warning and error messages that Perl gives us to determine their source.

To activate many of Perl's optional (but extremely useful) warnings, add
the line use warnings at the beginning of your program. For example:

```
#!/usr/bin/perl

use warnings;

print "The Eagle has landed!\n";
```

Because this program does not do anything suspicious or problematic, Perl does not produce any warnings when you run it.

CORE Note

Before version 5.6, use warnings *was activated with the* -w *flag. This still works, but is less flexible than* use warnings.

CORE Debugging

Activate use warnings *on all of your Perl programs, particularly during development. It will help you to find and remove problems.*

2.3   Statements and blocks

Perl programs are built from statements and blocks. A Perl *statement* is similar to an English-language sentence, and a *block* is similar to a paragraph.

2.3.1   Statements

The simplest Perl statement is empty, consisting of a trailing semicolon:

```
;
```

A statement can also be a single constant value, concluded by a semicolon:

```
"gazpacho";
```

The constant can be a number, rather than a string:

```
5;
```

A more useful statement assigns a value to a variable:

```
$color = 'blue';
```

The preceding line of code assigns the string **blue** to the global variable $color. The statement ends, as expected, with a semicolon.

Statements can contain arbitrary amounts of whitespace, which lets you break long statements across multiple lines. We can thus rewrite the preceding statement:

```
   $color         =
'blue'        ;
```

Comments, which are ignored by Perl but crucial to program maintenance, begin with a hash character (#) and extend to the end of the line.
For example:

```
$color = 'blue';     # Assign $color
```

An old rule is that comments should focus on *why*, rather than *what*. The
code should be clear enough to indicate what is happening; the comments
should indicate why you want to perform the task in question.

2.3.2   Blocks

A block is a collection of statements, placed between curly braces ({ and }).
The following is a simple block:

```
{
    print "Hello\n";
}
```

Blocks can consist of an arbitrary number of statements or blocks. You
can create a new block whenever you want. The following is thus legal, if a
bit strange:

```
{
    print "Big\n";
    {
        print "Bigger\n";
        {
            print "Biggest\n";
        }
    }
}
```

2.4   Variables

The C, C++, and Java compilers must know in advance which variables will
contain integers, which will contain strings, and which will contain floats.
In each of these languages, the type of a variable does not change until the

program exits. Even if a Java **String** only contains numeric digits, it cannot be used directly in calculations.

By contrast, Perl does not care what kind of data a variable contains. Use a variable to store whatever value you want, and Perl will do its best to handle it appropriately.

Perl's data types (scalars, arrays, and hashes), describe the way in which your data is organized, rather than what you are storing. Scalars contain a single value, arrays contain multiple scalars, and hashes contain pairs of scalars.

You can easily identify a variable's type by the symbol that comes before its name: Scalars begin with $, arrays begin with @, and hashes begin with %. This looks messy and confusing at first, but quickly becomes second nature.

2.4.1   Variable names

Variable names may contain any number of letters, numbers, and underscores (_), so long as they begin with a letter or underscore. Capitalization counts, so the variable $value is different from $Value, which in turn is different from $VALUE. In addition, a program can simultaneously work with a scalar $var, an array @var, and a hash %var.

Take advantage of Perl's willingness to allow long variable names. Rather than calling something $x or $i, describe it for what it is, such as $monthly_payment, $successfully_retrieved, or @incoming_messages. Appropriate use of long variable names can make programs much easier to understand.

The `perldata` documentation that comes with Perl contains a wealth of information about Perl's data types.

2.5   Scalars

A scalar contains a single value, such as a string, an integer, or a float. Examples of scalars are $variable, $this_is_a_scalar, and $a1.

If a scalar contains a number (or a string that begins with numeric digits), it can be used in calculations:

```
$scalar = 5;
print $scalar * $scalar;
```

This code assigns the value 5 to $scalar using =. Any previous value in $scalar is lost once the assignment is made.

When we assign a value to a scalar, we assign a type—integer, float, or string—along with it. Assigning '5' is thus different from assigning 5. (See Sections 2.5.4 and 3.4 for two examples of where this can bite you.) Perl automatically converts from the stored type to the needed type as necessary, allowing us to use integers as if they were strings or strings as if they were numbers. If a scalar contains a mixture of numbers and non-numbers, everything until the first non-digit is considered a number.

With warnings active, Perl will tell you if a scalar containing non-numeric characters is used in a mathematical context:

```perl
#!/usr/bin/perl

use warnings;

$scalar = "5a";
print $scalar * $scalar, "\n"; # prints 25, with a warning

$scalar = "a5";
print $scalar * $scalar, "\n"; # prints 0, with a warning

$scalar = "5a6b";
print $scalar * $scalar, "\n"; # prints 25, with a warning
```

To make numbers more legible, place an underscore (_) where you would normally put a comma (or period, as is the custom in some European countries):

```perl
1_234_567_890  # To Perl, the same as 1234567890
```

2.5.1 Using scalars

The following Perl program, scalar-assignment.pl, assigns and prints scalar values:

```perl
#!/usr/bin/perl
# filename: scalar-assignment.pl

use warnings;
```

```
$value = "one";              # Set $value to a string
print $value, "\n";          # Prints "one" and newline

$value = 1;                  # Set $value to an integer
print $value, "\n";          # Prints "1" and newline

$value = "a";                # Set $value to a string
print $value, "\n";          # Prints "a" and newline

$value = 1.2345;             # Set $value to a float
print $value, "\n";          # Prints "1.2345" and newline
```

`scalar-assignment.pl` produces the following output:

```
one
1
a
1.2345
```

This code demonstrates that print can take multiple arguments, separated by commas. Each invocation of print in `scalar-assignment.pl` has two arguments, the second one of which is NEWLINE, \n.

2.5.2   Working with scalars

Perl lets us move easily between the world of strings and the world of numbers. If we type:

```
perl -e '$x=1; $y=2; print $x+$y, "\n";'
```

Perl prints 3, which we might expect.

We can treat $x and $y as strings, rather than numbers, by replacing the + with the concatenation operator (.):

```
perl -e '$x=1; $y=2; print $x.$y, "\n";'
```

Perl treats $x and $y as strings, printing 12.

Perl's scalars grow and shrink as necessary, and have no maximum length. Perl's limits are imposed by your computer's memory, not by the language.

2.5.3 Simple variable interpolation

Inside of double quotation marks (""), variable names are replaced by their values via *interpolation*. For example:

```perl
#!/usr/bin/perl

use warnings;

# Get a random integer between 0 and 1,000
$raise = int rand 1000;

# Be the bearer of bad tidings
print "Uur sophisticated numerical techniques indicate\n";
print "that you should receive a raise of $raise dollars.\n";
```

This program uses the built-in **rand** function to get a random float ranging from 0 to 1,000 (not including 1,000 itself). We remove the non-integer portion with the built-in **int** function, and assign the resulting integer to $raise. Executing the program on my computer produces the following output:

```
Our sophisticated numerical techniques indicate
that you should receive a raise of 416 dollars.
```

Any legal variable name following $ is assumed to be a scalar, and is interpolated into a double-quoted string. If the variable does not exist, Perl creates it on the spot, and assigns it the undefined value, **undef** (see Section 2.5.9). This feature can come in handy, but it can also cause unexpected problems when you change or mistype a variable's name. **use warnings** will tell you when you inadvertently use a previously undefined variable.

If a $ is meant to be printed literally, you can escape it by preceding it with a backslash (\):

```perl
#!/usr/bin/perl

use warnings;

print "Our program uses \$foo as a variable.\n";
```

Similarly, escape double quotation marks by escaping them with a backslash:

```
print "This is \"in quotes\".";
```

Single quotation marks (') are similar to double quotation marks, except that no variable interpolation takes place. Everything is taken literally, except for \ and '. To insert ' into a single-quoted string, use \'. To insert \, use \\.

You can avoid \ entirely with the general-purpose single-quote operator, q. A similar qq operator exists for generalized double quotes. The first character following either q or qq becomes the delimiter, rather than ' or ":

```
$string1 = q|hello, $foo|;   # same as 'hello, $foo'
$string2 = qq|hello, $foo|;  # same as "hello, $foo"
```

Perl strings can contain any characters, including NEWLINE, control characters, and other unprintables:

```
# Contains two newlines and no interpolated variables
$single_quoted = q#hello,
$foo\n#;

# Contains one newline and one interpolated variable
$double_quoted = qq!hello $foo!;
```

If the opening delimiter is {, <, (, or [, then its matching closing delimiter closes the string:

```
$string1 = q{$foo};   # literal $foo, same as '$foo'
$string2 = qq<$foo>;  # value of $foo, same as "$foo"
```

CORE Approach

qq is particularly useful in Web applications, which have output that requires both interpolation and double quotes:

```
print qq{<input type="text" name="$foo">\n};
```

2.5.4 Octal numbers

Perl assumes that any number beginning with a 0 is in base 8, known as *octal*. You can assign an octal value as easily as a decimal one:

```
$number = 01234;     # Assigns decimal 668
```

Perl always displays numbers using decimal:

```
$dec = 72;
print "72 dec = $dec dec\n";

$oct = 072;
print "72 oct = $oct dec\n";
```

Perl exits with a compilation error if it detects a non-octal digit in an octal number:

```
$dec = 78;
print "78 dec = $dec dec\n";

$oct = 078;
print "78 oct = $oct dec\n";
```

The assignment to $oct results in a fatal "illegal octal digit" compilation error.

Any scalar value can be treated as if it were an octal number with the oct function:

```
print oct(123), "\n";     # Same as 0123, prints 83

$input = "500";
print oct($input), "\n"; # Same as 0500, prints 320

$input = 583;
print oct($input), "\n"; # Same as 0583, prints 5
```

oct produces a warning (but does not exit with a fatal error) when its argument contains a non-octal digit.

CORE Note

When Perl treats a string as a number, it uses base 10 regardless of any leading 0. So 0123 is an octal number, but "0123" is not. Use oct *when the input is a decimal number or a string, to treat it as an octal without the leading 0. But don't use* oct *on an octal number with a leading 0, because the argument will first be turned into a decimal number—and you may be surprised by the confusing results:*

```
print 0123 * 1, "\n";        # prints 83
print '0123' * 1, "\n";      # prints 123
print "0123" * 1, "\n";      # prints 123
print oct("0123") * 1, "\n"; # prints 83
print oct(0123) * 1, "\n";   # prints 0; same as oct(83)
print oct(123) * 1, "\n";    # prints 83
```

2.5.5   Hexadecimal numbers

Hexadecimal numbers have digits ranging from 0 to 9, and then A to F (capital or lowercase). Here is how to count from 0 to 17 in hexadecimal:

```
0, 1, 2, 3, 4, 5, 6, 7, 8, 9, A, B, C, D, E, F, 10, 11
```

Each digit represents a power of 16, so hex 123 is $3 \times 16^0 + 2 \times 16^1 + 1 \times 16^2$, or $3 + 32 + 256 = 291$ decimal.

Perl treats any number as hexadecimal if it begins with 0x or 0X:

```
print 0x123, "\n";  # prints 291
print 0XAB5, "\n";  # prints 2741
```

To treat an arbitrary scalar as a hexadecimal number, use hex:

```
$hex1 = hex(123);        # 291
$hex2 = 0x123;           # 291, in a different way
print "hex1 = $hex1, hex2 = $hex2\n";
```

2.5.6   Math operators

Perl does not force programmers to choose between integers and floats. It automatically switches into floating-point mode if one or more arguments is a non-integer, or if we divide one integer by another.

Basic arithmetic The four basic mathematical operators are + (addition), - (subtraction), * (multiplication), and / (division). These operators have the precedence that you might expect: Expressions are evaluated from left to right, with multiplication and division performed before addition and subtraction. Parentheses can change the default order of operations (see Section 3.7). For example:

```
$arg1 = 3;
$arg2 = 8.2;
$sum = $arg1 + $arg2;
$difference = $arg2 - $arg1;
$product = $arg1 * $arg2;
$quotient = $arg1 / $arg2;
```

All of these operators can be combined with =, as in C. For example:

```
$account_balance = $account_balance - $taxes;
```

That line could be rewritten as follows:

```
$account_balance -= $taxes;
```

The empty string "" is equivalent to 0 when evaluated as a number.

The remainder from a division operation is known as the *modulus*, and can be retrieved with %:

```
print 10 % 2, "\n";      # prints 0
print 10 % 3, "\n";      # prints 1
```

% is useful when determining if one number is divisible by another number:

```
print "You're even!\n" if ($number %2 == 0);
```

See Section 3.4.2 for information about postfix conditionals.

** performs exponentiation. The first argument is the base, and the second is the exponent. For example, the following line of code prints 2^3:

```
print 2**3, "\n";  # Prints 2 cubed
```

Use log to get natural logarithms (i.e., using base e) and exp to perform exponentiation:

```
perl -e 'print log 1000, "\n";'            # Prints 6.90775527898214
perl -e 'print exp 6.90775527898214, "\n";' # Prints 1000
```

Scientific notation

Perl uses scientific notation for very large and small numbers. For example:

```
perl -e 'print 2**60, "\n";' # Prints 1.15292150460685e+18
```

You can also use scientific notation as input:

```
$val1 = "1.12589990684262e+15";
$val2 = $val1;
print $val1 * $val2, "\n";   # 2**50 * 2**50 = 2**100
```

Negation

Unary minus negates a number:

```
$arg = 1234;

$arg = -$arg;               # Flip it once
print "arg = '$arg'\n";     # Print the result

$arg = -$arg;               # Flip it again
print "arg = '$arg'\n";     # Print the original number
```

Exponentiation binds more tightly than unary minus:

```
#!/usr/bin/perl

use warnings;

$answer = -2**10;    # -1024; same as -(2**10)
print $answer, "\n";
```

Change the priority with parentheses:

```
#!/usr/bin/perl

use warnings;

$answer = (-2)**10; # 1024
print $answer, "\n";
```

abs returns a number's absolute value:

```
$price = -5.35;
print abs $price, "\n";     # Prints 5.35
```

Trigonometric operators

Perl comes with a number of trigonometric operators. These operate in radians, where 2π radians $= 360°$.

sin returns the sine of its argument. The following prints the sine of $45°$ ($\pi/4$ radians):

```perl
$pi = 3.1415927;  # An approximation, of course
$degrees = 45;
$sine = sin ($degrees / ($pi * 2));
print "Sine = $sine\n";
```

cos similarly returns the cosine. To find the tangent, divide the sine by the cosine:

```perl
$tan = $sin / $cos;
```

Section 6.4.1 describes Math::Trig, a module that provides a tan subroutine.

Integers and floats

As we saw earlier, int removes the floating-point part of a number:

```perl
$random_number = rand 100;        # Get a random float
$random_int = int $random_number; # Remove the non-integer part
print $random_int, "\n";
```

We can combine these into a single line of code:

```perl
$random_int = int rand 100;
print $random_int, "\n";
```

You can get the non-integral part of a number by subtracting its integer portion:

```perl
#!/usr/bin/perl

use warnings;

$random_num = rand 100;
$random_int = int $random_num;
$random_frac = $random_num - $random_int;
print $random_frac, "\n";
```

2.5.7   Auto-increment and auto-decrement

Perl allows for auto-increment and auto-decrement, as in C. This is done by putting ++ or -- before or after a variable name. If ++ or -- is placed before the variable name, the value is changed before the expression is evaluated. If ++ or -- is placed after the variable name, the value is changed after the expression is evaluated. For instance:

```
# Auto-increment
$new = $old++;  # Same as $new = $old; $old = $old + 1;
$new = ++$old;  # Same as $old = $old + 1; $new = $old;

# Auto-decrement
$new = $old--;  # Same as $new = $old; $old = $old - 1;
$new = --$old;  # Same as $old = $old - 1; $new = $old;
```

Perl can also auto-increment strings:

```
$string = "a";  $string++; print "$string\n";  # Sets $string to "b"
$string = "Z";  $string++; print "$string\n";  # Sets $string to "AA"
$string = "z";  $string++; print "$string\n";  # Sets $string to "aa"
$string = "z9"; $string++; print "$string\n";  # Sets $string to "aa0"
```

CORE Note

Auto-decrement does not work with strings.

2.5.8   Special characters

NEWLINE is represented by \n inside of double quotes. Other special characters have similar nicknames (see Table 2.1).

These characters are interpolated into double-quoted strings (see Section 2.5.3). They are treated literally in single-quoted strings, meaning that \n will be treated as two literal characters.

```
#!/usr/bin/perl

use warnings;

print 'foo\n', "\n";    # Prints literal 'foo\n', then newline
```

Table 2.1	Nicknames for Special Characters

Character	Description
\a	Alarm bell (CONTROL-G)
\c$x$	Control character (CONTROL-x)
\e	ESCAPE (CONTROL-[)
\f	Form feed (CONTROL-L)
\n	NEWLINE (CONTROL-J)
\r	Carriage return (CONTROL-M)
\t	TAB (CONTROL-I)
\xxx	Character with octal ASCII code xxx
\x$xx$	Character with hex code xx

2.5.9 undef

Perl automatically creates variables as they are mentioned. These variables are given a value of undef by default, indicating that they contain no value.

undef is not the same as the empty string or 0. However, if Perl is forced to use an undefined value in an expression, it will provide either the empty string or 0, as appropriate:

```
#!/usr/bin/perl

use warnings;

print "Undefined value is '$undefined'.\n";
print "undefined * 5 = ", $undefined * 5, "\n";
```

use warnings tells us when we try to use an undefined value, but does not stop us from doing so.

To undefine an existing variable, use undef as a function:

```
undef $foo;
```

2.6 Lists and arrays

Perl allows us to group together scalars in a *list*, and to store a list value in an *array*. Just as scalar variable names begin with $, array variable names begin with @. $foo and @foo are unrelated, and both can be used in a program.

2.6.1 Creating arrays

List values are always surrounded by parentheses. The simplest array contains a list with no elements, which is thus depicted as an empty set of parentheses:

```
@the_empty_array = ();
```

We can assign elements by putting a comma-separated list of scalars between the parentheses:

```
@array_of_stuff = ("abc", 123, 3.14159, $foo);
```

See Figure 2.1 for a graphic depiction of @array_of_stuff.

qw ("quote words") returns a list of elements that are implicitly quoted. qw can take any delimiter, much like q and qq:

```
@array_of_stuff = qw(abc 123 3.14159);
```

This example sets @array_of_stuff to a list of three values: abc, 123, and 3.14159. qw takes everything literally, except for whitespace:

```
@array_of_stuff = qw(abc, 123, 3.14159);      # Wrong
```

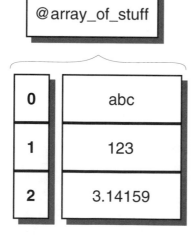

Figure 2.1   An array can contain any number of scalars. @array_of_stuff contains three items, with indexes 0, 1, and 2.

The preceding code assigns the values 'abc,', '123,', and '3.14159' to @array_of_stuff, including the trailing commas! See Figure 2.2 for a graphic depiction of this assignment. If use warnings is active, it tells us of a "Possible attempt to separate words with commas" in such a situation.

To create a list of the numbers from 1 up to and including 100, use the .. (*range*) operator. For example, the following assigns the list of integers from 1 to 10 to @integers:

```perl
@integers = (1 .. 10);
```

The range operator can fill in letters as well as numbers:

```perl
@last_half = ('n' .. 'z');
```

The easiest way to view the contents of an array is to interpolate the array's name inside of a set of double quotes:

```perl
#!/usr/bin/perl

use warnings;
```

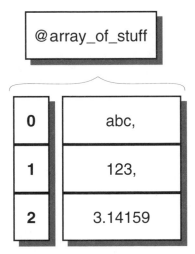

Figure 2.2   Do not separate elements with commas when creating a list with qw. The commas will be considered part of the elements' values rather than separators.

```
@integers = (1 .. 10);
print "@integers\n";
```

The preceding program prints the contents of @integers, with elements separated from each other by spaces. Because print takes a variable number of arguments, you can also give it @integers as an argument:

```
print @integers, "\n";
```

This code displays each of the elements of @integers, without any white-space between them.

Perl's foreach loop iterates over the elements of a list, one by one, executing a block of code. We can thus display the elements of an array as shown in the following example:

```
#!/usr/bin/perl

use warnings;

@integers = (1 .. 10);

foreach $int (@integers)
{
    print "$int\n";
}
```

(See Section 3.8.1 for more about foreach.)

2.6.2   *Array size*

To find the highest index in @array, use the special value $#array. Array indexes start at 0, so if @array_of_stuff contains three elements, $#array_of_stuff returns 2:

```
@array_of_stuff = qw(Peter Paul Mary);
print "Highest index = $#array_of_stuff\n";    # Prints 2
```

Assigning to $# changes the length of the array, which is normally unnecessary.

If @array_of_stuff is empty, $#array_of_stuff is -1.

You can also get the size of @array_of_stuff (which is one more than $#array_of_stuff) by assigning it to a scalar:

```
@array_of_stuff = qw(Peter Paul Mary);
$how_much_stuff = @array_of_stuff;
print "There are $how_much_stuff elements.\n";
```

This assignment takes advantage of Perl's idea of context, described in Section 4.2.5.

2.6.3 Accessing array elements

The following code demonstrates how to retrieve individual elements from @array_of_stuff:

```
$first_element = $array_of_stuff[0];
$second_element = $array_of_stuff[1];
$third_element = $array_of_stuff[2];
```

The $ indicates that we want to retrieve a scalar value from @array_of_stuff, and does *not* mean that we are working with a scalar named $array_of_stuff. The square brackets ([and]) tell Perl to retrieve from an array.

In the following code, $a and $b are assigned values from two completely different sources:

```
$a = $array_of_stuff;    # Value of scalar $array_of_stuff
$b = $array_of_stuff[0]; # First element of @array_of_stuff
```

Using @ rather than $ produces an *array slice*, a subset of the array. Because an array slice is a list, we can assign its value to a new array:

```
@array_of_stuff = ("abc", 123, 3.14159);
@new_array = @array_of_stuff[0];    # one-element array slice
```

Although a one-element array slice is pretty useless, slices can be quite helpful. For example, they can be used to reverse elements of an array:

```
@array[5,8] = @array[8,5]  # Swap $array[5] and $array[8]
```

More than two elements can be swapped:

```
@array[1, 3, 5] = @array[5, 1, 3]; # 5->1, 1->3, 3->5
```

The following uses the range operator to select all but the first element from @array:

```
@new_array = @array[1 .. $#array];
```

Array slices need not retrieve consecutive elements:

```
@new_array = @array[0, 2, 3..10, 15..22, $#array];
```

2.6.4 Flattening arrays

Lists can contain only scalars, not other lists. Lists inside of other lists are "flattened":

```
@how_now_brown_cow = ('how', 'now', 'brown', 'cow');

@how_now = ('how', 'now');
@brown_cow = ('brown', 'cow');
@new_array = (@how_now, @brown_cow);    # same as @how_now_brown_cow
```

In this example, @new_array contains four elements, not two.

2.6.5 Conversion between scalars and lists

You can turn a list into a scalar using join, and a scalar into a list using split. split treats a scalar as a record of variable-length fields. Given the scalar:

```
$scalar = "The rain in Spain falls mainly on the plain";
```

Break it into individual words by splitting across SPACE characters:

```
@words = split / /, $scalar;
```

@words is now an array of nine elements. No whitespace from the original scalar is retained in @words. The record separator is a text pattern (see Chapter 5).

If $scalar contains two whitespace characters in a row, the returned list will have one additional (and empty) element:

```
# Two spaces between "rain" and "in"
$scalar = "The rain  in Spain falls mainly on the plain";
@words = split / /, $scalar;
```

split's optional third argument puts an upper limit on the size of the returned list:

```
@array = split /,/, "a,b,c,d,e,f", 3;  # No more than 3 in @array
```

In the preceding example, $array[0] will contain a, $array[1] will contain b, and $array[2] will contain c,d,e,f. split will not return more items than the specified maximum.

If you do not specify a scalar argument, split works on $_. The funny-looking variable $_ is automatically assigned values by many of Perl's built-in functions, so this comes in handy more often than you might expect:

```
@letters = split /,/;  # Assumes $_ as the scalar
```

We will see much more of $_ in Chapter 3.

join is the opposite of split. The following connects the numbers from 1 through 10 with a dash:

```
perl -e '@array = (1 .. 10); print join("-", @array), "\n";'
```

2.6.6   *Data structures with arrays*

We can use arrays to create stacks and queues, two simple and widely used data structures. In a *stack*, the most recent element stored is also the first one removed, like a stack of dishes at a cafeteria. A queue works like a line at the post office, in which the first person to arrive is also the first to leave. Stacks are often called LIFOs (last in, first out), while queues are also called FIFOs (first in, first out).

The built-in push and pop functions make it easy to use an array as a stack. push modifies an array by adding a new element to its end:

```
push @stack, $new_element;
```

Add multiple items to a stack by giving push a list rather than a scalar:

```
push @stack, $new_element1, $new_element2, $new_element3;
```

push returns the number of elements in the modified @stack. If we push three elements onto a 10-element @stack, push returns 13.

pop removes elements from the end of an array:

```perl
#!/usr/bin/perl

use warnings;

@stack = ("a" .. "z");
print "Length: ", $#stack + 1, "\n";     # prints 26
$popped = pop @stack;
print "Popped: $popped\n";               # prints z
print "Length: ", $#stack + 1, "\n";     # prints 25
```

Here is a simple program that demonstrates stacks:

```perl
#!/usr/bin/perl

use warnings;

# Create an empty stack (LIFO)
@stack = ();

# Add elements to the stack with push
push @stack, 1; print "Stack: @stack\n";
push @stack, 2; print "Stack: @stack\n";
push @stack, 3; print "Stack: @stack\n\n";

# Remove elements from the stack with pop
print "\tRemoved: ", pop @stack, "\n"; print "Stack: @stack\n";
print "\tRemoved: ", pop @stack, "\n"; print "Stack: @stack\n";
print "\tRemoved: ", pop @stack, "\n"; print "Stack: @stack\n\n";
```

shift is similar to pop, but removes an element from the front of an array:

```perl
@alphabet = ("a" .. "z");
print "Length: ", $#alphabet + 1, "\n";

# Remove the first element of @alphabet
$letter_1 = shift @alphabet;
print "Letter 1: $letter_1\n";
print "Lengthx: ", $#alphabet + 1, "\n";

# Remove the second element of @alphabet
$letter_2 = shift @alphabet;
```

```
print "Letter 2: $letter_2\n";
print "Length: ", $#alphabet + 1, "\n";

# Remove the third element of @alphabet
$letter_3 = shift @alphabet;
print "Letter 3: $letter_3\n";
print "Length: ", $#alphabet + 1, "\n";
```

We can create a queue using push and shift:

```
#!/usr/bin/perl

use warnings;

# Create an empty queue (FIFO)
@queue = ();

# Add elements to the queue with push
push @queue, 1; print "Queue: @queue\n";
push @queue, 2; print "Queue: @queue\n";
push @queue, 3; print "Queue: @queue\n\n";

# Remove elements from the queue with shift
print "\tRemoved: ", shift @queue, "\n"; print "Queue: @queue\n";
print "\tRemoved: ", shift @queue, "\n"; print "Queue: @queue\n";
print "\tRemoved: ", shift @queue, "\n"; print "Queue: @queue\n\n";
```

To add an element to the front of an array, use unshift:

```
#!/usr/bin/perl

use warnings;

@array = ();                  # Create an empty array

unshift @array, 1;            # Add an element with unshift
print "@array\n";             # Print the current state

unshift @array, 2;            # Add another element with unshift
print "@array\n";             # Print the current state

unshift @array, 3;            # Add a third element with unshift
print "@array\n";             # Print the current state
```

```
print shift @array, "\n";       # Remove the first element
print "@array\n";               # Print the current state

print shift @array, "\n";       # Remove the second element
print "@array\n";               # Print the current state

print shift @array, "\n";       # Remove the final element
print "@array\n";               # Print the current state
```

2.6.7   splice

The built-in splice function adds or removes elements from an array. With
two arguments, splice removes all of the elements of the array, beginning
with the element at the specified index:

```
@array = qw(a b c d e f g);
splice @array, 3;               # Removes d, e, f, g
print "@array\n";               # Prints 'a b c' and newline
```

With the optional third argument, splice removes a specified number of
elements:

```
@array = qw(a b c d e f g);
splice @array, 3, 2;            # Removes only d, e
print "@array\n";               # Prints 'a b c f g' and newline
```

Arguments following the third are treated as a list to be inserted in place
of those that splice removed:

```
@array = qw(a b c d e f g);
splice @array, 3, 2, Z, Q;      # Replaces d, e with Z, Q
print "@array\n";               # Prints 'a b c Z Q f g' and newline
```

The number of elements inserted into the array does not have to equal
the number removed:

```
@array = qw(a b c d e f g);
splice @array, 3, 2, 'Z', 'Q', 6, 15;   # Replaces d, e with stuff
print "@array\n";                         # a b c Z Q 6 15 f g +newline
```

2.6.8 undef *and arrays*

We can undefine an array just as we did a scalar, by using undef as a function:

```
undef @array;    # Undefines @array
```

An empty array is not undefined, just as the empty string is a distinct value from undef. However, the use of defined test (see Section 3.4.4) is deprecated on arrays, meaning that the best way to remove an array is to assign it the empty list:

```
@array = ();
```

We can undefine individual elements of @array:

```
undef $array[5];
```

Undefining $array[5] has no effect on $array[4], $array[6], or the length of @array.

2.7 Hashes

One of the main drawbacks of an array is the fact that elements are only accessible by a numeric index. To determine whether an element exists in an array, you might have to iterate through all of its elements.

One solution to this problem is to use a *hash*, sometimes known as an *associative array* or *hash table*. A hash associates a value with a *key*, which can be any scalar value. Hashes allow for keys like tom, dick, and harry. This is less restrictive than an array's numeric indexes.

2.7.1 Hash characteristics

Just as scalar names begin with $ and array names begin with @, hash names begin with %. Use the following syntax to create the hash depicted in Figure 2.3:

```
%hash = ("key1", "value1",    # key-value pair 1
         "key2", "value2",    # key-value pair 2
         "key3", "value3");   # key-value pair 3
```

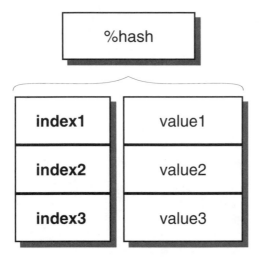

Figure 2.3   A graphical depiction of the hash %hash. It has three keys, each of which points to a scalar value.

A synonym for , is =>, which makes the initialization easier to understand:

```
%hash = ("key1" => "value1",
         "key2" => "value2",
         "key3" => "value3");
```

You can retrieve the value held at key1 with the following syntax:

```
print $hash{"key1"}, "\n";
```

Because we are retrieving a scalar value, we use a $ before the hash's name. Because we are retrieving from a hash, we surround the index with { and }. If the key does not contain whitespace, we can even drop the quotes:

```
print $hash{key1}, "\n";
```

The built-in keys function takes a hash as an argument and returns a list containing the hash's keys:

```perl
#!/usr/bin/perl

use warnings;

# Create the hash
%hash = ("elephant" => "trunk",
         "anteater" => "snout",
         "toucan" => "beak");

# Get the keys
@keys = keys %hash;

# Print the keys
print "Keys: @keys\n";
```

CORE Warning

keys *returns hash keys in the same order as Perl stores them internally, not the order in which they were stored. For this reason, never depend on the order of keys in a hash.*

Once we have the list of keys, we can use Perl's built-in **sort** function (see Section 3.9) to order them:

```perl
#!/usr/bin/perl

use warnings;

# Create the hash
%hash = ("elephant" => "trunk",
         "anteater" => "snout",
         "toucan" => "beak");

# Get the keys, in sorted order
@keys = sort keys %hash;

# Print the keys
print "Keys: @keys\n";
```

Because sort keys returns a list, we can iterate over the keys in a foreach loop:

```
#!/usr/bin/perl

use warnings;

%hash = ("elephant" => "trunk",
         "anteater" => "snout",
         "toucan" => "beak");

# Print keys and values, sorted by keys
foreach $key (sort keys %hash)
{
    print qq{"$key" => "$hash{$key}"\n};
}
```

As the preceding example demonstrates, we can interpolate individual hash elements inside of a double-quoted string. However, hashes themselves are not interpolated:

```
print "ENV is %ENV\n";      # Prints literal '%ENV'
```

Assigning a hash to a scalar actually assigns a description of how full the hash is:

```
#!/usr/bin/perl

use warnings;

# Create the hash
%hash = ("elephant" => "trunk",
         "anteater" => "snout",
         "toucan" => "beak");

# Assign the hash to a scalar
$scalar = %hash;

# Print the scalar
print "$scalar\n";
```

This program prints 3/8, meaning that three of the hash's available eight "buckets" are filled. Perl increases the number of buckets dynamically as new key–value pairs are added to the hash.

2.7.2 undef *and hashes*

Just as we can undefine a scalar or array, we can undefine a hash:

```
undef %hash;
```

The built-in defined test (see Section 3.4.4) is deprecated on hashes as well as arrays. For this reason, it is often best to remove an array by assigning it the empty list, rather than using undef:

```
%hash = ();
```

Undefining a particular hash key keeps the key in place, but removes the value:

```
undef $hash{foo};    # Keeps the key, undefines the value
```

More often, you will want to to remove an entire key–value pair. The built-in delete function does this, returning the deleted value.

```perl
#!/usr/bin/perl

use warnings;

%hash = ("elephant" => "trunk",
         "anteater" => "snout",
         "toucan" => "beak");

$deleted_value = delete $hash{toucan};
@keys = sort keys %hash;
print "@keys\n";
print qq{deleted value = "$deleted_value"\n};
```

The built-in exists function can tell you whether a given key is defined for a given hash. It returns TRUE or FALSE, for which we test using if (see Section 3.4):

```
#!/usr/bin/perl

use warnings;

%hash = ("elephant" => "trunk",
         "anteater" => "snout",
         "toucan" => "beak");

print "Toucan exists before\n" if (exists $hash{toucan}); # Will print
delete $hash{toucan};
print "Toucan exists after\n" if (exists $hash{toucan});  # Won't print
```

2.7.3   Hashes and arrays

We can use a hash where a list value is expected. For example:

```
@hash_contents = %hash;
```

@hash_contents now contains an even number of elements. The even-indexed (0, 2, and 4) elements are the keys from %hash, and the odd-indexed elements are the associated values.

We can find the number of key–value pairs in %hash by assigning keys %hash to a scalar (see Section 2.6.2):

```
%hash = ("elephant" => "trunk",
         "anteater" => "snout",
         "toucan" => "beak");

$number_of_pairs = keys %hash;

print "$number_of_pairs pairs in %hash.\n";
```

2.8   References

Programs often need more complex data structures than simple arrays and hashes. What happens, for example, if we try to create a multidimensional array?

```
#!/usr/bin/perl

use warnings;
```

```
@foo = (0 .. 50);
@bar = (900 .. 1000);

# Try to stuff @bar into $foo[100]
$foo[50] = @bar;

print $foo[50], "\n";    # Displays 101
```

Because an array element can only be a scalar, Perl did what it always does when assigning a list value to a scalar variable—it used the length of the list, rather than the contents of the list. Because @bar contains 101 elements, $foo[50] was assigned 101.

2.8.1   What are references?

It is obvious from the preceding example that we cannot simply stick an array into another array. To create complex data structures, we must use *references*, which are scalar values that point to other data structures. Because references are scalars, they can be stored inside of arrays and hashes. (References are not pointers! For example, there is no Perl equivalent to pointer arithmetic. Because Perl shields programmers from the computer's internals, Perl programs are more robust than their C counterparts.)

Given a a variable $scalar, we can create a reference to it:

```
$scalar = "hello";
$scalarref = \$scalar;
```

Prefacing $scalar with a backslash returns a reference to it. We can store that reference in $scalarref, as references are scalar values. What happens if we print $scalarref?

```
SCALAR(0x80bcee8)
```

This is Perl's way of indicating that $scalarref contains a scalar reference value. To retrieve the original value, dereference $scalarref by adding another $:

```
print $$scalarref;    # Prints 'hello'
```

We now have two ways to modify the value of $scalar: directly, by assigning it a value, or by assigning a value via our reference:

```
$scalar = "goodbye";          # Modifies $scalar directly
$$scalarref = "hello again";  # Modifies $scalar via the reference
```

We can create a reference to any scalar value, including a constant:

```
$scalarref = \10;
print $$scalarref, "\n";    # Prints 10
```

We can use { and } to separate the reference's name from the dereferencing prefix:

```
print ${$scalarref};
```

2.8.2   Array references

We can create an array reference with square brackets, instead of regular parentheses:

```
$arrayref = [0 .. 100];
```

We can retrieve the list value to which **$arrayref** points by dereferencing it with @:

```
@array = @$arrayref;  # Same as @array = @{$arrayref};
```

The following retrieves the element at index 32 from the array to which **$arrayref** points:

```
$element_32 = @{$arrayref}[32];
```

More simply, we can say:

```
print $$arrayref[32];
```

Alternatively, we can use ->:

```
print $arrayref->[32];
```

We can modify the referenced array using any of these methods:

```
$arrayref->[32] = 5000;    # Assigns the value via $arrayref
```

2.8.3 Hash references

Just as array references are created using [and], hash references are created using { and }:

```
$hashref = {"elephant" => "trunk",
            "anteater" => "snout",
            "toucan" => "beak"};
```

We can dereference $hashref, depicted in Figure 2.4, and copy its contents to a hash:

```
%hash = %{$hashref};  # Same as '%hash = %$hashref'
```

We can also retrieve elements directly from a hash reference, using -> and curly braces ({}):

```
print $hashref->{elephant}; # Same as '$$hashref{elephant}'
```

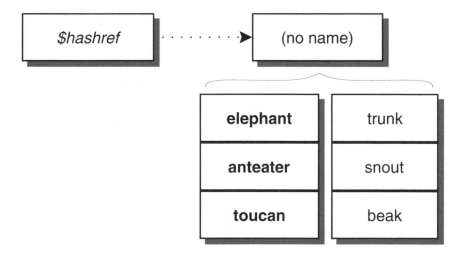

Figure 2.4 $hashref is a hash reference that points to the contents of a hash. However, that hash is anonymous, and can only be accessed indirectly via the reference.

2.8.4   *References to existing non-scalars*

To create a reference to an existing array, preface the array name with a backslash:

```
@abc = ('a', 'b', 'c');
$abcref = \@abc;
```

We can now transport $abcref—a scalar value—until we need access to the contents of @abc. Then we can dereference it, retrieving one or more elements of the list (see Figure 2.5).

We can create a reference to an existing hash in the same way, as shown in Figure 2.6:

```
%hash = {"firstname" => "Reuven", "lastname" => "Lerner"};
$hashref = \%hash;
```

Because $hashref points to %hash, changes to %hash will be reflected when we dereference $hashref.

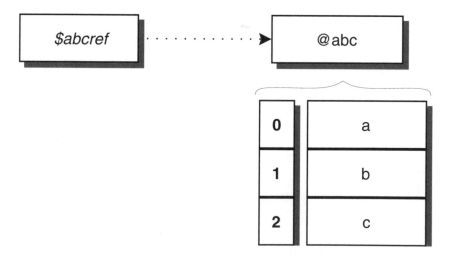

Figure 2.5   To use @abc where a scalar value is required, create $abcref, a reference to @abc. The values from @abc can always be dereferenced and retrieved from $abcref.

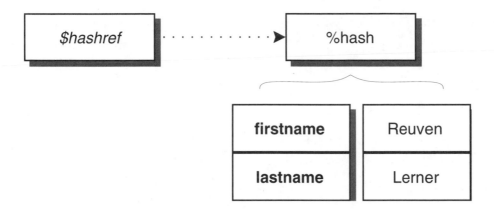

Figure 2.6 $hashref is a reference that points to %hash. Any changes in %hash will be reflected in $hashref as well.

2.8.5 Complex data structures

We can use scalar, array, and hash references to create arbitrarily complex data structures, including arrays of arrays and hashes of hashes.

For example, we can use references to create a two-dimensional array by creating an array of array references:

```
@array = ([0, 1, 2, 3, 4],
          [10, 11, 12, 13, 14],
          [20, 21, 22, 23, 24],
          [30, 31, 32, 33, 34]);
```

We can access individual elements of this two-dimensional array:

```
print $array[3][0], "\n";  # Get '30' from row 3, column 0
```

We can similarly assign values to individual elements:

```
$array[3][0] = 50;  # Assign '50' to row 3, column 0
```

We can also create a nickname for the first row by creating an array reference that points to it:

```
$row0 = $array[0];   # Point to the array reference
```

Since $row0 is an array reference, we can use it to retrieve any element from that row:

```
print $row0->[3];
```

This process can be repeated indefinitely to create other multidimensional arrays.

We can also store hash references in arrays. Here is a telephone book in which each person is represented by a hash reference:

```
#!/usr/bin/perl

use warnings;

# Define our first user as a hash reference
$person1 = {firstname => 'George',
            lastname => 'Washington',
            email => 'george@alum.whitehouse.gov'};

# Define our second user as a hash reference
$person2 = {firstname => 'Abraham',
            lastname => 'Lincoln',
            email => 'abe@alum.whitehouse.gov'};

# Add both users to our database
push @users, $person1, $person2;

# Display all entries by iterating over @users
foreach $user (@users)
{
    print qq{First name: "$user->{firstname}"\n};
    print qq{Last name: "$user->{lastname}"\n};
    print qq{E-mail: "$user->{email}"\n};
    print "\n";
}
```

If @users contains many elements, it can take a while to determine if a particular user is listed. We can speed up such a search by replacing the array with a hash, using e-mail addresses as keys. (It would be a mistake to use the first or last name, because those are not necessarily unique.)

```perl
# Define two users
$person1 = {firstname => 'George',
            lastname => 'Washington',
             email => 'george@alum.whitehouse.gov'};


$person2 = {firstname => 'Abraham',
            lastname => 'Lincoln',
             email => 'abe@alum.whitehouse.gov'};

foreach $person ($person1, $person2)
{
    # Get the user's email address
    $email = $person->{email};

    print "Storing with $email\n";

    # Store information about this user, with
    # the e-mail address as key
    $users{$email} = $person;
}
```

To retrieve the first and last names of a user with the e-mail address $email, use it as the key to %users:

```perl
print $users{$email}->{firstname}, "\n";
print $users{$email}->{lastname}, "\n";
```

We can also assign and modify values in this way:

```perl
$users{'abe@alum.whitehouse.gov'}->{lastname} = 'Lincoln';
```

See Section 8.3.1 for a description of MLDBM, a Perl module that makes it possible to store arbitrarily complex data structures on disk.

2.8.6   Casting types

What happens if we try to dereference a reference as the wrong type?

```perl
#!/usr/bin/perl

use warnings;
```

```
my @array = qw(a b c d);
my $arrayref = \@array;
my %hash = %{$arrayref};
print $hash{a}, "\n";
```

Perl complains that it cannot "coerce array into hash," and exits with a fatal runtime error. You can, however, use a dereferenced hash as a list value (see Section 2.7.3):

```
#!/usr/bin/perl

use warnings;

my @array = qw(a b c d);
my $arrayref = \@array;

# Turn the array ref back into an array
my @dereferenced = @$arrayref;

# Turn the array into a hash, where even-numbered indexes contain
# keys, and odd-numbered indexes contain the values
my %hash = @dereferenced;

print $hash{a}, "\n";    # Displays 'b'
```

2.9   Lexicals and globals

Until now, all of the Perl programs in this book have used global variables. As the name implies, globals are visible everywhere in a program. More important, their values can be retrieved and set in any statement or block. This makes program maintenance difficult, because any code can modify any variable.

Perl solves these problems with *lexical variables*, also known as *temporary variables*.

We create a lexical variable by prefacing its first appearance with my. When its innermost enclosing block ends, the variable disappears, going "out of scope." Lexicals defined at a program's top level go out of scope when the program exits.

In some programs, there is no obvious difference between a global and a lexical:

```
#!/usr/bin/perl

use warnings;

my $name = 'George Washington';

print "I am '$name'\n";
```

2.9.1   Lexicals and scope

Lexicals exist only as long as the block in which they were declared exists. When their innermost enclosing block goes away, the lexical also goes away. This can sometimes lead to confusion, as the following code demonstrates:

```
#!/usr/bin/perl

use warnings;

print $x;          # Global $x

{
    my $x = 5;     # Lexical $x
}                  # End of block; Lexical $x goes out of scope

print $x;          # Global $x
```

This code fragment produces two warnings, but no output. $x is only defined—and only has a value—within its innermost enclosing block. Outside of that block, it does not exist.

Consider the following:

```
#!/usr/bin/perl

use warnings;

# Create a new lexical $lexical
my $lexical = 10;
print "$lexical\n";
```

```
{
    # Print the value of $lexical -- refers to the outer
    # one, because no new $lexical has been declared yet
    print "$lexical\n";

    # Declare a new lexical $lexical
    my $lexical = 5;
    print "$lexical\n";
}

# Back in outer scope, $lexical is 10
print "$lexical\n";
```

When it first begins to execute this code, Perl sees a variable named $lexical, assigns the value 10 to it, and prints its value.

Then we open a new block. Before we do anything else, we **print** the value of $lexical. No variable named $lexical has yet been declared in this block, so Perl looks at the enclosing block to find a value. It prints 10.

When we declare $lexical in the inner block, Perl forgets everything it ever knew about the outer $lexical. Setting or retrieving the value of $lexical now affects the inner variable alone. The outer $lexical is unreachable until the end of the block.

When the block ends, the inner $lexical disappears. The only remaining variable named $lexical is the outer one, and this value is displayed on the screen.

Any type of Perl variable—scalar, array, or hash—can be a lexical or a global. Lexicals make programs faster, more memory efficient, and easier to maintain.

As we have seen, Perl automatically creates an array or hash the first time that we store or retrieve one of its elements. However, this is not true for lexicals; we must first declare a lexical array or hash, and then work with it. For example, the following code will not compile:

```
#!/usr/bin/perl

use warnings;

$global{key} = 'value';     # Automatically creates %global, and
                            # inserts key => value

my $lexical{key} = 'value'; # Compilation error
```

The preceding code must be written as follows:

```
#!/usr/bin/perl

use warnings;

$global{key} = 'value';     # Automatically creates %global, and
                            # inserts key => value

my %lexical;                # Declare a lexical hash
$lexical{key} = 'value';    # Works just fine
```

For an excellent introduction to the idea of lexical variables, including Perl's use of globals and lexicals, read "Coping with Scoping," an article by Mark-Jason Dominus at http://perl.plover.com/FAQs/Namespaces.html.

2.10   Conclusion

This chapter described some of the basics of Perl programming, with a particular emphasis on data structures. You should now know:

- How to write a basic Perl program, either on the command line or within an executable file;

- All about scalars, arrays, and hashes, including how to use them to store and retrieve data;

- How to use arrays to create stacks and queues with push, pop, shift, and unshift;

- The differences between quotation marks, including the generic quoting operators q and qq;

- How references can be used to create complex data structures; and

- Basic differences between lexical and global variables.

This is enough to start writing programs in Perl. However, these programs will be limited by the small number of built-in Perl functions and variables we have discussed. The next chapter introduces you to such items, as well as conditional execution and more robust error handling.

EXTENDING YOUR PERL VOCABULARY

Topics in This Chapter

- Basic input and output
- Comparison operators
- Conditional execution
- Logical operators
- Order of operations
- Looping constructs
- Sorting
- Introduction to files
- Built-in variables
- Special identifiers
- Executing system commands
- Processes, environment variables, and signals
- Evaluating Perl code within running Perl programs

Chapter 3

In Chapter 2, we learned how to write simple Perl programs, and looked at Perl's data types. In this chapter, we take a closer look at Perl's built-in functions, including conditional execution, reading and writing text files, and loops. We also take an initial look at Perl's map and grep operators, which apply a function or test to each member of a list.

By the end of this chapter, you should feel comfortable writing small- and medium-sized Perl programs. You will not yet have all of the tools that are necessary for handling large jobs, but your vocabulary will include most of the ideas necessary for basic Perl programming.

3.1   Basic output

As we saw in the last chapter, we can use print to display a scalar:

```
print "This is a string.\n";
```

Because print accepts a list of arguments, this code could be rewritten as:

```
print ("This ", "is ", "a ", "string.\n");
```

When passing a list of arguments to a function, we can drop the parentheses:

```
print "This ", "is ", "a ", "string.\n";
```

Strings can contain any character, including NEWLINE. Using print with multiline strings can look odd. Perl's "here document" syntax allows us to create strings that include NEWLINE in a more natural way:

```
print <<END;
This is text I want to send
to the user's display.
END
```

The << tells print to take input from a *here document*. The symbol END indicates the end of the multiline string. The semicolon (;) following the symbol's name is mandatory.

The here document is treated as a double-quoted string for the purposes of interpolation:

```
my $user = "Reuven";
print <<END;
This is text I want to send
to $user.
END
```

Any symbol can be substituted for END:

```
print <<CHICKPEA;
This is text I want to send
to the user's display.
CHICKPEA
```

CORE Alert

The symbol indicating the end of a here document is sensitive to case and whitespace. If the ending symbol is END, make sure that it is not indented in the source code. Such symbols are traditionally written in upper-case letters, but this is a convention, not a rule. The first mention of the symbol's name must come immediately after << without any intervening whitespace.

3.1.1   *Arguments to* print

We saw earlier that print expects a list of inputs. This is not quite true: print takes two optional arguments, the second of which is a list. Until now, we have ignored the first optional argument.

That first argument is a *filehandle*, a data structure through which programs communicate with files. Although programs can create as many filehandles as they want, Perl automatically provides three: STDIN (standard input), STDOUT (standard output), and STDERR (standard error output). We discuss filehandles at greater length in Section 3.10 and Chapter 9; for now, it is sufficient to know that they are a Perl data type whose name is traditionally written in CAPITAL letters.

By default, print sends output to STDOUT, which is normally connected to the user's screen. For print to send data to another filehandle, we must name it explicitly.

The second optional argument is a list of scalars that should be printed. Without that list, print uses $_, the scalar variable that Perl sets automatically in certain situations, such as inside of loops.

Given these defaults, here are four ways to accomplish the same thing:

```
print;            # Assumes STDOUT and $_
print $_;         # Assumes STDOUT
print STDOUT;     # Assumes $_
print STDOUT $_;  # Assumes nothing
```

CORE Alert

No comma may appear between the filehandle and the beginning of the argument list.

The following will not work:

```
print LOG, "Hello,", $username, "!\n"; # Illegal: Extra comma
print "Hello," $username, "!\n";       # Illegal: Missing comma
```

print returns 1 on success and 0 otherwise, not the string that was printed.

Perl also includes printf, which displays formatted output. As with print, the first argument to printf is an optional filehandle. The next argument is a string describing how the remaining arguments should be formatted. A

% character in the formatting string, followed by a letter, tells Perl how to interpolate the data. For example, %d interpolates a decimal value, whereas %f interpolates a floating-point value:

```
printf "I squashed %d bugs today.\n", $bug_counter;
```

This could be rewritten to use print:

```
print "I squashed $bug_counter bugs today.\n";
```

printf can often be ignored in favor of print. One exception involves truncating floating-point numbers:

```
my $earnings = 100.125;
printf "I earned %.2f dollars today.\n", $earnings;
```

This code displays $earnings to two decimal places. This is not the same as rounding to the nearest number.

The related sprintf function returns a formatted string to its caller, rather than sending it to a filehandle:

```
my $earnings_declaration =
    sprintf "I earned \$%.2f today.\n", $earnings;
print $earnings_declaration;
```

A full list of the formatting strings for printf and sprintf is available by reading `perldoc -f sprintf`.

3.1.2   length

The built-in length function returns the length of a scalar:

```
print length "abcdefghijklmnopqrstuvwxyz", "\n"; # Prints 26

my $scalar = 'rhinoceros';
print length $scalar, "\n";                       # Prints 10
```

If no variable is specified, $_ is measured:

```
print length, "\n";  # Same as print length $_, "\n";
```

CORE Alert

length *is meant for scalars, not arrays. Using* length *with an array will treat the array as a scalar, invoking* length *on the array's length.* length *will thus return the number of digits in the array's length:*

```
@array_of_stuff = (1, 2, 3, 4, 5);
print length @array_of_stuff, "\n"; # Prints 1
```

3.2   Time

At its heart, all time in Perl revolves around the built-in time function. time returns the number of seconds since the *epoch*, which is January 1, 1970 on most platforms.

To get the local time and data from time, as well as to retrieve a text string that humans can understand, use the built-in localtime function. localtime takes a single optional argument, which it takes to be a number of seconds since the epoch. Assigned to a scalar variable, localtime returns a human-readable scalar:

```
my $now = localtime time;
print "$now\n";        # Prints 'Fri Sep  3 01:08:57 1999' +newline

my $then = localtime 12345678;
print "$then\n";       # Prints 'Sat May 23 23:21:18 1970' + newline
```

When its output is treated as a list, localtime returns a list of numbers representing the date and time. The list is shown in Table 3.1.

For example:

```
my @now = localtime time;
my $hour = $now[2];
my $minute = sprintf "%02d", $now[1];   # Zero-fill tens digit
my $second = sprintf "%02d", $now[0];   # Zero-fill tens digit

print "The time is $hour:$minute:$second\n";
```

Table 3.1	List of Numbers Representing Date and Time
Array position	*Contents*
0	seconds
1	minutes
2	hours
3	day of the month
4	month, where January is 0 and December is 11
5	number of years since 1970
6	day of the week, where Sunday is 0 and Saturday is 6
7	day of the year, where 0 is the first day of the year
8	an indication of whether Daylight Savings Time is in effect

CORE Alert

Do not try to display the current date and time with print localtime. localtime *thinks that you are trying to assign it to an array (because* print *takes a list of objects) and displays a list of numbers, rather than a human-readable string. See Section 4.2.5 for more information.*

3.3   Basic input

Most interesting programs base their output on some input, either from a user or an external data source. Perl gives us two choices when reading input, allowing us to retrieve a fixed or variable number of bytes. When reading a variable number of bytes, the input is normally terminated with NEWLINE.

The built-in **read** function retrieves a fixed number of bytes from a file-handle. It takes three arguments: the filehandle (see Section 3.10) from which to read, a scalar variable into which the retrieved data is placed, and the number of bytes to retrieve. For example, the following code retrieves 50 bytes from standard input (STDIN) and places them in $buffer:

```
read STDIN, $buffer, 50;  # Read 50 bytes from STDIN into $buffer
```

If you are not sure how many bytes you want to read and are willing to wait until the user presses ENTER, use the <> operator. Perl reads bytes from the named filehandle up to and including the first NEWLINE:

```
my $userdata = <STDIN>;     # Assigns the user's input to $userdata
```

Perl retains the trailing NEWLINE character at the end of the line. To remove it, use the built-in chomp function:

```
my $userdata = <STDIN>;     # Assigns the user's input to $userdata
chomp $userdata;            # Removes a trailing newline, if one exists
```

If the final character is not NEWLINE, chomp has no effect. The related chop function removes the last character from a scalar, regardless of what it is.

chomp returns the number of characters it removed from the target string.

CORE Note

chomp *determines the current end-of-line character by checking the built-in special variable* $/. *Changing* $/ *will also change the behavior of* chomp. *See* perldoc perlvar *for more information about* $/, *and* perldoc perlport *to learn how non-Unix platforms use* $/.

3.4 **Conditional execution**

The most basic conditional operator is if, which performs a traditional if-else:

```
if ($condition_is_true)
{
    do_something;
}
elsif ($some_other_condition_is_true)
{
    do_something_else;
}
else
{
    do_the_default;
}
```

In the preceding code, exactly one of the three blocks will be executed. Perl allows for any number of elsif clauses. Both elsif and else are optional.

CORE Alert

Perl requires that if, elsif, and else be followed by a block, not a statement. If you use if without the corresponding curly braces, Perl exits with a compilation error.

For a full description of if, see `perldoc perlsyn`.

Perl defines FALSE as 0 or the empty string (""). Anything else is TRUE. This can sometimes confuse new Perl programmers:

```
$true_1    = 1;       # 1 is true
$false_1   = 0;       # 0 is false

$true_2    = 'a';     # non-empty string is true
$false_2   = '';      # empty string is false

$true_3    = '0.0';   # Non-empty string is true
$false_3    = 0.0;    # 0.0 is the same (numerically) as 0, thus false

$false_4 = $true_3 + 0;  # This assigns the number 0 to $false_4,
                         # which is false
```

This means that we can easily test to see if a scalar is equal to 0 or the empty string:

```
#!/usr/bin/perl

use warnings;

print "Enter your user name: ";
my $username = <STDIN>;
chomp $username;

# If $username is the empty string, then wag our finger at the user
if ($username)
{
    print "Hello, $username!\n";
}
else
{
    print "You did not enter a user name!\n";
}
```

Because Perl also considers 0 to be FALSE, this program does not distinguish between input of 0 and the empty string. Section 3.5.2 describes how to avoid this, with the eq operator.

Undefined scalar values are FALSE. This leads many Perl programmers to believe that variables are automatically defined when they are first used, and that they are automatically initialized to 0 or "". However, this is not the case: Undefined variables have the value undef, which is to say no value at all. When forced to provide a value where none exists, Perl supplies 0 or "", as appropriate. This makes logical sense, because undef is FALSE, which is (by definition) either 0 or "":

```
#!/usr/bin/perl

use warnings;

print $foo, "\n";                  # Warning: undefined value
print $foo * 5, "\n";              # Warning: undefined value

if ($foo)                          # No warning; undef is false
{
    print "We have foo";
}


$foo = "2";                        # Define a value

print $foo, "\n";                  # No warning
print $foo * 5, "\n";              # No warning

if ($foo)                          # Now $foo is true
{
    print "Now we have foo";
}
```

3.4.1 *Logical "not" and* unless

To invert the results of a test, turning TRUE into FALSE (and vice versa), use !. For example:

```
if (!0)        # Same as ''if (1)'', which is always true
{
    print "Hello\n";
}
```

Perl's unless accomplishes the same thing as inverting the test for an if:

```
unless (0)        # Same as ''if (1)'', which is always true
{
    print "Hello\n";
}
```

You can use else with unless, but it is unusual to do so.

3.4.2 Postfix conditionals

Perl allows you to place if or unless after a statement, thus improving the code's readability. For example, given the following simple if statement:

```
if ($money_in_the_bank)
{
    print "You have money.\n";
}
```

This can be rewritten as:

```
print "You have money.\n" if ($money_in_the_bank);
```

The same trick can be used with unless:

```
print "No money!\n" unless $bank_balance;  # Prints if $balance != 0
```

3.4.3 ?:

Perl provides a *trinary operator* ?:, similar to the operator of the same name in C. ?: takes three arguments: a condition, a statement that is evaluated if the condition is TRUE, and a statement that is evaluated if the condition is FALSE. Given the following code:

```
if ($argument)
{
    print "Argument exists\n";
}
```

```
else
{
    print "No argument\n";
}
```

This can be written as:

```
print $argument ? "Argument exists\n" : "No argument\n";
```

3.4.4 defined

We can test to see if a scalar is defined with the built-in defined function. defined returns FALSE if the scalar contains undef and TRUE otherwise.

```
print "Defined" if (defined $foo);
```

CORE Warning

Do not use defined on arrays or hashes.

CORE Note

Remember that 0 and the empty string (" ") are defined but FALSE.

3.5 Comparison operators

Perl provides a number of operators that compare two scalars. Each operator returns TRUE or FALSE, which means that it can be used inside of an if statement.

Perl gives you the option of comparing scalars numerically or as strings. Many scalars are numerically equivalent but differ as strings, such as 5.0 and 5, or A and B (which are both numerically 0).

3.5.1 Comparing numbers

Perl has three numeric comparison operators: == (equality), < (less than), and > (greater than). These can be combined to create the <= (less than or equal) and >= (greater than or equal) operators. Finally, there is also != (not equal), which returns the opposite of ==. This sample program demonstrates the use of these operators:

```perl
#!/usr/bin/perl
# filename: numeric-compare.pl

use warnings;

# Get a number from the user
print "Enter a number: ";
my $user_number = <STDIN>;
chomp $user_number;

# Compare $user_number with 1, 50, and 100
foreach $number (qw(1 50 100))
{
    if ($number > $user_number)
    {
        print "$number is bigger than $user_number\n";
    }
    elsif ($number == $user_number)
    {
        print "$number is equal to $user_number\n";
    }
    else
    {
        print "$number is smaller than $user_number\n";
    }
}
```

CORE Alert

= *assigns, whereas* == *compares. If* use warnings *is active, Perl issues a warning when* = *appears in conditional statements.*

3.5.2 String comparison

What happens if we compare two strings with ==?

```
$s1 = "aardvark";
$s2 = "xylophone";

print "$s1 == $s2\n" if ($s1 == $s2);  # Prints
print "$s1 != $s2\n" if ($s1 != $s2);  # Does not print
```

This code compares $s1 and $s2 numerically, producing a warning if use warnings is active. However, these strings are both numerically equal to zero (see Section 2.5). Perl solves this problem by offering a set of text comparison operators (see Table 3.2).

Table 3.2	Text Comparison Operators

Text comparison operator	Description
eq	equality
ne	inequality
gt	greater than
ge	greater than or equal
lt	less than
le	less than or equal

These operators work similarly to their numeric cousins:

```
$s1 = "aardvark";
$s2 = "xylophone";

print "$s1 eq $s2\n" if ($s1 eq $s2);  # Does not print
print "$s1 ne $s2\n" if ($s1 ne $s2);  # Prints
```

Perl compares strings according to their ASCII character values, so A precedes both a and B.

3.5.3 Case-modification operators

You can modify the case of one or more characters in a double-quoted string by using a number of special backslash operators (see Table 3.3).

For example:

```
my $text = 'aBcD';
print "\l$text\E$text\n";              # prints aBcDaBcD
```

```
print "\L$text\E$text\n";          # prints abcdaBcD
print "\u$text\E$text\n";          # prints ABcDaBcD
print "\U$text\E$text\n";          # prints ABCDaBcD
```

Table 3.3	Special Backslash Operators

Operator	Description
\l	make the next character lowercase
\L	make the rest of the string (or until \E) lowercase
\u	make the next character uppercase
\U	make the rest of the string (or until \E) uppercase
\E	end the effects of \L, \U, or \Q (see Section 5.3.1)

CORE Note

The case-modifying operators have no effect on non-letters.

Using these backslash operators, we can compare two strings in a case-insensitive fashion:

```
my $text1 = "ABC";
my $text2 = "abc";


# Compare including case
print "'$text1' is the same as '$text2'"
    if ($text1 eq $text2);


# Compare ignoring case
print "'\L$text1' is the same as '\L$text2'"
    if ("\L$text1" eq "\L$text2");
```

3.6   Logical operators

We can test more than one logical condition inside of an if or unless using the Boolean operators || (for logical "or") and && (for logical "and").

&& and || are both *short-circuit operators*. If the first argument to &&
is FALSE, the second argument is not evaluated, because it cannot affect the
outcome. By the same token, if the first argument to || is TRUE, the second
argument is not evaluated.

Just as parentheses can modify the order of mathematical operations
in a statement, they can force a new order of logical operations. Without
parentheses, && has higher priority than ||. Thus the expression:

```
$a || $b && $c || $d
```

is the same as:

```
$a || ($b && $c) || $d
```

CORE Approach

*Use parentheses when the order of operations might be misinterpreted by
other programmers.*

3.6.1 English equivalents

&& can be written as and, and || can be written as or. There is no logical
difference between the two versions of each operator, but the words have
lower precedence than their symbolic counterparts (see Section 3.7). This
often means that parentheses used to force the order of operations can be
removed by replacing && with and.

A similar not operator performs the same task as !. Like its verbose
cousins, not has lower precedence than the symbolic equivalent.

3.6.2 Return values from logical operators

&& and || return the last evaluated value, rather than a simple TRUE or
FALSE. Perl programmers often take advantage of this to assign variable
values or conditionally execute code. For example, assume that our program
has a parameter $username. The function get_id retrieves the user ID for that
user name. If the user name does not exist, it returns FALSE. The function
create_id creates and returns a new ID for the user name:

```
$id = get_id($username) || create_id($username);
```

The above line of code will always assign an appropriate value to $id. It will never return FALSE, because create_id will always return a value. But the TRUE value returned will always be a nonzero user ID from one of these two functions.

3.7 Order of operations

In Section 2.5.6, we saw that Perl performs multiplication and division before addition and subtraction. Like all programming languages, Perl has a fixed order in which operations take place. Knowing this order can reduce the number of parentheses in your programs, thus making them more readable.

Table 3.4 shows Perl's order of operations, including items that we have not yet covered in this book. The type of precedence indicates the associativity of the operator. A left-associative operator works from left to right, as we expect in most basic mathematical operations. But some are right-associative, meaning that they operate from right to left. Some operators are nonassociative, meaning that the idea of left-to-right or right-to-left has no meaning.

3.8 Loops

Perl has a number of loop operators, one of which (foreach) we discussed in Section 2.6.1. This section describes Perl's loops and discusses the differences between them.

3.8.1 foreach

As we have already seen, foreach iterates through the elements of a list:

```
foreach $number (0 .. 10)
{
    print $number, "\n";
}
```

foreach normally takes three arguments: an iterating variable ($number, in the preceding example), a list ((0..10), in the preceding example), and a block of code. The block is executed once for each list element, so the block is executed 11 times. During each iteration, $counter is assigned a different

Table 3.4	Perl's Order of Operations

Type of precedence	*Operators*
left	"Terms," including strings, variables, function calls, subroutine invocations, and eval {}
left	->, used for dereferencing
non-associative	++ and - -
right	**
right	!, ~ (bitwise negation), \ (creating a reference), unary +, and unary -
left	=~ (pattern matching) and !~ (pattern non-matching)
left	*, /, %, and x (repeated string)
left	+, -, and .
left	<< and >>
non-associative	Unary operators, including those that look like functions Examples: -t, -M, caller, eval, exit, ref, rmdir, and sin
non-associative	<, >, <=, >=, lt, gt, le, and ge
non-associative	==, !=, <=> (numeric comparison), eq ne cmp (string comparison)
left	&
left	| ^
left	&&
left	||
non-associative	.. (range and Boolean flip-flop) and ... (specialized version of ..)
right	?:
right	= += -= *= and other operate-and-assign combinations
left	, and the equivalent =>
non-associative	Right side of list operators
right	not
left	and
left	or xor

value from the list. After the final iteration, the global variable $counter has the value 10, and execution continues with the statement following the end of the loop block.

If we omit an iterating variable, $_ is used:

```
foreach (0 .. 10)
{
    print $_, "\n";  # $_ is the iterating variable
}
```

Making the iterator a lexical rather than a global helps to avoid maintenance issues. We do this by preceding its name with my:

```
foreach my $number (0 .. 10)
{
    print $number, "\n";    # $number is lexical
}
```

$number is lexical within the loop block, meaning that it goes out of scope when the loop ends.

The list in a foreach can come from an existing array:

```
my @numbers = (0 .. 10);

foreach my $number (@numbers)
{
    print $number, "\n";    # $number is lexical
}
```

CORE Note

Parentheses are always required around the foreach *list value.*

3.8.2 Nonstandard loop exits

You can exit from a loop prematurely with last:

```
foreach my $number (0 .. 10)
{
    print $number, "\n";
```

```
    last if ($number == 8); # Exit the loop after printing 8
}
```

Similarly, next skips to the next iteration, ignoring everything until the end of the code block:

```
foreach my $number (0 .. 6)
{
    # Skip today, where Sunday = 0 and Saturday = 6
    next if ($number == (localtime time)[6]);

    print $number, "\n";
}
```

The preceding code will print the numbers 0 through 6, except for the number corresponding to the day on which you run it.

redo returns to the top of a loop block without evaluating the test case or resetting the iterating variable. This can be useful when you want to modify the value of the iterator or otherwise evaluate the loop block a second time. For example:

```
my @usernames = qw(Tom@foo.com Dick@foo.com harry@foo.com);
foreach my $username (@usernames)
{
    # Print the name for debugging
    print "\tIn loop: username = '$username'\n";

    # If $username is not lowercase, change it and start again
    if ($username ne "\L$username")
    {
        $username = "\L$username";
        redo;
    }

    # Say that we will check this user's records
    print "Will check records for '$username'\n";
}
```

That program produces this output:

```
        In loop: user name = 'Tom@foo.com'
        In loop: user name = 'tom@foo.com'
Will check records for 'tom@foo.com'
        In loop: user name = 'Dick@foo.com'
        In loop: user name = 'dick@foo.com'
Will check records for 'dick@foo.com'
        In loop: user name = 'harry@foo.com'
Will check records for 'harry@foo.com'
```

3.8.3   Nested loops

Loops can be nested infinitely deep. Inside of nested loops, next and last apply to the innermost loop in which they appear:

```
foreach my $i (0 .. 6)                          # Outer loop begins
{
    foreach my $j (0 .. 6)                      # Inner loop begins
    {
        # Skip today, where Sunday = 0
        next if (0 == localtime(time)[6]);  # next $j, not next $i

        print "($i,$j) ";
    }

    print "\n";
}
```

next and last can apply to a block other than the innermost one. To do this, the target block must have a name, traditionally written in capital letters and always followed by a colon (:). The target block is then named as an argument to next or last. For example:

```
#!/usr/bin/perl

use warnings;

my @now = localtime time;  # Get the current time
my $day = $now[6];         # Get the day
my $hour = $now[2];        # Get the hour

OUTER:
    foreach my $i (0 .. 6)
```

```
    {

INNER:
    foreach my $j (0 .. 6)
    {
        # Skip Wednesdays (Sunday is 0) -- same as "next INNER"
        next if ($day == 3);

        # Skip to the end of this week, if after noon
        next OUTER if ($hour > 12);

        print "($i,$j) ";
    }

    print "\n";
}
```

next and last are also common within while loops, described in Section 3.8.5.

3.8.4 for

Perl also provides C-style for loops, whose arguments are a semicolon-separated set of three statements and a code block. The first statement is evaluated once before the first iteration, the second determines whether the block is evaluated again, and the third is evaluated after each iteration. For example:

```
for (my $counter = 0 ; $counter<10 ; $counter++)
{
    print $counter, "\n";
}
```

CORE Approach

In C, you loop over an array by iterating over the array's indexes. Perl, by contrast, provides foreach, *which allows you to loop over the array elements themselves. This approach is typically easier to understand and debug.*

3.8.5   while

Another common looping construct is while, which takes two arguments—a test that returns TRUE or FALSE, and a block of code that is executed repeatedly until the test returns FALSE:

```
while ($counter++ < 10)
{
    print "$counter\n";
}


print "Final value is '$counter'\n";    # Prints 11
```

If the test returns FALSE during the loop's first iteration, the code block is never executed:

```
my $temp = 55;

while ($temp > 65)            # Returns 'false', since $temp is 55
{
    $air_conditioning = 1;    # Never executes
}
```

Just as if has its counterpart in unless, while has a negative counterpart until. Both while and until can be used in a postfix form:

```
$bid_price += $increment until ($bid_price >= $highest_bid);
```

3.8.6   map

One of Perl's most powerful functions is map, which executes a code block on each of a list's elements. The current element from the input list is assigned to $_.

For example, the code assigns @cubes the list of cubes for 1 through 10:

```
my @cubes = map {$_ ** 3} (1 .. 10);
print "@cubes\n";
```

CORE Alert

No comma should appear between the code block and the input list.

Because **map** returns a list, and because a list can contain any scalar value, we can modify the block such that it returns a string, taking advantage of both variable interpolation and the . (concatenation) operator:

```
my @cubes = map {"\n$_ -> " . $_ ** 3} (1 .. 10);
print "@cubes\n";
```

Because **print** accepts a list of arguments, we don't even have to assign the resulting list to **@cubes**. Our code can be compressed into a single line:

```
print map {"\n$_ -> " . $_ ** 3} (1 .. 10);
```

The following example places single quotes around each element of the input list:

```
my @words = qw(beef hubcap luge);
my @quoted = map {"'$_'"} @words;
print "@quoted\n";        # Prints 'beef' 'hubcap' 'luge'
```

If the code block returns an empty list for a given iteration, no element is added to the output list:

```
my @words = qw(beef hubcap luge);
my @quoted = map {$_ eq "beef" ? $_ : ()} @words;
print "@quoted\n";        # Prints '"beef"'

my $length = @quoted;
print "$length element(s)\n";
```

The resulting list can even be longer than the original one, if the code block returns a list containing more than one element:

```
my @words = qw(beef hubcap luge);
my @doubled = map {($_, $_)} @words;
print "@doubled\n";     # Prints 'beef beef hubcap hubcap luge luge'
```

3.8.7 grep

grep is similar to map, in that it applies a code block to each element of a list. However, grep expects its code block to return TRUE or FALSE for each element of the input list. If the block returns TRUE, $_ is placed in the output list:

```
my @letters = ('a' .. 'z');
my @before_m = grep {$_ lt 'm'} @letters;  # True for a through l
print "@before_m\n";    # Prints 'a b c d e f g h i j k l'
```

CORE Alert

As with map, *no comma should appear between the code block and the input list.*

Here is another example:

```
my @animals = ("aardvark", "armadillo", "zebra", "crocodile");
@has_nine_letters = grep { length($_) == 9 } @animals;
print "@has_nine_letters\n";  # Prints 'armadillo' and 'crocodile'
```

3.9   Sorting

As we saw in Section 2.7.1, Perl's built-in sort function takes a list as input and returns a list as output: sort:

```
@sorted = sort @unsorted;
```

The input and output lists will always be of the same length. sort does not remove identical items, as the following example demonstrates:

```
my @characters = qw(a w b q # - = z w);
my @sorted = sort @characters;
print join '..', @sorted;  # Prints '#..-..=..a..b..q..w..w..z'
print "\n";
```

3.9.1   Sorting numerically

By default, sort compares items by ASCII code, rather than numerically. This can result in unexpected results:

```
@count = sort (10, 9, 8, 7, 6, 5, 4, 3, 2, 1);

print join '..', @count;    # Prints '1..10..2..3..4..5..6..7..8..9'
print "\n";
```

Because 10 and 1 start with the same character, they are sorted similarly to the strings a and an.

The algorithm sort uses can be modified by inserting a code block immediately before the input list. sort repeatedly invokes the code block on pairs of elements from the input list, where the first element is called $a and the second one $b. (The variables $a and $b are special, and their names cannot be changed.) The code block must return -1 (indicating the $a comes before $b), 0 (indicating that $a and $b are equal), or 1 (indicating the $a comes after $b). By default, sort uses Perl's built-in cmp operator, which compares any two scalars by their ASCII value. We could thus rewrite the preceding code as:

```
@count = sort {$a cmp $b} (10, 9, 8, 7, 6, 5, 4, 3, 2, 1);

print join '..', @count;    # Prints '1..10..2..3..4..5..6..7..8..9'
print "\n";
```

To sort the elements of a list numerically, we use Perl's <=> (numeric comparison, or "spaceship") operator:

```
@count = sort {$a <=> $b} (10, 9, 8, 7, 6, 5, 4, 3, 2, 1);
print join '..', @count;    # Prints '1..2..3..4..5..6..7..8..9..10'
print "\n";
```

An easy way to reverse the output from sort is to swap $a and $b:

```
@count = sort {$b <=> $a} (1 .. 10);
print join '..', @count;    # Prints '10..9..8..7..6..5..4..3..2..1'
print "\n";
```

3.9.2   Custom sort routines

A code block used with sort can be as sophisticated as we want. For example, we know that we can display the contents of a hash in key order:

```perl
#!/usr/bin/perl

use warnings;

%hash = ("elephant" => "trunk",
         "anteater" => "snout",
         "toucan" => "beak");

# Print keys and values, sorted by keys
foreach $key (sort keys %hash)
{
    print "'$key' => '$hash{$key}'\n";
}
```

With a custom routine, we can display the hash in value order. To do this, we compare $hash{$a} and $hash{$b}, rather than $a and $b:

```perl
#!/usr/bin/perl

use warnings;

%hash = ("elephant" => "trunk",
         "anteater" => "snout",
         "toucan" => "beak");

# Print keys and values, sorted by values
foreach $key (sort {$hash{$a} cmp $hash{$b}} keys %hash)
{
    print "'$key' => '$hash{$key}'\n";
}
```

A subroutine name (see Chapter 4) can be substituted for a code block. This is useful when the same routine will be used in multiple places.

CORE Note

$a $b are special variables in sort *routines.   They do not need to be declared, even if* use strict *(see Section 6.1.3) is active.*

CORE Approach

Avoid using the variable names $a and $b in your programs, so as to avoid potential confusion inside of custom sort *routines.*

3.10   Files

In Section 3.1.1, we took an initial look at filehandles, which allow Perl to read from and write to files. Filehandles' names are traditionally in ALL CAPS. Chapter 9 discusses files in great depth; in this section, we will get a basic taste for working with them.

3.10.1   Opening files

To create a filehandle and associate it with a file, use Perl's built-in open command:

```
open FILE, "/www/index.html";
```

If successful, this line opens the file /www/index.html for reading, makes its contents available via the filehandle FILE, and returns TRUE. If unsuccessful, FILE remains undefined, and open returns FALSE. The following is thus a common Perl idiom:

```
my $file = "/www/index.html";    # Put filename in scalar

open FILE, $file
    or die "Could not open '$file' for reading: $! ";
```

If open is successful, Perl's short-circuit or operator exits without evaluating its second argument (see Section 3.6). If open fails, it returns FALSE—in which case or evaluates its second argument, a call to die.

die immediately aborts a program's execution, indicating that an error occurred to its parent process. die takes an optional list of arguments, which are sent to STDERR before the program exits. Arguments to die often contain the special variable $!, which contains the latest error message.

CORE Approach

If the final argument to die ends with something other than NEWLINE, Perl automatically adds the name of the program and the number of the line on which the error occurred.

Note that the preceding idiom uses or, rather than ||. Because && and || bind to their arguments more closely than their English counterparts, parentheses are necessary to accomplish the same thing with ||:

```
my $file = "/www/index.html";

open (FILE, $file)              # Use parens with || to avoid problems
    || die "Could not open '$file' for reading: $! ";
```

Because open returns FALSE when it fails to open a file, it can also be placed in an if statement:

```
if (FILE, $file)
{
    print "The file is open!\n";
}
else
{
    print "Ack!  Something terrible happened!  Abandon ship!\n";
    die "Perl's message: $! ";
}
```

This is a useful technique when you need to execute multiple statements if open fails.

CORE Note

A tutorial on the use of open *is available by typing* perldoc perlopentut.

3.10.2   Writing and appending

Thus far, we have only opened files for reading. To open a filehandle for writing, use the same syntax as before, but preface the filename with >. To write data to that file, use print and specify the filehandle:

```
my $file = "/www/index.html";

open FILE, ">$file"
    or die "Could not open '$file' for writing: $! ";

print FILE "This sentence is written to '$file'.\n";
```

Opening a filehandle for writing destroys any contents that the associated file might contain. We can instead append to a file, adding to any content that might already be there, by prefacing the filename with >>. The file is created if it did not previously exist. For example:

```
my $file = "/www/index.html";

open FILE, ">>$file"
    die "Could not open '$file' for appending: $! ";

print FILE "This sentence is appended to '$file'.\n";
```

You can optionally prefix the filename with < to open the file for reading. In the absence of > or >>, < is assumed.

3.10.3   Closing filehandles

When you have finished with a filehandle, use close and the filehandle name:

```
close FILE;
```

When a program exits, any open filehandles are closed automatically. In theory, this means that a program need not close filehandles explicitly. However, because open filehandles consume memory, it is best to use close.

3.10.4   Iterating through a file with <>

Many Perl programs read text files one line at a time, performing a task on each line before moving on to the next one. The <> operator is the most common way to accomplish this in Perl.

In Section 3.3, we saw how to use <> to retrieve a single line of input, terminated with NEWLINE. In a while loop, <> reads a file one line at a time into $_. When no unread lines remain, <> returns undef (which is treated as FALSE), thus exiting from the loop. For example:

```
my $filename = 'file.txt';
open FILE, $filename or die "Cannot read '$filename': $! ";

while (<FILE>)      # Iterate through FILE, one line at a time
{
    print $_;      # Prints current line to STDOUT
}

close FILE;
```

Because print assumes STDOUT and $_ if it is given no arguments, and because while (<FILE>) places successive lines of FILE in $_, we can display the contents of FILE with a single line of code:

```
print while (<FILE>);
```

If <> is used where a list is expected (see Section 4.2.5), it returns the entire file as a list, with one line in each element. For example:

```
my $filename = "/www/index.html";
open FILE, $filename or die "Cannot read '$filename': $! ";

@contents = <FILE>;  # Each line of FILE is an element of @contents
close FILE;

print @contents;     # Displays the contents of $file
```

print takes a list of arguments, and <FILE> can return a list value. We can thus display the contents of the file directly:

```
my $filename = "/www/index.html";
open FILE, $filename or die "Cannot read '$filename': $! ";

print <FILE>;  # Display the contents of $filename
```

We can sort the lines of a file by invoking **sort** between **print** and <>:

```
my $filename = "/www/index.html";
open FILE, $filename or die "Cannot read '$filename': $! ";

print sort <FILE>;  # Display the sorted lines of $filename
```

3.10.5   *Sending data to a program*

To send text to another program's standard input, put | ("vertical bar" or "pipe") before the program name, and **open** it like a file:

```
my $sendmail = '/usr/lib/sendmail -t';

open SENDMAIL, "|$sendmail " or
    die "Cannot open '$sendmail': $! ";
```

Any text sent to SENDMAIL will be treated as input to the **sendmail** program's STDIN. Because **sendmail** expects to receive an e-mail message on its STDIN, we can send mail in the following way:

```
print SENDMAIL 'From: reuven@lerner.co.il', "\n";
print SENDMAIL 'To: president@whitehouse.gov', "\n";
print SENDMAIL "\n"; # Separate headers from the mail body
print SENDMAIL "Howdy!\n";
close SENDMAIL;
```

We can similarly read from an external program's standard output. Put the pipe character (|) after the program name, and invoke it as usual:

```
my $ls = '/bin/ls';
open (LISTING, "$ls|") or die "Cannot open '$ls': $! ";

print while (<LISTING>);

close (LISTING);
```

This program iterates through each of the lines produced by **ls**, printing them to STDOUT.

3.11   Built-in variables

Perl has many built-in variables, most of which have funny-looking names that consist entirely of symbols. The best known is $_, which often takes on default scalar values. This section describes some of these variables, and how you can use them in your programs. For a full list of Perl's built-in variables, see `perldoc perlvar`.

3.11.1   Command-line arguments

Any command-line arguments that were passed to the program are placed in @ARGV. For example, this program prints its command-line arguments:

```perl
#!/usr/bin/perl
# filename: print-args.pl

use warnings;

my $counter = 0;
foreach my $arg (@ARGV)
{
    print "$counter) $arg\n";
    $counter++;
}
```

The following code ensures that at least one argument was passed to the program:

```perl
die "No arguments here!\n" unless @ARGV;
```

Because unless expects a scalar argument, @ARGV provides one—the number of elements in @ARGV (see Section 2.6.2). If that number is 0 (or FALSE), then the unless invokes die.

3.11.2   Current program name

The special variable $0 contains the name of the program as it was currently invoked, including its full path. A program can always identify itself with $0:

```perl
#!/usr/bin/perl
use warnings;
print "My name is '$0'\n";
```

CORE Alert

C programmers might expect $ARGV[0] to contain the program name. It does not. Rather, it contains the first argument.

A single-line program run with the -e flag has a program name of -e:

```perl
perl -e 'print $0;'    # Prints -e
```

3.11.3   Current process ID

The special variable $$ contains the process ID of the currently executing Perl process. Modern operating systems typically assign a unique process ID to each executing program.

To create a temporary file with a low chance of colliding with another process, combine $$ with time and a random number:

```perl
my $time = time;
my $random = int rand 1000;
$filename = "/tmp/$$-$time-$random";
open TEMP, ">>$filename"
    or die "Cannot append to '$filename': $! ";
```

Even if several copies of the same program execute simultaneously, each copy has a unique process ID. (See Section 9.3.6 for a more reliable method of creating temporary files with the IO::File object.)

It is often a good idea to specify the process ID in a logfile:

```perl
open LOG, ">>$logfile" or die "Cannot append to '$logfile': $! ";

print LOG "[$0 / $$]: Error ($error_message)\n";  # Name and process ID
close LOG;
```

3.11.4   Autoflushing output

When a Perl program invokes print, the output is not immediately written to the filehandle. Rather, it is placed in a variable known as a *buffer*. When the buffer fills, data is emptied, or *flushed*, to the file.

To flush output automatically after every call to print, set the built-in Perl variable $| to TRUE:

```
$| = 1;
```

In Perl jargon, this is sometimes known as making a filehandle hot.

3.11.5   Environment variables

Operating systems commonly keep track of process information using *environment variables*. Each process has its own environment, some of which are set by the operating system (such as PPID, indicating the ID of the parent of the current Unix process). Other environment variables, such as PATH, can be modified by individual users and programs. Environment variables are normally passed from a parent process to its children.

Perl provides access to environment variables with the %ENV hash. The keys are the names of environment variables, and the values are those variables' values. For example, the current PATH is available with $ENV{PATH}.

The following program displays the current environment:

```perl
#!/usr/bin/perl

use warnings;

foreach my $key (sort keys %ENV)
{
    print "'$key' => '$ENV{$key}'\n";
}
```

CORE Note

Modifying an environment variable in a process only affects that process, and perhaps the children of that process. It has no effect on other processes.

3.12   Data manipulation functions

Perl provides a number of built-in functions that manipulate lists and scalars. This section describes some of the most common and useful functions.

3.12.1   pack *and* unpack

Two of Perl's most powerful functions are pack and unpack. Like join and split, pack turns a list of values into a scalar, and unpack turns a scalar into a list. However, whereas join and split treat a scalar as a record with variable-length fields, pack and unpack work with fixed field lengths.

For instance, assume a simple banquet roster in which each record contains a 21-character name field, a 20-character description field, a two-digit table number, and a one-digit indication of whether the person will be coming:

```
Barbara Lerner         Mother                1 Y
Bill Clinton           Former president      96N
Arnold SchwarzeneggerBig actor & director25N
```

unpack can turn each line of the this information into a list of values. unpack takes two arguments: The first is a template describing the type of data in the input, and the second contains the data itself.

An unpack template is a string containing letters (optionally separated by a SPACE characters) in which each letter indicates the type of data that field contains. The template a a a a indicates four character fields, each one character long. The length of each field can be changed from the default of 1 by putting a number after each character. Thus a21 a20 a2 a describes our banquet roster—a 21-character text field, followed by a 20-character text field, followed by a two-character text field, followed by a one-character text field.

If the preceding roster is read into the filehandle ROSTER, the columns can be retrieved and displayed with:

```
while (<ROSTER>)
{
    # Unpack $_ into  a 21-char string, a 20-char
    # string, a 2-char string, and a 1-char string
    @people = unpack "a21 a20 a2 a", $_;

    # Print them
    print join("\t", @people), "\n";
}
```

Using the H template character, unpack can turn an ASCII string into a list of hex values:

```
$hex = unpack "H10", "howdy";   # Hex string, high nybble first
print "$hex\n";                 # prints "686f776479"
```

To separate the hex digits, use H2 five times (once for each digit), assign the output to an array, and interpolate the array into a double-quoted string:

```
@hex = unpack "H2 H2 H2 H2 H2", "howdy";
print "@hex\n";                 # prints "68 6f 77 64 79"
```

Even better, we can use join:

```
print join ' ', unpack "H2 H2 H2 H2 H2", "howdy";
```

pack does the opposite of unpack, encoding a list of arguments into a single scalar based on a template. For example:

```
$output = pack "A7", "abcdefg";  # Grab a seven-character string
print "'$output'\n";             # prints abcdefg
```

If the template specifies more characters than exist in the input, the A template adds SPACE characters to its output:

```
$output = pack "A10", "abcdefg"; # Grab more characters than exist
print "'$output'\n";             # prints 'abcdefg   '
```

The a template adds NULL characters (ASCII 0) instead of SPACE:

```
$output = pack "a10", "abcdefg"; # Grab more characters than exist
print "'$output'\n";             # prints "abcdefg^@^@^@" +newline
```

If the template specifies fewer characters than the input provides, the remaining characters are ignored:

```
$output = pack "a3", "abcdefg";  # Grab 3 characters, when 7 exist
print "'$output'\n";             # prints "abc" +newline
```

pack can be used to turn binary digits into text, with the b template:

```
$greeting = pack "b16", "0001011010010110"; # Pack 16 binary digits
print "'$greeting'\n";                       # prints "hi"
```

The u template allows pack to encode a string in *uuencode* format. Using * rather than a number tells pack to grab all of the characters:

```
my $string = 'hello, Reuven!';
my $uuencoded = pack "u*", $string;
print $uuencoded, "\n";
```

We can uudecode with unpack:

```
$uudecoded = unpack "u*", $uuencoded;
```

The full list of template characters for pack and unpack is available by typing perldoc -f pack.

3.12.2   reverse

reverse returns a new list whose elements are in the opposite order from the input list.

```
@array = ("abc", "def", "ghi", "jkl");

# prints 'Old: abc def ghi jkl'
print "Old: ", join ' ', @array, "\n";

@reversed_array = reverse @array;

# prints 'New: jkl ghi def abc'
print "New: ", join ' ', @reversed_array;
print "\n";
```

> **CORE Note**
>
> reverse *does not modify its input. Like* sort, *it returns a list value that is based on its input.*

reverse can also reverse a scalar:

```
$scalar = "abcdefghijkl";
print "Old: $scalar\n";          # prints 'Old: abcdefghijkl'
$reversed = reverse $scalar;
print "New: $reversed\n";        # prints 'New: lkjihgfedcba'
```

Using reverse on a hash turns its keys into values and vice versa:

```
%by_value = reverse %by_key;
```

Once this code has been executed, they keys of %by_value are the values of %by_key, and vice versa.

Unlike the keys of a hash, the value need not be unique. Reversing a hash thus has the potential to clobber one or more values in your hash.

3.12.3   substr

substr lets us work with a subset of characters in a string. With two arguments (a string and an index), it returns the string beginning with that index. The index of the first character in a string is 0:

```
$string = "abcdefghij";
$substring = substr($string, 6);
print $substring, "\n";                    # Prints 'ghij' +newline
```

An optional third argument indicates the maximum number of characters to return:

```
$string = "abcdefghij";
$first_three = substr($string, 0, 3);      # 3 chars, starting with 0
print $first_three, "\n";                   # Prints 'abc' +newline
```

Use a negative offset to retrieve characters from the end of the string:

```
$string = "abcdefghij";
$last_four = substr($string, -4, 4);
print $last_four, "\n";                     # Prints 'ghij' +newline
```

If the length is negative, substr will leave that many characters:

```
$string = "abcdefghij";
$past_c = substr($string, 3, -2);
print $past_c, "\n";                        # Prints 'defgh' +newline
```

If used on the left-hand side of an assignment, substr can modify one or more characters of a scalar:

```
$string = "abcdefghij";
substr($string, 2, 3) = "QQQQ";
print $string, "\n";                        # Prints 'abQQQQghij' + newline
```

Notice how the number of removed characters does not have to equal the number of inserted characters.

3.12.4   index *and* rindex

index and rindex search for a string in a scalar, returning the index of the first match found:

```
print index "elephant", "p";     # Prints 3
```

Similarly:

```
print index "elephant", "t";     # Prints 7
```

index returns the position of the first occurrence of the search target. rindex returns the position of the final occurrence of the search target. Thus:

```
print index "banana", "n";      # Prints 2
print rindex "banana", "n";     # Prints 4
```

CORE Alert

If the search target is not found, index *returns -1. Because of this property, do not say:*

```
print "Found!"
   if (index $string, $substring);  # Will not work
```

Rather, use:

```
print "Found!"
   unless (index $string, $substring == -1);  # Will
work
```

The Unix commands `dirname` and `basename` extract the directory name and filename from a full path name. Given the file /usr/bin/emacs, `dirname` would return /usr/bin, and `basename` would return emacs. rindex and substr make it possible to emulate these commands:

```
my $path name = "/usr/bin/emacs";
my $last_slash = rindex $path name, "/";
my $dirname = substr $path name, 0, $last_slash;
my $basename = substr $path name, ($last_slash + 1);
```

```
print "Dirname: '$dirname'\n";
print "Basename: '$basename'\n";
```

We could also have used split and join:

```
my $path name = "/usr/bin/emacs";
my @path = split '/', $path name;
my $basename = $path[$#path];
my $dirname = join '/', @path[0 .. ($#path-1)]; # Array slice

print "Dirname: '$dirname'\n";
print "Basename: '$basename'\n";
```

The second version of this program is approximately four times slower than the first, so although there might be more than one way to accomplish your task, consider the impact on program efficiency. Converting a scalar to a list and back is slower than simply working with the scalar.

index and rindex can search for any string, not just a single character:

```
print index "abracadabra", "ac";    # Prints 3 ('ac' begins at 3)
```

rindex works similarly, and returns the index of the first character in the matching string:

```
print rindex "abracadabra", "ac";    # Prints 3
```

3.13   Running external programs

Perl has often been seen as a "glue" language, making it possible to tie together other programs. In this section, we discuss some of the ways in which we can interface with other programs.

3.13.1   Backticks

Section 2.5.3 described the difference between single and double quotes. Perl also supports a third kind of quotes, known as *backticks* (`). The contents of backticks are treated as a program (and arguments) to be executed from the operating system's shell. The backticks return anything that the command might have sent to its standard output.

For example, Linux systems have a program /usr/bin/uptime that displays the system load and how long the computer has been running. Using backticks, we can place the output from uptime in a scalar variable:

```
my $load = '/usr/bin/uptime'; # $load has /usr/bin/uptime output
print $load;                   # Prints the load, including newline
```

Any program can be executed inside of backticks. The returned scalar value can contain more than one line of text:

```
my $listing = 'ls /usr/local/apache';   # Listing contains newlines
print $listing;                         # Prints the listing
```

If we assign the backticks to an array, each line of the return value is assigned to an element of that array:

```
my @listing = 'ls /usr/local/apache';   # Assign listing to @listing

# Sort the directory contents
foreach my $filename (sort @listing)
{
    print "$filename";
}
```

We can compress that all to a single line:

```
print sort 'ls /usr/local/apache';
```

See Section 9.11.3 for built-in Perl functions that allow us to work with directories.

CORE Note

If the named program is not in your Perl program's PATH (i.e., $ENV{PATH}), the backticks will return undef. For this reason, as well as for your system's security, use programs' full path names rather than depending on the PATH. If use warnings is active and the named program cannot be found, Perl will complain appropriately.

3.13.2 qx

Variables are interpolated into backticks, as with double quotes:

```
my $directory = '/usr/local/apache';
my $listing = `ls $directory`;        # Assigns (multiline) listing
print $listing;                       # Prints the listing
```

qx is the generic backtick operator, similar to q and qq, and allows for the same delimiters:

```
my $load1 = qx{/usr/bin/uptime};    # Matching parens
my $load2 = qx|/usr/bin/uptime|;    # Also good
my $load3 = qx=/usr/bin/uptime=;    # Legal, but confusing
```

To execute an external program without retrieving its value, use the built-in system command.

Passed a single scalar argument, system either hands the argument to the shell (if the argument contains shell metacharacters) or executes it on its own. The executed program can display things on the screen by writing to standard output. For example:

```
system "ls $directory";    # Better passed as a list; see below
```

Passed a list of arguments, system assumes that the first argument is the name of the program to execute, and that the remainder of the list should be passed as arguments to the external program. For example:

```
system $progname, $arg1, $arg2, $arg3;
```

CORE Warning

Working with system and exec (described in the next section) can be tricky and can have security implications. Read the Perl security documentation (perldoc perlsec) before using these functions on a production system.

3.13.3 exec

To replace the currently running program with another one, use exec. exec, like system, can accept one or multiple arguments. Using exec ends a program's execution:

```
print "Before exec.\n";    # Will print something
exec "/bin/date";          # Will execute /bin/date
print "After exec.\n";     # Will never execute
```

use warnings, when active, will indicate that the third line cannot be executed:

```
Statement unlikely to be reached at - line 3.
    (Maybe you meant system() when you said exec()?)
Before exec.
Wed Mar  7 12:42:53 IST 2001
```

If the named program does not exist, exec fails and returns control to the Perl program:

```
print "Before exec.\n";
exec "/bin/foo/bin/date";  # Does not exist!
print "After exec.\n";     # Prints, because exec failed
```

To avoid warnings, use or and die, displaying $! as necessary:

```
print "Before exec.\n";    # Will print
exec "/bin/foo/bin/date" or die "exec did not work: $! ";
print "After exec.\n";     # Will not print
```

3.13.4 *Return codes from* exec *and* system

system and exec do not return output from the program they execute. However, they do return a *status code* indicating success or failure. (Of course, exec will never return a successful status code.) A status code of 0 indicates that the program exited successfully:

```
$result = system "/bin/date";
print "Result = '$result'\n";
```

On my machine, I get:

```
Wed Mar  7 12:53:37 IST 2001
Result = '0'
```

The built-in variable $? also contains the status code, and is more reliable:

```
system "/bin/date";
print "Result = '$?'\n";    # More reliable
```

We must normally divide the status code by 256 to get its actual meaning. For example, the following code attempts to execute an external Perl program that consists solely of a die:

```
system "die.pl";                            # Does not exist
print "Result code = '$?'\n";               # Print code
print "Translated code = ", $?/256, "\n";   # Translate code
```

You can also use $? to determine whether a program was killed by a signal, which signal was responsible, and whether the program left a core dump behind. See perldoc perlvar, under the heading for $?, for a full description.

3.14   fork

Modern computers can execute two programs at the same time. Perl's built-in fork function clones the current program, creating two identical processes where one previously existed. The two processes continue their execution on the line following fork, and have access to the same filehandles and environment variables (see Section 3.11.5).

fork returns twice, once in each process. In the parent, fork returns the process ID of the new child, whereas in the child, fork returns 0.

3.14.1   *An example of* fork

This program demonstrates fork, including a method for distinguishing between the parent and child processes. Notice how we use Perl's built-in getppid function to get the parent process ID of the new child:

```
#!/usr/bin/perl
# filename: test-fork.pl

use warnings;
use strict;

$| = 1;    # Keep buffers "hot"

print "Before forking\n";
```

```
# Clone this process
my $result = fork;

# Get the parent process ID
my $ppid = getppid;

# If $result is 0, this is the child
if ($result == 0)
{
    print "I am the child (result == $result), ";
    print "PID $$, PPID $ppid.\n";
}

# Otherwise, this is the parent
else
{
    print "I am the parent; child's ID is ";
    print "$result, I am $$, PPID $ppid.\n";
}

print "After forking\n";
```

My computer displayed the following results from the preceding code:

```
Before forking
I am the parent; child's ID is 3290, I am 3289, PPID 2209.
I am the child (result == 0), PID 3290, PPID 3289.
After forking
After forking
```

The text **Before forking** is printed once, as there is only one process at that point. The text **After forking** is printed twice, as two processes (the parent and child) execute that code.

CORE Note

fork *is not guaranteed to work on all operating systems. Check* perldoc
perlport *for more information.*

Unix programs often use a combination of fork and exec to launch an external process. The parent invokes fork, and the spawned child then replaces itself with another program, invoked with exec:

```perl
#!/usr/bin/perl
# filename: test-fork-and-exec.pl

use warnings;
use strict;

# Print a short message
print "Before forking\n";

# Fork and get the result
my $result = fork;

# Get the parent process ID
my $ppid = getppid;

if ($result == 0)
{
    print "I am the child (result == $result), ";
    print "PID $$, PPID $ppid.\n";
    exec "/bin/date";
}
else
{
    print "I am the parent; child's ID is ";
    print "$result, I am $$, PPID $ppid.\n";
}

print "After forking.\n";
```

After forking will only be displayed once, because the child will never reach that line. It will instead replace itself with /bin/date, which will execute and exit:

```
Before forking
I am the parent, result 506, PID 505.
```

After forking.
I am the child, result 0, PID 506.
Sun Aug 16 01:05:07 IDT 1998

3.14.2   *Zombies*

As we saw in Section 3.13.4, a process returns a status code when it exits. A program can set its exit status with exit:

```
exit;                    # Returns an exit status of 0
```

exit can take an argument to indicate abnormal status:

```
exit 1;                  # Returns an exit status of 1
```

This value is what programs can retrieve using $?.

Unix systems normally keep a child around until the exit status is retrieved by its parent. If the parent never retrieves that status, the child process remains a *zombie*. If the exit status is never collected, the zombie process remains, cluttering the process list and unnecessarily using system resources.

See Section 4.7.4 for some techniques for avoiding the creation of zombies.

3.15   eval

One of Perl's most powerful functions is eval. eval can be particularly confusing, not only because it opens the door to great mischief, but also because its behavior differs depending on its arguments.

3.15.1   *Scalar versus block invocation*

If eval is passed a scalar argument, its contents are compiled and executed each time the eval is encountered:

```
foreach my $counter (1 .. 10)
{
    eval qq{print "hello\n"};     # Same as saying: print "hello\n"
}
```

During each loop iteration, eval is invoked with a scalar argument, a double-quoted string. eval compiles and executes the small program inside of that argument. In the preceding case, executing that argument produces output on STDOUT.

The other version of eval takes a block as input:

```
foreach my $counter (1 .. 10)
{
    eval {print "hello\n"};    # Argument is a block, not a string
}
```

The block version of eval parses its argument only once, along with the surrounding Perl program. A block argument to eval must contain valid Perl when the program is compiled, whereas a string argument is only checked at execution time.

3.15.2   String interpolation

Here is another example of eval with a scalar argument:

```
my $eval_string = "print 5 + 5";
eval $eval_string;
```

Because the evaluated code is treated as if it were inside of the current block, variables (lexicals and globals) are available:

```
my $number = 5;
eval "print $number + $number";    # Lexicals are available
```

Lexicals defined in an eval string fall out of scope once the eval ends. For example:

```
my $number = 5;
eval "my $number = 10; print $number + $number";
print "\nNumber is now $number\n";
```

The code inside of an eval string can modify globals, however.

3.15.3   Error codes

If there is an error when running eval, the variable $@ contains this error message:

```
eval "pritn 5+5";                    # Intentionally misspelled
print "Trapped error: '$@'\n" if $@;
```

This code produces the following error message:

```
Number found where operator expected at (eval 1) line 1, near "pritn 5"
        (Do you need to predeclare pritn?)
Trapped error: 'syntax error at (eval 1) line 1, near "pritn 5"
'
```

If we use the block form of eval, rather than the string form, the preceding code fails to compile, and never executes:

```
eval { pritn 5+5 };                     # Intentionally misspelled
print "Trapped error: '$@'\n" if $@;
```

Because a program can use die within an eval, and because an eval block is checked at compile time, many Perl programmers use the combination as a simple form of exception handling. See Section 4.2.6 for some examples.

3.16   Conclusion

This chapter outlined many of the functions and operators that are central to programming in Perl. We discussed the following:

- Basic output with print,

- Retrieving basic input from the user,

- Here documents,

- Functions for working with lists and scalars,

- Working with the current time and date,

- Comparison operators,

- Case modifiers,

- Conditional execution and logical operators,

- Looping constructs foreach, for, while, map, and grep,

- Sorting lists,

- Reading from and writing to files,

- Perl's built-in variables,

- Working with backticks, system, and exec,

- Using fork to clone the current process, and

- Using eval to execute small Perl programs.

You are now prepared to handle many of the basic programs that Perl programmers write every day. However, several key elements are still missing. In the next chapter, we will see how to define Perl subroutines, and how to use them intelligently in programs.

SUBROUTINES

Chapter 4

This chapter describes subroutines, Perl's name for functions and procedures. By the end of this chapter, you should feel comfortable writing and using Perl subroutines.

Until now, the differences between Perl's lexical and global scopes have probably seemed largely irrelevant. Subroutines make the differences between scopes much more obvious, particularly when we want to create or use variables within a subroutine. We will look at what happens when a subroutine references lexical variables within its enclosing scope, as opposed to creating new lexicals within its own scope.

Subroutines are especially useful when they can return a value to their caller. After looking at ways in which subroutines can return one or more values, we will look at *context*, Perl's notion that a subroutine can alter its return value depending on what the caller is expecting to receive.

Finally, we will look at several advanced subroutine-related topics, such as subroutine references, BEGIN and END blocks, private variables, recursion, and signal handlers.

4.1   Subroutine basics

Subroutines, which put commonly executed code in a single place, are an essential part of modern programming. They allow us to work at a high level of abstraction, ignoring low-level implementation details. They make code more maintainable by reducing clutter and putting each piece of functionality in a single location. And they allow us to optimize and debug algorithms once, rather than having to do so in multiple locations.

To declare a subroutine in Perl, preface a block of code with the keyword sub and the name of the subroutine. The name can contain alphanumeric characters (including _), and is case-sensitive, so Print_Status is different from print_status.

Here is a simple subroutine, named print_now, which displays the current time and date:

```
sub print_now
{
    my $now = localtime;    # Get the current time
    print "$now\n";         # Print the current time
}
```

A program can invoke print_now by prefacing its name with an ampersand (&):

```
&print_now;  # Leading "&" denotes subroutine
```

Modern versions of Perl allow us to drop the &, if we then add parentheses:

```
print_now(); # Don't need & if we have ()
```

Perl looks for subroutines during its compilation phase. This means that subroutine declarations do not need to be placed at the top of a program file, but can be anywhere. Indeed, it is traditional to put them at the bottom of a program. For example:

```
print_now();    # Invocation of print_now

sub print_now   # Declaration of print_now
```

```
{
    $now = localtime;
    print "$now\n";
}
```

4.2   Return values

A subroutine can return a scalar or list value to its caller with return. Without arguments, return returns undef or the empty list, depending on context (see Section 4.2.5).

The following code demonstrates how a subroutine can return a scalar value, and how that value can then be assigned to a variable:

```
my $five = return_five();     # Invoke the subroutine,
                              # assigning its return value

print "Five = $five\n";

sub return_five               # Define a simple subroutine
{
    return 5;                 # Return a scalar
}
```

If a subroutine returns a list value, we can similarly assign the return value to an array, or to a list of scalars:

```
# Invoke the subroutine, assigning its return value to an array
my @stuff = return_five_and_ten();
print "Five = $stuff[0], Ten = $stuff[1]\n";

# Invoke the subroutine, assigning its return value to two scalars
my ($five, $ten) = return_five_and_ten();
print "Five = $five, Ten = $ten\n";

sub return_five_and_ten    # Define the subroutine
{
    return (5, 10);        # Return a list value
}
```

If a subroutine returns a hash, the hash is turned into a list of key–value pairs. Keys and values will always be kept together in this list (see Section 2.7.3), but the order of those pairs depends on Perl's internal storage. Because we can use a list to assign a hash, we can then use the returned value to create a new hash. For example:

```
%hash = return_hash();    # Assign a hash from return value

sub return_hash           # Define the subroutine
{
    %sub_hash = ("key1" => "value1", "key2" => "value2");

    return (%sub_hash);   # Return the hash
}
```

4.2.1   Implicit return values

Without return, the value of a subroutine is the value of the final executed statement:

```
sub return_number
{
    $number = 5;    # Implicitly returns 5
}
```

CORE Approach

This implicit behavior makes subroutines more compact, but increases the difficulty of maintaining the code.

4.2.2   Flattening list results

If a subroutine returns two or more lists, they are flattened into a single list (see Section 2.6.4). In the following code, @everything is a single flattened array:

```
my @everything = return_list();
print "@everything\n";    # Prints '1 2 3 4 5 6'
```

```
sub return_list
{
    my @first_list = (1, 2, 3);
    my @second_list = (4, 5, 6);

    # Combine the two arrays into a single list, and return
    # that single list value
    return (@first_list, @second_list);
}
```

4.2.3 Returning both scalars and lists

Perl allows us to assign multiple scalars by placing them in a list:

```
my ($first, $second) = (1, 2);
```

If the final element of the left-hand list is an array, it is assigned whatever leftovers might come from the right-hand side:

```
my ($first, $second, @rest) = (1 .. 100);
```

In the preceding example, $first is assigned 1, $second is assigned 2, and @rest is assigned the list of values (3 .. 100).

A list value returned by a subroutine can thus be assigned to one or more scalars, followed by one array. For example:

```
my ($first, @rest) = sub_returning_a_list();
```

When assigning multiple variables to a list value, make sure that the array comes at the end. If we were to place @rest before $first, it would grab the entire list, leaving nothing in the scalar:

```
my (@first, $last) = sub_returning_a_list();  # $last is undef
```

In this code, @first is assigned everything returned by the subroutine, and $last is assigned undef as a result.

4.2.4 Returning references

Because references (see Section 2.8) are scalars, subroutines can return them, too:

```perl
# Return value is an array reference
my $fruits = return_array_reference();

# Dereference it and print its contents
foreach my $fruit (@$fruits)
{
    print "$fruit\n";
}

sub return_array_reference
{
    my @array = qw(kiwi passionfruit papaya mango);
    return \@array;
}
```

By returning a list of two array references, a subroutine can avoid the effects of flattening:

```perl
# Return value is an array reference
my ($tropical_fruits, $berries) = return_array_references();

# Print each tropical fruit
foreach my $fruit (@$tropical_fruits)
{
    print "Tropical fruit: $fruit\n";
}

print "\n";

# Dereference it and print its contents
foreach my $berry (@$berries)
{
    print "Berry: $berry\n";
}

sub return_array_references
{
    my @tropical_fruits = qw(kiwi passionfruit papaya mango);
    my @berries = qw(cranberries blueberries cherries loganberries);

    return (\@tropical_fruits, \@berries);
}
```

As we saw in Section 2.8.5, we can build complex data structures (e.g., arrays of arrays, arrays of hashes, and hashes of hashes) using references. A subroutine can return one or more references to such structures:

```
# Get the data structure
my $presidents = return_presidents();

# Print information about each president
foreach my $president (@$presidents)
{
    print "First name: $president->{FirstName}\n";
    print "Last name: $president->{LastName}\n\n";
}

# Define the subroutine
sub return_presidents
{
    # Create two anonymous hash references
    my $hash1 = {FirstName => "George", LastName => "Washington"};
    my $hash2 = {FirstName => "Thomas", LastName => "Jefferson"};

    # Create an array of two anonymous hash references
    my @presidents = ($hash1, $hash2);

    # Return a reference to our complex data structure
    return \@presidents;
}
```

4.2.5 Context and return values

In Perl, a function can see what sort of return value the caller expects to receive, and can vary the return value accordingly. This functionality, known as *context*, is powerful, but can be confusing to the uninitiated.

For example, the built-in localtime function returns a human-readable string when in scalar context—that is, when the item to the left of localtime expects a scalar value:

```
my $localtime = localtime time;
print "$localtime\n";    # Prints 'Thu Sep  9 22:02:00 1999'
```

If we invoke localtime where a list value is expected, known as *array context*, it returns a list of numbers representing the current time and date:

```
my @now = localtime time;  # @now gets current date/time

foreach my $element (@now)
{
    print "$element\n";     # Prints each element on a line by itself
}
```

Because functions look to their immediate left to determine context, we can force scalar context by preceding the function name with the scalar keyword:

```
my @now = scalar localtime time;  # Scalar context, even though @now
                                  # is an array

foreach my $element (@now)
{
    print "$element\n";           # Prints only one line
}
```

In the preceding example, @now contains a single element, the text string that localtime returns in scalar context. We can similarly force list context by surrounding the left side with parentheses:

```
my ($stuff) = localtime time;  # Forces list context
print "Stuff = '$stuff'\n";    # Prints number of seconds in current time
```

Because localtime returns a list (see Section 3.2) in array context, $stuff is assigned the first element of that list—the number of seconds from the current time.

Just as Perl's built-in functions can modify their output based on context, so too can user-written subroutines, by using the built-in wantarray function. wantarray can return undef (also known as *void context*, when no value is expected), FALSE (in scalar context), or TRUE (in array context). The following program demonstrates the use of wantarray and context:

```
#!/usr/bin/perl

use strict;
use warnings;

do_we_want_an_array();                # No context

my @array1 = do_we_want_an_array();       # Array context
```

```
my @array2 = scalar do_we_want_an_array();  # Force scalar context

my $scalar1 = do_we_want_an_array();        # Scalar context
my ($scalar2) = do_we_want_an_array();      # Force list context

# Define subroutine
sub do_we_want_an_array
{
    if (! defined(wantarray))    # Not defined
    {
        print "No return value expected.\n";
    }

    elsif (wantarray)            # Defined and true
    {
        print "An array return value expected.\n";
    }

    elsif (!wantarray)           # Defined and false
    {
        print "A scalar return value expected.\n";
    }
}
```

Context also explains why we can write:

```
if (@array1 == @array2)
{
    print "They are of equal lengths.\n";
}
```

The == operator forces its arguments into scalar context. Because an array in scalar context returns its length, the previous code compares the lengths, and not their contents.

By contrast, print takes a list of arguments, which means that its arguments are always in array context. That explains why we should not write:

```
print localtime, "\n";    # Probably not what we want
```

We can avoid having to assign the output from localtime to a scalar by invoking it in scalar context:

```
print scalar localtime, "\n";    # Forces scalar context
```

localtime looks to the left, sees the scalar keyword, and executes in scalar context. Without scalar, localtime would only see print, which is array context.

4.2.6 *Exceptions*

What should a subroutine return if an error occurs? In C and C++, it is common to return 0 or -1 to indicate a problem. But if a subroutine returns 0, how can we tell the difference between a legitimate 0 value and an error? Many Perl programmers opt to return undef to indicate that an error has occurred. For example, the following subroutine allows us to differentiate between user input of 0 and the empty string:

```
sub get_input
{
    print "Enter something: ";   # Print a message to the user
    my $input = <>;              # Get a number
    chomp $input;                # Remove the trailing newline

    if ($input eq "")            # Return undef if $input is empty
    {
        return undef;
    }
    else                         # Otherwise return the input
    {
        return $input;
    }
}
```

Although it is common for Perl subroutines to indicate an error or exceptional situation by returning undef, advanced programmers often use other techniques. For example, a subroutine can indicate an exception with die, and its caller can trap that exception with eval (see Section 3.15.3). You can read a full explanation of this technique in perldoc -f eval.

4.3   Variables within subroutines

Until now, the differences between lexicals and globals have seemed relatively small. However, the two act very differently when combined with subroutines.

CORE Note

Variable scoping, and particularly its interaction with subroutines, often confuses new Perl programmers. Pay close attention to the distinction between lexicals and globals, to avoid confusion.

4.3.1   Lexicals in a subroutine

Lexicals declared in a subroutine go out of scope when the subroutine returns, as we might expect. Using lexicals, we can thus create variables that exist only within our subroutine:

```
# Before the subroutine
print "foo is ", (defined $foo ? "" : "un"), "defined\n";

# Invoke the subroutine
subroutine();

# After the subroutine
print "foo is undefined\n" unless (defined $foo);

sub subroutine
{
    my $foo = 10;
    print "foo is ", (defined $foo ? "" : "un"), "defined\n";

}
```

$foo, a lexical, is declared and assigned a value inside of subroutine. Because it is a lexical, we do not need to worry about $foo's value affecting our program after the subroutine exits. For this reason alone, lexicals are almost always preferable over globals.

If a subroutine declares a lexical with a name that is the same as a lexical in the enclosing block, the inner (subroutine) lexical overshadows the outer one. The outer one is inaccessible from within the subroutine:

```
my $x = 5;                   # $x is a lexical, value 5

print "Before, x = '$x'.\n";  # $x is 5
print_during();              # Calls the subroutine
```

```
print "After, x = '$x'.\n";      # $x is 5, since subroutine's $x
                                 # went out of scope
sub print_during
{
    my $x = 10;                  # New $x overshadows other $x
    print "During, x = '$x'.\n"; # Prints inner $x
}
```

CORE Approach

Using the same variable name in a subroutine and its caller is legal and does not produce any warnings. However, using the same variable name can make code difficult to maintain. Using long, explicit variable names can reduce the potential for such confusion.

Of course, a subroutine may access and assign to lexicals defined in an enclosing block. If we remove the my declaration from the preceding program, then print_during is no longer assigning a value to a new lexical $x, but is rather changing the value of $x in the enclosing block. Even after the subroutine exits, this new value remains:

```
my $x = 5;                       # $x is a lexical, value 5

print "Before, x = '$x'.\n";     # $x is 5
print_during();                  # Calls sub, which assigns $x
print "After, x = '$x'.\n";      # $x remains 10

sub print_during
{
    $x = 10;                     # No $x in this block, so
    print "During, x = '$x'.\n"; # caller's $x is modified
}
```

4.3.2   *Globals in a subroutine*

Because globals are in scope until the program exits, the value of a global variable defined or modified in a subroutine does not go out of scope:

```
$x = 5;                          # $x is a global, value 5

print "Before, x = '$x'.\n";     # $x is 5
```

```perl
print_during();                 # Subroutine assigns $x
print "After, x = '$x'.\n";     # $x remains 10

sub print_during
{
    $x = 10;                    # Modify the global $x
    print "During, x = '$x'.\n";
}
```

CORE Warning

It is possible to declare a subroutine within a subroutine, a feature known as nested subroutines. *However, this feature should only be used by experienced Perl programmers who understand the implications. One particularly common problem with nested subroutines occurs when the inner subroutine refers to a lexical variable in the outer subroutine. When this happens, the two subroutines no longer refer to the same variable, a situation that can cause great confusion. For more information, see the explanation in the* mod_perl *guide, at* http://perl.apache.org/guide/perl.html#my_Scoped_Variable_in_Nested_S.

4.3.3   my and local

Many built-in Perl variables must be globals and thus cannot be declared or overshadowed with my. To give a variable a temporary value, use the confusingly named local statement.

local gives an existing global variable a temporary value through the end of the current block. This temporary value sticks around even when execution passes to a subroutine. For example:

```perl
#!/usr/bin/perl

use strict;
use warnings;
use vars qw($global);    # Allow the global $global

$global = 1000;
```

```
print "Global before block is '$global'\n";
print_global();
{
    # Temporarily assign $global a new value
    local ($global) = 5555;
    print "Global after local() call is '$global'\n";

    print_global();

    # After the block, $global reverts to its previous value
}
print "Global after block is '$global'\n";
print_global();

sub print_global
{
    print "Global inside of print_global() is '$global'\n";
}
```

This program displays 1000 everywhere except during the two print statements between local and the end of the block. The same program, rewritten to use my instead of local, has a totally different effect:

```
#!/usr/bin/perl

use strict;
use warnings;

my $lexical = 1000;

print "Lexical before block is '$lexical'\n";
print_lexical();
{
    # Temporarily assign $lexical a new value
    my ($lexical) = 5555;
    print "Lexical after my() call is '$lexical'\n";

    print_lexical();
```

```
}
print "Lexical after block is '$lexical'\n";
print_lexical();

sub print_lexical
{
    print "lexical inside of print_lexical() is '$lexical'\n";
}
```

The my declaration inside the block creates an entirely new variable $lexical with a value that is completely separate from the top-level $lexical. Within that block, $lexical has the value 5,555. But when we invoke print_lexical, it has no knowledge of the $lexical within the executing block. Rather, it only knows of the top-level $lexical, with a value of 1,000.

You can read more about local and global variables in perldoc perlsub under the heading "Temporary Values via local()." Mark-Jason Dominus also wrote an excellent article on the subject, available at http://perl.plover.com/local.html.

4.4 Subroutine arguments

Subroutines are much more interesting and useful when they can receive parameters, which are passed as a comma-separated list, between parentheses, following the subroutine name. For example:

```
subroutine_name($scalar);                  # One argument
subroutine_name($scalar1, $scalar2, $scalar3); # List of arguments
```

4.4.1 Retrieving arguments

A subroutine receives arguments in the special array @_. Subroutine arguments are typically retrieved with shift (see Section 2.6.6), which removes and returns the first element of @_ by default:

```
sub subroutine
{
    my $first = shift;    # Removes and returns the 1st argument
    my $second = shift;   # Removes and returns the 2nd argument
    my $third = shift;    # Removes and returns the 3rd argument

    print "First = '$first', Second = '$second', Third = '$third'\n";
```

```
}

# Invoke the subroutine with three arguments
subroutine (1, "a b c", "sunflower");
```

As you can see from this example, subroutine parameters are defined more loosely in Perl than in other languages. A subroutine can be invoked with any number of arguments; it is up to the subroutine to determine if it was called with too few or too many. In addition, parameter names are determined within the subroutine, rather than by a subroutine prototype or declaration.

Subroutine arguments are passed by value. Thus in the preceding example, modifying $first, $second, or $third will affect those variables within subroutine, but not the values within the caller's environment.

CORE Warning

It is possible for a subroutine to access its arguments by directly accessing elements of @_. This is generally a bad idea, because it can easily lead to unmaintainable code. It is better to simply pass a reference, as described in the next section.

4.4.2   Passing references

If a subroutine is passed a reference as an argument, it can access and modify the referenced value in the caller's environment. For example:

```
my $x = 5;

print "Before, x = '$x'.\n";
modify_x(\$x);                          # Pass a reference to $x
print "After, x = '$x'.\n";

sub modify_x
{
    my $ref_x = shift;
    $$ref_x = $$ref_x * $$ref_x;
}
```

We can also pass array and hash references as subroutine arguments. Here is an example of an array:

```perl
# Set lexical @x
my @x = (9, 6, 4, 10, 7, 5, 2, 1, 8, 3);

# Display @x
print "Before, x = '@x'.\n";

# Invoke a subroutine with one parameter, a reference to @x
modify_array(\@x);

# Display @x
print "After, x = '@x'.\n";

sub modify_array
{
    # Get the array reference
    my $ref_x = shift;

    # Sort the list, and assign the output to @x via $ref_x
    @{$ref_x} = sort {$a <=> $b} @{$ref_x};
}
```

4.4.3 Pseudo-formal parameters

Perl does not support named subroutine parameters, but it is possible to simulate them by passing a hash as an argument to a subroutine. When a subroutine is passed a hash as an argument, it unravels the hash into a list of key–value pairs. This list can be turned back into a hash by assigning a new hash to @_. For example, the following program takes three pseudo-named parameters (first, last, and phone):

```perl
#!/usr/bin/perl

use strict;
use warnings;

print_params('first' => 'Reuven', 'last' => 'Lerner');
print_params('phone' => '08-973-0394', 'first' => 'Atara');

sub print_params
{
    my %parameters = @_;      # Use @_ to create a lexical hash
```

```
    print "First name: $parameters{first}\n" if $parameters{first};
    print "Last name: $parameters{last}\n" if $parameters{last};
    print "Phone number: $parameters{phone}\n" if $parameters{phone};
    print "\n";
}
```

4.5   Subroutine references

Assume the following subroutine:

```
sub print_something
{
    print "something\n";
}
```

We can create a reference to print_something by prefacing its name with &
and a backslash. This is sometimes known as a *code reference*, or simply as a
subroutine reference. Whereas the & is optional when invoking subroutines,
it is mandatory when referencing them:

```
my $something_sub = \&print_something;
```

CORE Alert

Do not say:

```
my $something_sub = \print_something(); # Not what we
want
```

This executes print_something, *and assigns the return value to*
$something_sub.

4.5.1   *Dereferencing code references*

To dereference and invoke a code reference, preface its name with &:

```
# Define a subroutine
sub print_something
```

```
{
    print "something\n";
}

# Create a reference to the subroutine
my $sub_ref = \&print_something;

# Invoke the subroutine reference
&$sub_ref;
```

Alternatively, we can use the same arrow (->) we used with array and hash references:

```
$sub_ref->();
```

We can also invoke a subroutine with arguments, given a reference:

```
sub print_something
{
    # Get an argument
    my $something = shift;

    print $something, "\n";
}

my $print_something = \&print_something;
&$print_something("hello");           # Prints 'hello'
```

4.5.2   Passing subroutines as arguments

Using code references, a subroutine can be passed as an argument to another subroutine. This is the definition of **repeat**, which takes an integer and a code reference as arguments. Any additional parameters are used as input to the subroutine reference. The subroutine is dereferenced and executed as many times as indicated in the first argument:

```
sub repeat
{
    my $howmany = shift;  # Get the integer
    my $routine = shift;  # Get the subroutine reference
```

```
    # Stop if $howmany is less than 1
    return if ($howmany < 1);

    # Decrement the counter
    $howmany--;

    # Call the routine
    &$routine(@_);

    # Call ourselves, but with the updated counter
    repeat($howmany, $routine, @_);
}
```

Using **repeat**, we can invoke a subroutine any number of times:

```
sub say_hi
{
    print "Hi!\n";
}


repeat (10, \&say_hi);     # Say "Hi" 10 times
```

This code will print *Hi!* 10 times. We can also write our subroutine such that it takes an additional argument:

```
sub say_hi_name
{
    my $arg = shift;    # Get the first argument
    print "Hi, $arg\n"; # Print a message
}


# Say "Hi" to to Elvis five times
repeat (5, \&say_hi_name, "Mr. Presley");
```

4.5.3   *Anonymous subroutines*

Just as we can create anonymous array and hash references, we can create anonymous code references. To create an anonymous subroutine, leave off the name in the declaration:

```
my $subref = sub { print "Hi\n"; } # Anonymous subroutine reference
```

Because a code reference is just a scalar, subroutines can return other subroutines:

```
sub return_sub
{
    # Return an anonymous code reference
    return sub { print "hi\n"; }
}
```

The preceding can be invoked as follows:

```
my $sub = return_sub();  # Get the anonymous subroutine reference
&$sub;                   # Execute the subroutine
```

We can use anonymous subroutine references wherever a subroutine reference is expected. For example, we could invoke **repeat** with an anonymous code reference, rather than defining and passing a reference to say_hi_name:

```
# Print "foo" five times
repeat (5, sub {print "foo\n"});
```

4.6 BEGIN **and** END

A number of subroutines get special treatment in Perl if they are defined. The most common are BEGIN and END; a full list of special subroutines is available in `perldoc perlmod`. These subroutines' names consist entirely of capital letters, and do not need to be prefaced by the keyword **sub**.

A BEGIN block is executed during compilation, immediately after Perl finishes reading its definition. Multiple BEGIN blocks are run in the order in which they appear in your program, with the first executing before the second is even parsed by Perl's compiler.

END blocks are similarly executed just as a program is exiting. However, multiple END blocks are executed in the reverse order of their appearance in your program.

Here is a trivial example of both kinds of blocks:

```perl
#!/usr/bin/perl

# filename: multiple-begin-end.pl

print "Place 0\n";

use strict;
use warnings;

print "Place 1\n";

BEGIN { print "Hello 1!\n";}
BEGIN { print "Hello 2!\n";}
BEGIN { print "Hello 3!\n";}

print "Place 2\n";

END { print "Goodbye 1!\n";}
END { print "Goodbye 2!\n";}
END { print "Goodbye 3!\n";}

print "Place 3\n";
```

The output from this program is the following:

```
Hello 1!
Hello 2!
Hello 3!
Place 0
Place 1
Place 2
Place 3
Goodbye 3!
Goodbye 2!
Goodbye 1!
```

BEGIN blocks can be useful for modifying the environment of a program during the compilation phase. For example, it would normally be impossible to conditionally use a module (see Section 6.2.2) in an if statement, because use happens at compile time, whereas if happens during execution. Placing such code inside of a BEGIN block allows it to work.

4.6.1 *Private variables*

Lexical variables declared within a BEGIN block are only visible to subroutines defined within that block. However, those subroutines are available to the entire program. In this way, we can create private variables, with values that cannot be modified directly by any other part of the program. (This is similar to the "nested subroutines" issue we discussed in Section 4.3.2, but is less confusing because a BEGIN block only executes once.) For example:

```perl
#!/usr/bin/perl

use strict;
use warnings;

BEGIN
{
    # Declare a lexical variable
    my $variable = 5;

    sub print_variable
    {
        print "variable = '$variable'\n";
    }
}

print_variable();
```

Because lexical variables fall out of scope as soon as a block ends, $variable is inaccessible outside of the BEGIN block. However, subroutine names do not fall out of scope. So although we can print the current value of $variable with print_variable, we cannot access it directly.

We can, of course, define print_variable such that it returns a reference to $variable. This effectively makes our private variable public, allowing us to set and retrieve its value via the reference. For example:

```perl
#!/usr/bin/perl

use strict;
use warnings;

BEGIN
{
    # Declare a lexical variable
    my $variable = 5;

    sub print_variable
    {
        print "variable = '$variable'\n";
        return \$variable;
    }
}


# Get a reference to our variable
my $var_ref = print_variable();

# Dereference it, and assign it a value
$$var_ref = 10;

# Now see what our hidden variable has to say for itself!
print_variable();
```

4.7   Signals

A program generally runs from start to finish, without any interference from the operating system. The exception is a *signal*, which interrupts a program's execution with an important message. Consider how a cellular telephone can interrupt a conversation, and you will understand the gist behind signals.

When a signal is sent to a running Unix program, the program can ignore the signal or act on it. The action taken depends on something known as a *signal handler*. If no signal handler is installed, then the operating system executes its own default handler. Perl programs can define signal handlers by assigning anonymous code references to elements of %SIG.

4.7.1 Handling signals

In Unix, pressing CONTROL-C typically sends the *interrupt signal*, abbreviated as SIGINT. If no handler is installed for SIGINT, the system terminates the program.

The following is a short Perl program that loops infinitely. After it receives a text string as input, the program sends the string to STDOUT. Because no signal handler is installed, it terminates when CONTROL-C is pressed.

```perl
#!/usr/bin/perl
# filename: infinite-loop.pl

use strict;
use warnings;

my $phrase = "";     # Get input

while (1)
{
    print "Enter a phrase:: ";
    chomp($phrase = <STDIN>);
    print "You entered: '$phrase'\n\n";
}
```

We can replace the default behavior of SIGINT (i.e., program termination) by assigning a signal handler:

```perl
$SIG{"INT"} =
    sub { print "You pressed control-C!\n"; }
```

CORE Note

Avoid changing global variable values inside of a signal handler, unless you are sure that the global values will not be used or modified anywhere else.

4.7.2   Built-in signal handlers

If a program has modified the signal handler for SIGINT, it can restore the original behavior by assigning the string DEFAULT:

```
$SIG{"INT"} = "DEFAULT";
```

A program can ignore a signal by assigning the string IGNORE:

```
$SIG{"INT"} = "IGNORE";
```

4.7.3   Pseudo-signals

Several keys in %SIG correspond to Perl events, rather than Unix events. This makes for a more consistent interface, even if it means that signal handlers are unrelated to Unix signals.

For example, a code reference assigned to $SIG{__WARN__} will be executed every time Perl generates a warning message:

```
#!/usr/bin/perl
# filename: demo-warn.pl

use warnings;

$SIG{__WARN__} =
    sub {
        print STDERR "Perl is warning us!\n";
    };

print "Foo = $foo;\n";    # Undefined variable causes warning
```

Running this program produces the following output:

```
Name "main::foo" used only once: possible typo at ./foo.pl line 9.
Perl is warning us!
Foo = ;
```

Signal handlers for $SIG{__WARN__} are passed a single argument, containing the warning message that will be printed. A handler to $SIG{__WARN__} could thus translate warning messages into another language or filter out unimportant messages.

$SIG{__DIE__}, another pseudo-signal, is invoked when a fatal error occurs—either a runtime error, or an explicit invocation of die. $SIG{__DIE__} is not invoked if die is called from within the signal handler.

4.7.4 Zombies and signals

When a Unix process exits, the operating system sends its parent the SIGCHLD (or SIGCHILD signal). The parent can then retrieve the child's exit status with wait, which is implemented in a Perl function of the same name. If the child's exit status is never retrieved by the parent, it becomes a *zombie*, taking up room in the system's process table without doing anything useful. Perl programs that invoke fork (see Section 3.14) need to take this into account, to avoid creating zombies.

A common solution is to install a signal handler for SIGCHLD. The signal handler calls wait immediately, allowing the child process to exit. Here is one possible implementation:

```
# Define a signal-handling subroutine
sub REAPER
{
    # Find out which process exited and exit silently
    my $which_process = wait;

    # Re-install the signal handler, in case we are running
    # under a version of Unix that requires it
    $SIG{CHLD} = \&REAPER;
}

# Install the signal handler initially
$SIG{CHLD} = \&REAPER;
```

See the `perldoc perlipc` manual pages for much more information about fork, wait, signal handlers, and zombies.

4.8 Conclusion

In this chapter, we learned about Perl subroutines. In particular, we saw:

- How to declare subroutines,

- How lexical and global variables work within subroutines,

- How subroutines return values,

- How Perl's context works,

- How to pass subroutine arguments, including those with semiformal parameter names,

- How to store code in subroutine references,

- How the BEGIN and END subroutines work when included in your programs,

- How to use signal handlers.

In the next chapter, we discuss text patterns, one of the most important tools for a Perl programmer. Patterns allow programs to perform sophisticated matches on text, and they are at the heart of Perl's strength as a text-processing language.

TEXT PATTERNS

Topics in This Chapter

- Introduction to patterns
- Metacharacters
- Character classes
- Backslashes
- Parentheses
- Substitution with s///
- Grabbing parts of a string
- Greediness
- Options for matching and substituting
- Making patterns easier to read
- Regexp objects
- Character transformations with tr///
- Substituting across multiple files

Chapter 5

In Chapter 3, we learned about eq, ne, and other string-comparison operators. However, these operators only allow us to compare a variable with one value. How can we compare a variable with multiple values, or with a general pattern of characters?

The solution is to use *text patterns*, sometimes known as *regular expressions* or *regexps*. Patterns provide much of Perl's renowned flexibility and power when working with text, and are central to Perl's matching (m//) and substitution (s///) operators.

This chapter describes the language of Perl's text patterns. We will look at *metacharacters*, built-in character classes, user-defined character classes, and optional arguments that we can pass to m// and s///.

Although you can probably be an accomplished C or Java programmer without thinking too much about regular expressions, this is not true for Perl. By the end of this chapter, you should have a good understanding of how text patterns work, why they are central to Perl, and how to use them in your programs.

5.1   What are text patterns?

Perl's text patterns—also known imprecisely as *regular expressions* or *regexps*—allow us to compare a text string with a general formula, rather a static text string. We can thus look for any word beginning with a, or filenames ending with p, or lines of a text file containing a vertical bar but lacking a numeric digit.

Let's begin by looking at the simplest possible patterns, which consist entirely of alphanumeric characters. For example, houseboat is a perfectly acceptable pattern. To determine whether $_ matches this pattern, use the m// ("match") operator:

```
m/houseboat/    # Looks for "houseboat" in $_
```

m// returns TRUE or FALSE, depending on whether a match was found. Remember that m// does not tell us if the $_ equals our pattern, but rather if it matches our pattern. Thus m/houseboat/ returns TRUE even if $_ contains the string XXXhouseboatYYY.

The leading m is optional if slashes are used as delimiters:

```
/houseboat/    # Same as m/houseboat/
```

Keeping the m makes it possible to use other delimiters:

```
m|houseboat|    # Same as m/houseboat/
```

If the opening delimiter is {, <, (, or [, then the closing delimiter is its matching right character:

```
m{houseboat}
m<houseboat>
```

To treat a delimiter as a literal character within a pattern, escape it with a backslash (\):

```
/\/usr\/bin\/perl/;  # Looks for /usr/bin/perl (hard to read)
```

However, it is usually a better idea to simply switch delimiters:

```
m|/usr/bin/perl|;    # Looks for /usr/bin/perl (easy to read)
```

5.1.1   *Searching for matches*

To look for a match in a string other than $_, precede m// with the =˜
operator. For example, this code compares the string ABC to the pattern
/houseboat/:

```
if ("ABC" =~ /houseboat/)
{
    print "We have a match!\n";    # Will not print this
}
else
{
    print "Sorry, no dice.\n";     # Will print this
}
```

m/houseboat/ will return TRUE for all of the following strings:

```
houseboat
houseboats
let's buy a houseboat, shall we?
```

m/houseboat/ will return FALSE for all of the following strings:

```
houseboa
ouseboat
Houseboat
HouseBoat
```

CORE Note

*When using the =˜ operator, the string goes on the left, and the pattern
goes on the right.*

The left side of =˜ can be any scalar value, not just a string literal:

```
my $residence = "houseboat";
if ($residence =~ /houseboat/)
{
    print "We have a match!\n";    # Prints
}
```

```
else
{
    print "Sorry, no dice.\n";     # Does not print
}
```

5.1.2 Interpolation

Delimiters around a pattern act like double quotes for purposes of variable interpolation. (This is not the case if you use single quotes as delimiters.) For example, the following pattern searches for a literal a, followed by the contents of the scalar variable $b, followed by a SPACE, followed by a literal c:

```
print if /a$b c/;    # $b is interpolated as in double quotes
```

5.1.3 Matching lines of a file

Here is a simple program that searches through the file /etc/passwd, which traditionally holds user information on a Unix system. The user enters a pattern, and the program displays all of the lines in /etc/passwd that match the pattern:

```
#!/usr/bin/perl

use strict;
use warnings;

my $filename = '/etc/passwd';
open PASSWD, $filename or die "Cannot read '$filename': $! ";

print "Enter a pattern for which to search: ";
my $pattern = <>;  # Get user input
chomp $pattern;    # Remove the trailing newline

while (<PASSWD>)    # Iterate over the file
{
    # "print" without arguments prints the current value of $_
    print if (/$pattern/);
}
close PASSWD;
```

5.2   Metacharacters

As we have seen, characters normally match themselves in a pattern. However, *metacharacters*, as they are known, are special, matching multiple characters or modifying the number of times another character must appear.

5.2.1   Matching any character

In a pattern, . (period) matches any ASCII character except NEWLINE. (To match a literal ., escape it with a preceding backslash.) The pattern a.c thus matches any string in which an a is followed by any non-NEWLINE character, and then c, including:

```
abc
qaBcz
ttttaaczzzqa
a c
a~c
```

It does not match the following:

```
ac
acb
a\nc
```

The first nonmatching string contains only two characters, the second lacks a c in the third slot, and the third contains a NEWLINE, which . does not match.

Patterns return TRUE when they find the first (i.e., leftmost) match. If there are multiple possible matches, m// ignores all but the first of them. See Section 5.10.1 to change this behavior.

5.2.2   Making characters optional

How can we construct a pattern that matches both abc and ac? The easiest solution is to use the question mark (?) metacharacter, which makes the preceding character optional. (Put differently, ? indicates that the preceding character may appear 0 or 1 times). To match a literal ?, precede it with a backslash.

The pattern ab?c will thus match both abc and ac. The pattern dictates that a must be followed by an optional b, followed by a mandatory c.

A related pattern, a.?c, matches any string in which a is followed by an optional non-NEWLINE character, and then a mandatory c.

The pattern a?.c matches an optional a, followed by a (mandatory) non-NEWLINE character, and then c. It matches qc, abc, aac, and a7c, but not iic or Ac.

? can appear multiple times in a pattern, following different characters. So the pattern be?a?t matches the strings bet, bat, beat, and bt.

CORE Alert

A ? cannot immediately follow another ?.

5.2.3   Matching zero or more times

The * metacharacter is similar to ?, in that it makes the preceding character optional. However, the character may also repeat any number of times. To match a literal *, precede it with a backslash.

The pattern caa*r thus matches car, caar, and caaar. The pattern ca*d*r matches any number of a and d characters between c and r, as in cr, cadr, and caaddr.

CORE Alert

*A * cannot immediately follow another *.*

* always matches, regardless of how many times a character appears—or if it appears at all. The pattern Q* is found in zebra, because Q appears zero or more times:

```
print "'Q' found in zebra!\n" if ("zebra" =~ /Q*/);
```

5.2.4   Matching one or more times

Similar to * is +, which indicates that the preceding character must appear one or more times. + only matches if the character appears at least once. To match a literal +, precede it with a backslash.

For example, the pattern a+b*c ("one or more a characters, followed by zero or more b characters, followed by a single c") matches all of the following:

```
abc
ac
aabc
aabbc
aaaaaaaaaaaaaaaaaaaaaaaaabc
abbbbbbbbbbbbbbbbbbbbbbbbc
```

Core Alert

*As with ? and *, Perl will not allow two + characters in a row.*

5.2.5 Custom ranges

* and + define ranges of "0 or more" and "1 or more," respectively. Perl allows for custom ranges with {*min,max*}, in which *min* and *max* are integers between 0 and 65535. The pattern br{2,5} thus matches brr, brrr, brrrr, and brrrrr. The pattern will also match the text string brrrrrr, but that is because our pattern matches the first six characters (one b and five r), and ignores the rest. So although our pattern will match brrrrrr, it will also match brrrrrQ and QbrrrrrQ.

Removing *max* removes any upper limit from the range. The patterns br{1,} and br+ are thus identical. Similarly, {0,1} is the same as ?, and {0,} is identical to *.

To specify that a character must match a particular number of times, use a single number, as in br{3}.

5.2.6 Alternation

How can a pattern match both Congress and congress, but nothing else? .ongress comes close, but also matches kongress and qongress, as well as zongress.

A simple solution is to use |, known as the *alternation* metacharacter, which operates as a logical "or" inside of a regexp. To insert a literal | in a pattern, precede it with a backslash.

The alternatives allowed by | are bounded by the ends of the pattern, by | characters, and by parentheses ((and)). We can thus search for a, b, or c with a|b|c. We can search for ab, cd, or ef with ab|cd|ef. We can match bat, bet, or but with b(a|e|u)t.

To match `congress` or `Congress`, we can thus use the pattern `(C|c)ongress`. Without the parentheses, our pattern will match either `C` or `congress`. This might trick us into believing that our pattern worked, because the one-character pattern `C` matches the string `Congress`.

5.3   Anchoring searches

Perl provides metacharacters that anchor the match to the beginning (ˆ) or end ($) of a line. These anchors, which match a location without consuming any characters, can be used to ensure that the pattern matches at the beginning or end of the target string. For example, `ˆabc` matches any text string beginning with `abc`, and `xyz$` matches any text string ending with `xyz`.

ˆ and $ only have these special meanings at the beginning or end of a pattern. The pattern `$1,000,000` thus begins with a literal dollar sign, not the end-of-string anchor.

5.3.1   Ignoring metacharacters

If a pattern must escape many metacharacters in a row, it is often easiest to turn off their special properties altogether for an extended run with \Q and \E. Metacharacters between \Q and \E are treated literally.

For instance, the pattern \Q3.14 + 2.71\E matches the literal string 3.14 + 2.71. Neither . nor + are treated as metacharacters. \Q and \E affect metacharacters, not variable interpolation.

CORE Note

Failing to include \E *after* \Q *results in an error.*

5.4   Character classes

Alternation is useful when there are only a few possibilities. However, as the number of possible matches increases, alternation makes the pattern difficult to read and maintain.

A solution to this problem is a *character class*, a set of characters placed inside of square brackets (`[]`) (To insert a literal `[` or `]`, precede the character with a backslash.) A character class matches any one character from within the set. Inside of a character class, metacharacters such as ., *, and + are not special, and others (e.g., ^ and -) become metacharacters with new meanings.

To match `congress` or `Congress` we could thus use the pattern [Cc]ongress. The pattern looks for one (but not both) of the characters inside of the class.

If ? appears after a character class, it means that any one of the class's elements may optionally appear. The pattern [abc]? thus matches a, b, c, or nothing at all. We can similarly place *, +, or {*min,max*}, after a character class.

The pattern [abc]+ will match any combination of the characters a, b, and c that is longer than one character long. For example, [abc]+ matches the string cba, as well as ccbbcc and baccab.

5.4.1 Ranges within classes

To match any of the letters from a through j, we can use the character class [abcdefghij]. But we can also write that class in an easier-to-read shorthand form, using the character class range operator, -. Using -, we can write our character class as [a-j].

To match American telephone numbers, we can use the pattern [0-9]3-[0-9]3-[0-9]4. This represents three digits, a hyphen, another three digits, another hyphen, and four final digits.

To include a literal - inside of a character class, make it the first or final character, or escape it with a backslash. For example, the character class [-+*/] matches all four arithmetic operators. Notice how + and * are not metacharacters inside of the character class.

5.4.2 Negative character classes

It is sometimes useful to specify which characters should not match, rather than which should. We can negate the elements of a character class by placing a ^ as the initial character. (^ is treated normally everywhere but the first position in a character class.) We can thus match any character but j with the pattern [^j], and any character but a through j with [^a-j].

As a further example, the set of four- to six-letter words beginning with any letter other than X is [^X][a-z]{3-5}. The pattern [^Xx][a-z]{3-5} matches any four- to six-letter word beginning with any letter other than x or X.

5.5   Predefined character classes

Perl includes many predefined character classes, saving you the effort of creating them yourself. These character classes can be used in a pattern or within a user-defined character class. All predefined classes are named with a backslash (\) and a letter. In many cases, the capitalized form of a character class is the inverse of the lowercase form. For instance, \w is the opposite of \W, and \d is the inverse of \D. For a full list of predefined character classes, see `perldoc perlre`.

5.5.1   Alphanumeric characters

Any alphanumeric character matches \w (same as [A-Za-z90-9_]), and any non-alphanumeric character matches with \W (same as [^\w] or [^A-Za-z90-9_]). A license plate consisting of any combination of seven alphanumeric characters can be matched with \w{7}.

The following program displays all of the lines of $filename that contain at least one alphanumeric character:

```perl
#!/usr/bin/perl

use strict;
use warnings;

my $filename = '/tmp/foo.txt';
open FILE, $filename or die "Cannot read '$filename': $! ";

while (<FILE>)          # Iterate through the file
{
    print if /\w/;     # Print lines that contain a character
}
close FILE;
```

___

CORE Note

\w and \W automatically adapt themselves to the locale in which they are run. Thus \w will always match alphabetic characters, regardless of the alphabet in question. See `perldoc perllocale` *for more information on locales in Perl.*

To match decimal digits alone, use \d. Our pattern that matches American telephone numbers could thus be rewritten as \d{3}-\d{3}-\d{4}. We can match hexadecimal numbers with [\da-fA-f]+.

The inverse class \D matches any character other than a decimal digit.

5.5.2 Matching whitespace

Whitespace characters normally match themselves. However, it is sometimes advantageous to match any whitespace, regardless of if it is a SPACE, NEWLINE, or TAB. This is possible with the \s character class, which matches any whitespace character. Its inverse, \S, matches any non-whitespace character.

The following code displays all lines in $filename, ignoring those that contain only whitespace:

```
open FILE, $filename or die "Cannot read '$filename': $! ";
while (<FILE>)
{
    print if /\S/; # Only if a non-whitespace character is found
}
close FILE;
```

The following code displays only those lines that contain two or more words:

```
open FILE, $filename or die "Cannot read '$filename': $! ";
while (<FILE>)
{
    print if /\w+\s+\w+/;
}
close FILE;
```

Notice how this example uses + to search for multiple characters. This means that words can consist of multiple letters, and that the words can be separated by multiple whitespace characters.

5.5.3 Finding word boundaries

Just as ^ matches the beginning of a string and $ matches the end of a string, \b matches the boundary between words, defined as the point between an alphanumeric character and a non-alphanumeric character. \b also matches the boundary between an alphanumeric character and a string's beginning or end.

We can thus search for the word `cat` with `\bcat\b`. This will match `cat`, but not `catsup` or `concatenation`.

CORE Note

Within a character class, \b means backspace, not word boundary. Because the boundary version of \b does not match any characters, it makes sense that it could not appear within a character class. However, the use of the same metacharacter to mean different things depending on context can be confusing.

To match something that is not a word boundary (i.e., the inverse of \b), use \B.

5.6   Parentheses

We have already seen how parentheses ((and)) can be used to limit the alternation metacharacter |. However, parentheses have other uses in patterns: They can "capture" parts of a pattern for later use, or group multiple characters together for modification by another metacharacter.

5.6.1   Capturing matches

Consider a configuration file in which name–value pairs are separated by colons. We can display valid lines in this file with:

```
while (<CONFIG>)
{
    print if /^\s*\w+\s*:\s*.+$/;
}
```

Until now, we have not seen any way to extract data from the input line—except, perhaps, using split. Using parentheses, we can capture part or all of a match, saving it for later use:

```
my ($name, $value);
if (/^\s*(\w+)\s*:\s*(.+)$/)
```

```
{
    $name = $1;     # Assigned to \w+
    $value = $2;    # Assigned to .+
}
```

If the pattern matches the input string, then everything that was matched by \w is assigned to $1, and everything that was matched by .+ is assigned to $2. We can then assign these values to variables of our choosing and display or modify them as appropriate.

Text captured by the first set of parentheses is stored in $1, by the second set in $2, and by the 35th set in $35. Because parentheses can be nested, count left parentheses (() to determine which variable contains which text.

5.7 Grabbing parts of a string

When a pattern successfully matches a string, we can divide that string into the text preceding the match, the matched text, and the text following the match. Perl makes these strings available to us in three variables: $` contains the preceding text, $& contains the matched text, and $' contains the following text. This code demonstrates these variables:

```
my $string = 'abcdefghij';
if ($string =~ /def/)
{
    print "Before: $`\n";    # Prints 'abc'
    print "Matched: $&\n";   # Prints 'def'
    print "After: $'\n";     # Prints 'ghij'
}
```

Similarly, $+ contains text captured in the final set of parentheses. Given the pattern ^\s*(\w+)\s*:\s*(.+)$, $+ will be set to the contents of what .+ matched.

Computing ($`, $&, $', and $+) forces Perl to work harder than usual, so it is best to avoid these variables when possible. However, using any one of them forces the rest of them to be created. If a program uses any of them, it may use the rest without any additional penalty.

CORE Approach

When debugging text patterns, it is often useful to print the content of $',
$&, $', and $+. Using these variables, you can double-check that you are
capturing the text that you want to capture.

5.7.1   Backreferences

A form of capturing, known as *backreferences*, is also available within patterns. For instance, a naive programmer might look for a doubled vowel using the pattern [aeiou]{2}. However, this will find any two vowels, rather than a repeated vowel. So although the pattern will match bees, it will also match bears.

With backreferences, we capture part of a match with parentheses, and then refer to that match later in the same pattern. Just as we can refer to captured text outside of the pattern with $1 and $2, we can refer to captured text within the pattern with \1 and \2.

To match a doubled vowel, we would thus use the pattern ([aeiou])\1. The pattern captures a vowel as part of a character class, and stores that in the first pair of parentheses. \1 refers to whatever was captured by the first set of parentheses. For example:

```
@words = qw(bees claw bears acetone books scads crowbar piece);
foreach my $word (@words)
{
    if ($word =~ /([aeiou])\1/)
    {
        print "$word has a doubled vowel.\n";
    }
    else
    {
        print "$word does not have a doubled vowel.\n";
    }
}
```

5.7.2   Grouping with parentheses

Normally, the metacharacters ?, +, and * affect only one character. Using parentheses, these metacharacters can affect groups of characters.

For example, the pattern bana+na matches banana and banaana, because + modifies the preceding a. In the similar pattern ba(na)+na, the + modifies the phrase (na), not just a, and thus matches banana, bananana, and banananana. The + tells Perl to search for one or more occurrences of the two-letter combination na, in order.

ba(na)+na and ba[na]+na are similar patterns, but work differently. In the first pattern, + modifies the group (na), matching any number of occurrences of na. In the second pattern, + modifies the character class [na], matching any number of occurrences of either n or a. So although both of these patterns would match bananana, only the second would match baaaaaana.

Using groups and ?, we can make an entire word optional:

```
I am( very)? hungry today\.
```

Notice how the SPACE between am and very must be optional, to avoid having too much or too little whitespace between words.

A pattern can use parentheses for both grouping and capturing:

```
if ($string =~ /I got a( high)? grade of (\d+)\./)
{
    $grade = $2;
}
```

To use parentheses for grouping without capturing their contents, put ?: immediately after the opening parenthesis:

```
my $variable = "do re mi";
if ($variable =~ /(\w+)?\s+(?:\w+)?\s+(\w+)?/)
{
    print "First: $1\n";    # Prints "do"
    print "Second: $2\n";   # Prints "mi"
    print "Third: $3\n";    # Prints nothing
}
```

The second pair of parentheses is only used by the ? following it. Because it is a non-capturing group, the third set of parentheses can be retrieved with $2—and $3 is left undefined.

5.8   Substitution

So far, this chapter has demonstrated patterns for searching through text strings. However, they can also be used with Perl's substitution operator, s///, to replace matching text with something else:

```
s/replace_me/with_me/;
```

As with m//, the initial s is optional when / is used as a delimiter. As with m//, other characters can be used as delimiters:

```
$string =~ s|/usr/local/bin|/usr/bin|;
$string =~ s{find me} {and replace with me};
```

Both the pattern and the replacement text support variable interpolation, except when ' is the delimiter:

```
my $foo = "foo";
my $bar = "bar";
my $foobar = "foobar";
$foobar =~ s/$foo/$bar/;
print $foobar, "\n";    # Prints "barbar";
```

This program customizes a text string based on user input:

```
#!/usr/bin/perl
# filename: fill-in-blank.pl

use strict;
use warnings;

my $sentence = "Hi, USERNAME.  How are you feeling today?";

# Get the user's name
print "Please enter your name: ";
my $username = <STDIN>;

# Remove trailing newline
chomp $username;
```

```
# Replace the generic string with the user's input
$sentence =~ s/USERNAME/$username/;

print $sentence, "\n";
```

If the substitution text is empty, text that matched the pattern is removed:

```
s/what_you_don't_what//;
```

s/// substitutes the entire match with the replacement text. Using text captured from parentheses, we can effectively replace only part of the matched text:

```
my $string = "yes no yes";
$string =~ s/(\w+)\s+no\s+(\w+)/$1 maybe $2/;
print $string;     # Prints "yes maybe yes"
```

5.9 Greediness

By nature, Perl's patterns are "greedy," meaning that they try to match the maximum possible number of characters. For example, new programmers sometimes try to remove HTML tags with the following code:

```
my $input = "Yes, <b>sir<b>!";
$input =~ s/<.*>//;           # Removes more than you think!
print "$input\n";
```

Because * is greedy, .* in our pattern matched everything between the initial < and the final >:

```
Yes, !
```

One solution is to use the negative character class [^>], which ensures that * cannot contain more than one HTML tag:

```
my $input = "Yes, <b>sir<b>!";
$input =~ s/<[^>]*>//;
print "$input\n";
```

A superior solution is to make the operator non-greedy, forcing it to match the minimum possible occurrences rather than the maximum number. *, +, ?, and {*min,max*} are greedy by default, and can be made non-greedy by appending ?. For example:

```
my $word = "brrrrr";

if ($word =~ m/(br+?)/)
{
    print "Non-greedy matched '$1'\n"; # Prints br
}

if ($word =~ m/(br+)/)
{
    print "Greedy matched '$1'\n";      # Prints brrrrr
}
```

5.10   Options for matching and replacing

You can modify the behavior of m// and s/// with single-character options, which are placed following the final delimiter. For example, we can modify m// with the /i (case-insensitive search) option:

```
$string =~ /findme/i;     # /i option to m//
```

We can place multiple options after the final delimiter, in any order:

```
$string =~ s|replace me|with me|gm;   # /g and /m options to s///
```

Specifying a nonexistent option results in a compilation error:

```
$string =~ s/foo/bar/u;    # /u does not exist; will not compile
```

5.10.1   /g

m// and s/// usually stop after the first match. The /g option modifies this behavior, such that m// returns and s/// replaces all of the matches that they find in the target string.

Using /g with s/// is similar to performing a global search-and-replace operation in a word processor. Every time the search pattern is encountered, it is replaced with the replacement text. For example:

```
my $text = "a b a b a b a b a b";
$text =~ s/a/b/g;
print "$text\n";   # Prints 'b b b b b b b b b b'
```

With /g active, m// returns a list of matches found in the target string. (In scalar context, it returns the number of matches that were found.) For example:

```
my $string = "claw cab acetone scads crowbar cent piece";

# Find words in which c is followed by a vowel
@results = ($string =~ m/\b\w*c[aeiou]\w*\b/g);
print "@results\n";    # Prints 'cab acetone scads cent piece'
```

Within a while loop, m//g iterates once for each match:

```
my $string = "claw cab acetone scads crowbar cent piece";

# Iterate over words in which 'c' is followed by a vowel
while ($string =~ m/\b(\w*c[aeiou]\w*)\b/g)
{
    print "$1\n";    # Print the captured word
}
```

5.10.2   /i

Patterns are normally case-sensitive, treating a and A as distinct characters. When /i is active, searches no longer treat them differently. The following code replaces both abc and ABC with xyz:

```
$string =~ /abc|ABC/xyz/;
```

Using /i, this code could be rewritten as follows:

```
$string =~ /abc/xyz/i;
```

/i only affects the search string. Case is preserved in the replacement string, regardless of the case of the matched text.

5.10.3   /m

Normally, ^ and $ match the beginning and end of a line, respectively. /m modifies this definition, matching at the beginning and end of a string. This is known as *multiline mode*, because /m is only relevant when the target string contains NEWLINE characters.

For example, this code tests whether **end** is at the end of **$string**, rather than just before NEWLINE within **$string**:

```
if ($string =~ /end$/m)
```

Without /m, a pattern can match the beginning and end of a string with \A and \Z.

When both /m and /g are active, ^ and $ retain their usual definitions.

5.10.4   /s

/s puts Perl in *single-line mode*, modifying . to include NEWLINE.

This is useful for searching through the contents of a file, including across line boundaries:

```
my $filename = 'phrases.txt';
open FILE, $filename or die "Cannot open '$filename' for reading: $! ";

@contents = (<FILE>);    # Grab the file's contents as a list of lines

my $contents = join "", @contents;

close FILE;

print "Oxymoron!\n"
    if ($contents =~ /military.intelligence/is);
```

The preceding code searches for the words "military" and "intelligence," separated by any character. Because /s is active, that character can be a NEWLINE.

CORE Note

Avoid confusing /m and /s. The former redefines ^ and $. The latter redefines . to include NEWLINE.

5.10.5   /o

Perl compiles patterns into an internal format before using them. Normally, this is performed only the first time a pattern is encountered. However, if a variable is interpolated into a pattern, Perl compiles the pattern each time, since it cannot be sure whether the variable will change in value before the pattern is next needed. /o overrides this judgment, telling Perl that the search string can be compiled even though it contains an interpolated variable. For example:

```
if ($string =~ /$variable/o)
```

/o is only useful if the search string contains an interpolated variable.
  See Section 5.11 for information on the related **study** function.

5.10.6   /e

/e is only useful with s///. It evaluates the replacement string as a small Perl program, substituting the result of this program's evaluation for the matched text. The syntax of the substitution expression is checked at compile-time.
  For example, the following code reverses five-letter words, leaving others in place:

```
my $string = "claw cab acetone scads crowbar cent piece";
print "Old string = '$string'\n";

$string =~ s/\b(\w{5})\b/reverse $1/eg;

print "New string = '$string'\n";
```

  Each /e forces a further evaluation of the result string. Thus one /e (as we saw earlier) evaluates the replacement text once, whereas /ee would evaluate the evaluation of the replacement text. There is no limit to the number of /e options you can use, but it is unusual to use more than one or two.

5.10.7   /x

/x extends the pattern syntax, ignoring whitespace and anything following #. Whitespace or # with a preceding backslash is treated as usual. In addition, SPACE characters are not ignored inside of character classes. Comments inserted using /x may contain any character except for a closing search delimiter. /x has no effect on the replacement string in s///, which continues to be treated as a double-quoted string. Without /x, long patterns can be difficult to understand and debug.

For example, consider the pattern (abc)*\s+(def)+[ghi]{3,7}. With /x, we can make it much more readable and understandable:

```
m/(abc)*      # Find zero or more occurrences of 'abc',
  \s+         # separated by one or more whitespace characters,
  (def)+      # followed by one or more occurrences of 'def',
  [ghi]{3,7}  # with 3-7 letters from the set 'ghi'.
 /x
```

You can also insert inline comments into a pattern, inside of parentheses whose first two characters are ?#:

```
next unless /^\d\.\d\d(?# Only two decimals)$/;
```

5.11   study

Scalars compared with patterns are normally parsed each time m// or s/// is invoked. study analyzes the scalar in advance, removing the need for such parsing upon each comparison.

study takes a single argument, the scalar to parse. Without an argument, it defaults to $_. If the variable's value changes, the effects of study are lost.

Because study builds a linked list describing how often each character occurs in the target scalar, it takes some time to execute. Only use study if a scalar will often be the subject of m// or s///.

CORE Note

Do not confuse study *with* /o, *the option that optimizes searches.* study *examines the scalar, whereas* /o *examines the pattern. Use* study *if a scalar value will be compared with many patterns. Use* /o *if a pattern contains an unchanging interpolated variable.*

5.12   Regexp objects

Recent versions of Perl make it possible to create and compile *pattern objects* using qr. The return value from qr is a string that remembers the options with which it was created. For example:

```
my $regexp = qr/abc/i;

print "Found in 1\n" if ($text1 =~ /$regexp/);
print "Found in 2\n" if ($text2 =~ /$regexp/);
```

The pattern in this code is only compiled once, when qr is invoked. Without qr, Perl would have to compile the pattern twice, once for each if statement.

Moreover, qr remembers the options with which a pattern was compiled. Therefore, even though our m// statements do not explicitly invoke /i for case-insensitive searching, the fact that $regexp was created with qr and /i means that the search will ignore case.

5.13   tr///

Perl's tr/// function substitutes characters rather than patterns. (For historical reasons, tr/// can also be written as y///.)

For example, all of the a characters in $string can be turned into b with:

```
$string =~ tr/a/b/;
```

This task could be performed equally well with s///. However, s/// cannot simultaneously turn a's into b's and vice versa. Because tr/// works in parallel, the following is possible:

```
my $string = 'banana';        # Prints 'Before: banana'
print "Before: $string\n";
$string =~ tr/ab/ba/;
print "After: $string\n";     # Prints 'After: abnbnb'
```

tr/// returns the number of replacements it made. To count how many times a character appears in a string, use tr/// to replace the character with itself:

```
$string = "aaabbbcccaaabbbcccd";
$count = ($string =~ tr/a/a/);
print $count, "\n";              # Prints 6
```

5.13.1   *Using* tr///

tr/// substitutes each character in the match string with the character in
the same position of the substitution string.

If the match string is longer than the substitution string, the extra characters are turned into the final character of the latter:

```
my $string = 'banana';          # Prints 'Before: banana'
print "Before: $string\n";
$string =~ tr/abn/ba/;
print "After: $string\n";       # Prints 'After: ababab'
```

The rot-13 mode used for hiding potentially offensive postings on Usenet
is performed with:

```
$article =~ tr/m-za-l/a-z/;
```

This example demonstrates the use of ranges with tr///. Although the
match string uses two ranges and the substitution string has a single range,
the fact that both have 26 characters makes for a one-to-one correspondence
when translating.

tr/// builds its translation table during compilation, and thus cannot
interpolate variables within its match and substitution strings. This can be
emulated using eval:

```
$forwards = "abcdefg";
$backwards =   "zyxwvut";

$_ = "gfedcba";
eval "tr/$forwards/$backwards/";

print "$_\n";
```

tr/// does not handle metacharacters. For instance, the following will
remove s from $string, rather than the expected whitespace:

```
$string =~ tr/\s//;
```

5.13.2   /c

Like m// and s///, tr/// supports options that modify its behavior.

/c forces tr/// to complement the search list, much like a negative character class. The following code turns all letters but g and r into Z:

```
$string = join '', ("a" .. "z");
$string =~ tr/gr/Z/c;
print $string;       # Prints 'ZZZZZZgZZZZZZZZZZrZZZZZZZZ'
```

5.13.3   /d

The /d option tells tr/// that if the search list is longer than the replacement list, the extra characters should be deleted rather than replaced. For example:

```
my $string1 = 'aaabbbcccdddeeefffgggaaaa';
my $string2 = 'aaabbbcccdddeeefffgggaaaa';

$string1 =~ tr/abcdef/z/;    # Without /d
$string2 =~ tr/abcdef/z/d;   # With /d

print "1: $string1\n";    # zzzzzzzzzzzzzzzzzzgggzzzz
print "2: $string2\n";    # zzzgggzzzz
```

5.13.4   /s

/s "squashes" repeated occurrences of the same replacement into a single one:

```
my $string = 'I have  a   secret   to    tell     you.';
$string =~ tr/ / /s;
print "$string\n";
```

5.14   Substituting across multiple files

Several common Perl idioms make it easy to modify one or more files from the command line, much like the traditional Unix program sed. To activate this behavior, use the either the -n or -p command-line switch, as well as the -e switch followed by a string of Perl code.

Any remaining arguments are treated as filenames. Perl opens each file in sequence, iterating through its lines as if in a while loop. Each line is placed in $_, and the argument to -e is then executed. The -p switch tells Perl to print $_ after each line is modified, and the -n switch keeps Perl silent by default. For example, the following replaces every occurrence of abc in foo.txt with 123. A modified version of foo.txt is sent to STDOUT:

```
perl -p -e 's/abc/123/;' foo.txt
```

Neither -n nor -p changes the original file. The modified output can be piped to another program or redirected to create a new file:

```
perl -p -e 's/abc/123/;' foo.txt > new-foo.txt
```

To modify the input files themselves, use the -i flag in conjunction with -n or -p. For example:

```
perl -ip -e 's/abc/123/;' foo.txt
```

This modifies foo.txt, turning all occurrences of abc into 123. Because of the danger of making a mistake, -i takes an argument. If the argument exists, then the original version of the file is saved with the suffix indicated. For example:

```
perl -i.bak -p -e 's/abc/123/;' foo.txt
```

The file foo.txt will be modified, with the original version retained as foo.txt.bak.

5.15   grep

Section 3.8.7 described grep, which allows us to filter through elements of a list by using a code block. However, the first argument to grep can be a pattern, rather than a code block. In such a case, grep returns those list elements that match the pattern. For example, here is how we can find words beginning with a:

```
my @animals = ("aardvark", "armadillo", "zebra", "crocodile");
@starts_with_a = grep /^a/, @animals;
print "@starts_with_a\n";  # Prints 'aardvark' and 'armadillo'
```

Notice how we need not surround the pattern with braces ({ and }). We do need to insert a comma between the pattern and the input list, however.

5.16   Conclusion

This chapter introduced the notion of patterns and Perl's m//, s///, and tr/// operator. Patterns are central to Perl, and one of its most complex topics. For a complete discussion of patterns, including a complete list of Perl's built-in character classes and extensions to the pattern syntax, see `perldoc perlre`. In this chapter, we discussed the following:

- Text pattern basics,

- Metacharacters,

- User- and system-defined character classes,

- The m// and s/// operators,

- Using parentheses for capturing and grouping,

- Optional arguments to m// and s///,

- tr/// and its arguments, and

- How to substitute text in multiple files from the command line.

In the next chapter, we will conclude our discussion of Perl basics with a discussion of modules and object-oriented programming.

MODULES

Topics in This Chapter

- Packages

- Modules

- Exporting values

- Creating simple constants

- Version numbers

- Some example modules

Chapter 6

Over the years, Perl has grown to include many new features. These features make the language richer and more useful—but they also make it more complex for programmers and the Perl maintainers.

Perl 5 partly solved this problem by making the language extensible with modules that range widely in complexity, adding anything from convenience variables to sophisticated database clients and Web development environments. Modules have made it possible for Perl to improve incrementally without changing the language itself.

This chapter begins with a discussion of Perl packages, which allow us to place variables and subroutines in a namespace hierarchy. Once we have discussed packages, we begin to discuss modules—how to use them, how to write them, and how to improve them.

By the end of this chapter, you should understand not just how Perl modules work, but also how you can use them effectively in your programs.

6.1   Packages

Programmers working on large projects often discover that a variable or subroutine name is being used by someone else. Perl and other languages provide *packages*, or *namespaces*, which make it easier to avoid such clashes. Packages are analogous to surnames in human society, allowing more than one David or Jennifer to coexist unambiguously.

6.1.1   Packages

Every global variable in Perl exists within a package, with the default package being main. The global variable $x is actually shorthand for $main::x, where main is the package, $x is the variable, and :: separates the package name from the unqualified variable name.

We can similarly refer to variables in other packages. For example, $fruit::mango, @fruit::kiwi, and %fruit::apple are all in the fruit package. As you can see, symbols representing a data type ($, @, or %) precede the package name, not the unqualified variable name. As with variables, packages spring to life when they are first referenced.

Package names may contain ::, allowing us to create what appear to be hierarchies. For instance, $fruit::tropical::kiwi is the variable $kiwi in the package fruit::tropical. However, these names are only significant to programmers; Perl does not notice or enforce hierarchies. As far as Perl is concerned, two unrelated modules can be under the same package hierarchy, and two related modules can be in completely different packages.

At any time in our program, we can set or retrieve the value of any global variable by giving its fully qualified name:

```
$main::x = 5;
$blueberry::x = 30;

print "main::x = $main::x\n";
print "blueberry::x = $blueberry::x\n";
```

6.1.2   Lexicals and packages

Lexicals exist outside of a package, in a separate area known as the *scratch-pad*. They have nothing to do with packages or global variables. There is no relationship between $main::var and the lexical $var, except in the mind of a programmer. This program is perfectly legal, but hard for programmers to understand:

```perl
#!/usr/bin/perl
# filename: globals-and-lexicals.pl

use warnings;

$main::x = 10;                     # Global
my $x = 20;                        # Lexical

print "x = '$x'\n";                # Prints 20 (lexical)
print "main::x = '$main::x'\n";    # Prints 10 (global)
```

Once the lexical $x is declared, $main::x must be retrieved with its fully qualified name. Otherwise, Perl will assume that $x refers to the lexical $x, rather than the global $main::x.

6.1.3   use strict

use strict tells the Perl compiler to forbid the use of unqualified global variables, avoiding the ambiguity that we saw in the preceding program. When use strict is active, $x must refer to a lexical explicitly declared with my. If no such lexical has been declared, the program exits with a compilation error:

```perl
#!/usr/bin/perl
# filename: counter.pl

use strict;
use warnings;

# Declare $counter lexical within the foreach loop
foreach my $counter (0 .. 10)
{
    print "Counter = $counter\n";
    $counter++;
}

# $counter has disappeared -- fatal compilation error!
print "Counter at the end is $counter\n";
```

We can fix this program by declaring $counter to be a top-level lexical:

```
#!/usr/bin/perl
# filename: new-counter.pl

use strict;
use warnings;

# Declare $counter to be lexical for the entire program
my $counter;

# Declare $index to be lexical within the foreach
foreach my $index (0 .. 10)
{
    print "Counter = $counter\n";
    $counter++;
}

# Counter still exists
print "Counter at the end is $counter\n";
```

6.1.4   use vars *and* our

Experienced Perl programmers include use strict in their programs, because of the number of errors it traps. However, referring to globals by their full names quickly gets tedious.

use vars helps by making an exception to use strict. Variables named in the list passed to use vars can be referred to by their unqualified names, even when use strict is active. For example, the following code tells Perl that $a, $b, and $c in the current package do not need to be fully qualified:

```
use vars qw($a $b $c);
```

In the case of a conflict between my and use vars, the lexical has priority. (After all, you can always set and retrieve the global's value using its fully qualified name, but the lexical has only one name.) The following program demonstrates this:

```
#!/usr/bin/perl
# filename: globals-and-lexicals-2.pl
```

```
use strict;
use warnings;
use vars qw($x);    # Allows us to write $main::x as $x

$x = 10;            # Sets global $main::x
my $x = 20;         # Sets lexical $x
$x = 30;            # Sets lexical $x, not global $main::x

print "x = '$x'\n";          # Prints 30 (lexical)
print "main::x = '$main::x'\n"; # Prints 10 (global)
```

As of Perl 5.6, use vars has been deprecated in favor of our. our is similar to my, in that its declarations only last through the current lexical scope. However, our (like use vars) works with global variables, not lexicals. We can rewrite this program as follows using our:

```
#!/usr/bin/perl
# filename: globals-and-lexicals-with-our.pl

use strict;
use warnings;
our $x;             # Allows us to write $main::x as $x

$x = 10;            # Sets global $main::x
my $x = 20;         # Sets lexical $x
$x = 30;            # Sets lexical $x, not global $main::x

print "x = '$x'\n";          # Prints 30 (lexical)
print "main::x = '$main::x'\n"; # Prints 10 (global)
```

6.1.5 Switching default packages

To change to a new default package, use the package statement:

```
package newPackageName;
```

A program can change default packages as often as it might like, although doing so can confuse the next person maintaining your code. Remember that package changes the default namespace; it does not change your ability to set or receive any global's value by explicitly naming its package.

There is a subtle difference between use vars and our that comes into play when we change packages. use vars ceases to have effect when you change to a different default package. For example:

```
package foo;        # Make the default package 'foo'
use vars qw($x);    # $x is shorthand for $foo::x

$x = 5;             # Assigns $foo::x

package bar;        # Make the default package 'bar'
print "'$x'\n";     # $x refers to $bar::x (undefined)

package foo;        # Make the default package 'foo' (again)
print "'$x'\n";     # $x refers to $foo::x
```

In this code, use vars tells Perl that $x is shorthand for $foo::x. When we switch into default package bar, $x no longer refers to $foo::x, but $bar::x. Without use strict, Perl allows us to retrieve the value of an undeclared global variable, which has the value undef. When we return to package foo, $x once again refers to $foo::x, and the previous value is once again available.

By contrast, global variables declared with our remain available with their short names even after changing into a different package:

```
package foo;        # Make the default package 'foo'
our $x;             # $x is shorthand for $foo::x

$x = 5;             # Assigns $foo::x

package bar;        # Make the default package 'bar'
print "'$x'\n";     # $x still refers to $foo::x
```

For $x to refer to $bar::x, we must add an additional our declaration immediately following the second package statement:

```
package foo;        # Make the default package 'foo'
our $x;             # $x is shorthand for $foo::x

$x = 5;             # Assigns $foo::x

package bar;        # Make the default package 'bar'
```

```
our $x;             # $x is now shorthand for $bar::x
print "'$x'\n";     # $x now refers to $bar::x
```

6.1.6 *Subroutines*

When we declare a subroutine, it is placed by default in the current package:

```
package abc;
sub foo {return 5;}    # Full name is abc::foo
```

This means that when working with more than one package, we may need to qualify subroutine names:

```
package numbers;        # Default package is "numbers"
sub gimme_five { 5; }   # Define a subroutine


package main;           # Default package is now "main"


my $x = gimme_five();   # Fails to execute main::gimme_five()
print "x = '$x'\n";     # Prints 5
```

This code exits with a fatal error, with Perl complaining that no subroutine main::gimme_five has been defined. We can fix this by invoking the subroutine with its fully qualified name:

```
package numbers;               # Default package is "numbers"
sub gimme_five { 5; }          # Define a subroutine

package main;                  # Default package is now "main"

my $x = numbers::gimme_five(); # Qualify gimme_five() with a package
print "x = '$x'\n";            # Prints 5
```

6.2   Modules

Modules make it easy to reuse Perl code in multiple programs. Writing a Perl module involves defining a set of variables and subroutines within a package, and then making those definitions available for public consumption. Just as you can avoid repeating code within a program by using subroutines, you can avoid repeating code within a set of programs by writing a module. In this section, we will see just how easy it is to create and use Perl modules.

6.2.1   Creating a module

To write a module, create a file with a `.pm` suffix. The file should define global variables and subroutines, all within a package with a name that is the same as the filename. If the file is named `Foo.pm`, then it should define variables and subroutines in the package `Foo`. (User-defined module and package names traditionally begin with capital letters.)

If the package name contains ::, such as Food::Cooking, then the file should be named `Cooking.pm`, placed within a directory named `Food`. Perl translates the hierarchy separator :: into a directory separator, regardless of what platform you're running. Food::Cooking would thus be in `Food/Cooking.pm` on a Unix system, and `Food\Cooking.pm` on a Windows system. Within a Perl program, these platform-specific differences are normally invisible.

A module will normally begin with a `package` statement, naming the package in which the module's variables and subroutines will be placed. So in Food::Cooking, the first line would be:

```
package Food::Cooking;
```

The last line of a module must evaluate to TRUE. This is traditionally done by putting the number 1 on the final line:

```
1;
```

The following is a perfectly legal definition of the Mathtest module, which defines two variables and a subroutine:

```
use strict;

package Mathtest;
our ($pi, $e);

$pi = 3.14159;    # Define $Mathtest::pi
$e = 2.7182818;   # Define $Mathtest::e

sub circle_area   # Declare a subroutine
{
    # Get the argument to our subroutine
    my $radius = shift;
```

```
    # Return the calculated area
    return ($pi * $radius * $radius);
}


1;                 # Loaded successfully
```

6.2.2 Using our module

Once Mathtest has been created, a program can use it with the compile-time use statement:

```
use Mathtest;
```

A program can also use the -M command-line argument:

```
perl -MMathtest -e 'print "$Mathtest::pi\n";'
```

This could be rewritten as:

```
perl -e 'use Mathtest; print "$Mathtest::pi\n";'
```

6.2.3 Details of module loading

The array @INC lists the directories in which Perl should look for modules. When it encounters a use statement, Perl looks through the directories in @INC sequentially, stopping when it finds a match.

The following one-liner displays the contents of @INC:

```
perl -e 'print join "\n", @INC, "\n";'
```

On my computer, this program displayed the following:

```
/usr/local/lib/perl5/5.6.1/i686-linux
/usr/local/lib/perl5/5.6.1
/usr/local/lib/perl5/site_perl/5.6.1/i686-linux
/usr/local/lib/perl5/site_perl/5.6.1
/usr/local/lib/perl5/site_perl/5.6.0/i686-linux
/usr/local/lib/perl5/site_perl/5.6.0
/usr/local/lib/perl5/site_perl
```
.

If `Mathtest.pm` is in any of these directories, then use `Mathtest` within our program will work. If Perl cannot find `Mathtest.pm` in any of these directories, the program exits with a fatal compilation error. . represents the current directory, meaning that Perl will normally look for modules in the same directory as an executing program. Activating taint mode (see Section 13.3) removes . from @INC, as a safety precaution.

A program can add a directory to @INC with use lib:

```
use lib "/usr/random/directory";
```

use lib adds directories to the front of @INC, giving them priority over the default directories. Command-line programs can have the same effect with -I:

```
perl -I/usr/local/perl/modules -I/home/joeuser/modules -MJoe -w
```

When Perl finds and loads a module with use, it adds a key–value pair to %INC. Each key in %INC is a module name, and its corresponding value is the file from which it was loaded. This ensures that each module is loaded only once, even if it appears in two use statements.

6.2.4 Using modules

Once a module is loaded, its variables and subroutines are available to a program. For example:

```
use Mathtest;

my $log_base = $Mathtest::e;
print "Log base: $log_base\n";      # Prints 2.7182818

my $radius = 10;
my $area =
    Mathtest::circle_area($radius);
print "Area = $area\n";             # Prints 314.159
```

Globals declared in a module are no different from any other global variables. We can thus modify global variables defined in a module, as the following code demonstrates:

```
use Mathtest;          # Import the module
$Mathtest::pi = 4;     # Redefine pi!

my $radius = 10;
my $area = Mathtest::circle_area($radius);
print "$area\n";       # Prints 400
```

It is generally a bad idea to redefine variables defined by a module unless the module's documentation encourages such behavior explicitly.

6.2.5   *Lexicals in modules*

Lexical variables, as we have already seen, look similar to global variables but act quite differently. Every global is associated with a package and lasts until the program exits. By contrast, lexicals do not have any associated package and disappear when their enclosing block goes out of scope.

Because they lack a package, lexical variables defined at a module's top-level scope are invisible to programs outside of the module. This can sometimes be useful, but it usually leads to confusion—particularly for the programmer who cannot figure out why he or she cannot access a module's variables!

Understanding the difference between globals and lexicals is a key part of programming in Perl, and this is especially true when working with modules. Although it is normally a good idea to use lexicals wherever possible, this does not include module variables that must be visible to the outside world.

6.3   Exporting symbols

As we saw earlier, Perl programs have full access to variables and subroutines defined within imported modules. However, it quickly becomes tedious to use fully qualified names for every variable and subroutine that a module defines.

Perl's Exporter module allows modules to "export" identifiers (i.e., variable and subroutine names) into the calling program's namespace. Once exported, an identifier has two names—one in the module's package and another in the importing program's package.

Importing symbols is potentially dangerous: A module that exports $x will trample $x in the calling program's package. This is known as *namespace pollution*, and we will soon see how Perl helps us to avoid such problems.

6.3.1   Basic export functionality

For a module to export one or more identifiers into a caller's namespace, it must:

- use the Exporter module, which is part of the standard Perl distribution,

- declare the module to inherit Exporter's capabilities, by setting the variable @ISA (see Section 7.3.1) to equal ('Exporter'), and

- indicate under which circumstances identifiers should be exported, by setting one or more of the variables @EXPORT, @EXPORT_OK, and %EXPORT_TAGS.

@EXPORT is the easiest way to export identifiers, but also the most dangerous: Any identifier in @EXPORT will be exported to the calling program's namespace, unless the caller indicates otherwise. For example, the following defines MyModule, which exports $a and @b by default:

```
package MyModule;

use Exporter;           # Gain export capabilities
our (@EXPORT, @ISA);    # Global variables

@ISA = qw(Exporter);    # Take advantage of Exporter's capabilities
@EXPORT = qw($a @b);    # Export $a and @b by default

$a = 5;                 # Assign some values
@b = (1, 2, 3);

1;                      # Always return a true value
```

When a program invokes use MyModule, the variables $a and @b will be available as $MyModule::a and @MyModule::b, and also as $main::a and @main::b. (This assumes, of course, that the default package when executing use is main.) Any existing values for $main::a and @main::b are overwritten.

A calling program can override the value of @EXPORT by explicitly passing a list of identifiers that should be exported. For example:

```
use MyModule qw($a);    # Only imports $a
```

The preceding code imports $a, but not @b, from MyModule. We can import a module without any of its identifiers by passing an empty list:

```
use MyModule ();        # Don't import into the current package
```

To avoid potential namespace pollution, place exportable identifiers in
@EXPORT_OK. @EXPORT_OK is just like @EXPORT, except that its contents are only exported when explicitly requested.

A module can also create named groups of identifiers that can be exported
in a single chunk. Group names are known as *export tags*, and these form
the keys of %EXPORT_TAGS. The value associated with each key is an array
reference listing the identifiers belonging to that group. Identifiers named in
%EXPORT_TAGS must appear in either @EXPORT or @EXPORT_OK.

For example, the below Conversions module shown here declares four
subroutines (inch2cm, gal2liter, dollar2pound, and dollar2mark) as exportable,
by listing them in @EXPORT_OK:

```
package Conversions;

use Exporter;           # Gain export capabilities

our (@ISA, @EXPORT,     # Declare some global variables
    @EXPORT_OK, %EXPORT_TAGS,
    $inch2cm, $gal2liter, $dollar2pound, $dollar2mark);

@ISA = qw(Exporter);    # Take advantage of Exporter's capabilities

@EXPORT_OK =            # Exported, if explicitly requested
    qw($inch2cm $gal2liter $dollar2pound $dollar2mark);

%EXPORT_TAGS =          # Tag groups
    ("metric" => [qw($inch2cm $gal2liter)],
    "currency" => [qw($dollar2pound $dollar2mark)]);

# Subroutine definitions go here

1;                      # Always return a true value
```

We can import dollar2pound and dollar2mark by naming their their tag
group in our use statement, preceding the tag name with a colon (:):

```
use Conversions qw(:currency);    # Imports 'currency' tag group
```

perldoc Exporter describes the Exporter module more thoroughly, including advanced ways to selectively import symbols.

6.4   Some example modules

The Perl distribution comes with many modules, and CPAN (see Section 1.6) offers thousands of others. This section describes a few of these modules and how to use them.

6.4.1   Math::Trig

The Math::Trig module, which was written by Jarkko Hietaniemi and Raphael Manfredi, defines subroutines that fill in some of Perl's missing trigonometric functions. All of its subroutines are exported by default to the caller's package.

Among the subroutines defined by Math::Trig are tan, which returns the tangent of an angle in radians, and deg2rad, which converts degrees to radians. Here is an example of how to use this module:

```perl
#!/usr/bin/perl

use strict;
use warnings;

use Math::Trig;

my $angle_degrees = 30;
my $angle_radians = deg2rad $angle_degrees;
my $tangent = tan $angle_radians;

print "Tangent of $angle_degrees degrees is $tangent.\n";
```

6.4.2   File::Compare

File::Compare, written by Nick Ing-Simmons, compares two files. It returns 0 if the files are equal, 1 if the files are different, or -1 if there was an error.

By default, File::Compare exports the compare subroutine to the caller's package. The following program uses File::Compare to compare two files:

```perl
#!/usr/bin/perl
# filename: compare-files.pl

use strict;
```

```perl
use warnings;
use File::Compare;

# What files should we compare?
my $file1 = "/home/reuven/.bashrc";
my $file2 = "/home/reuven/.bash_profile";

# Compare the files, and get a result
my $result = compare($file1, $file2);

if ($result == 0)
{
    print "'$file1' and '$file2' are identical.\n";
}
elsif ($result == 1)
{
    print "'$file1' and '$file2' are different.\n";
}
elsif ($result == -1)
{
    die "Problem running File::Compare::compare: $! ";
}
else
{
    die "Error!  Result of '$result' from File::Compare: $! ";
}
```

6.4.3 Getopt::Long

Getopt::Long, written by Johan Vromans and available on CPAN (see Section 1.6), makes it easy for Perl programs to accept command-line arguments. Unix programs often allow an option to be invoked with a single-letter argument or an equivalent, one-word argument. For example, GNU `cat` sees the -n and –number options as equivalent.

Command-line arguments often take values. For example:

```
program --number=5
```

Getopt::Long automatically exports the subroutine GetOptions. GetOptions takes a hash as an argument, in which the keys describe the data types and the values are references to variables that should be assigned the argument's value. For instance, a program can automatically place the integer argument to the –number flag in the $number variable with:

```perl
GetOpt("number=i" => \$number);
```

To make –number and -n aliases for one another, separate the possibilities with a vertical bar (|). The following program demonstrates how to integrate this feature into a program:

```perl
#!/usr/bin/perl
# filename: test-getopt.pl

use strict;
use warnings;
use Getopt::Long;

# Declare the variable, giving a default value
my $number = 0;

# Get the options
my $success = GetOptions("number|n=i" => \$number);

# Use the variable
print "Option was $number\n" if $success;
```

If this program is invoked without –number or -n, GetOptions does not modify $number. GetOptions also tests the type of data passed in –number, exiting with a fatal error if the user passes a string or float.

The manual for Getopt::Long, available after installation with `perldoc Getopt::Long`, describes the module's type checking in detail.

6.4.4   Data::Dumper

Data::Dumper, written by Gurusamy Sarathy and available from CPAN (see Section 1.6), makes it possible to store, pass, and retrieve complex data structures. By default, Data::Dumper exports its Dumper subroutine.

The following program demonstrates how Data::Dumper stores an array of arrays:

```perl
#!/usr/bin/perl
# filename: demo-dumper.pl

use strict;
use warnings;
use Data::Dumper;

# Translate 0-1-2-3 (English, Spanish, Hebrew)
my @array0 = qw(zero cero efes);
my @array1 = qw(one uno achat);
my @array2 = qw(two dos shtayim);
my @array3 = qw(three tres shalosh);

# Create a reference to our array of arrays
my $numbers_ref = [\@array0, \@array1, \@array2, \@array3];

print Dumper($numbers_ref), "\n";
```

The output from demo-dumper.pl looks like this:

```
$VAR1 = [
          [
            'zero',
            'cero',
            'efes'
          ],
          [
            'one',
            'uno',
            'achat'
          ],
          [
            'two',
            'dos',
            'shtayim'
          ],
          [
            'three',
            'tres',
```

```
            'shalosh'
        ]
    ];
```

Data::Dumper is particularly useful for saving data structures to disk and then reading them back again. The following program reads this structure from the file /tmp/output-file, retrieves it into a lexical with eval, and then displays its contents:

```perl
#!/usr/bin/perl
# filename: read-dumped-data.pl

use strict;
use warnings;

my $VAR1;

# What file is it?
my $file = "/tmp/output-file";

# Open a filehandle
open FILE, $file or die "Cannot read '$file': $! ";

# Grab the whole file at once
undef $/;

# Read the contents
my $contents = (<FILE>);

# Close the filehandle
close FILE;

# Evaluate the contents into a new array ref
eval $contents;

foreach my $number (@$VAR1)
{
        print "English: $number->[0]\n";
        print "Spanish: $number->[1]\n";
```

```
    print "Hebrew: $number->[2]\n";
    print "\n";
}
```

6.5   Documenting modules with POD

Perl documentation is generally well written and complete. This is partly because of POD, the "plain old documentation" format that allows documentation to be interspersed in Perl modules. POD can be read by a number of different programs, including several that come with Perl—`perldoc`, `pod2html` (for HTML output), `pod2latex` (for LATEX output), and `pod2man` (for Unix-style `man` pages).

6.5.1   POD definitions

POD directives are placed directly inside of a Perl module. POD recognizes three kinds of lines:

- Regular lines of text are kept verbatim.

- Indented lines of text are kept verbatim, but indented.

- POD commands begin in the first column, and with an equals sign (=). This is how Perl distinguishes between code and documentation.

Each POD command typically affects a single paragraph of text. For example:

```
package Howdy;

=head1 NAME

    Howdy - A module for testing cowboy-speak

=head1 SYNOPSIS

    This module allows programs to display error messages
    in cowboy-speak, as well as plain ol' English.

=head1 DESCRIPTION
```

```
    If you want to know what to say when tipping your 10-gallon hat,
    you can use this module.
```

=cut

This module consists entirely of a package statement and POD documentation. POD's =head1 command introduces a first-class headline, and is used for the highest-level section headings. (There is a similar =head2 command for smaller headlines.) Headline text in =head1 sections is traditionally capitalized.

6.5.2   Writing and reading POD

The =cut command ends a section of POD. If the module contains several POD sections, it may contain several =cut commands. For example, the following module has three POD sections, each of which ends with =cut:

```
package PodTest;

=head1 NAME

    PodTest - Demonstrates POD module

=head1 SYNOPSIS

    use PodTest;
    my $variable = $PodTest::a;

=head1 DESCRIPTION

    This module demonstrates how to write POD documentation.  It
    doesn't do anything else.  If you use this module, you deserve
    what you get.

=cut

use vars qw($a $b $c);

$a = 1;
$b = 2;
$c = 3;

=head2 $a
```

```
    The C<$a> variable contains 1.

=head2 $b

    The C<$b> variable contains 2.

=cut

sub return_five
{
    return 5;
}

1;

=head2 return_five

    The subroutine C<return_five> returns C<5>.

=cut
```

The above module demonstrates single-letter POD commands, such as C and I, which modify the way in which a particular letter or word is displayed. C treats the text between < and > as literal code, I italicizes it, and B (not shown in the preceding example) makes it bold. Variable, subroutine, and module names are typically displayed using C<>.

Another useful single-letter command is L, which creates a link to another file, document, or section of a manual page.

`perldoc`, which comes with Perl, is the easiest way to read POD documentation. Typing `perldoc Module` will look for that module in @INC, displaying its POD documentation. If the module does not exist, `perldoc` exits with an error message.

6.6   Conclusion

In this chapter, we have looked at Perl's namespaces, and how we can take advantage of them to write reusable modules. In particular, we discussed the following:

- Perl namespaces, and how to use `package`,

- Creating Perl modules,

- How to retrieve information about the environment from which a subroutine was called,

- How Perl searches for modules,

- How to selectively export and import names into the current package, and

- How to write module documentation using POD.

OBJECTS

Topics in This Chapter

- Objects
- Defining methods
- Inheritance
- Creating a class

Chapter 7

In the last chapter, we saw how easy and convenient it is to create Perl modules, bundling variables and subroutines under a namespace. In the last 20 years, however, procedural programming has given way to object-oriented programming. Objects combine data and code into neat packages, making it easier to work with complex data structures.

This chapter explains how to turn a Perl module into a class file. We will look at constructors, instance variables, methods, and inheritance. We will also discuss some of the differences between objects in Perl and other languages, such as destructors and private instance variables.

Finally, we will go through the process of creating some of our own objects, reflecting on those design decisions and how they affect programmers who use our classes.

When you have finished this chapter, you should be comfortable with Perl's modules and objects. You will understand where they can be helpful and how to incorporate them into your own programs.

7.1   Objects

A programmer does not have to know how a subroutine is implemented to invoke it. Indeed, this is one of the great advantages of subroutines: So long as the interface remains stable, the implementation can change, adding functionality, increasing speed, and removing bugs.

Objects similarly separate their interface from their implementation, except that they hide data along with the code that manipulates that data. As long as an object's interface remains stable, its implementation—the internal representation of data and the methods that modify that data—can improve and grow.

7.1.1   A quick introduction to objects

In procedural programming, you pass a subroutine one or more parameters:

```
foo($data);          # Invoke subroutine foo on $data
```

Object-oriented programming turns this around, making the data structure, or *object*, the central focus:

```
$object->foo();    # Ask $object to invoke its foo method
```

The preceding code asks $object to invoke its foo method. (Presumably, there is a foo method associated with $object. If there isn't, our program will exit with a runtime error.) Different objects can have identically named methods that may or may not have similar effects:

```
$triangle->draw();    # Tells $triangle to draw itself
$hexagon->draw();     # Tells $hexagon to draw itself
$cowboy->draw();      # Tells $cowboy to draw his gun
```

Each type of object is known as a *class*, and objects of that type are known as *instances*. There is no limit to the number of times an object can be "instantiated" in a program, just as there is no limit to the number of scalars, arrays, and hashes that we can create.

7.1.2   How do Perl objects work?

In Perl, each class is defined in its own module (see Chapter 6). Each instance of the class is typically a hash reference whose key-value pairs contain the object's *instance variables*, or unique state.

To retrieve the value from an instance variable, treat the object as a simple hash reference:

```
$variable = $object->{variable};
```

The same is true for assigning new values to instance variables:

```
$object->{variable} = $new_value;
```

CORE Note

Any scalar can be used as a hash key, which means that instance variable names may contain SPACE *characters and unprintable symbols.*

For full information about objects in Perl, see the online documentation. `perldoc perltoot` is a tutorial about Perl objects, and `perldoc perlobj` is a more complete reference about Perl objects.

7.2   Methods

To define a class in Perl, create a module with subroutines that are actually methods. A method differs from a subroutine in only one way: When a method is invoked, Perl invisibly assigns the first argument to be the invoking object. Consider, for example, the following line of code:

```
$value = $object->mymethod($arg1, $arg2);  # Invoke mymethod on $object
```

If $object is an instance of Class, the preceding code will be silently rewritten as:

```
$value = Class::mymethod($object,          # Rewritten method call
                    $arg1, $arg2);
```

The definition of mymethod must take this rewriting into account, treating the first argument as an object. By convention, the object is called $self. For example, the following simple definition for mymethod always returns the number 5:

```perl
sub mymethod
{
    # Grab the object itself
    my $self = shift;

    my $param1 = shift; # Gets value of $arg1
    my $param2 = shift; # Gets value of $arg2

    return 5; # Returns the number 5
}
```

Once our method has a reference to $self, we can invoke methods, set instance variables, and retrieve instance variable methods:

```perl
sub another_method
{
    # Grab the object itself
    my $self = shift;

    my $param1 = shift; # Gets value of $arg1
    my $param2 = shift; # Gets value of $arg2

    # Sets instance variables
    $self->{var1} = $param1;
    $self->{var2} = $param1 * $param2;

    # Invoke mymethod on $self
    $self->mymethod();

    # Returns instance variable "var2"
    return $self->{var2};
}
```

7.2.1 Constructors

We have now seen how to set and retrieve instance variables, and how to write methods. But one crucial item is missing: How can we instantiate a new object?

Every object has at least one *constructor* method, traditionally called new. A constructor creates a new instance of a class, and initializes its data to a known default. For example, here is a simple constructor:

```perl
sub new
{
    # Get the (implicitly passed) class
    my $class = shift;

    # Create a blank object, a ref to an anonymous hash
    my $self = {};

    # Set three instance variables
    $self->{scalar} = "hello";
    $self->{array} = [1, 2, 3];
    $self->{hash} = {"one" => 1, "two" => 2};

    # Turn it into an object
    bless $self, $class;
}
```

We will soon discuss the details of how this constructor works; for now, understand that new returns an instance of the class. If this new method is defined in Test.pm, we can create a new instance of the Test class with:

```perl
use Test;
```

```perl
my $object = Test->new(); # The -> invokes it as a method, not a sub
```

Perl also allows us to put a method name before a class name, which can sometimes be more readable:

```perl
my $test1 = new Test;      # Create one instance
my $test2 = new Test;      # Create a second instance
```

In the above code, $test1 and $test2 are two instances of Test.

7.2.2   *Inside the constructor*

As we have seen, Perl silently rewrites method calls such that the object is the first parameter. But constructors are invoked on a class, rather than an instance—so the first implicitly passed parameter will be the name of the class, rather than the object instance itself. Our example new constructor thus assigns its implicit first parameter to $class. We use $class when invoking bless on our object, described later.

Once we have assigned $class, we begin to assemble the object itself. As we have already seen, an object in Perl is typically based on a hash reference. To create our new instance, we thus create a new hash reference ($self), populating it with keys (instance variable names) and values (instance variable values).

In our example new above, we assign three instance variables to $self: scalar (which contains a scalar value), array (which contains an array reference), and hash (which contains a hash reference). As this demonstrates, we can store any scalar value, including a reference, in our instance variables—including an instance of another object. Just as we can create arbitrarily complex data structures (see Section 2.8.5), we can compose arbitrarily complex objects, with instance variables that point to other objects.

7.2.3   Blessing the new object

The built-in bless function turns a reference (normally a hash reference) into an object. It takes two arguments, the reference and the class name, and returns a new instance of the reference as an instance of that class. After invoking bless, we can invoke methods on $self, in addition to setting and retrieving its data. Because bless returns the newly created object, its invocation is often the last line of new.

Constructors can take arguments, just like any other method. For example, the following constructor takes a single argument, the value of which it places verbatim in the arg instance variable:

```
sub new
{
    # Get our type
    my $class = shift;

    # Get our argument
    my $arg = shift;

    # Create a blank object, a ref to an anonymous hash
    my $self = {};

    # Set an instance variable
    $self->{arg} = $arg;
```

```
    # Turn it into an object
    bless $self, $class;
}
```

If this constructor is defined for the Object class, our program can do the following:

```
use Object;

my $thing_a = new Object(10);      # arg is 10
print $thing_a->{arg}, "\n";       # prints 10

my $thing_b = new Object(20);      # arg is 20
print $thing_b->{arg}, "\n";       # prints 20
```

Here is how this code could be written using ->:

```
use Object;

my $thing_a = Object->new(10);     # arg is 10
print $thing_a->{arg}, "\n";       # prints 10

my $thing_b = Object->new(20);     # arg is 20
print $thing_b->{arg}, "\n";       # prints 20
```

7.2.4   Destructors

Because Perl manages memory automatically, it does not require a *destructor* method to remove allocated objects. However, we can optionally define a DESTROY method for our object. DESTROY is invoked implicitly by Perl when our object is removed from memory—which by definition will only be after we have finished using it.

Most Perl objects do not need a DESTROY method, and we ignore it for the rest of this book. `perldoc perltoot` has a good primer on the subject, as does `perldoc perlobj`.

7.3   Inheritance

Object-oriented programming makes it possible for one class to *inherit* characteristics from another, much as children inherit traits from their parents.

Inheritance is possible when one class is a more specific version of another, known as a *subclass*, in something known as an *is-a* relationship.   This is different from a *has-a* relationship, which implies that one object contains another.

Thus Car is-a Vehicle (and inherits from it), whereas Car has-a Trunk. We represent a has-a relationship with an instance variable, and an is-a relationship with inheritance.

CORE Note

Programmers new to object-oriented programming often confuse the notion of ownership with inheritance. Children retain their parents' traits even when they are in school, playing with friends, or watching television. Similarly, an object's traits and inheritance characteristics do not change when one object contains another.

7.3.1   @ISA

Perl defines is-a relationships with the global array @ISA, which lists the objects from which our object inherits. Because it is a global, @ISA must belong to a package; in this case, it belongs to the same package as the class it describes. We say that Car is-a Vehicle by defining @Car::ISA:

```
package Car;

our @ISA = qw(Vehicle);    # Car is-a Vehicle
```

When a program invokes a method, Perl first tries to locate a method by that name in the object's package. If no such method exists, Perl iterates through @ISA until it finds a matching object. If no matching method name is found, the program exits with a fatal runtime error.

For example, here is a definition for the class Class, which defines the method get_vegetable:

```
package Class;

sub new
{
    # Get the class
    my $class = shift;
```

```perl
    # Create $self
    my $self = {};

    # Set an instance variable
    $self->{vegetable} = 'broccoli';

    # Turn this hash into an object
    bless $self, $class;
}

sub get_vegetable
{
    # Get myself
    my $self = shift;

    # Return the vegetable
    return $self->{vegetable};
}

1;
```

A program can create an instance of Class and invoke its get_vegetable method as follows:

```perl
use Class;

my $variable = new Class;
print $variable->get_vegetable(), "\n";    # Prints broccoli
```

As its name implies, the following SubClass inherits from Class—in other words, SubClass is-a Class:

```perl
package SubClass;

our @ISA = qw(Class);    # Global @ISA in package SubClass

use Class;               # Import the class from which we inherit

sub new                  # Define a constructor
{
    # Get the class
    my $class = shift;
```

```
    # Define myself
    my $self = {};

    # Give myself a vegetable
    $self->{vegetable} = 'fennel';

    # Bless the new instance
    bless $self, $class;
}

1;
```

SubClass defines the constructor new, but no other methods. Invoking any method but new on an instance of SubClass will be referred to Class. Perl knows that SubClass inherits from Class because of @SubClass::ISA is set.

Consider the following code:

```
use SubClass;

my $variable = new SubClass;
print $variable->get_vegetable(), "\n";    # Prints 'fennel'
```

This code prints **fennel**, reflecting the different constructor (but the common get_vegetable method).

A class and its subclasses might understand the same questions, but they will often provide different answers—much as a parent and child will both know how to speak the same language, but will often answer the same question in different ways.

CORE Note

Perl provides for method inheritance, but not for data inheritance, as is the case in some other languages. In the preceding example, SubClass *inherited the method* get_vegetable, *but not the value of the* vegetable *instance variable itself.*

If a subclass defines a method with the same name as its parent, we say that it has *overridden* the method. Inheritance only applies when an invoked method is not defined by a subclass. If the subclass does define the method, then the parent class's method is ignored completely.

An object can inherit from more than one class by naming multiple parents in @ISA. For example:

```
our @ISA = qw(Vehicle ConsumerGood);
```

When an object is descended from more than one parent, Perl searches through @ISA in the order in which they are named, using a "depth-first" search. The second item in @ISA is only consulted if neither the first item nor any of the first item's ancestors provides the named method.

7.3.2   UNIVERSAL

Every object automatically inherits from the implicit UNIVERSAL class. UNIVERSAL defines several useful methods, including isa, which returns an object's type at runtime. For example:

```
print "Yes, it's a vehicle"
    if (UNIVERSAL::isa($object, "Vehicle"));
```

Because every object inherits from UNIVERSAL, the following syntax is also acceptable:

```
print "Yes, it's a vehicle"
    if $object->isa("Vehicle");
```

UNIVERSAL::isa also works with references to built-in data types, which are considered objects of type SCALAR, ARRAY, and HASH.

The built-in ref function returns a string describing an object's type. For example:

```
my $object = new Foo;
my $ref = ref $object;

print "object is a '$ref'\n";    # Prints "query is a 'Foo'"
```

7.3.3   *Testing for methods*

The universal method can indicates whether an object understands a particular method. can returns a reference to the method if it exists, or undef if it does not. For example:

```
use Class;
my $object = new Class;

# Is there a get_vegetable method for object?
$result = $object->can("get_vegetable");

# If so, invoke it
if ($result)
{
    print "Calling get_vegetable...\n";

    # Dereference and invoke the method call
    &{$result};
}

# Otherwise, complain
else
{
    print "get_vegetable not defined.\n";
}
```

7.4   Creating and working with objects

The most important part of writing an object happens before any coding takes place. During the planning stages, consider what the object's interface should be to the outside world. What methods will be necessary? What is the most natural way to store data in this new object or to retrieve existing data from it?

The implementation can change over time, as it is hidden beneath an abstraction layer—but so long as the interface remains the same, programs using an object never have to know when this happens. With careful planning, an object's interface can remain stable, while its implementation improves.

For example, consider a Book class that describes books. Before implementing this class, think about information the class will contain and what interfaces will be available to access it. What state should each instance keep in its instance variables? What methods will be used to access, modify, and store values in these instance variables? How will the object be used? Then there are the corner cases: Should each volume in a multivolume series be considered separately? Should hardcover and paperback versions be considered the same object or different ones?

These issues should be fleshed out as much as possible before beginning to implement an object. In particular, ensure that the interface is as complete as possible. Object-oriented programming works best when the interface remains stable, which is impossible until its design is complete.

7.4.1 *Implementing* Book

A full definition of Book would be too long for this chapter, so we'll have to keep things relatively brief. The idea, however, is that our Book class can be used in a variety of applications, such as a library inventory system, an online bookstore, or a bibliography. Just as a physical book can be used in many circumstances, so too can an instance of our Book object.

If we keep things simple—incorrectly assuming, for example, that each book has only one author and that its price never changes—Book requires only a few instance variables:

- title

- author

- publisher

- isbn

- price_in_dollars

- pages

Each instance variable corresponds to information that an external user may want to retrieve, assign, or modify. The object will thus have to include at least one "getter" and "setter" method for each instance variable. There are several styles for writing such methods. My preferred naming convention involves writing two methods for each instance variable, one beginning with get_ and the second beginning with set_. Thus a method to set the title instance variable would be called set_title, and a method to retrieve the current value of the title would be called get_title.

CORE Approach

Perl cannot prevent a program from violating an object's abstraction barrier and directly manipulating its instance variables. The best defense against such behavior is to provide a rich interface with many useful methods. The better an object's interface, the greater the chances that programmers using it will take advantage of available methods.

Now that the basic design is out of the way, we can begin to write the object itself. Here is the beginning of a definition for Book, including the constructor new and two methods, get_title and set_title:

```perl
package Book;

sub new
{
    # What class is this?
    my $class = shift;

    # Get some basic arguments
    my $title = shift || "";
    my $author = shift || "";
    my $publisher = shift || "";
    my $isbn = shift || "";
    my $price_in_dollars = shift || 0;
    my $pages = shift || 0;

    # Title and author are required
    return undef unless ($title and $author);

    # Create the object hash
    my $self = {};

    # Name all of the instance variables, setting some
    $self->{title} = $title;
    $self->{author} = $author;
    $self->{publisher} = $publisher;
    $self->{isbn} = $isbn;
```

```perl
    $self->{price_in_dollars} = $price_in_dollars;
    $self->{pages} = $pages;

    # Create the object, and return it
    bless $self, $class;
}

sub get_title
{
    # Get myself
    my $self = shift;

    # Return the title
    return $self->{title};
}

sub set_title
{
    # Get myself
    my $self = shift;

    # Get the new title
    my $new_title = shift;

    # Title must contain at least one non-whitespace character
    return undef unless ($new_title =~ /\S/);

    # Set the title
    $self->{title} = $new_title;

    # Return $self to indicate success
    return $self;
}

1;
```

This code implements a primitive form of Book, with only three methods. If saved as Book.pm somewhere in @INC, this object can be used in a program.

The constructor takes up to five explicit arguments, as well as the silent first argument. Using || to test whether each argument is FALSE (i.e., the empty string or 0), we can assign default values within our method. But of course, not all arguments are optional: For example, every Book object must have a title and author. If one or both of these is missing, new returns undef.

get_title is a simple example of a "getter" method, providing an external interface to an instance variable. It does not take any arguments, and returns the current value.

The "setter" method, set_title, requires an argument, which is tested to see if it contains at least one non-whitespace character. If the new title is blank, set_title returns undef.

The following program creates an instance of Book and retrieves its title twice. Between the two invocations of get_title, the program uses set_title to modify that instance variable. The fact that the title is stored in an instance variable is irrelevant to the caller—all that matters is that the interface for retrieving and modifying a book's title is clearly defined:

```perl
#!/usr/bin/perl
# filename: demo-book-1.pl

use strict;
use warnings;
use Book;

# Create a book
my $book = new Book("Programming Perl", "Wall and Christiansen",
                    "O'Reilly and Associates", "1-56592-149-6",
                    39.95)
    or die "Fatal error when creating book";

# Print the title
my $title = $book->get_title;
print "Title is '$title'.\n";

# Set the title to something new
$book->set_title("Camel Book")
    or die "Fatal error when setting title";

# Print the new title
my $new_title = $book->get_title;
print "Title is now '$new_title'.\n";
```

7.4.2 *Using* Book

The simple Book class can be extended in any number of directions from the earlier examples. For example, it could be used to model books on a shelf:

```perl
#!/usr/bin/perl
# filename: bookshelf.pl

use strict;
use warnings;
use Book;

my @shelf = ();

# Add some books to the shelf
push @shelf, new Book("Philip and Alex's Guide to Web Publishing",
                    "Philip Greenspun", "Morgan-Kaufmann",
                    "1-55860-534-7", 44.95);

push @shelf,
    new Book("Structure and Interpretation of Computer Programs",
            "Abelson and Sussman", "MIT Press",
            "0-262-01153-0", 65);

push @shelf, new Book("Essentials of User Interface Design",
                    "Alan Cooper", "Prentice-Hall",
                    "1-56884-322-4", 29.99);

# Print the titles, sorted alphabetically
foreach my $book (sort {$a->get_title cmp $b->get_title} @shelf)
{
    print $book->get_title, "\n";
}
```

This program not only demonstrates that objects can be stored in arrays just like any other data, but also that results can be ordered using custom sort routines.

The program would be even more useful if it provided users with an interactive method for entering books, rather than hard-wiring all of the

information inside of a program. Alternatively, the program could read
information about books from a TAB-delimited file:

```perl
#!/usr/bin/perl
# filename: better-bookshelf.pl

use strict;
use warnings;
use Book;

my @shelf = ();

# Tab-delimited file containing book information
my $file = '/tmp/books';

open BOOKS, $file or die "Cannot read '$file': $! ";

while (<BOOKS>)
{
    # Remove a trailing newline
    chomp;

    # Get the book info
    my @book_info = split /\t/, $_;

    # Turn the book information into a new instance of Book
    my $new_book = new Book(@book_info);

    if (defined $new_book)
    {
        push @shelf, $new_book;
    }
    else
    {
        print STDERR "Warning: Error on line $. of '$file'.\n";
    }
}

close BOOKS;
```

```
# Print the titles, sorted alphabetically
foreach my $book (sort {$a->get_title cmp $b->get_title} @shelf)
{
    print $book->get_title, "\n";
}
```

This program reads the information in /tmp/books, turns each line into a new instance of Book, and adds it to @shelf. If a line fails to contain a title or author's name, the program prints a warning, using the built-in $. variable to indicate the line on which the error occurred.

For example, here is a sample version of /tmp/books, reformatted slightly to fit the page width. The two lines describing books are separated by a blank line, which the program cannot parse:

```
Philip and Alex's Guide to Web Publishing        Philip Greenspun
    Morgan-Kaufmann 1-55860-534-7    44.95

Essentials of User Interface Design     Alan Cooper
    Prentice-Hall    1-56884-322-4    29.99
```

Given this input, the improved book-listing program will produce the following output:

```
Warning: Error on line 2 of /tmp/books.
Essentials of User Interface Design
Philip and Alex's Guide to Web Publishing
```

7.4.3 *Subclassing* Book

Once created, Book can also be subclassed for more specific objects. Because a textbook is-a book, a TextBook class could inherit from Book, adding appropriate methods. For example:

```
package TextBook;

use Book;

# Inherit from Book
our @ISA = qw(Book);

# Constructor for TextBook
sub new
```

```perl
{
    # What class is this?
    my $class = shift;

    # Get some basic arguments
    my $title = shift || "";
    my $author = shift || "";
    my $publisher = shift || "";
    my $isbn = shift || "";
    my $price_in_dollars = shift || 0;
    my $pages = shift || 0;
    my $course = shift || "";

    # Title and author are required
    return undef unless ($title and $author);

    # Create the object hash
    my $self = {};

    # Name all of the instance variables, setting some
    $self->{title} = $title;
    $self->{author} = $author;
    $self->{publisher} = $publisher;
    $self->{isbn} = $isbn;
    $self->{price_in_dollars} = $price_in_dollars;
    $self->{pages} = $pages;
    $self->{course} = $course;

    # Create the object, and return it
    bless $self, $class;
}

sub get_course
{
    # Get myself
    my $self = shift;

    # Return the course
```

```
        return $self->{course};
}

sub set_course
{
    # Get myself
    my $self = shift;

    # Get the new course
    my $new_course = shift;

    # Course must contain at least one non-whitespace character
    return undef unless ($new_course =~ /\S/);

    # Set the course
    $self->{course} = $new_course;

    # Return $self to indicate success
    return $self;
}

1;
```

This TextBook class defines its own instance variables, as Perl does not provide for data inheritance. However, it does not need to redefine set_title and get_title, as those are no different from the methods defined in its parent class. By contrast, TextBook does need get_course and set_course methods, as these apply to an instance variable that does not exist in Book.

Because each instance of TextBook is also an instance of Book, both types of objects could be used interchangeably in a university library administration program. However, a program to handle university course assignments would have to use TextBook, which provides capabilities unavailable in Book. Every instance of TextBook is-a Book, but not every Book is-a TextBook.

Just as several instances of Book were placed in @shelf earlier, it would also be possible to create a Shelf class, representing a shelf. Such an object would need a single instance variable, shelf, that would contain a reference to an array of instances of Book:

```
# Constructor for Shelf
sub new
```

```
{
    # What class is this?
    my $class = shift;

    # Get the initial books, or the empty list
    my @books = @_;

    # Create the object hash
    my $self = {};

    # Create an instance variable reprenseting the shelf
    $self->{books} = \@books;

    # Create the object, and return it
    bless $self, $class;
}
```

This demonstrates a has-a relationship, as described in Section 7.3. A Shelf has-a Book. However, it is not correct to say that Shelf is-a Book. The Shelf class is known as a container class, since it is used to provide easy access to other objects. With appropriately defined methods, such as get_titles, add_book, and get_by_publisher, Shelf quickly becomes more useful than a simple array.

Because they put code and data together in neat, reusable packages, objects make it easy to play around with such ideas. One object can be used in a number of different programs, just as one subroutine can be used in several places within the same program.

7.5 Conclusion

In this chapter, we have looked at Perl's object-oriented capabilities. As we saw, these capabilities stem directly from a clever combination of packages and references—but this trickery works well, and gives us a great deal of flexibility. In particular, we looked at the following:

- What objects are (and aren't) in Perl,

- How to work with objects,

- Writing and invoking methods,
- Working with instance variables,
- Inheritance and @ISA, and
- Designing maintainable objects.

TYING

Topics in This Chapter

- Tied variables
- Tied scalars
- Tied hashes
- DBM files
- Tied arrays

Chapter 8

U ntil now, this book has looked at two types of abstraction, procedural and object-oriented. In the procedural world, subroutines are black boxes, performing tasks on our data within an established interface. In the object-oriented world, the data and its associated methods act as a single unit.

Perl provides a third type of abstraction, known as *tying*. Any scalar, array, or hash may be tied to a Perl object. A tied variable retains the same interface as other scalars, arrays, and hashes. However, its implementation is controlled by a Perl object. Tied variables thus make it possible to work transparently with relational databases and files on disk, as well as to modify the behavior of Perl's built-in data types.

In this chapter, we look at the classic example of tying hashes to DBM files. But we also consider other possibilities, including the creation of an object that makes Perl arrays act like circular buffers.

8.1   Tying

Perl has long made it possible to associate a hash with a DBM file on disk. (DBM files store data on a filesystem similar to how hashes store data in memory.) When a hash is associated with a DBM file, changes to the hash are automatically reflected in the DBM file, and vice versa.

Modern versions of Perl go one step further, allowing us to associate any scalar, array, or hash with a class. This lets us associate hashes with DBM files, but also means that we can connect hashes to relational databases, or create "magical" variables that trigger events when their values are set or retrieved.

8.1.1   tie *and* untie

We associate a variable with a class using the built-in tie function. The association continues until the program exits, or until we invoke untie on the variable.

Consider IO::Dir, an object from the Perl distribution that connects a hash to a directory. We can connect the %dir hash to the directory /home/reuven by invoking tie as follows:

```
tie %dir, IO::Dir, "/home/reuven";
```

Once tie goes into effect, modifying %dir changes the contents of the directory, and vice versa.

In the preceding example, tie took three arguments: the name of the variable to be tied, the name of the class with which to associate our variable, and the name of the tied directory. Of these, the first two are always mandatory when using tie. Additional parameters may be required by the class.

Once a variable is tied, every retrieval or modification of its value results in a behind-the-scenes method call. Actually, the first implicit call takes place when we first invoke tie: Perl automatically calls a constructor-style method within the object class. Which pseudo-constructor is invoked depends on the type of variable we are tying; Perl automatically decides whether to call TIESCALAR, TIEARRAY, or TIEHASH. (There is also a TIEHANDLE function, but we do not discuss tied filehandles in this chapter. See `perldoc perltie` for a full discussion of tying, including a description of tied filehandles.)

8.2   Tying a scalar

You can really do only two things with a scalar variable: assign a value to it or retrieve the existing value. As such, a class that implements tied scalar behavior only needs to define two methods, named FETCH and STORE. As you might guess, FETCH is invoked whenever someone attempts to read the tied scalar's value, and STORE is invoked when we assign it a new value. When the scalar is finally destroyed—because it goes out of scope or the program ends—the DESTROY method is called, giving us a chance to clean up. (This DESTROY method is no different from the one described in Section 7.2.4.)

Here is Squealer, an object that expects to be tied to a scalar. Every time a program retrieves or modifies the scalar's value, a message is written to STDERR:

```
package Squealer;

sub new
{
    # Get the class
    my $class = shift;

    # Create the object
    my $self = {};

    # Set an instance variable
    $self->{value} = 0;

    # Bless myself into a class
    bless $self, $class;
}

sub TIESCALAR
{
    # Get the class, just like with "new"
    my $class = shift;

    # Create $self by calling the constructor
    my $self = $class->new;
```

```perl
    # Report on current activities
    print STDERR "Activating Squealer tie\n";

    # Return the object
    return $self;
}

sub FETCH
{
    # Get myself
    my $self = shift;

    # Get the current value
    my $value = $self->{value};

    # Report on current activities
    print STDERR "Retrieving Squealer value\n";

    # Return value
    return $value;
}

sub STORE
{
    # Get myself
    my $self = shift;

    # Get the new value
    my $new_value = shift;

    # Report on current activities
    print STDERR "Storing Squealer value\n";

    # Set the value as necessary
    $self->{value} = $new_value;

    # Return myself
    return $self;
}
```

```perl
sub DESTROY
{
    print STDERR "Squealer is going away!\n";
}

1;
```

Squealer defines a constructor, conventionally called new. However, new will never be called directly. Rather, it will be invoked by TIESCALAR, which is itself called by tie.

Here is an example of using Squealer:

```perl
#!/usr/bin/perl
# filename: squealer.pl

use strict;
use warnings;
use Squealer;

my $variable;
my $status;

tie $variable, "Squealer";

# Store a simple value
$variable = 5;

# Retrieve, print "5"
print $variable, "\n";

# Restrieve and store
$variable += 100;

# Retrieve, print "105"
print $variable, "\n";

untie $variable;
```

Aside from the initial call to tie and the final call to untie, it looks like the program is accessing a simple scalar. That is just the point: It looks like we are working with a scalar, but underneath it all, we are doing many other things. We have created a magical variable, in which performing one action can trigger a number of others.

squealer.pl produces the following output:

```
Activating Squealer tie
Storing Squealer value
Retrieving Squealer value
5
Retrieving Squealer value
Storing Squealer value
Retrieving Squealer value
105
Squealer is going away!
```

8.2.1   Another example of tying scalars: RandomNumber

Next we see RandomNumber, another example of tying scalars. Each time a scalar tied to RandomNumber is retrieved, a new random number is returned. RandomNumber's constructor expects two arguments, representing the maximum random number that should be returned and the number of places after the decimal point that will be allowed.

Here is the class definition:

```
package RandomNumber;

# Constructor
sub new
{
    # Get the class
    my $class = shift;

    # Get the maximum number and number of decimals
    my $max = shift;
    my $decimals = shift || 0;

    # Make sure that $max is positive
    return undef unless ($max > 0);

    # Make sure that $decimals is an integer
    return undef unless ($decimals == int $decimals);
```

```perl
    # Make sure that $decimals is non-negative
    return undef unless ($decimals >= 0);

    # Create the object
    my $self = {};

    # Set instance variables
    $self->{max} = $max;
    $self->{decimals} = $decimals;

    # Return the blessed object
    bless $self, $class;
}

sub TIESCALAR
{
    # Get the class
    my $class = shift;

    # What is the maximum number?
    my $max = shift;

    # How many decimals will we allow?
    my $decimals = shift;

    # Create the object
    my $self = $class->new($max, $decimals);

    return $self;
}

sub FETCH
{
    # Get myself
    my $self = shift;

    # Get the number of decimals
    my $decimals = $self->{decimals};
```

```
    # Create an sprintf string
    my $sprintf = "%.$decimals" . "f";

    # Return a random number, with limited decimals
    return sprintf($sprintf, rand $self->{max});
}

sub STORE
{
    # Get myself
    my $self = shift;

    # Issue a warning
    warn "Illegal attempt to assign to RandomNumber.\n";

    # Return undef, just in case
    return undef;
}

1;
```

RandomNumber demonstrates how to associate state with a tied variable using instance variables. The max and decimals instance variables are carried around with each instance of RandomNumber, but are invisible to the user.

In addition, STORE prevents users from storing values in a tied variable. It is not hard to imagine how a Constant class could be written to take advantage of tie and create true constants in Perl.

Following is a short program that uses RandomNumber. It creates a random-number generator, returning values between 0 and 1000 and with a single digit following the decimal point. Each time a new value is retrieved, a different random number is returned.

```
#!/usr/bin/perl
# filename: random.pl

use strict;
use warnings;
use RandomNumber;
```

```
# Make $rand a random-number generator
my $rand;
tie $rand, "RandomNumber", 1000, 1;

# Make sure that $rand it was defined
die "Problem creating $rand"
    unless (defined $rand);

# Retrieve 50 values
foreach my $index (1 .. 50)
{
    print "$index: $rand\n";
}

# Try to assign to it
$rand = 50.3;

# Retrieve 10 more values
foreach my $index (1 .. 10)
{
    print "$index: $rand\n";
}
```

8.3   Tying a hash

Tying a hash is similar to tying a scalar, except that the additional complexity means that we need more methods:

TIEHASH is the constructor invoked when a hash is first tied. This is similar to TIESCALAR, invoking a constructor, or returning a new instance itself.

FETCH gets a single argument, the key. It normally returns a value associated with that key.

STORE receives two arguments, a key and its associated value.

EXISTS gets a single argument, the key. Like exists, it should return a TRUE or FALSE value, indicating whether the key is defined.

DELETE receives one argument, the key of the element to be deleted (like delete).

CLEAR is invoked when the entire data structure should be deleted.

FIRSTKEY returns the first key–value pair for the first key in the hash. This is invoked when keys or each are run. Despite its name, FIRSTKEY returns a key–value pair, and not only the key.

NEXTKEY keys and each invoke, FIRSTKEY once, and then NEXTKEY repeatedly until the latter returns undef (or the empty list, depending on context). Despite its name, FIRSTKEY returns a key–value pair, and not only the key.

DESTROY is invoked when the tied variable is destroyed or goes out of scope.

Here is a hash analogy to Squealer, called HashSquealer, which makes it clear just when the various methods are being invoked:

```perl
package HashSquealer;

sub TIEHASH
{
    # Get the class, just like with "new"
    my $class = shift;

    # Create $self directly
    my $self = {};

    # Report on current activities
    print STDERR "\tActivating HashSquealer tie\n";

    # Return the object
    bless $self, $class;
}

sub FETCH
{
    # Get myself and the key
    my $self = shift;
    my $key = shift;
```

```
    # Get the current value for that key
    my $value = $self->{$key};

    # Report on current activities
    print STDERR "\tGetting '$key' => '$value' (HashSquealer)\n";

    # Return value
    return $value;
}

sub STORE
{
    # Get myself, the key, and the value
    my $self = shift;
    my $key = shift;
    my $new_value = shift;

    # Report on current activities
    print STDERR "\tStoring '$key' => '$new_value' (HashSquealer)\n";

    # Set the value as necessary
    $self->{$key} = $new_value;

    # Return myself
    return $self;
}

sub EXISTS
{
    # Get myself and the key
    my $self = shift;
    my $key = shift;

    # Does that key exist?
    my $exists = exists $self->{$key};

    # Report on current activities
    print STDERR "\tChecking existence of $key in HashSquealer\n";

    # Return the value
    return $exists;
}
```

```perl
sub DELETE
{
    # Get myself and the key
    my $self = shift;
    my $key = shift;

    # Delete the key
    delete $self->{$key};

    # Report on current activities
    print STDERR "\tDeleted '$key' in HashSquealer\n";

    # Return ourself
    return $self;
}

sub CLEAR
{
    # Get myself
    my $self = shift;

    # Delete everything from $self!
    %$self = ();

    # Report on current activities
    print STDERR "\tCleared contents of HashSquealer\n";

    # Return the object
    return $self;
}

sub FIRSTKEY
{
    # Get myself
    my $self = shift;

    # Report on current activities
    print STDERR "\tRunning FIRSTKEY in HashSquealer\n";

    # Get the keys for %self, and reset the "each" counter
    my @keys = sort keys %$self;

    # Return "each" of %$self
    return each %$self;
}
```

```perl
sub NEXTKEY
{
    # Get myself
    my $self = shift;

    # Report on current activities
    print STDERR "\tRunning NEXTKEY in HashSquealer\n";

    # Return "each" of %$self
    return each %$self;
}

sub DESTROY
{
    print STDERR "\tHashSquealer is going away!\n";
}

1;
```

Information printed by HashSquealer is sent to STDERR, and preceded by a TAB character. This makes it easier to understand what is being printed by the calling program, and what is being printed by HashSquealer.

Notice how there is no new constructor for HashSquealer. Rather, that job is performed by TIEHASH. As indicated in Section 7.2.1, it is a convention to call constructors new—but there is no requirement that there be only one constructor, or that it be named new.

The following program, called `hashsquealer.pl`, demonstrates which methods in HashSquealer are invoked for various actions on a hash:

```perl
#!/usr/bin/perl
# filename: hashsquealer.pl

use strict;
use warnings;
use HashSquealer;

my %hash;
tie %hash, "HashSquealer";
```

```perl
# Make one assignment
print "Make one assignment\n";
$hash{q} = 2000;

# Clear the whole thing
print "Clear the whole thing\n";
%hash = ();

# Add several key-value pairs
print "Make three assignments\n";
$hash{a} = 1;
$hash{b} = 2;
$hash{c} = 3;

# Test exists
print "Check for key 'a'\n";
if (exists $hash{a})
{
    print "Hash 'a' exists.\n";
}
else
{
    print "Hash 'a' does not exist.\n";

}

print "Check for key 'z'\n";
if (exists $hash{z})
{
    print "Hash 'z' exists.\n";
}
else
{
    print "Hash 'z' does not exist.\n";

}
```

```
# Test each
print "Using each in while loop\n";
while (my ($key, $value) = each %hash)
{
    print "each test: key = '$key', value = '$value'\n";
}

# Delete a key
print "Deleting key 'a'\n";
delete $hash{a};

# Test each keys
print "Using keys in foreach\n";
foreach my $key (sort keys %hash)
{
    print "keys test: key = '$key', value = $hash{$key}\n";
}
```

Even programmers uninterested in tie should examine the output from
hashsquealer.pl. It demonstrates some properties of Perl that might not
be immediately obvious, such as the fact that sort keys %hash returns a list
of keys to foreach before the loop body is evaluated.

If a program only needs to override one or two of the functions normally
associated with a tied hash, it can subclass Tie::Hash, which comes with
the Perl distribution. By itself, Tie::Hash does not do anything interesting.
However, it ensures that all of the tie-related methods are defined, avoiding
potential fatal runtime errors.

8.3.1 DBM Files

DBM files, which were the original inspiration for tie, are an efficient mechanism for storing key–value pairs on disk. Because of their similarity to
hashes, Perl has long provided a mapping between hashes and DBM files.

CORE Note

*There are many versions of DBM, each with its own quirks, advantages,
and disadvantages. Perl comes with classes that handle a number of these–
–NDBM_File, DB_File, GDBM_File, SDBM_File, and ODBM_File.
Which you choose depends on the DBM implementation that you choose.*

For example, the Sendmail program stores mail aliases in a Berkeley DB file called /etc/aliases.db on my computer. The following program prints the contents of that file, or of any other Berkeley DB file, on the screen:

```perl
#!/usr/bin/perl
# filename: print-db-file.pl

use strict;
use warnings;
use DB_File;

# Get our filename argument
my $file = $ARGV[0] or die "No argument!";

# Tie %data to the DB_File, or die trying
my %data = ();
tie %data, "DB_File", $file, O_RDONLY
    or die "Error tying %data: $! ";

# Print each of the key-value pairs
foreach my $key (sort keys %data)
{
    print "$key => $data{$key}\n";
}
```

This program will print any Berkeley DB file, assuming that the program has permission to read it. It passes only two arguments to tie, $file (containing the filename) and O_RDONLY, indicating that the file will only be opened for reading. Other possible access modes are O_RDWR (for read/write access) and O_WRONLY (for write-only access).

One difference between Perl's hashes and DBM files is that only plain scalars can be stored in the latter. This makes it difficult or impossible to store references and complex data structures in a hash. The solution is to use MLDBM, a class designed for this purpose and included with the Perl distribution. MLDBM requires Data::Dumper (see Section 6.4.4) to function correctly.

Here is a rewritten version of print-db-file.pl, using MLDBM. It performs the same function, but can read complex values, as well as simple ones:

```perl
#!/usr/bin/perl
# filename: mldbm-print-db-file.pl

use strict;
use warnings;
use Fcntl;

# Indicate which underlying mechanism to use
use MLDBM qw(DB_File);

# Get our filename argument
my $file = $ARGV[0] or die "No argument!";

# Open the DBM file
my %data;
tie %data, "MLDBM", $file, O_RDONLY
    or die "Error tying %data: $! ";

# Print each of the key-value pairs
foreach my $key (sort keys %data)
{
    print "$key => $data{$key}\n";
}
```

mldbm-print-db-file.pl differs from its predecessor in only a few ways. First, it uses the Fcntl module, which exports O_RDONLY and other symbols into the current package. In addition, the use MLDBM statement must be followed by a list of the DBM classes to be used. In this particular case, because the files use DB_File, that class is named in the use statement.

Here is a similar program, which modifies a DBM file (or creates one, if none exists). Notice how it can store references and non-scalars:

```perl
#!/usr/bin/perl
# filename: store-mldbm.pl

use strict;
use warnings;
use Fcntl;
```

```perl
# Indicate which underlying mechanism to use
use MLDBM qw(DB_File);

# Get our filename argument
my $file = $ARGV[0] or die "No argument!";

# Open the DBM file
my %data;
tie %data, "MLDBM", $file, O_RDWR|O_CREAT
    or die "Error tying %data: $! ";

# Create some variables
my $scalar = 100;
my @array = qw(a b c d e);
my %hash = ("z" => 26, "y" => 25, "x" => 24);

# Store references to these variables
$data{scalar} = \$scalar;
$data{array} = \@array;
$data{hash} = \%hash;

# Untie %data, which will store it
untie %data;
```

The data stored by the preceding program can be read with this one:

```perl
#!/usr/bin/perl
# filename: read-mldb.pl

use strict;
use warnings;
use Fcntl;

# Indicate which underlying mechanism to use
use MLDBM qw(DB_File);

# Get our filename argument
my $file = $ARGV[0] or die "No argument!";
```

```perl
# Open the DBM file
my %data;
tie %data, "MLDBM", $file, O_RDONLY
    or die "Error tying %data: $! ";

# Print each of the key-value pairs
foreach my $key (sort keys %data)
{
    print "$key => $data{$key}\n";
}
```

When run, the preceding program produces this output:

```
array => ARRAY(0x823add8)
hash => HASH(0x82383dc)
scalar => SCALAR(0x8233280)
```

The printed representations indicate that the data was stored correctly, but make it difficult to retrieve and print the data. Using UNIVERSAL::isa makes it easier:

```perl
#!/usr/bin/perl
# filename: read-mldbm.pl

use strict;
use warnings;
use Fcntl;

# Indicate which underlying mechanism to use
use MLDBM qw(DB_File);

# Get our filename argument
my $file = $ARGV[0] or die "No argument!";

# Open the DBM file
my %data;
tie %data, "MLDBM", $file, O_RDONLY
    or die "Error tying %data: $! ";
```

```perl
# Print each of the key-value pairs with an appropriate method
foreach my $key (sort keys %data)
{
    # Get the data
    my $ref = $data{$key};

    # Handle scalars
    if (UNIVERSAL::isa($ref, "SCALAR"))
    {
        print "$key -> $$ref\n";
    }

    # Handle arrays
    elsif (UNIVERSAL::isa($ref, "ARRAY"))
    {
        my @array = @$ref;
        print "$key -> @array\n";
    }

    # Handle hashes
    elsif (UNIVERSAL::isa($ref, "HASH"))
    {
        my %hash = %$ref;
        print "$key ->\n";

        foreach my $subkey (sort keys %hash)
        {
            print "\t$subkey -> $hash{$subkey}\n";
        }
    }
    else
    {
        print "Error!\n";
    }
}
```

8.4 Tying an array

Arrays can be tied to objects, just like scalars and hashes. A class that provides for tied arrays must define the TIEARRAY constructor and FETCH and STORE methods, which operate similarly to their scalar and hash counterparts. Unique to tied arrays are the FETCHSIZE and STORESIZE methods, which return the number of stored elements and the number of available storage slots. FETCHSIZE corresponds to the special $\#$ syntax, which returns the highest numbered element in an array. STORESIZE returns the number of slots that are defined for an array, as returned when an array is placed in scalar context. Finally, the class may include an optional DESTROY method, which is invoked when the variable is untied.

A number of other methods handle special cases—POP, PUSH, SHIFT, UNSHIFT, SPLICE, and EXTEND. To avoid implementing such features, a class can inherit from Tie::Array. This class, like Tie::Hash, implements the basic functions associated with a data type. Any method not overridden by the subclass is handled in the standard way.

Consider a class, CircularBuffer, which turns an array into a circular buffer of arbitrary size. A circular buffer works something like a clock, rolling over to the beginning when it reaches the end. A circular buffer of size 5 can only contain five elements. The sixth element overwrites what was previously in position 0, the seventh overwrites what was previously in position 1, and so on.

An array tied to CircularBuffer works just like a regular array, except when it comes to assignments. The STORE method ignores the index at which the new data should be stored, instead placing it at the next available element. Instance variables handle the housekeeping that takes place behind the scenes, keeping track of the last index at which an element was placed, and ensuring that the buffer never goes beyond its defined boundaries. Here is one possible implementation of CircularBuffer:

```
package CircularBuffer;

use Tie::Array;
use vars qw(@ISA);

@ISA = qw(Tie::Array);
```

```
sub TIEARRAY
{
    # Get the class name
    my $class = shift;

    # Get the size from the user
    my $size = shift;

    # Buffer must be an integer and positive
    return undef unless ($size == int $size);
    return undef unless ($size > 0);

    # Create an empty hash
    my $self = {};

    # Set the size
    $self->{size} = $size;

    # Set the current pointer
    $self->{pointer} = 0;

    # Set the current contents
    my @contents = ();
    $self->{contents} = \@contents;

    # Bless the new object, and return it
    bless $self, $class;
}

sub FETCHSIZE
{
    # Get myself
    my $self = shift;

    # Return the size of the circular buffer
    return $self->{size};
}

sub STORESIZE
{
    # Get myself
    my $self = shift;
```

```
    # Return the size of the circular buffer
    return $self->{size};
}

sub STORE
{
    # Get myself
    my $self = shift;

    # Get index, which we will ignore
    my $ignored_index = shift;

    # Get the new value
    my $new_value = shift;

    # Get the current pointer
    my $pointer = $self->{pointer};

    # Now set the new value
    $self->{contents}->[$pointer] = $new_value;

    # Update the pointer
    $self->{pointer}++;

    # Make the pointer circular
    $self->{pointer} = 0 if ($self->{pointer} == $self->{size});

    # Return the index of the udpated item
    return $pointer;
}

sub FETCH
{
    # Get myself
    my $self = shift;

    # Get the index
    my $index = shift;

    # Make sure that $index is an integer
    return undef unless ($index == int $index);

    # Make sure that $index is positive and less than size
    return undef if ($index < 0);
    return undef if ($index >= $self->{size});
```

```
    # Return the item at $index
    return $self->{contents}->[$index];
}

1;
```

The following is a simple demonstration of how an array operates when tied to CircularBuffer:

```perl
#!/usr/bin/perl
# filename: use-circular-buffer.pl

use strict;
use warnings;
use CircularBuffer;

# Create a five-element circular buffer
my @array;
tie @array, "CircularBuffer", 5;

# Add items with push
foreach my $number (1 .. 10)
{
    push @array, $number;
}

# Print some statistics
print "@array\n";
print "highest index is $#array\n";

# Add several elements -- notice how the
# index is ignored completely
$array[0] = 100;
$array[0] = 200;
$array[0] = 300;

# Print some more statistics
print "@array\n";
print "highest index is $#array\n";
```

8.5   Conclusion

Tying allows us to pretend that an object is a built-in Perl type. Instead of directly invoking methods on our object, we use it as we would a scalar, array, or hash. The methods are invoked automatically and behind the scenes. This chapter described the following:

- What tied variables are, and how to use them,

- How the built-in tie function connects a variable to an object class,

- How to tie scalars,

- How to tie hashes,

- How to tie hashes to DBM files, including multilevel DBM files, and

- How to tie arrays.

WORKING WITH FILES

Topics in This Chapter

- Iterating through files
- Random file access
- Filehandles
- IO::File
- Globbing
- Permissions
- suid and sgid
- Unary test operators
- stat
- Locking
- Directories
- Renaming and deleting files
- Links

Chapter 9

Perl makes it natural and easy to work with disk files. You can read them line by line, or in one fell swoop. You can read and write text in a variety of formats, from tab-delimited to XML. You can even work with binary files.

In this chapter, we explore many of the ways in which we can work with files from within Perl programs. After reviewing the <> operator, we look at permissions, ownership, and locking. We also look at directories, which are similar to files but have their own quirks.

Modern versions of Perl provide object classes (IO::File and IO::Dir) that replace the old filehandle and dirhandle data types. We look at these, demonstrating how they can be used in programs to replace a number of separate functions.

By the end of this chapter, you should have a good understanding of how to work with the underlying filesystem from within Perl, and how to incorporate it into your programs.

9.1   Basic file access

As we saw in Section 3.10, the following code creates the filehandle FILE, which lets us read from the filename assigned to $file. We can iterate through and display each line of $file with the following:

```
open FILE, $file or die "Cannot read '$file': $! ";
print while (<FILE>);
close FILE;
```

9.1.1   <>

The <> operator is normally used with a filehandle (or a scalar reference to a filehandle, described in Section 9.3.6). In scalar context, each invocation of <> retrieves one line from the filehandle, where the end-of-line character is determined by $/ (see Section 9.1.2). When <> reaches the end of the file, it returns FALSE. We can thus iterate through the lines of FILE with:

```
while (<FILE>)
{
    print $_;
}
```

In list context, <> returns a list of unread lines from the filehandle, with one line per list element:

```
@lines = <FILE>;
```

We can take advantage of this to operate on each line of a file:

```
@alphabetized_lines = sort <FILE>;
```

We can place the contents of a file in a scalar variable with:

```
my $contents = join '', <FILE>;    # Empty string is join character
```

9.1.2 $/

The built-in $/ variable defines the end-of-line marker, also known as the *record separator*. By default, $/ is set to ASCII 10 (the LINEFEED character,

CONTROL-J). In scalar context, <> returns everything up to and including the next occurrence of $/ (or the end of the file, if that appears first).

Changing $/ thus changes the way that Perl reads lines. For example, assume the input file /tmp/test-input:

```
This is yet another of my many tricks to
demonstrate that Perl is versatile.  Viva
le Perl!
```

Now consider the following code, which reads /tmp/test-input:

```
#!/usr/bin/perl

use strict;
use warnings;

my $filename = "/tmp/test-input";
open FILE, $filename or die "Cannot read $filename: $! ";
$/ = "a";               # lines end with "a", not control-J
while (<FILE>)
{
    print "=>$_<=", "\n";
}
```

On my computer, the output is:

```
=>This is yet a<=
=>nother of my ma<=
=>ny tricks to
demonstra<=
=>te tha<=
=>t Perl is versa<=
=>tile.  Viva<=
=>
le Perl!
<=
```

Notice how NEWLINE is treated just like any other character, and a marks the end of each line. chomp would remove the trailing a, rather than NEW-LINE.

Setting $/ to the empty string ("") forces <> to operate in *paragraph mode*. Each iteration of <> will retrieve all of the characters up to and including any blank lines. (A blank line is one consisting of a single NEWLINE character.) Paragraph mode treats multiple blank lines as a single blank line.

CORE Note

Paragraph mode is not the same as setting $/ to \n\n. The former will squeeze together multiple blank lines. By contrast, setting $/ to \n\n tells Perl to look for exactly two NEWLINE characters.

To "slurp" the contents of a file in one fell swoop, undefine $/:

```
undef $/;          # Eliminate record separator
$contents = <FILE>; # Now $contents contains the whole file
```

CORE Note

Unix systems separate lines with ASCII 10. The Macintosh OS, by contrast, separates lines with ASCII 13, known as CARRIAGE RETURN (or CONTROL-M). Be careful when reading files that might have been produced on other operating systems! See `perldoc perlport` *for important tips regarding $/, NEWLINE, and portable Perl programming.*

9.2   Random file access

Sometimes, our programs need to move forward and backward through a file. Perl provides several functions that give us random access capabilities.

9.2.1   seek

The built-in seek function provides random access with three arguments: a filehandle, an offset (counted in bytes), and the base of the offset. We can thus move five bytes forward of the current position (known as SEEK_CUR), or 1,000 backward from the end of the file (known as SEEK_END), or even 15,000 bytes forward from the beginning of the file (known as SEEK_SET). (You can import the various SEEK symbols from IO::Seekable.) seek returns TRUE or FALSE to indicate whether it executed successfully.

The following code demonstrates how to move through a file with seek:

```perl
#!/usr/bin/perl

use strict;
use warnings;

# Import those symbols
use IO::Seekable qw(SEEK_SET SEEK_CUR SEEK_END);

# Open our file for random access
my $filename = "/tmp/foo";
open FILE, "$filename" or die "Cannot read '$filename'\n";

my $successful;

# Move to the beginning
$successful = seek FILE, 0, SEEK_SET;
die "Cannot seek: $! " unless $successful;

# Move to 15 characters before the end
$successful = seek FILE, -15, SEEK_END;
die "Cannot seek: $! " unless $successful;

# Move forward five characters
$successful = seek FILE, 5, SEEK_CUR;
die "Cannot seek: $! " unless $successful;

close FILE;
```

The preceding program demonstrates seek in a read-only file. To open a file for read-write access, preface the < with a + symbol. For example:

```perl
open (FILE, "+<$filename");
```

CORE Warning

> While +> opens a file for reading and writing, it first removes the file's existing contents.

The built-in **tell** function returns the current position within the file. **tell** takes an optional argument of a filehandle:

```
my $current_position = tell FILE;
```

9.2.2 truncate

The built-in **truncate** function shrinks a file to the requested number of characters. For example, the following deletes a file's contents:

```
truncate FILE, 0;
```

CORE Note

Unlike print, truncate *requires a comma following its filehandle argument.*

The following removes everything following the first 50 characters from FILE:

```
truncate FILE, 50;
```

CORE Note

Some operating systems do not support truncate. *On such systems,* truncate *causes a fatal runtime error.*

truncate makes it easy to rewrite a file from scratch after reading its contents. This program alphabetizes the lines of /tmp/foo:

```
#!/usr/bin/perl
# filename: alphabetize-foo.pl

use strict;
use warnings;

# What file do we want to alphabetize?
my $filename = "/tmp/foo";
```

```
# Open the file for reading and writing
open FILE, "+<$filename"
    or die "Cannot open $filename for reading and writing: $! ";

# Grab the contents of FILE
my @lines = (<FILE>);

# Chop the file
truncate FILE, 0;

# Separate lines with newline
$" = "\n";

# Write the sorted lines
print FILE sort @lines;

# Close the filehandle
close FILE;
```

9.3 Filehandles

Filehandles might appear to be simple datatypes, but they can sometimes be tricky to work with. This section summarizes a number of facts about filehandles and offers some tips for working with them.

9.3.1 The null filehandle

When <> is invoked without any filehandle, it is called the *null* filehandle. In such a case, Perl iterates through each line of each file in @ARGV (see Section 3.11.1). Indeed, the ARGV filehandle is an alias for the null filehandle, so one can substitute for the other. The filename currently being processed is placed in $ARGV.

For example, the following prints each line of each file named on the command line:

```
#!/usr/bin/perl
# filename: demonstrate-null-filehandle.pl

use strict;
use warnings;
```

```
while (<ARGV>)
{
    print "Current file: '$ARGV'\n";
    print "Current line: $_\n";
}
```

If there are no command-line arguments, <> reads from STDIN. The value of $ARGV in such cases is -.

When using <>, command-line arguments are assumed to be filenames. Perl complains if an argument is not a valid filename, or if the file cannot be opened. However, it continues to iterate through @ARGV until reaching the end. For instance:

```
./demonstrate-null-filehandle.pl not-a-file also-not-a-file
Can't open not-a-file: No such file or directory
Can't open also-not-a-file: No such file or directory
```

9.3.2   *Duplicating and redirecting filehandles*

It is sometimes useful to take advantage of the default behaviors attached to STDIN, STDOUT, and STDERR, while modifying the default settings. For instance, we might want warn to write to a global logfile. Or we might want STDERR and STDOUT to be synonyms.

To connect two filehandles, invoke open as you usually would—but in place of a filename, use > & and the name of the existing filehandle. For example, we can turn STDERR into an alias for STDOUT:

```
open STDERR, ">&STDOUT";
```

This works for all filehandles, not just predefined ones:

```
open LOG, ">>/tmp/logfile";  # LOG appends to /tmp/logfile
open LOG2, ">&LOG";          # LOG2 is an alias for LOG
```

LOG and LOG2 might point to the same file, but they are not aliases for one another. If one is closed, the other remains open.

9.3.3   DATA

The DATA filehandle allows you to read input from the Perl program itself, following a __DATA__ token. The DATA filehandle does not need to be created with open. For example:

```perl
#!/usr/bin/perl
# filename: data-filehandle.pl

use strict;
use warnings;

while (<DATA>)
{
    print if /5/;
}
__DATA__
100 bottles of beer
50 states in the USA
billions and billions of stars
e is 2.171828
pi is 3.14159
```

The preceding program only prints lines containing 5, which is to say only the second and last lines in the __DATA__ segment.

9.3.4 fork *and filehandles*

Section 3.14 described fork, which splits a currently running program into two identical processes, each of which continues execution following the call to fork. Any filehandles that were owned by the original program are shared by the two resulting processes.

For example:

```perl
#!/usr/bin/perl
# filename: demo-fork-filehandles.pl

use strict;
use warnings;

# Name the file to which we will write
my $output = "/tmp/logfile";

# Open the file
open FILE, ">$output"
    or die "Cannot write '$output': $! ";
```

```
print FILE "Before fork from process $$\n";

# Split into two programs
my $pid = fork();

# Child
if ($pid == 0)
{
    print FILE "Hello from the child, pid $$\n";
}

# Parent
else
{
    print FILE "Hello from the parent, pid $$\n";
}


# Both programs print this, and close the filehandle
print FILE "Closing filehandle, pid $$\n";
close FILE;
```

Here is some sample output from this program:

```
Before fork from process 8797
Hello from the parent, pid 8797
Closing filehandle, pid 8797
Before fork from process 8797
Hello from the child, pid 8798
Closing filehandle, pid 8798
```

Sharing filehandles in this way can lead to problems: The two processes also share file pointers, meaning that using seek from one program will affect the other. Programs that will move through a file using seek should close the filehandle after fork returns to avoid confusion and potential errors.

9.3.5 *Filehandles as subroutine parameters*

As a general rule, we can pass filehandles as subroutine parameters:

```
my $logfile = '/tmp/log.txt';
open LOG, ">>$logfile" or die "Cannot open '$logfile' for writing: $! ";

print_to_filehandle(LOG);   # Passing the filehandle to a sub

sub print_to_filehandle
{
    # Get the filehandle
    my $fh = shift;

    # Send data to the filehandle $fh
    print $fh "Hello from the subroutine!\n";
}
```

However, $fh in the preceding program does not contain a copy of LOG. Rather, it contains a *symbolic reference* to LOG. As it turns out, print can work with symbolic references just as easily as standard filehandles. However, because symbolic references are an advanced, potentially dangerous feature (described fully in `perldoc perlref`), they are outlawed by use strict. The program just shown will thus fail to compile if use strict is in place.

9.3.6 IO::File

To avoid the sorts of issues associated with use strict and passing filehandles to subroutines, we can use the IO::File object, which comes with the Perl distribution. Using IO::File is straightforward for anyone familiar with Perl objects:

```
use IO::File;

my $file = '/home/reuven/.emacs';
my $fh = new IO::File;
$fh->open($file) or die "Could not open '$file' for reading: $! ";

while (<$fh>)
{
    print;
}

$fh->close;
```

It is not hard to follow what is happening in this code: The program creates a new instance of IO::File, which attempts to open the file /home/reuven/
.emacs. An instance of IO::File can be placed inside of <>, just like an or-
dinary filehandle.

The open method in IO::File lets you specify read, write, or append mode
using the C-style letters (r, w, and a), rather than the shell-style <, >, and
>>. An optional third argument specifies the octal permissions with which
the file should be opened.

You can combine new and open into a single operation by passing additional parameters to new:

```perl
my $fh = new IO::File $filename, "w", 0666;
```

Check for errors by checking to see if $fh is defined:

```perl
my $fh = new IO::File $filename, "w", 0666
    || die "Cannot open $filename for writing: $! ";

if (defined $fh)
{
    print $fh "Hello\n";
}
else
{
    print "Error: $! ";
}
```

IO::File provides a new_tmpfile constructor for creating temporary files.
When the instance of IO::File goes out of scope, the file is destroyed. For
example:

```perl
use IO::File;

my $fh = new_tmpfile;

if (defined $fh)
{
    print $fh "Hello\n";
}
else
```

```
{
    print "Error: $! ";
}
```

IO::File provides a number of methods that correspond to built-in Perl functions. For instance, close closes a filehandle, eof indicates whether a program has reached the end of a filehandle, and read reads from a filehandle. Other methods are described in from `perldoc IO::File`.

9.3.7 Buffered output

When Perl encounters the following code:

```
print FILE "Hello\n";
```

The string Hello is not immediately sent to FILE. Rather, it is stored in a holding area, known as a *buffer*. When it fills up, the buffer is emptied (flushed) into the file. Because the start-up cost of sending data to a file is much greater than the overhead for each additional character, buffered output helps programs to run more efficiently.

9.3.8 Flushing buffers

Perl flushes a buffer automatically when it is full. A program using IO::File can force a flush with the flush method. For example:

```
#!/usr/bin/perl
# filename: flushing-buffers.pl

use strict;
use warnings;
use IO::File;

my $filename = "/tmp/foo.txt";
my $fh = new IO::File;

$fh->open(">$filename") or
    die "Could not open for writing: $! ";
```

```
foreach my $counter (1 .. 60)
{
    print $fh "hello $counter\n";
    sleep 1;
}

$fh->close;
```

9.4   Globbing

Globs are text patterns designed for matching filenames. Perl's globs use the syntax from **csh**, the "C shell" from BSD Unix. The built-in **glob** function returns a list of filenames in the current directory that match its argument (or **$_**), if it is invoked without an argument.

The most commonly used glob characters are * and ?, which represent "zero or more characters" and "one character," respectively. glob('*.html') returns a list of all of the files ending in .html, and glob('a*b*.html') returns a list of files beginning with a, containing b, and ending with .html.

[ ] allow us to create a glob-style character class (see Section 5.4), in which any of the enclosed characters can match. Thus the sequence [abc] will match a, b, or c, but not more. Glob character classes can match a sequence by putting a - between items. Thus the glob [a-z] matches any one of the letters between a and z.

Any glob can be negated by prefacing it with ^. Thus [^abc] matches any single character other than a, b, or c, and a[^b]* matches filenames beginning with a in which b is not the second letter.

CORE Note

Negation (^) does not work if the glob contains {, }, or ˜.

If the characters { and } contain a comma-separated list, the glob is turned into a list of strings containing all of the possibilities. Thus the glob q{r,x,t,u}v is shorthand for the filenames qrv, qxv, qtv, and quv.

Finally, the character ˜ at the beginning of a glob expands to the current user's home directory.

For instance, the following one-liner lists the files beginning with **w** in the directory **Foo** under the user's home directory, except for those files ending with ~. Notice how ~ only has a special meaning at the beginning of a glob:

```
perl -e 'print join "\n", sort glob("~/Foo/w*[^~]")'
```

9.5   Real and effective IDs

Unix identifies each user is with a numeric ID, or *uid*, and a group ID, or *gid*. These are known as the "real" uid and gid, because they can never be changed. Under some circumstances (see Section 9.7), a program will temporarily pretend to be running as another user or group, setting what are known as the user's *effective uid* and *effective gid*.

The real uid and gid are available from the built-in $< and $(variables, respectively. The effective uid and gid are similarly available from the built-in $> and $) variables, respectively.

CORE Note

Perl's Unix heritage is particularly clear when working with file ownership and permissions. Issues having to do with uids and gids are meaningless on some other platforms, including Macintosh and Windows, and file permissions can have very different meanings. Consult `perldoc perlport` *before using these functions.*

9.5.1   File ownership

Each file is typically owned by a single uid/gid pair, indicating which user and group owns the file. To change a file's owner, use the built-in chown function:

```
chown $uid, $gid, $filename;
```

The following assigns $filename the uid and gid of the current user:

```
chown $<, $(, $filename;
```

chown accepts a list of filenames:

```
chown $<, $(, @files;
```

The first two arguments are integers reflecting uid and gid, and not the names associated with those numbers. Thus the following will not work:

```
chown "reuven", "staff", $file;  # Wrong
```

chown returns the number of files whose ownership was successfully changed.

9.5.2 *Retrieving user information*

The built-in getpwnam function retrieves user information from the operating system, given a user name. getpwnam returns the uid in scalar context, and a list of information about the user in list context:

```
my ($name, $password, $uid, $gid, $quota,
    $comment, $gcos, $dir, $shell) = getpwnam("reuven");
```

Not all list elements will be filled on all systems. On my Linux computer, which has no quota, $quota would be set to the empty string.

The preceding example sets $gcos to the GCOS field, which contains system-dependent information. It normally includes the user's address, telephone number, and nickname. Under Linux, elements of the GCOS field are separated by commas, so a program can retrieve the individual elements as follows:

```
# Grab the uid, and then the GCOS field
my @uid = getpwnam("reuven");
my $gcos = $uid[6];

# Print the full value of the GCOS field
print "gcos = '$gcos'\n";

# Split the scalar into an array across commas
my @gcos = split /,/, $gcos;

# Print each GCOS sub-field for Linux machines
print "Name: $gcos[0]\n";
print "Address: $gcos[1]\n";
print "Office phone: $gcos[2]\n";
print "Home phone: $gcos[3]\n";
```

Unix systems normally store less information about each group than about each user. However, this information can be retrieved with getgrnam, which takes a group name as an argument:

```
my ($name, $password, $gid, $members) = getgrnam("wheel");
```

To list a group's members, split $members across whitespace:

```
my @members = split /\s+/, $members;
```

getpwnam and getgrnam return undef if the parameter does not match an existing user or group.

The getpwuid and getgrgid functions return the same information as the getpwnam and getgrnam, except that they take a uid or gid as a parameter, rather than a user name or group name.

9.6   File permissions

Three different sets of permissions are associated with each file on a Unix (or Linux) system: one for the file's owner, a second for the file's group, and a third for everyone else.

For instance, assume that a file has uid joeuser and gid staff. If someone tries to access the file, Unix first checks the user's identity. If the user has uid joeuser, then the user permissions apply. If the user has gid staff, then the group permissions apply. If neither of these applies, then the other permissions apply.

9.6.1   Symbolic permissions

User, group, and other permissions are further divided into read, write, and execute privileges. These can be written symbolically as rwxrwxrwx, where the first rwx refers to user permissions, the second to group permissions, and the third to other permissions. In this scheme, a – means that a permission is lacking. So rw-rw-rw- means that anyone can read or write a file, and rwx------ means that although the owner can read, write, or execute a file, other users are forbidden from all of these activities.

Text files often have permissions of rw-rw-r--. This lets the owner and owner's group modify the file, and allows everyone else to read it. Executable programs frequently have permissions of rwxr-xr-x, allowing everyone to read and execute them but only allowing the owner to modify them.

9.6.2   Octal permissions

File permissions are often written using octal numbers, rather than the symbolic notation used earlier. Each octal digit represents the user, group, or other permissions, and comes from summing the applicable privileges, where r = 4, w = 2, and x = 1. We can thus describe a file's permissions as shown in Table 9.1.

Table 9.1	File Permissions	
Symbol	**Octal**	**Description**
rwxrwxrwx	0777	read, write, execute for all
rwxr-xr-x	0755	read and execute for all, write only by user
rw-rw-rw-	0666	read, write by all
rwx------	0700	read, write, execute only by user
rw-rw-r--	0664	read by all, write by user and group

9.6.3   chmod

Perl's built-in chmod function modifies the permissions of one or more files. The following code allows all users to read, write, and execute foobar:

```
chmod 0777, "foobar";    # Symbolic: rwx,rwx,rwx
```

Always include the initial 0 when using octal permissions (see Section 2.5.4). For example:

```
chmod 777, "foobar";                      # BAD: No loading 0
$mode = "0777"; chmod $mode, "foobar";   # BAD: Quotes ignore 0
```

Like chown, chmod can affect multiple files, and returns the number of files successfully modified:

```
my @files_to_change = qw(foo.txt bar.txt baz.txt etc.txt);
my $howmany = chmod 0700, @files_to_change;
print "Files change: $howmany\n";
```

Although less efficient, the following makes it easier to pinpoint errors:

```
@files_to_change = qw(foo.txt bar.txt baz.txt etc.txt);

foreach my $file (@files_to_change)
{
    my $was_changed = chmod 0700, $file;
    print "Error with 'chmod $file': $! " unless $was_changed;
}
```

9.6.4   umask

When a program creates a file, the effective uid and gid define the file's owner and group. The file's permissions are defined by the *umask*, an octal number that is bitwise-anded with 0666. For example:

```
umask 000;  # Creates files with permission 0666
my $file = '/tmp/testing';
open FILE, ">>$file"
    or die "Cannot append to '$file': $! ";
close FILE;
```

To create files with permission 0640 (`rw-,r--,---`), set the umask to 026:

```
umask 026;  # Creates files with permission 0640
my $file = '/tmp/testing';
open FILE, ">>$file"
    or die "Cannot append to '$file': $! ";
close FILE;
```

CORE Note

Execution bits are unaffected by the umask, and must be turned on explicitly with chmod.

Without any argument, umask returns the current umask:

```
my $umask = umask;
```

9.7   suid and sgid

Normally, a program inherits its uid and gid from the user who executes the program. An suid program, however, inherits its permissions from the owner and group of the program file. If a program is suid joeuser, then every user executing that program has an effective uid of joeuser. It is relatively common to make programs suid root, giving users root permission without having to know the superuser password.

CORE Warning

Buggy suid root *programs are a major source of security problems on Unix systems. Avoid making programs suid in general, and suid* root *in particular, unless it is unavoidable.*

Just as suid programs run with the permissions associated with the file's owner, sgid programs run with permissions associated with the file's group.

Because only executable programs can be suid or sgid, these permissions are represented symbolically with an s in place of the x.

9.7.1   Assigning suid and sgid permissions

We can assign suid permissions, like all others, with chmod. The octal digit for suid is 04000, and sgid is 02000. So assign $filename 0755 permissions plus suid, set it to 04755:

```
chmod 04755, $filename;  # rws,r-x,r-x
```

To give the same file 0755 permission and sgid, set it to 02755:

```
chmod 02755, $filename;  # rwx,r-s,r-x
```

9.7.2   The "sticky" bit

The octal value 01000 is known as the *sticky bit*, because it historically told Unix systems that a program should be retained in memory. Now, the sticky bit is mostly used for directories; see Section 9.11.4 for a full description of permissions on directories.

9.8 Unary file tests

Perl comes with a variety of tests for files and filehandles. Many of these are unary (i.e., one-argument) operators, with names that consist of - followed by a single letter. These tests return TRUE if the file passed the test, FALSE if it failed the test, and undef if the file does not exist.

For example, -e returns TRUE if the named file exists:

```
print "$file exists" if (-e $file);
```

Unary tests can help to improve your program's error messages by pinpointing problems. For example, the following code uses -W to see if a file is writable before invoking open:

```
# Can we write to $logfile?
if (-W $logfile)
{
    open LOG, ">>$logfile"
        or die "Could not open '$logfile': $! ";
    close LOG;
}
else
{
    print STDERR "Cannot write to '$logfile'; we won't even try.\n ";
}
```

9.8.1 File permissions and effective IDs

Several tests, shown in Table 9.2, indicate whether the current program's effective uid and gid allow it to read, write, or execute a file.

Table 9.2	Unary Tests for uid and gid File Permissions
Unary test	**Description**
-r	File can be read by the effective user ID or group ID
-w	File can be written to the effective user ID or group ID
-x	File can be executed by the effective user ID or group ID
-o	File is owned by effective user ID

For example, assume the following file:

```
-rw-r--r-- 1 root root 454325 Oct 14 1998 /boot/vmlinuz-2.0.34-0.6
```

Here is a short program that tests this file:

```
my $file = "/boot/vmlinuz-2.0.34-0.6";

print "Can read '$file'\n" if (-r $file);
print "Can write '$file'\n" if (-w $file);
print "Can execute '$file'\n" if (-x $file);
print "I own '$file'\n" if (-o $file);
```

Running as user **reuven**, group **reuven**, this code produces the following output:

```
Can read "/boot/vmlinuz-2.0.34-0.6"
```

Running as user **root**, group **root**, the program produces the following output:

```
Can read "/boot/vmlinuz-2.0.34-0.6"
Can read "/boot/vmlinuz-2.0.34-0.6"
I own "/boot/vmlinuz-2.0.34-0.6"
```

9.8.2   File permissions and real IDs

Other functions check to see whether the real uid/gid can read, write, or execute a file. These are identical to their effective counterparts, but use capital letters rather than lowercase ones (see Table 9.3).

Table 9.3	Unary Tests for real uid and gid File Permissions

Unary test	*Description*
-R	File can be read by the real user ID or group ID
-W	File can be written to the real user ID or group ID
-X	File can be executed by the real user ID or group ID
-O	File is owned by real user ID

9.8.3   Checking file attributes

Several unary tests, shown in Table 9.4, indicate if a file exists, as well as its current size.

Table 9.4	Unary Tests for File Presence and Size

Unary test	Description
-e	Returns TRUE if the file exists
-z	Returns TRUE if the file has zero length
-s	Returns FALSE if the file has zero length, otherwise returns the file's size

9.8.4   Determining a file type

Unix contains many types of files, the most prominent of which are standard files and directories. Some other types are sockets (see Section 10.2.1), named pipes (see Section 10.1.4), and links (see Section 9.13). These functions help us to determine a file's nature and are shown in Table 9.5.

Table 9.5	Unary Tests for File Type

Unary test	Description
-f	returns TRUE if a plain file
-d	returns TRUE if a directory
-l	returns TRUE if a symbolic link
-p	returns TRUE if a named pipe
-S	returns TRUE if a socket
-b	returns TRUE if a block-oriented device, such as a disk device
-c	returns TRUE if a character-oriented device, such as a keyboard
-t	returns TRUE if its argument is a tty

9.8.5   Checking special permissions

The tests in Table 9.6 check if a special (suid, sgid, or sticky) bit has been set.

9.8.6   Checking a file's contents

Perl can determine, using a rough algorithm, whether a file is binary, or if it contains ASCII text (see Table 9.7). The -T and -B operators, which are logical negatives of each other, check to see if a file contains more than 30%

Table 9.6	Unary Tests for a Special Bit

Unary test	*Description*
-u	returns TRUE if the suid bit is set
-g	returns TRUE if the sgid bit is set
-k	returns TRUE if the sticky bit is set

Table 9.7	Unary Test for Text or Binary Data

Unary test	*Description*
-T	returns TRUE for text files
-B	returns TRUE for binary files

alphanumeric characters. If it does, then the file is considered to contain text. Otherwise, it is considered binary.

9.8.7   Retrieving file dates and times

Unix filesystems typically record three different timestamps for each file:

- the creation date, meaning the date on which the file was first created,

- the access time, meaning the last time that the file was accessed in any way, and

- the modification time, meaning the last time that the file was modified.

If a file is created and never again touched, these three times are identical. If a file is created and read from a number of times, then the modification and creation dates remain the same, but the access time changes. If the file is modified, then the creation date becomes the odd man out, with the other two timestamps updated to reflect the changes.

The three unary operators shown in Table 9.8 return these pieces of information.

For example:

```
$filename = "/home/reuven/.emacs";
print "Age of file: ", (-M $filename), "\n";
print "Last access: ", (-A $filename), "\n";
print "Last modification: ", (-C $filename), "\n";
```

Table 9.8	Unary Tests for File Dates and Times

Unary test	*Description*
-M	Age of file, in days, when the program started
-A	Access time, in days, when the program started
-C	Inode time, in days, when the program started

Because these operators' results are measured in days, the preceding code will produce this sort of output:

```
Age of file: 16.5249537037037
Last access: 0.0132523148148148
Last modification: 16.5249537037037
```

The file was created or modified 16.52 days ago, and was last accessed 0.01 days ago (or 0.23 hours ago).

9.9 stat

stat, based on the Unix function call of the same name, takes a filename or filehandle as an argument (defaulting to $_ if no argument is passed). stat returns a 13-element list describing the named file or filehandle. If the file does not exist, or if there is some other error, then stat returns an empty list.

The array elements are shown in Table 9.9.

stat is typically invoked as follows:

```
my $filename = "/home/reuven/.emacs";
my ($dev, $ino, $mode, $nlink, $uid
    $gid, $rdev, $size, $atime,
    $mtime, $ctime, $blksize, $blocks) = stat $filename;
```

In scalar context (see Section 4.2.5), stat returns TRUE to indicate that it executed successfully, and FALSE otherwise.

Information from the latest invocation of stat is cached in the special filehandle _. Once you have used stat, speed up your programs by passing _ as an argument to unary file operators.

Table 9.9	Unary Tests for stat File Descriptions

Unary test	Description
0	filesystem device number
1	inode number (inodes are the basic building blocks of Unix filesystems)
2	mode (type and permissions of the file)
3	number of hard links to the file
4	uid for this file
5	gid for this file
6	device identifier, for "special" device files
7	size of the file, in bytes
8	last time the file was accessed (like -A)
9	last time the file was modified (like -M)
10	last time the inode was changed (like -C)
11	preferred block size
12	number of blocks used for this file

9.10   Locking

Nothing unusual happens if two processes read from a file simultaneously. However, if they both write a file at the same time, the result is impossible to predict. One solution is for programs to lock a file before writing to it, guaranteeing exclusive access.

Perl offers *advisory locks*, meaning that all programs accessing the file agree to check for a lock before modifying a file. Advisory locks only work if all of the processes agree to abide by the same rules. If even one process ignores the locks, all bets are off.

9.10.1   Using advisory locks

To lock or unlock a file, use the built-in flock function. flock takes two arguments, a filehandle and one or more constants from the :flock tag group in the Fcntl module (see Table 9.10).

9.10.2   Locking examples

To read from a file, use a shared lock:

```
use Fcntl qw(:flock);
```

Table 9.10	flock **Arguments**

Symbol	*Description*
LOCK_SH	Requests a "shared lock," otherwise known as a lock for reading; to read from a file without writing to it, request a shared lock
LOCK_EX	Requests an exclusive lock, which ensures that no other process will write or append to the file
LOCK_UN	Releases a lock
LOCK_NB	Forces the call to flock not to block

```
my $file = '/tmp/foo';
open FILE, $file
    or die "Cannot open '$file' for reading: $! ";

# Lock the file for reading (shared lock)
flock FILE, LOCK_SH ||
    die "Cannot lock '$file' for reading: $! ";

# Read from the file
print while (<FILE>);

# Unlock the file
flock FILE, LOCK_UN;
```

This call to flock can have three possible results:

1. The call returns TRUE immediately, meaning that the program successfully locked the filehandle. The program continues to execute.

2. The call waits for another program to release its lock, and then return TRUE when that happens. There is no way to know how long flock will "block," or wait, for the current owner of the lock to give it up. To avoid blocking, use LOCK_NB (described later).

3. The call to flock returns FALSE, meaning that it was unable to get a lock on FILE. If this happens, close the file immediately, rather than continuing to use it.

Under most circumstances, LOCK_SH and LOCK_EX will block. If a file is already locked, the program will wait to open the file until the lock is released. To change the behavior of flock such that it will not block, use a bitwise "or" (|) with LOCK_NB. For example:

```
use Fcntl qw(:flock);

my $file = '/tmp/foo';
open FILE, ">$file"
    or die "Cannot open '$file' for writing: $! ";

# Lock the file for non-blocking read (exclusive lock)
flock (FILE, (LOCK_EX | LOCK_NB)) ||
    die "Cannot lock '$file' for writing: $! ";

# Print to the file
print FILE "Hello there!\n";

# Unlock the file
flock FILE, LOCK_UN;
```

Locks are released automatically when a program exits normally.

9.11   Directories

Perl provides a number of functions for working with directories, which parallel those that work with files. This section describes some of them and demonstrates how to use them.

9.11.1   Creating directories

To create a directory, use the built-in mkdir function. mkdir expects to receive two arguments, the name of the directory to create, and an octal number representing its permissions. It returns TRUE or FALSE, depending on whether the directory was created.

```
my $was_created = mkdir "/tmp/newdir", 0666;
if ($was_created)
```

```
{
    print "It was created.\n";
}
else
{
    print "It was not created.\n";
}
```

The the initial permissions of a new directory are affected by the umask (see Section 9.6.4).

9.11.2   Changing directories

Unix filesystems are a hierarchy, beginning with the root node / and additional / characters indicating subdirectories. /usr/bin/program.pl thus refers to the file program.pl in the bin subdirectory of usr, which is a subdirectory of /.

Without a leading slash, a file is assumed to exist in the current directory. The built-in chdir function changes the current directory:

```
chdir "/tmp";    # Makes /tmp current directory
```

Without an argument, chdir sets the current directory to the value of $ENV{HOME}. (If neither is defined, chdir does nothing.) chdir returns TRUE if it is successful, and FALSE otherwise.

9.11.3   Opening and reading directories

Under Unix, a directory is a special file containing the names of other files. We can open and read that list with the opendir function. For example:

```
opendir DIR, $directory
    or die "Cannot open directory '$directory': $! ";
```

Directory handles ("dirhandles") and filehandles look identical, but are kept in different namespaces. A program can simultaneously work with a filehandle LOG and a dirhandle LOG, although common sense would suggest against it.

The readdir takes a dirhandle as an argument, and returns a list of the filenames in that directory. Use grep (see Section 3.8.7) to filter that list:

```
opendir DIR, $directory
    or die "Cannot open '$directory' for reading: $! ";
my @html_files = grep /\.html$/, readdir(DIR);
closedir DIR;

foreach my $file (@html_files) { print "$file\n"; }
```

9.11.4 Permissions and directories

Directory permissions determine whether a user can read or modify the list of the files it contains (see Table 9.11).

Table 9.11	Directory Permissions

Permission	*Description*
read	Permission to list the names of files in a directory
write	Permission to modify the list of files in a directory—including creating new files, renaming files, moving files into and out of the directory, and deleting files
execute	Permission to access the files themselves

`r--` permission lets a user see which files are in a directory without giving them access to the files. `--x` permission lets a user access files if he or she knows their names—but without read permission on the directory, a user cannot read the list of files.

On many systems, giving a directory sgid permission means that newly created files are placed in the same group as the directory.

On a directory, the sticky bit prevents users from deleting any files other than their own. This is often used in the Unix `/tmp` directory, where all users' temporary files are stored. The sticky bit ensures that users cannot delete each others' files.

9.11.5 IO::Dir

Just as IO::File provides an object-oriented interface to files, IO::Dir gives us an object-oriented interface to directories.

To read through a directory's contents, invoke the **read** method on an instance of IO::Dir. Like <> (see Section 9.1.1), each invocation of **read** returns a filename or **undef**:

```
use IO::Dir;

# Set directory to my homedir
my $dir = '/home/reuven';

# Create an instance of IO::Dir
my $dh = new IO::Dir "$dir";

# If undefined, there was an error
if (defined $dh)
{
    # Print each filename in the directory
    while (defined($filename = $dh->read))
    {
        print "$filename\n";
    }
}

# Report any errors
else
{
    print "Error listing dir '$dir': $! ";
}
```

9.11.6 *Tying* IO::Dir

IO::Dir is designed to be used both as a standalone object class and when tied to a hash (see Section 8.1). The keys to the tied hash are the filenames in the directory. Each element of the hash is itself a hash reference, in which the keys are the various elements returned by lstat (see Section 9.13.2).

For example, the following code lists the files in a directory followed by each file's inode:

```
use IO::Dir;

tie %dir, IO::Dir, "/home/reuven";
foreach my $filename (keys %dir)
{
    print $filename, " " , $dir{$filename}->ino,"\n";
}
```

Assigning to an existing element of the tied hash changes the associated file's modification time to the current time, not the filename. (If the file does not already exist, then it will be created.) Assigning a numeric value sets the access time along with the modification time:

```
tie %dir, IO::Dir, "/home/reuven";
foreach my $filename (keys %dir)
{
    $dir{$filename} = time;
}
```

CORE Warning

To avoid accidents, IO::Dir will only delete files if the DIR_UNLINK option is passed in the call to tie.

9.12   Renaming and deleting

This section describes Perl's functions for renaming and deleting files and directories.

9.12.1   rename

The rename function renames a file or directory, returning TRUE or FALSE according to its success:

```
my $oldname = "oldfoo";
my $newname = "newfoo";
my $successful = rename $oldname, $newname;
print "Failed to rename: '$oldname' to '$newname': $! "
    unless $successful;
```

Moving a file to a different directory is no different from giving it a new name that begins with a different path:

```perl
my $oldname = "/usr/local/bin/oldfoo";
my $newname = "/usr/bin/newfoo";
my $successful = rename $oldname, $newname;
print "Failed to rename: $! "
    unless $successful;
```

CORE Note

The preceding code will only work if /usr/local/bin *and* /usr/bin *are in the same filesystem. To avoid problems, it is often better to copy a file (perhaps using* File::Copy*) and then* unlink *it (see Section 9.12.2).*

9.12.2   Deleting files and directories

To delete one or more files, use unlink followed by a list of filenames. Without an argument, $_ is used as the filename. unlink returns the number of files successfully deleted:

```perl
my $number_deleted = unlink 'foo.html', 'bar.html';
print "Just deleted $number_deleted files.\n";
```

Deleting a directory with unlink is potentially dangerous to your filesystem. Perl will only allow the superuser to unlink a directory, and only if the -U option must be invoked.

Instead, you should delete directories with rmdir, which takes one optional argument, defaulting to $_. It deletes the directory, but only if the directory is empty. If the directory is not empty, rmdir returns FALSE:

```perl
my $doomed_dir = "/tmp/foodir";
my $success = rmdir $doomed_dir;
print "Successfully deleted $doomed_dir!\n"
    if $success;
```

9.13   Links

Most modern operating systems provide a way to refer to a file with more than one name. Unix has two such systems, both known as *links*. Links fill the same role that aliases do on the MacOS and shortcuts do under Windows.

Hard links associate a new filename to the same file contents. To create a hard link, use the built-in link function. link takes two arguments (the name of the file to which the link should point, and the name of the link), and returns TRUE or FALSE to indicate whether the link was successful:

```
my $was_created = link "/tmp/foo", "/tmp/link-to-foo";
```

Hard links have several limitations that are overcome by *symbolic links*. To create a symbolic link, use the built-in symlink function. symlink takes the same inputs as link, and returns TRUE or FALSE, as well:

```
my $symlink_was_created =
    symlink "/tmp/foo", "/tmp/sym-to-foo";
```

9.13.1   Problems with symbolic links

Using symlink on systems that lack symlink support results in a fatal runtime error. As the Perl documentation suggests, use eval to test for symlink before using it:

```
$symlink_exists = (eval {symlink("","")};, $@ eq '');

if ($symlink_exists)
{
    # Create a symlink
}
else
{
    # Somehow get around the issue
}
```

You can find out where a symbolic link points with the built-in readlink function:

```
print readlink "/tmp/sym-to-foo";     # prints /tmp/foo
```

9.13.2   stat *and symbolic links*

stat assumes that a user is not interested in the link itself, but rather in the file to which it points. To find out information about a link, use lstat, which returns the same information as stat. Here are the results from stat and lstat when called on `file.txt` and the symlink `link-to-file.txt`:

```perl
my @orig_stat = stat "file.txt";
my @stat = stat "link-to-file.txt";
my @lstat = lstat "link-to-file.txt";

print "Original: @orig_stat\n";
print "Regular:  @stat\n";
print "Lstat:    @lstat\n";
```

The preceding code gives the following result on my system:

```
Original: 769 8093 33206 1 500 500 0 0 903863329 903863329 903863329
Regular:  769 8093 33206 1 500 500 0 0 903863329 903863329 903863329
Lstat:    769 8180 41471 1 500 500 0 8 903863750 903863335 903863335
```

The differences between the two files are in stat indexes 2 (type and permissions), 7 (size of the file), 8 (access time), 9 (modification time), and 10 (change time).

Ironically, the link in this example contains more bytes than the file itself! The file itself contains zero bytes, whereas a symlink contains the name of the file to which it points. Because our symbolic link points to `file.txt`, the length of our link is 8 bytes.

9.14 Conclusion

In this chapter, we looked at Perl's many built-in operators and functions for working with files and directories. In particular, we examined:

- Basic file access, including advanced uses for <>,

- How to use $/ to "slurp" files and read them in paragraph mode,

- Random file access with seek,

- Built-in, null, and duplicated filehandles,

- IO::File and IO::Dir,

- Globbing,

- Users, groups, and permissions, and

- How to use flock for advisory file locking.

NETWORKING AND INTERPROCESS COMMUNICATION

Topics in This Chapter

- Anonymous pipes

- Named pipes (FIFOs)

- Network communication with sockets

- IO::Socket

- Writing network servers and clients

- Writing forking servers

- Working with Internet protocols

- Using LWP

Chapter 10

So far, all of our programs have been designed to work by themselves. However, programs often need to communicate with other programs, on the same computer or other computers connected by a network.

This chapter describes some of the ways in which Perl programs can communicate with others. We begin by looking at one-way anonymous pipes, followed by one-way named pipes. We then look at IO::Socket, which makes it easy to create a network client or server.

The remainder of the chapter is spent looking at the most popular Internet protocols, including FTP (File Transfer Protocol), Telnet, and SMTP (simple mail transfer protocol). We will also look at LWP, the library for Web programming that makes it easy to write HTTP (Hypertext Transfer Protocol) clients.

Unfortunately, not all of the tools introduced in this chapter are available on all operating systems. Before writing a networked application that must be as portable as possible, read `perldoc perlport`, which describes many of the pitfalls that await unsuspecting programmers.

10.1   Pipes

Section 3.10.5 demonstrated how to send data to another program (or read data from it) using open. Such programs demonstrate how two processes on the same computer can communicate. Behind the scenes, open links the two programs with a "pipe," connecting a write-only filehandle on one process with a read-only filehandle on another process.

10.1.1   Simple anonymous pipes

Anonymous pipes take advantage of the fact that following a fork, the parent and child processes share the parent's filehandles. The built-in pipe function opens two filehandles, the first of which is read-only and the second of which is write-only (see Figure 10.1). If the process invokes fork following the call to pipe, the parent and child can then communicate, with one process writing to the pipe and the other process reading from it (see Figure 10.2). Both processes have access to both filehandles following the fork; to avoid confusion and potential hangs, each process should close the filehandle that it will not use (see Figure 10.3).

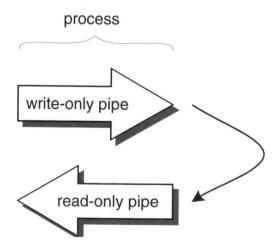

Figure 10.1   When pipe is first invoked, it creates two pipes—one is a read-only filehandle, and the other is a write-only filehandle.

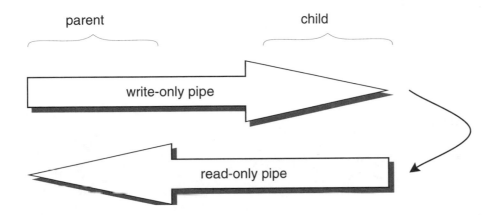

Figure 10.2   After the invocation of fork, the parent and child processes share the read-only and write-only pipes.

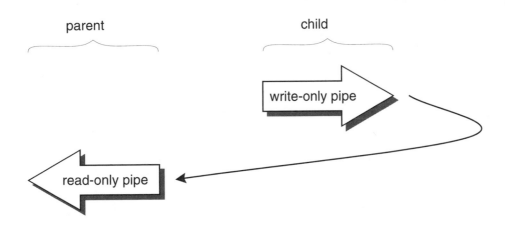

Figure 10.3   Following the fork, one process closes its copy of the read-only pipe, and the other closes its copy of the write-only pipe. This example demonstrates how the child process can then send messages to its parent, but the opposite is also possible.

This program demonstrates how a program can communicate with its child process using pipe:

```perl
#!/usr/bin/perl
# filename: anonymous-pipe.pl

use strict;
use warnings;

# Create some pipes
pipe(READONLY, WRITEONLY);

# Fork!
my $pid = fork();

# Make sure that fork worked
die "Cannot fork: $! " unless (defined $pid);

# I am the child, and will write to the parent
if ($pid == 0)
{
    # Close the read-only filehandle
    close READONLY;

    # Send a message to the parent
    print WRITEONLY "Hello from the child, PID $$!\n";

    # Always close the filehandle
    close WRITEONLY or die "Error closing: $! ";

    exit;
}

# I am the parent, and will read from the child
else
{
    # Close the write-only filehandle
    close WRITEONLY;
```

```
    # Get the message from the child
    print while (<READONLY>);

    # Always close the filehandle
    close READONLY or die "Error closing: $! ";

    exit;
}
```

If READONLY is closed while data is still being written to WRITEONLY, the writing process will receive the PIPE signal, known as SIGPIPE. For example:

```perl
#!/usr/bin/perl
# filename: sigpipe-demo.pl

use strict;
use warnings;

# Install a signal handler for SIGPIPE
$SIG{PIPE} =
    sub { print "\nProcess $$ caught SIG{PIPE}: $! "; exit;};

# Create some pipes
pipe(READONLY, WRITEONLY);

# Fork!
my $pid = fork();

# Make sure that fork worked
die "Cannot fork: $! " unless (defined $pid);

# I am the child, and will write to the parent
if ($pid == 0)
{
    # Close the read-only filehandle
    close READONLY;

    my $counter = 1;

    # Infinite loop!
    while (1)
```

```perl
        {
            $counter++;
            print WRITEONLY "This is child $$, on loop $counter.\n";
        }

        # Close the filehandle, and check for errors
        close WRITEONLY or die "Error closing: $! ";

        exit;
    }


# I am the parent, and will read from the child
else
{
    # Close the write-only filehandle
    close WRITEONLY;

    # Read one line from the child
    my $message = <READONLY>;
    print $message;

    # Close the filehandle, and check for errors
    close READONLY or die "Error closing: $! ";

    exit;
}
```

10.1.2   Two-way communication

Pipes can be useful for sending messages from one process to another, but what if the receiving process wants to send a message back to its peer? The simple solution is to create two pairs of pipes, one for each direction:

```perl
#!/usr/bin/perl
# filename: two-anonymous-pipes.pl

use strict;
use warnings;

# Create some pipes
pipe(PARENT_READ, CHILD_WRITE);
pipe(CHILD_READ, PARENT_WRITE);
```

```perl
select CHILD_WRITE; $| = 1;   # Autoflush CHILD_WRITE
select PARENT_WRITE; $| = 1;  # Autoflush PARENT_READ
select STDOUT;

# Fork!
my $pid = fork();

# Make sure that fork worked
die "Cannot fork: $! " unless (defined $pid);

# I am the child, and will write to the parent
if ($pid == 0)
{
    # Close the parent's sides of the pipe
    close PARENT_READ;
    close PARENT_WRITE;

    # Send a message to the parent
    print CHILD_WRITE "This is child $$, saying hello!\n";

    # Get a message from the parent
    my $message = <CHILD_READ>;
    print "Child received message '$message' from parent\n";

    # Always close the filehandles
    close CHILD_READ or die "Error closing: $! ";
    close CHILD_WRITE or die "Error closing: $! ";

    exit;
}

# I am the parent, and will read from the child
else
{
    # Close the child's sides of the pipe
    close CHILD_READ;
    close CHILD_WRITE;

    # Send a message to the parent
    print PARENT_WRITE "This is parent $$, saying hello!\n";

    # Get a message from the child
    my $message = <PARENT_READ>;
    print "Parent received message '$message' from child\n";
```

```
    # Always close the filehandles
    close PARENT_READ or die "Error closing: $! ";
    close PARENT_WRITE or die "Error closing: $! ";

    exit;
}
```

This program uses the built-in **select** function to set the default filehandle. This affects not only **print**, but values set to **$|** as well (see Section 3.11.4). Without setting **$|** in this way, text sent by our program would not fill the output buffer. The parent and child would block waiting for each other, causing the program to hang forever. Turning on autoflush mode ensures that this will not happen.

10.1.3   socketpair

A better solution to this problem is the built-in **socketpair** function, which creates two bidirectional pipes, known as *sockets*. Sockets are normally discussed in the context of network communication (see Section 10.2.1), but are also useful for two-way communication on a single computer:

```
#!/usr/bin/perl
# filename: socketpair.pl

use strict;
use warnings;
use Socket;

# Create a pair of two-way sockets
socketpair(CHILD_TO_PARENT, PARENT_TO_CHILD,
           AF_UNIX, SOCK_STREAM, PF_UNSPEC)
    or die "Cannot create socketpair: $! ";

select CHILD_TO_PARENT; $| = 1;
select PARENT_TO_CHILD; $| = 1;
select STDOUT;

# Fork!
my $pid = fork();

# Make sure that fork worked
die "Cannot fork: $! " unless (defined $pid);
```

```perl
# I am the child, and will write to the parent
if ($pid == 0)
{
    # Send a message to the parent
    print CHILD_TO_PARENT "This is child $$, saying hello!\n";
    close CHILD_TO_PARENT
        or die "Cannot close CHILD_TO_PARENT: $! ";

    # Get a message from the parent
    my $message = <PARENT_TO_CHILD>;
    print $message;
    close PARENT_TO_CHILD
        or die "Cannot close PARENT_TO_CHILD: $! ";

    exit;
}

# I am the parent, and will read from the child
else
{
    # Send a message to the parent
    print PARENT_TO_CHILD "This is parent $$, saying hello!\n";
    close PARENT_TO_CHILD
        or die "Cannot close PARENT_TO_CHILD: $! ";

    # Get a message from the parent
    print while (<CHILD_TO_PARENT>);
    close CHILD_TO_PARENT
        or die "Cannot close CHILD_TO_PARENT: $! ";

    exit;
}
```

socketpair takes five arguments, the first two of which are sockets (implemented as Perl filehandles). The remaining arguments are numbers, normally written as constants exported by the Socket module, that describe the type of sockets to create. In this particular case, the sockets will be in the Unix domain (i.e., between two processes on the same computer), and will be stream oriented, rather than consisting of individual, unrelated packets.

10.1.4 Named pipes

All of the aforementioned techniques require that the reader and writer were originally part of a single process that invoked fork. A named pipe, by contrast, allows two unrelated programs to communicate with each other. A named pipe is sometimes known as a FIFO, as data is received in the same order as it is sent.

To the casual observer, a named pipe looks and acts like a file. Rather than being stored anywhere, however, data sent to a named pipe is sent to a process reading from it. By the same token, a process reading from the named pipe is actually receiving data from a program.

Named pipes require support from the underlying operating system. Modern versions of Unix support the `mkfifo` command, which creates a named pipe in the filesystem. Once created, any program can use the named pipe. On my Linux system, I can create a named pipe with:

```
mkfifo /tmp/random
```

Unix systems lacking `mkfifo` instead use `mknod`, adding the "p" option to create a named pipe. For example:

```
mknod /tmp/random p
```

A named pipe is typically created in conjunction with a program that acts as a constant data source or sink. For example, if we connect the following program to `/tmp/random`, programs can retrieve data from `/tmp/random` for a random number between 1 and 1,000:

```perl
#!/usr/bin/perl
# filename: random-pipe.pl

use strict;
use warnings;

# What file is our named pipe (FIFO)?
my $pipe_filename = "/tmp/random";

# What is the maximum random number to return?
my $max_random = 1000;

while (1)
{
    # Blocks on open until someone reads the file
    open OUTPUT, ">$pipe_filename"
        or die qq|Cannot open "$pipe_filename": $! |;
```

```
    # Send a random number to the output
    my $number = rand $max_random;
    print OUTPUT $number, "\n";

    # Close it
    close OUTPUT;
}
```

In each iteration of the while loop, we open the named pipe for output, as if we were writing to a file. However, open blocks until another process opens the FIFO for reading. At that point, we send a random number and ending with NEWLINE. The program closes the OUTPUT filehandle before returning ot the top of the while loop. A program can get a stream of random numbers by reading one or more lines from /tmp/random.

Named pipes are useful, but they do have drawbacks—in particular, there is no way to identify which process is on the other side of the pipe. FIFOs are also not designed for multiple programs to send (or receive) large amounts of data. The POSIX standard does guarantee that some minimal number of bytes will be sent uninterrupted over a FIFO, but this number is generally too small to be of real use.

10.2   Network communication

So far, we have only looked at ways in which two processes on the same computer can communicate. Today, programs can communicate with one another via networks. Perl supports a variety of network protocols, most of which are based on TCP/IP.

TCP/IP, the lingua franca of the Internet, is actually two protocols: the Transmission Control Protocol, and the Internet Protocol. IP contains the addressing information, and TCP ensures reliability and that packets arrive in order. If you are willing to trade speed for reliability, you can substitute UDP (the User Datagram Protocol). UDP has less overhead than TCP, but does not guarantee that sent packets will arrive, or that they'll arrive in order.

A networked computer can carry on several simultaneous conversations. Each conversation, whether outgoing or incoming, is assigned a unique port number. A connection between two computers can thus be identified uniquely with four numbers—the first computer's IP address and port number, and its counterpart's IP address and port number. Programs that sit and wait for connections from the outside world are known as servers, and those that initiate connections are known as clients.

10.2.1 Sockets

Sockets, as we saw in Section 10.1.2, make it possible for two programs to communicate on the same computer. We can also use Perl's built-in socket function to create sockets that operate over a network. Using socket requires some platform-dependent code, which is why many programmers prefer the Socket module, which defines a number of standard constants that work on all platforms.

The easiest way to create socket-based clients and servers is the IO::Socket module, written by Graham Barr and included with Perl distributions beginning with 5.004. This module defines an object class that makes socket programming significantly easier than either socket or Socket. IO::Socket supports two different types of sockets, one for network communication (IO::Socket::INET) and one on the local computer (IO::Socket::UNIX).

10.2.2 Servers with sockets

A socket-based server is similar to a program that reads data from a named pipe: It waits to receive a connection, blocking until one arrives. Once the connection has been established, the socket provides a bidirectional interface through which the client and server can communicate.

As with anonymous pipes, it is possible for the client and server to deadlock, with each waiting for the other to send data. It is thus important to establish a protocol, describing when each computer must speak and when it must listen. The socket-based protocols used on the Internet, such as SMTP, FTP, and HTTP, include such provisions, removing the possibility of such a deadlock.

Here is a simple server that returns the current date and time to the connecting client:

```perl
#!/usr/bin/perl
# filename: socket-server.pl

use strict;
use warnings;
```

```perl
use IO::Socket;

# Create the server socket
my $socket = IO::Socket::INET->new(Proto => "tcp",
                                   LocalPort => 5555,
                                   Listen => SOMAXCONN,
                                   Reuse => 1);

print STDERR "Starting server...\n";

# Accept incoming connections
while (my $client = $socket->accept())
{
    # Read one line from the client
    my $buffer = <$client>;

    print STDERR qq|Received: "$buffer"\n|;

    # Get the current date
    my $date = localtime time;

    # Send something to the client
    print $client "Hello from the server on $date!\n";

    close $client;
}

print STDERR "Shutting down server...\n";
```

This example begins by creating a new instance of IO::Socket::INET. The constructor accepts about a dozen named parameters, four of which are assigned in the preceding program:

- Proto can be set to tcp or udp, and indicates which protocol should be used.

- LocalPort describes the port on which the server will reside. Unix systems traditionally restrict the first 1024 ports to the root user, leaving everything up to 65535 for other applications. Choose a unique port number for each application to avoid potential conflicts or confusion. This server uses 5555.

- Listen indicates how many incoming connections should be forced to wait while the current connection is being handled. An office telephone system can only say "Please hold—your call is important to us" to a finite number of callers; Listen sets that maximum number when working with sockets. We use the constant SOMAXCONN, defined by IO::Socket, to use the system's maximum.

- Reuse, when set to a nonzero value, indicates that the socket can be used by the system immediately after this client–server connection closes. Normally, a closed socket must remain closed for some time—two minutes, under Linux—before it can handle a new connection.

Once the socket has been created, the server waits for an incoming connection by invoking accept. accept blocks until a new connection arrives, returning either an instance of IO::Socket::INET or undef.

Once the connection has been established, $client functions as a bidirectional filehandle. The server can send data to $client with print, and can retrieve data from it with read or <>. In the preceding example, the server retrieves one line of text, sends a canned response, and closes the connection.

10.2.3   Clients with sockets

The code given earlier demonstrated how to write a simple socket-based server. Writing a client is similar, with the main difference being the lack of a call to accept.

The following example client connects to a server, to which it sends a short line of text. The server presumably sends something in return, which the client reads and prints. When this exchange ends, the client closes the connection and exits, freeing the server to accommodate another program:

```perl
#!/usr/bin/perl
# filename: socket-client.pl

use strict;
use warnings;
use IO::Socket;

# Create the socket
my $socket = IO::Socket::INET->new(Proto => "tcp",
                                   PeerAddr => "www.coreperl.com",
                                   PeerPort => 5555)
          or die "cannot connect: $! ";
```

```
# Get the current date
my $date = localtime time;

# Send some data to the server
print $socket "Hello from the client on $date!\n";

# Retrieve some data from the server
print while (<$socket>);
```

This code creates an instance of IO::Socket::INET, specifying the Proto keyword. However, the client must also specify the IP address and port on which the server is running, using the PeerAddr and PeerPort keywords. PeerAddr can be a hostname or IP address, such as either www.lerner.co.il or 212.29.241.229.

10.2.4   Sample client: Finger

IO::Socket can be used to create clients and servers of arbitrary complexity. As an example, we will look at a finger client, which old-time Internet users might remember from the days that preceded home pages on the World Wide Web.

The finger protocol is simple: A client connects to a server on the well-known port 79, and sends a user name. The server responds by printing information about that user, sometimes including statistics about his or her login times and details about the system.

Here is the code for **finger.pl**, a simple finger client:

```
#!/usr/bin/perl
# filename: finger.pl

use strict;
use warnings;
use IO::Socket;

# Iterate over the arguments
foreach my $input (@ARGV)
{

    # Grab the user's input
    my ($username, $servername) = split /@/, $input;
```

```perl
    # Give empty variables a default value
    $username = $username || "";
    $servername = $servername || "localhost";

    # Create the socket
    my $socket = IO::Socket::INET->new(Proto => "tcp",
                                       PeerAddr => $servername,
                                       PeerPort => 79)
        or die "cannot connect: $! ";

    # It is traditional to print the hostname in brackets
    print "[$servername]\n";

    # Send some data to the server
    print $socket "$username\n";

    # Retrieve some data from the server
    print while (<$socket>);
}
```

Finger clients traditionally make it possible to learn about a host by leaving the user name blank. Conversely, a program can leave the hostname blank, in which case it defaults to the computer on which the client was invoked.

10.2.5 Sample server: HTTP

IO::Socket can also be used to create a simple server. In this case, the server will implement a small subset of HTTP, the hypertext transfer protocol widely used on the World Wide Web.

The server will receive a one-line request. The request begins with the keyword GET, is followed by whitespace, and ends with the name of a file to return. The server's response will be the contents of the file in question—or, in the case of an error, a message indicating what happened.

To avoid the risk of users retrieving arbitrary files, the server prepends a directory name to the beginning of every request. Here is one possible implementation of httpd.pl, a simple Web server:

```perl
#!/usr/bin/perl
# filename: httpd.pl
```

```perl
use strict;
use warnings;
use IO::Socket;

# Set the directory prefix
my $dir_prefix = "/usr/local/apache/htdocs/";

# Create the server socket
my $socket = IO::Socket::INET->new(Proto => "tcp",
                                   LocalPort => 8080,
                                   Listen => SOMAXCONN,
                                   Reuse => 1)
    or die "Error opening socket: $! ";

# Accept incoming connections
while (my $client = $socket->accept()) {

    # Grab the request from the client
    my $request = <$client>;

    # Drop the trailing newline
    chomp $request;

    # Split the request into a method and a filename, ignoring
    # anything that might come after it
    my ($method, $filename, $ignore) = split /\s+/, $request;

    # Make sure that the request is GET
    if ($method ne "GET")
    {
        print $client qq{Error!  Unknown method "$method"\n};
    }

    # If we got a GET request, return the
    # file's contents---if it exists
    else
    {
```

```
    # Remove leading . and / characters from the filename
    $filename =~ s|^[/.]+||g;

    my $full_filename = $dir_prefix . $filename;

    # Display the file if it exists
    if (open (FILE, $full_filename))
    {
        while (<FILE>)
        {
            print $client $_;
        }
    }
    # Otherwise report an error
    else
    {
        print $client "Error retrieving $filename: $!\n";
    }
}


# That's it!  Close up, and wait for the next connection
close $client;
}
```

10.2.6   Forking servers

Our server can only handle one incoming connection at a time. If a request arrives while one is being serviced, the new request must wait until the first request ends, which can be a long time. A common solution to this problem uses fork to create a new server process for each incoming connection.

The server invokes fork just after accept, creating a child process that handles the client connection. The parent is thus free to continue receiving and servicing new client connections.

Here is a version of our simple server that forks as it accepts incoming connections:

```
#!/usr/bin/perl
# filename: multi-socket-server.pl
```

```perl
use strict;
use warnings;
use IO::Socket;

# Create the server socket
my $socket = IO::Socket::INET->new(Proto => "tcp",
                                   LocalPort => 5555,
                                   Listen => SOMAXCONN,
                                   Reuse => 1);

# Define a subroutine that removes child processes
sub REAPER
{
    # Find out which process exited and exit silently
    my $which_process = wait;

    # Re-install ourselves, in case we are running
    # under a version of Unix that requires it
    $SIG{CHLD} = \&REAPER;
}

# Install the signal handler
$SIG{CHLD} = \&REAPER;

print STDERR "Starting server...\n";

# Accept incoming connections
while (my $client = $socket->accept()) {

    # Fork!
    my $pid = fork();
    die "Cannot fork: $! " unless (defined $pid);

    # The child continues to run
    if ($pid == 0)
    {
        # Read one line from the client
        my $buffer = <$client>;

        print STDERR qq|Received: "$buffer"\n|;

        # Get the current date
        my $date = localtime time;
```

```
        # Send something to the client
        print $client "Hello from the server on $date!\n";

        # Close the socket
        close $client;

        # The child must exit
        exit;
    }

    # The parent closes the socket and waits for a new connection
    close $client;
}

print STDERR "Shutting down server...\n";
```

Notice how this code avoids zombies (see Section 4.7.4) by installing a signal handler on SIG{CHILD}.

10.3   Working with Internet protocols

TCP/IP is the basis for all communication on the Internet. But sophisticated applications need higher level, application-layer protocols to function normally. Luckily, there are many such standard protocols on the Internet, including FTP (for file transfers), and SMTP (for sending e-mail). Better yet, Perl modules from the standard distribution and CPAN (see Section 1.6) make it easy for a Perl program to communicate using these protocols. This section briefly introduces some of the modules that handle these protocols.

10.3.1   Net::FTP

FTP allows two computers to exchange files via a socket. FTP works with an infinite loop of request–response pairs, in which the client sends a request and the server returns a response. Depending on the request, the response may be the contents of a file, a directory listing, or an error message. The socket is closed when the client requests an end to the link.

Files can be uploaded to the server with the put command, and can be downloaded from the server with the get command.

Net::FTP, a module written by Graham Barr and available on CPAN in the libnet package, provides an object-oriented interface for creating FTP clients.

To open an FTP connection, we first invoke the constructor new, passing the hostname of the FTP server to which the program should connect as an argument. If the connection fails, new returns undef and places the error message in $@.

Once the instance of Net::FTP has been created, log into the server with the login method. If this succeeds, we can use the put and get methods to send and retrieve files. We can also change to a different directory with the cwd method.

The following program uploaded the latest manuscript of this book to a Web site, from which my editors were able to retrieve it:

```perl
#!/usr/bin/perl
# filename: create-distribution.pl

use strict;
use warnings;
use Net::FTP;

$| = 1;

my $directory = "/coreperl-www/book/";

# Now that we have done all of the dirty work, let's upload
# these files to the right place
my $ftp = Net::FTP->new("www.lerner.co.il");

die "Cannot login: $@ " unless $ftp;

# Log into the server
$ftp->login("reuven", "*****");

# Change to the right directory
$ftp->cwd("/coreperl-www/book/")
    or die qq{Cannot switch to "$directory": $@ };

# Change to binary transfer mode
$ftp->binary;

# Turn on hash marks
$ftp->hash(1);

foreach my $filename ("$tarfile.gz", "$psfile.gz", "$dvifile.gz")
```

```
{
    print "About to upload $filename to $directory.\n";
    $ftp->put($filename);
    print "Done.\n";
}

$ftp->quit;
```

10.3.2   Telnet

Many computers allow users to log in remotely using the Telnet protocol. Telnet is particularly useful for system administrators, in that it allows full control of a system from anywhere in the world. The Net::Telnet module, available from CPAN and written by Jay Rogers, gives Perl programs the ability to log into remote computers using Telnet.

You can create an instance of Net::Telnet with the new constructor. One of the many optional arguments to new is Timeout, which indicates how long we should wait to connect to the Telnet server before giving up.

After creating a new object, use the open and login methods to connect to the server and create an interactive session. Once this is done, you can send commands to the remote server with the cmd method. cmd returns a list of text strings that were returned from the command. These strings can then be analyzed, printed, saved to a file, or discarded.

Here is an example program that uses Net::Telnet to run the finger command on a remote computer:

```
#!/usr/bin/perl
# filename: finger-via-telnet.pl

use strict;
use warnings;
use Net::Telnet;

# Set the username and password
my $username = "reuven";
my $password = "XXXXX";

# Create the session
my $session =
    new Net::Telnet (Timeout => 10);
```

```
# Open the Telnet session to localhost
$session->open("localhost");

# Log in as $username with $password
$session->login($username, $password);

# Send a command, and store its output
# in @result
my @result = $session->cmd("/usr/bin/finger");

# Print out the result
print @result;

$session->close;
```

10.3.3 SMTP

SMTP is the standard protocol for e-mail exchange on the Internet. Net::SMTP, written by Graham Barr, makes it possible for a Perl program to send mail using SMTP.

To create a new instance of Net::SMTP, pass the target mail server as a parameter to new:

```
use Net::SMTP;

# Connect to mail.coreperl.com
my $mailhost = 'mail.coreperl.com';
my $smtp = new Net::SMTP($mailhost)
    or die qq|Cannot connect to "$mailhost"|;
```

To ensure that the SMTP connection does not hang forever, pass new a named parameter of Timeout. This is the number of seconds to wait for a connection before giving up.

In addition, SMTP requires that a client first identify itself to the server. The Hello named parameter tells Net::SMTP what value to pass. If this parameter is not named, Net::SMTP guesses as best as it can.

CORE Note

Spammers often modify their SMTP clients to lie about their origins. Modern mail servers thus identify the client's hostname and IP address, as reported by DNS (the Domain Name System), for logging purposes.

Here is a version of the preceding code, rewritten to include both Timeout and Hello:

```
use Net::SMTP;

# Connect to mail.coreperl.com
my $mailhost = 'mail.coreperl.com';

# Try for 30 seconds, then give up
my $smtp = new Net::SMTP($mailhost, Timeout => 30)
    or die qq|Cannot connect to "$mailhost"|;
```

Once the client has identified itself, it can send mail to one or more recipients, using the mail method to identify the sender and the to method to identify the recipient. We can then send e-mail by putting the message in a list of strings, passing the data method that list. Here is a program that sends a file of the user's choice to a fixed e-mail address. The file must include the standard SMTP To and From headers, separated from the message with a blank line:

```
#!/usr/bin/perl
# filename: send-file.pl

use strict;
use warnings;
use Net::SMTP;

# Get the name of the file
print "Enter a filename: ";

my $filename = <>;
chomp($filename);
```

```
# Open the file
open FILE, $filename or die qq|Cannot open "$filename": $! |;

# Get the message contents
my @message = (<FILE>);

# Open a connection to the recipient's SMTP server
my $smtp = new Net::SMTP("mail.coreperl.com",
                         Timeout => 30)
    or die "Cannot connect to mail.coreperl.com";

# Indicate the sender and recipient
$smtp->mail('sendfile@coreperl.com')
    or die "Cannot set sender";

$smtp->to('getfile@coreperl.com')
    or die "Cannot set recipient";

# Send the message
$smtp->data(@message)
    or die "Cannot send message";

# Exit
$smtp->quit;

# Close the file
close FILE;
```

10.3.4   *Sending mail with* Mail::Sendmail

If you simply want to send e-mail, you may prefer to use a higher-level
module, such as Mail::Sendmail, written by Milivoj Ivkovic and available on
CPAN.

Mail::Sendmail exports the **sendmail** subroutine, which takes a single hash
argument. The hash's keys correspond to the e-mail headers—From, To,
Subject, and any others that the user wishes to define. The Body key points
to the message body.

If sendmail fails, it returns FALSE, and places the error message in the
variable $Mail::Sendmail::error. Full logging information is placed in $Mail::
Sendmail::log. Neither variable is exported to the caller's package.

The following program sends the contents of a text file to sendfile@coreperl.com:

```perl
#!/usr/bin/perl
# filename: better-send-file.pl

use strict;
use warnings;
use Mail::Sendmail;

# Get the name of the file
print "Enter a filename: ";

my $filename = <>;
chomp($filename);

# Open the file
open FILE, $filename or die qq|Cannot open "$filename": $! |;

# Slurp the entire file
undef $/;

# Get the message contents
my $message = (<FILE>);

# Close the file
close FILE;

# Send the message
sendmail(From => 'sendfile@coreperl.com',
         To   => 'getfile@coreperl.com',
         Body => $message)
    or die "Cannot send message: $Mail::Sendmail::error";
```

Mail::Sendmail automatically inserts a Date header indicating when the message was sent, as well as information about the type of contents being sent.

10.3.5   URLs

Each document on the World Wide Web is uniquely identified by its uniform resource locator, or URL. (URLs are sometimes called URIs, or uniform resource identifiers.) One example of a URL is:

```
http://the-tech.mit.edu/index.html
```

The above URL describes the file /index.html, sitting on the computer the-tech.mit.edu and available via HTTP. In the same way, the URL /pub/gnu/emacs-20.2.tar.gz points to a file on ftp.gnu.org, using FTP:

```
ftp://ftp.gnu.org/pub/gnu/emacs-20.2.tar.gz
```

By default, HTTP connections take place over port 80. To override this default, add a colon (:) and number to the hostname:

```
http://the-tech.mit.edu:8080/index.html
```

The above URL describes the document /index.html, retrieved via HTTP from the-tech.mit.edu on port 8080.

10.3.6   Retrieving files with LWP::Simple

The LWP abstraction that handles HTTP transactions is known as a user agent. A Web client sends its HTTP request to a user agent, which forwards it to the appropriate HTTP server. The response is returned to the user agent, which in turn makes it available to the calling program (see Figure 10.4).

LWP::Simple, the most basic user agent, exports its get subroutine into the caller's namespace. get retrieves the contents of a URL, which it takes as a mandatory parameter. If there is an error returning the document, get returns undef. For example:

```
use LWP::Simple;

my $url = "http://localhost/index.html";

# Display the contents of the URL, or die trying
print get $url
    || die qq|Error retrieving "$url"\n|;
```

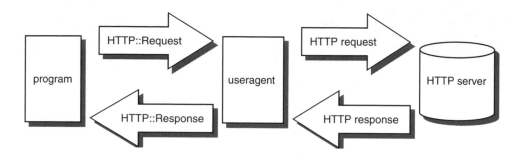

Figure 10.4   The user agent object handles HTTP requests on the program's behalf. The program sends it an instance of HTTP::Request, and receives an instance of HTTP::Response in return. The mechanics of connecting to the HTTP server are handled by the user agent object.

CORE Note

The preceding example uses || *rather than* or *because of their different precedences. Using* || *guarantees that the retrieved document will only be passed to* print *if it is defined; otherwise* die *will be invoked.*

getprint combines get and print into a single method, displaying the returned document on STDOUT or an error on STDERR. For example:

```
use LWP::Simple;
my $url = "http://www.perl.com";

# Print the document to STDOUT, or the error to STDERR
my $status = getprint $url;

# Always display the status code
print "Status code: '$status'\n";
```

Each HTTP response begins with a status code giving a full description of the transaction's success or failure. The status codes are typically numbers, but the Perl module HTTP::Status (available on CPAN) defines symbolic equivalents. You can thus refer to the OK status code as RC_OK. The "file not found" response code is similarly RC_NOT_FOUND.

By importing is_error, is_server_error, and is_client_error from HTTP::Status, a program can determine whether the request was serviced successfully. For example:

```
use LWP::Simple;
use HTTP::Status qw(is_client_error is_server_error);
my $url = "http://www.perl.com";
my $status = getprint $url;

# Cover server errors
if (is_server_error($status))
{
    print "Server error: $status (", status_message($status), ")\n";
}

# Cover client errors
elsif (is_client_error($status))
{
    print "Client error: $status (", status_message($status), ")\n";
}

# Cover non-client, non-server errors (which should not exist)
else
{
    print "Misc error: $status (", status_message($status), ")\n"
        if is_error($status);
}
```

LWP::Simple also provides the getstore subroutine, which saves the contents of a URL to disk. As with getprint, getstore returns the HTTP status code that it received when retrieving the file. For example:

```
use LWP::Simple;
my $url = "http://www.perl.com";
my $filename = "perl-home-page.html";
my $status = getstore ($url, $filename);

# Ignore "OK" status, which is 200
print "Status code: $status\n" unless ($status == RC_OK);
```

10.3.7   HTML

Most documents on the Web are written in HTML, the hypertext markup language. Each HTML *tag* describes a different section of the document.

For example, here is a simple HTML document:

```
<HTML>
<Head><Title>Hello!</Title></Head>

<Body>
<H1>Hello!</H1>

<P>This is a paragraph.</P>

<P>This paragraph contains a
    <a href="http://www.example.com/">link</a>.</P>

<P>Here is an image: <img src="foo.png"></P>

</Body>
</HTML>
```

This document contains most of the tags that a beginning Web author needs. Most tags come in pairs, with an opening (e.g., <HTML>) and a closing (e.g., </HTML>) version surrounding the designated text. There are six types of headlines, ranging from <H1> through <H6>. Paragraphs are marked with the <P> and </P> tags.

Many tags have *attributes*, name–value pairs that affect the tag's behavior. For instance, hyperlinks are created with the anchor tag (<a> and </a>), in which the target URL is marked with the href attribute. The <img> tag, which imports an image into the document, takes a src attribute.

In the above example, the word "link" is hypertext. Clicking on it brings the user to the URL http://www.example.com. The URL is not checked for accuracy until the browser tries to follow it.

To display literal < and > characters, HTML provides *entities*. Each entity begins with &, ends with ;, and has a unique code in the middle. Standard HTML entities include > (for >), < (for <), and & (for &). There are dozens of other standard entities, which are used when writing HTML-formatted pages in European languages.

10.3.8   Parsing HTML with LWP

Many client-side Web programs not only retrieve documents from the Web, but also analyze their structure and contents. LWP comes with several modules that help in this regard.

The most useful is HTML::LinkExtor, an object class that parses the links (i.e., <img> and <a> tags) in an HTML document.

The constructor for HTML::LinkExtor requires one argument, a reference to a subroutine (known as a *callback*) that will be invoked once for each link in the document. For example:

```
my $parser = HTML::LinkExtor->new(\&callback);
```

The following program parses the links of an HTML file, displaying tags and their attributes:

```perl
#!/usr/bin/perl
# filename: simple-extract.pl

use strict;
use warnings;
use LWP::Simple;
use HTML::LinkExtor;

# Get the URL from the command line
my $url = $ARGV[0];

# Retrieve the URL, or die trying
my $text = get($url)
    or die qq|Cannot retrieve "$url"|;

# Create the parser
my $parser = HTML::LinkExtor->new(\&callback);

# Parse the document, invoking callback on each HTML tag
$parser->parse($text);

sub callback
{
    # Get the tag type
    my $tag = shift;

    # Get the hash of attributes
    my %attributes = @_;
```

```
# Print information on the screen
print "$tag:\n";

foreach my $key (sort keys %attributes)
{
    print "\t$key: $attributes{$key}\n";
}
}
```

callback, which the parser invokes once for each tag, takes two arguments: a scalar containing the tag name, and a hash containing name–value pairs for the attributes. As the preceding program demonstrates, we can use these to display information about the tag, or to make decisions based on its contents.

10.3.9   More advanced user agents

For finer-grained control over the HTTP transaction than LWP::Simple provides, use the LWP::UserAgent class instead. LWP::UserAgent requires a deeper understanding of HTTP, but provides more opportunities for customization.

As the sample HTTP server in Section 10.2.5 demonstrated, an HTTP request consists of an action (known as a *request method*), followed by the name of a file. Modern versions of HTTP also indicate the highest supported version number, separating HTTP and the version number with a slash. The simplest and most common request method is GET, which consists of a URL and nothing more. For example:

```
http://the-tech.mit.edu/index.html
```

LWP describes this request in terms of objects, with an instance of HTTP::Request. Once created with new, the request object can be passed to an instance of LWP::UserAgent:

```
use LWP::UserAgent;
use HTTP::Request;

# Create the request
my $request =
        new HTTP::Request("GET", "http://www.lerner.co.il");
```

```perl
# Create the user agent
my $ua = new LWP::UserAgent;

# Send the request
my $response = $ua->request($request);
```

The request method returns an instance of HTTP::Response, which contains all of the information that the HTTP server returned to the client. We can retrieve the document contents from the response with the content method, defined in HTTP::Response. With the content in hand, we can analyze the returned document with HTML::LinkExtor. This program, for instance, displays a list of the hyperlinks in a document:

```perl
#!/usr/bin/perl
# filename: list-links.pl

use strict;
use warnings;
use LWP::UserAgent;
use HTTP::Request;
use HTML::LinkExtor;

# Get the URL from the command line
my $url = $ARGV[0]
    or die "No URL entered!";

# Create a request
my $request = new HTTP::Request("GET", $url);

# Create a user agent
my $ua = new LWP::UserAgent;

# Send the request to the server, and get a response
my $response = $ua->request($request);

# Create a parser
my $parser = new HTML::LinkExtor(\&parse_link);

# Parse the contents of the response
$parser->parse($response->content);
```

```
sub parse_link
{
    # Get the link information
    my ($type, %attributes) = @_;

    # Ignore everything but hyperlinks ("anchor" tags)
    return unless (lc $type eq "a");

    # Print where it goes
    print "\t", $attributes{href}, "\n";
}
```

10.4   Conclusion

In this chapter, we looked at Perl's functions for interprocess communication. We also discussed LWP, the library for Web programming that facilitates the creation of Web clients. In particular, we examined:

- One-way anonymous pipes,

- Two-way anonymous pipes and simple sockets,

- How to use named pipes to collect or send data,

- Network sockets, for communication between programs on different computers,

- Writing simple network servers and clients with sockets,

- Forking servers,

- Perl modules for working with FTP, Telnet, and SMTP protocols,

- The LWP model for creating HTTP clients,

- The user agents LWP::Simple and LWP::UserAgent,

- How to parse retrieved documents with HTML::LinkExtor,

- HTTP status codes, and

- Working with the contents of a document.

RELATIONAL DATABASES

Topics in This Chapter

- Relational databases and SQL
- Creating tables
- NULL
- Primary keys
- Inserting and retrieving data
- Joins
- Foreign keys
- Updating and deleting
- Indexes
- DBI
- Attributes
- Simple database applications

Chapter 11

As we have already seen, Perl excels at working with disk files. We can read and write fixed-length records (using **pack** and **unpack**), variable-length records (using **split** and **join**), and even DBM files (using **tie**). But using these types of files means writing (and documenting) special-purpose routines for storing and retrieving data, ensuring that the formatting is correct, and testing the data integrity. We also have to worry about locking the file to avoid corruption, because more than one program might try to store information in the file at the same time.

One popular solution to these problems is a relational database management system, or "RDBMS." Perl has long been able to communicate with the most popular database systems, especially those that accept queries written in Structured Query Language (SQL).

This chapter introduces relational databases from a Perl perspective, demonstrating how (and why) you would want to use a database from within your Perl program. We look at the **DBI** module, which provides a uniform interface to dozens of different databases.

By the end of this chapter, you should feel comfortable with relational databases, understand how to design a database containing one or more tables, and know how to use **DBI** to make your programs portable and efficient.

11.1   What is a relational database?

A *database* is a program that allows you to store and retrieve data flexibly, efficiently, and safely. A relational database does this by placing everything in two-dimensional tables. Each record is a row in a table, with each intersecting column describing a different type and length of data to be stored.

A table may contain zero, one, or infinitely many rows, with each row representing one record. The columns, by contrast, are defined when the table is created—and although you can change the columns later on, you have less freedom when modifying tables than when creating them.

Most databases contain more than one table, with the connections, or *relations*, drawn between similar fields in multiple tables. Indeed, relational databases are popular largely because of their ability to store data once and then refer to it many times. Relations make it easy to ensure the integrity and consistency of your data.

Like many modern programs, databases are divided into clients and servers. Database clients create and submit queries, whereas database servers receive, process, and execute the queries. Nearly any program can be a database client—a graphical user interface, Web server, or a stock-trading application.

Examples in this book use PostgreSQL, an open-source database available from http://www.postgresql.org/. PostgreSQL has proven itself to be fast, safe, and reliable over the years, and includes most of the standard SQL features. The code in this book was designed for and tested with PostgreSQL, but it should work on other systems—such as Oracle or Sybase—with few modifications. Documentation at the PostgreSQL Web site describes how to install the database client and server on a variety of operating systems.

11.2   Introducing SQL

Database clients send queries to a database server in SQL. SQL is a data manipulation language, rather than a programming language, which means that the SQL typically resides inside an executable program. The result of an SQL query is a table, containing the columns and rows that represent the database server's response to the query.

11.2.1   Creating a table

Because all information in a relational database resides in tables, the first logical step when working with an RDBMS is to create one or more tables. Next, we populate our tables with data. Finally, we will query the database server about our data.

> **CORE Note**
>
> *In the database world,* query *refers to any command that we send to a database. Queries allow us to modify a database, as well as retrieve information about it. This book sometimes uses the word* command *in place of* query.

Our first step is to create a database in which our tables will reside. (A database server can typically work with many databases simultaneously. Each database then contains many tables.) PostgreSQL comes with a command-line `createdb` utility; by typing `createdb coreperl`, we can create the coreperl database. (If you encounter errors while creating this database, read the "Getting Started" section of the PostgreSQL manual.)

After we create the coreperl database, we can work with it using the interactive `psql` tool. Any SQL queries we type into `psql` are sent to the database server, and any results the server returns are displayed on the screen. A semicolon tells `psql` that we have finished typing a query.

To create a table, we use the CREATE TABLE command in SQL. For example, the following creates a new table called AddressBook, with five columns that can contain textual data:

```
CREATE TABLE AddressBook
(
    first_name     TEXT,
    last_name      TEXT,
    address        TEXT,
    phone_number   TEXT,
    fax_number     TEXT
)
;
```

Each column in a database table has its own data type. In AddressBook, each column is of type TEXT.

We now insert a new row into AddressBook with the INSERT command. INSERT normally takes two sets of arguments—a comma-separated list of columns and a comma-separated list of values. For example:

```
INSERT INTO AddressBook
    (first_name, last_name, address, phone_number, fax_number)
VALUES
    ('Abraham', 'Lincoln', '1600 Pennsylvania Ave.', '202-555-1212',
    '202-555-1212')
;
```

11.2.2   NULL

Because we did not specify otherwise, all of the columns in AddressBook are optional. If we do not enter data into an optional column, we say that it contains NULL. NULL is distinct from any other value, including 0 and the empty string. Unlike Perl's undef, SQL never treats NULL as FALSE.

NULL is a necessary evil in the database world. Although it is useful, it complicates the logic of our queries and reduces our tables' efficiency. You should thus define as many columns as possible to forbid NULL values by including the NOT NULL keyword in your CREATE TABLE query. Those columns in which NULL is permitted should explicitly include the NULL keyword, rather than relying on the default behavior.

The following definition of AddressBook allows NULL values in the fax_number column—as some people lack a fax number—but forbids NULL in other columns:

```
CREATE TABLE AddressBook
(
    first_name      TEXT    NOT NULL,
    last_name       TEXT    NOT NULL,
    address         TEXT    NOT NULL,
    phone_number    TEXT    NOT NULL,
    fax_number      TEXT    NULL
)
;
```

CORE Note

In theory, you can freely mix NULL and NOT NULL columns in your table definition. However, some database servers work more efficiently if NULL columns are defined last.

11.2.3 Using a primary key

You can optionally assign a column to be the *primary key* of a table. Unlike other columns, the primary key must have a unique value in each row. Primary keys help us to locate and retrieve rows quickly and unambiguously.

Which column should be the primary key of AddressBook? We should not use first_name or last_name, because we may want to have more than one John or Smith in our table, and the primary key enforces uniqueness on that column. phone_number is similarly disqualified, as roommates and families often share a telephone number.

To avoid these sorts of problems, most tables include a column specifically meant to act as a primary key. Such "artificial" primary keys make it possible to uniquely identify a row with a single ID number without restricting other values in the table. Using an artificial primary key, two employees named John Smith are as different from each other as Ronald Reagan and Jimmy Carter. This is why the U.S. government began to use Social Security numbers years ago. It ensures that each citizen can be uniquely identified, even when they move or change their name.

Here is a new definition of AddressBook that includes an artificial primary key:

```
CREATE TABLE AddressBook
(
    person_id       NUMERIC(5,0)   NOT NULL,
    first_name      TEXT           NOT NULL,
    last_name       TEXT           NOT NULL,
    address         TEXT           NOT NULL,
    phone_number    TEXT           NOT NULL,
    fax_number      TEXT           NULL,

    PRIMARY KEY(person_id)
)
;
```

In this version of AddressBook, each person is identified uniquely by the person_id column. (We define person_id to be a five-digit integer, to accommodate up to 100,000 of our closest friends.)

To INSERT a row into AddressBook, we modify our previous query:

```
INSERT INTO AddressBook
    (person_id, first_name, last_name, address, phone_number, fax_number)
VALUES
    (1, 'Abraham', 'Lincoln', '1600 Pennsylvania Ave.', '202-555-1212',
    '202-555-1212')
;
```

11.2.4   Sequences

The preceding version of AddressBook might work in theory, but it requires that our program keep track of person_id. In particular, we must be careful not to insert two records with the same primary key. One solution to this problem is to let the database server keep track of the value, using a *sequence*. (Some databases refer to these as *identity* values, or as *auto incrementing* keys.) In PostgreSQL, the easiest way to use a sequence as a primary key is to use the SERIAL data type:

```
CREATE TABLE AddressBook
(
    person_id      SERIAL   NOT NULL,
    first_name     TEXT     NOT NULL,
    last_name      TEXT     NOT NULL,
    address        TEXT     NOT NULL,
    phone_number   TEXT     NOT NULL,
    fax_number     TEXT     NULL,

    PRIMARY KEY(person_id)
)
;
```

If we **INSERT** a new row into **AddressBook** without mentioning **person_id**, PostgreSQL automatically assigns the next unused integer:

```
INSERT INTO AddressBook
    (first_name, last_name, address, phone_number, fax_number)
VALUES
    ('Abraham', 'Lincoln', '1600 Pennsylvania Ave.', '202-555-1212',
    '202-555-1212')
;
```

11.3 SELECT

SELECT, the heavy workhorse of SQL, lets us retrieve information from tables in a variety of ways. We tell **SELECT** which tables we want to query and a list of criteria, and it returns a table containing zero, one, or more rows.

11.3.1 *Simple* SELECT *queries*

You can retrieve one or more columns from a table by listing them in a **SELECT** statement:

```
SELECT first_name, last_name
FROM AddressBook
;
```

On my computer, this query produces the following results:

```
 first_name | last_name
------------+-----------
 Abraham    | Lincoln
(1 row)
```

If there were 100 rows in AddressBook, our SELECT would have returned 100 rows. You can make the query more restrictive by adding a WHERE clause that includes one or more logical tests:

```
SELECT first_name, last_name
FROM AddressBook
WHERE last_name = 'Lincoln'
;
```

This query returns:

```
 first_name | last_name
------------+-----------
 Abraham    | Lincoln
(1 row)
```

A WHERE clause can test columns other than those named for retrieval. For example, the following query compares fax_number and phone_number, but displays first_name and last_name:

```
SELECT first_name, last_name
FROM AddressBook
WHERE fax_number = phone_number
;
```

As in Perl, conditions can be joined using logical AND and OR:

```
SELECT first_name, fax_number
FROM AddressBook
WHERE last_name = 'Lincoln'
AND fax_number = '202-555-1212'
;
```

11.3.2 Sorting rows

Relational databases do not store rows in any particular order. If we want the result from SELECT to be sorted, then we must add an ORDER BY clause. For example, we can sort the result by ascending last_name:

```
SELECT first_name, last_name
FROM AddressBook
ORDER BY last_name
;
```

To sort results in descending order, attach the DESC modifier after the column name. (ASC can similarly be used for ascending order, although it is rarely needed.)

ORDER BY can sort rows by multiple columns. For example, we can create a standard-style telephone book (in which Smith, James comes between Smith, Herbert and Smith, John) by saying:

```
SELECT last_name, first_name, phone_number
FROM AddressBook
ORDER BY last_name, first_name
;
```

11.3.3 SQL functions

SQL comes with a variety of mathematical functions that can be used in SELECT queries. For example:

```
SELECT person_id, person_id*2
FROM AddressBook;
;
```

This query returns a table with one row and one column:

```
 person_id | ?column?
-----------+----------
         1 |        2
(1 row)
```

As you can see, every column returned by SELECT needs a name. If it has no name, PostgreSQL automatically calls it ?column?.

Relational databases generally include *aggregate* functions as well, which take several rows as input and return a single result. For example, COUNT returns the number of rows in a table:

```
SELECT COUNT(person_id)
FROM AddressBook
;
```

This query returns the following result:

```
 count
-------
     1
(1 row)
```

CORE Note

COUNT *does not include* NULL *values.*

CORE Approach

Learn which SQL functions are supported by your brand of relational database server, and use those functions to simplify complex queries.

11.3.4   Comparison operators

SQL includes a large number of comparison operators, including = (equality), <> (inequality), < (less than), and > (greater than).

CORE Note

Perl uses == *to compare numbers and* eq *to compare strings, whereas SQL uses a single* = *to compare any type of data.*

SQL's comparison operators work not only on text and numbers, but also on dates. For example, the following Appointments table lets us schedule meetings. Notice the meeting_daytime column, which uses the PostgreSQL TIMESTAMP to store a date and time:

```
CREATE TABLE Appointments
(
    appointment_id     SERIAL     NOT NULL,
    meeting_with       TEXT       NOT NULL,
    meeting_daytime    TIMESTAMP  NOT NULL,
    meeting_notes      TEXT       NOT NULL,

    PRIMARY KEY(appointment_id)
)
;
```

The following query lists all of the appointments in our calendar, from earliest to latest:

```
SELECT meeting_daytime, meeting_with, meeting_notes
FROM    Appointments
ORDER BY meeting_daytime
;
```

To get a list of today's appointments, we can use the built-in PostgreSQL function CURRENT_DATE:

```
SELECT meeting_daytime, meeting_with, meeting_notes
FROM    Appointments
WHERE   meeting_daytime > CURRENT_DATE
AND     meeting_daytime < CURRENT_DATE + 1
ORDER BY meeting_daytime
;
```

We could instead use the built-in BETWEEN operator:

```
SELECT meeting_daytime, meeting_with, meeting_notes
FROM    Appointments
WHERE   meeting_daytime BETWEEN CURRENT_DATE AND (CURRENT_DATE + 1)
ORDER BY meeting_daytime
;
```

11.3.5 SQL regular expressions

The standard SQL operator for comparing strings is LIKE. LIKE searches for SQL regular expressions, much as m// searches for text patterns in Perl. However, SQL's regular expression syntax is more limited than Perl's: %

represents zero or more characters, and _ represents one character. (Prefacing either of these characters with \ turns them into literal characters, rather than metacharacters. To get a literal \, use \\.)

The following query retrieves last_name from any row whose first_name column begins with J:

```
SELECT last_name
FROM AddressBook
WHERE first_name LIKE 'J%'
;
```

To retrieve last_name where the first name contains four letters, starts with J and ending with n, use:

```
SELECT last_name
FROM AddressBook
WHERE first_name LIKE 'J__n'
;
```

This regular expression matches Joan, Jaon, Jenn, and John, but not Jane or Ralph.

PostgreSQL also supports Unix-style regular expressions (similar to the patterns described in Chapter 5), with the ~ and ~* operators, which are equivalent to Perl's m// and m//i, respectively:

```
SELECT last_name
FROM AddressBook
WHERE first_name ~ 'J..n';
```

11.3.6   Foreign keys

Consider a SocialSecurityNumbers table that keeps track of people's Social Security numbers:

```
CREATE TABLE SocialSecurityNumbers
(
    number      NUMERIC(9,0) NOT NULL,
    person_id   INTEGER       NOT NULL   REFERENCES AddressBook,
```

```
    PRIMARY KEY(number)
)
;
```

This table introduces several new ideas in our database:

- Our primary key is number, a nine-digit integer. We declare it using the standard SQL NUMBER syntax, which allows us to specify the total number of digits (nine, in this case) followed by the number of digits after the decimal point (zero, in this case).

- Our person_id column is of type INTEGER, which is the same four-byte integer value as PostgreSQL uses for storing sequences.

- person_id may only contain values that are assigned to the primary key of AddressBook. We say that person_id is a *foreign key* of AddressBook. Foreign keys ensure the integrity of our database; it is impossible for us to have an entry in SocialSecurityNumbers that doesn't correspond to an entry in AddressBook.

Let's now insert a row into SocialSecurityNumbers:

```
INSERT INTO SocialSecurityNumbers
    (number, person_id)
VALUES
    (123456789, 1)
;
```

CORE Note

If no record in AddressBook has a person_id of one, this INSERT will fail.

11.4 Joins

Relational databases are popular largely because of the ease with which we can join data from two or more tables. The ability to combine data on the fly is remarkably powerful and flexible, allowing you to analyze and retrieve data in a variety of ways.

For example, we might want to retrieve the first and last name of a user with a particular Social Security number. We can do this by joining together the AddressBook and SocialSecurityNumbers tables using their common person_id column, retrieving first_name and last_name from AddressBook, and using number in SocialSecurityNumbers. As the following query demonstrates, we can refer to columns in different tables by prefacing the column name with the table name and a . character:

```
SELECT AddressBook.first_name, AddressBook.phone_number
FROM AddressBook, SocialSecurityNumbers
WHERE SocialSecurityNumbers.number = 123456789
  AND AddressBook.person_id = SocialSecurityNumbers.person_id
;
```

We can make our query a bit more readable by giving each table a nickname in the FROM clause:

```
SELECT A.first_name, A.phone_number
FROM AddressBook A, SocialSecurityNumbers S
WHERE S.number = 123456789
  AND A.person_id = S.person_id
;
```

CORE Note

Without the final line of the preceding query, PostgreSQL creates the carte-sian product of AddressBook and SocialSecurityNumbers, matching each row in one table with each row in the other table. This has the double disadvantage of producing incorrect results and using more memory and processor time than is necessary. You can typically avoid this problem by checking that each table in the FROM clause is compared with something in the WHERE clause.

11.5   Updating and deleting

To change existing information, use the UPDATE command, naming a table and a comma-separated list of name–value pairs:

```
UPDATE AddressBook
SET    first_name = 'Thomas',
       last_name  = 'Jefferson'
WHERE  number     = 929602000
;
```

CORE Note

Always include a WHERE *clause in* UPDATE *queries! Without the* WHERE *clause, this* UPDATE *would have changed every row to have the name* Thomas Jefferson.

The **DELETE** command, which deletes rows from a table, should also be used only in conjunction with a **WHERE** clause:

```
DELETE FROM AddressBook
WHERE person_id = 987654321
;
```

To delete an entire table, including the table's definition, use the **DROP TABLE** command:

```
DROP TABLE AddressBook;
```

CORE Warning

There is no way to undo an UPDATE, DELETE, *or* DROP TABLE *command.*

11.6   Indexes

When a **SELECT** query includes a simple **WHERE** clause, the database server must search for the named value in the table. In a large table, such searches can take a long time. We can speed things up by creating an index on the column that will be searched.

In PostgreSQL, **CREATE INDEX** creates an index on a column in a table. For instance:

```
CREATE INDEX first_name_index ON AddressBook (first_name);
```

This query creates an index called name_index on first_name in AddressBook. Every time a row is inserted or modified, the database server updates the index, keeping track of which rows contain which values of first_name.

If an index speeds up comparisons so dramatically, why does indexing not occur by default? The answer is one of efficiency: Each time an indexed column is stored or modified, the database server must update both the table and the index. Because this overhead is not worthwhile for every column in a system, the database administrator must decide which columns deserve indexes.

11.7   Perl and databases

Perl programs have long been able to act as database clients, but Perl database programmers have been given a huge boost in recent years by DBI, the Perl Database Interface written largely by Tim Bunce.

DBI makes it possible to write a single program that works with any brand of database. Indeed, DBI makes it easy to write a program that reads data from one server and writes it to another. If your organization switches from one brand of database to another, existing Perl programs will work with minimal changes.

11.7.1   DBI, *the Perl Database Interface*

Once you have installed DBI from CPAN (see Section 1.6), your program can use it like any other module:

```
use DBI;
```

However, DBI does not do much by itself. Rather, it serves as an agent between Perl and a specific database driver, known as a DBD. Using DBI requires a DBD module for the specific database server you are using. DBDs for every major database server are available from CPAN. For example, the DBD for PostgreSQL is called DBD::Pg, and the DBD for Oracle is DBD::Oracle.

11.7.2   Connecting to a database

Most work with DBI is performed via two objects. The first, a *database handle*, represents a connection to a database server. A program typically creates only one database handle (traditionally called $dbh) during its lifetime.

In addition, each SQL query gets its own *statement handle*, traditionally called $sth. $sth is used to submit queries, as well as to retrieve any results from a query. It's common to reuse $sth over the course of a program's lifetime.

$dbh is returned by DBI->connect, which connects to a database server. Although DBI->connect is portable across all platforms, the number and format of its arguments depend almost entirely on the database server to which you are connecting. The first argument to DBI->connect is normally a text string that begins with dbi:, followed by the name of the specific DBD to use. Following that, you may need to specify a user name, password, port number, or server name.

For example, a program can connect to the coreperl PostgreSQL database with the following:

```
use DBI;

my $username = 'reuven';
my $password = '';
my $dbh = DBI->connect("DBI:Pg:dbname=coreperl", $username, $password);
```

After this code executes, $dbh will either be a database handle object (indicating success) or undef (indicating failure). DBI always places error messages in $DBI::errstr, allowing you to trap errors as follows:

```
use DBI;

my $username = 'reuven';
my $password = '';
my $dbh = DBI->connect("DBI:Pg:dbname=coreperl", $username, $password) ||
    die "Error connecting: '$DBI::errstr'";
```

To disconnect from a database, use the $dbh->disconnect method:

```
$dbh->disconnect();
```

11.7.3 Attributes

$dbh and $sth have *attributes* that serve as additional lines of communication with a program. Some attributes are read-only, whereas others are both readable and writable. Some attributes apply only to $dbh, others only to $sth, and still others to both handles.

Attributes can be read from and written to as if they were instance variables. For example, the following reads the value of the $dbh attribute PrintError:

```
my $current_print_error_status = $dbh->{PrintError};
```

Assigning a new value is similarly straightforward:

```
$dbh->{PrintError} = 0;  # Turn off error printing
```

Many DBI methods also let you pass a hash reference of attribute settings that override the defaults. For example, it's common to set attributes for a database handle when invoking DBI->connect:

```
use DBI;

my $username = 'reuven';
my $password = '';
my $dbh = DBI->connect("DBI:Pg:dbname=coreperl", $username, $password,
                  {'AutoCommit' => 1, 'PrintError' => 1}) ||
    die "Error connecting: '$DBI::errstr'";
```

This $dbh not only connects to the PostgreSQL database coreperl, but has its AutoCommit and PrintError attributes set to 1.

DBI provides a number of standard attributes, and each DBD can add some of its own. By convention, the capitalization of an attribute name indicates whether it is standard, and thus portable:

- An attribute name in CAPITALS refers to a standard from outside of DBI. One example is NULLABLE, which returns an array reference. The elements of this array reference describe the most recently accessed table, indicating whether its columns are null or not null. You can read about these attributes in `perldoc DBI`.

- If the attribute name begins with a capital letter, but is otherwise MixedUpperAndLower, it is a portable attribute within DBI. For example, the ChopBlanks attribute (available for both $dbh and $sth) indicates whether trailing whitespace should be deleted from fixed-length CHAR columns. You can read about these attributes in `perldoc DBI`.

- If the attribute name consists solely of lowercase letters, it is non-portable and works only within a particular DBD. Such non-portable, private attributes usually have names that begin with a suitable prefix, such as pg_ for PostgreSQL or ora_ for Oracle. For example, pg_cmd_status returns the type of query that was last executed. You can read about these attributes in the documentation for your specific DBD.

CORE Note

Setting or retrieving an attribute that does not exist causes a fatal runtime error.

11.7.4 AutoCommit, PrintError, **and** RaiseError

Three attributes—AutoCommit, PrintError, and RaiseError—provide a great deal of control over DBI's behavior.

AutoCommit is probably the most important of the three, because it indicates whether DBI should immediately commit each query as it is executed.

One of the most important qualities of a modern relational database is its ability to combine several queries together in a single, all-or-nothing group, known as a *transaction*. Without transactions, you would never be able to reliably perform a SELECT followed by an UPDATE: Someone else's query might execute after the SELECT but just before the UPDATE, potentially making the results of your SELECT irrelevant. Luckily, transactions are a part of every serious database, isolating client programs from each other and ensuring that power failures don't leave tables in a half-updated state. Thanks to transactions, banks can transfer money from one account to another without having to worry about funds being lost if the power goes out in the middle.

If AutoCommit is FALSE, you have the opportunity to create a transaction containing multiple queries. Following the final query, your program must invoke either $dbh->commit() to commit the changes, or $dbh->rollback() to restore the database to its state before the transaction began. By contrast, setting AutoCommit to TRUE means that DBI will treat each query as its own transaction, implicitly invoking $dbh->commit().

The default value of AutoCommit is TRUE, but the DBI documentation strongly encourages programmers to set an explicit value for it in DBI->connect(). With a database that lacks transactions, such as MySQL, setting AutoCommit to anything other than TRUE causes a fatal runtime error.

Two more useful attributes, PrintError and RaiseError, make it easier to debug Perl programs that use DBI. If PrintError is set, then DBI errors are trapped and sent to Perl's built-in warn function.

RaiseError works similarly, except that it sends DBI to die, resulting in a fatal error. This might seem like a recipe for havoc, with programs exiting whenever a database error occurs. However, programs that set RaiseError generally trap DBI method calls inside of eval blocks, checking the value of $@ after each method call. If $@ is TRUE, then the program can die gracefully. See `perldoc DBI` for a full description of this technique.

11.8   Simple DBI programs

This section introduces the basics of writing programs that use DBI, using a database to store persistent data.

11.8.1   Inserting data

Inserting data into a database table involves three steps: connecting to the database, preparing the query, and executing the INSERT. Each of these steps corresponds to a DBI method, as demonstrated in this program:

```perl
#!/usr/bin/perl
# filename: dbi-insert.pl

use strict;
use warnings;
use DBI;

# Connect to the database
my $username = 'reuven';
my $password = '';
my $dbh = DBI->connect("DBI:Pg:dbname=coreperl", $username, $password,
                       {'AutoCommit' => 1, 'PrintError' => 1}) ||
    die "Error connecting: '$DBI::errstr'";

# What data will we INSERT?
my $first_name = 'Franklin';
my $last_name = 'Roosevelt';
my $address = '1600 Pennsylvania Avenue, Washington DC';
my $phone_number = '202-555-1234';
my $fax_number = '202-555-1235';

# Create the SQL query
my $sql = "INSERT INTO AddressBook ";
$sql .= "(first_name, last_name, phone_number, address, fax_number) ";
$sql .= "VALUES (?, ?, ?, ?, ?) ";
```

```
# Prepare the statement
my $sth = $dbh->prepare($sql) ||
    die "Error preparing: $DBI::errstr";

# Execute the statement
$sth->execute($first_name, $last_name, $phone_number, $address, $fax_number) ||
    die "Error executing: $DBI::errstr";

# Indicate success
print "Successfully inserted $first_name $last_name into AddressBook!\n";

# Finish with the statement
$sth->finish;

# Disconnect from the database
$dbh->disconnect;
```

This program connects to the coreperl database on the local computer's PostgreSQL server. After connecting successfully, we create an INSERT query as $sql. Our query does not contain legal values, however: Instead, we put a comma-separated list of unquoted question marks (?), known as *placeholders* in DBI. Using placeholders has a number of advantages, the main one of which is that Perl automatically quotes non-numeric data for us.

We replace the placeholders with values when we execute the query with $sth->execute(). The method's first argument is assigned to the first placeholder, the second to the second placeholder, and so forth. Perl will exit with a fatal error if the number of placeholders does not match the number of arguments to $sth->execute().

CORE Approach

Placeholders make it possible to prepare an SQL statement once, and to execute it multiple times with different values. This can be significantly faster than preparing and executing the query each time, particularly if your database caches queries.

$sth->execute() returns undef to indicate that the query execution failed. If it succeeds, our program closes $sth and $dbh before exiting.

11.8.2   Selecting rows

SELECT works similarly to INSERT, except that we must retrieve and parse the server's response to our query. We can retrieve that response in a number of forms, including an array, array reference, and hash. For example, the following program displays the first names and telephone numbers of all entries in AddressBook in alphabetical order:

```perl
#!/usr/bin/perl
# filename: dbi-select.pl

use strict;
use warnings;
use DBI;

# Connect to the database
my $username = 'reuven';
my $password = '';
my $dbh = DBI->connect("DBI:Pg:dbname=coreperl", $username, $password,
                       {'AutoCommit' => 1, 'PrintError' => 1}) ||
    die "Error connecting: '$DBI::errstr'";

# Now that we have connected, create the query
my $sql = "SELECT first_name, phone_number ";
$sql .= "FROM AddressBook ";
$sql .= "ORDER BY first_name ";

# Prepare the statement
my $sth = $dbh->prepare($sql) ||
    die "Error preparing: $DBI::errstr";

# Execute the statement
my $result = $sth->execute ||
    die "Error executing: $DBI::errstr";

# Iterate through resulting rows
while (my $rowref = $sth->fetchrow_arrayref)
{
    my ($name, $phone) = @{$rowref};
    print "$name\t\t$phone\n";
}

# Finish with the query
$sth->finish;

# Disconnect from the database
$dbh->disconnect;
```

The only new method in this code is fetchrow_arrayref, which works similarly to <> (see Section 9.1.1). With each invocation, fetchrow_arrayref returns the next unread row from our SELECT, or undef if there are no more rows. In each iteration, we assign the returned row to the array reference $rowref. Inside the body of the while loop, we dereference $rowref and assign the individual fields to lexical variables, printing them on the screen in our desired format. DBI represents NULL as undef, so you may have to use defined on any columns defined as NOT NULL.

fetchrow_arrayref is not the only method for retrieving rows from a database, but it is the most efficient. fetchrow_array, for example, works like fetchrow_arrayref but returns an array.

Another retrieval method is fetchrow_hashref, which places the returned row in a hash reference with keys as the column names. For example, here is the while loop from the preceding program, rewritten to use fetchrow_hashref:

```
while (my $rowref = $sth->fetchrow_hashref)
{
    print "$rowref->{first_name}\t\t$rowref->{phone_number}\n";
}
```

Although fetchrow_hashref makes programs more readable, it is substantially slower than the other retrieval methods.

11.9   Conclusion

In this chapter, we have covered quite a bit of ground. In particular, we discussed:

- What a relational database is, and why someone might want to use one,

- How to use SQL to manipulate database tables,

- How Perl's DBI allows us to communicate with a database using a common set of objects and methods,

- How to embed SQL within a Perl program, and

- How to use DBI within an application to INSERT and SELECT data from the database.

The next chapter describes how to use these techniques in more sophisticated ways—for example, as the back end of an object, or in creating sophisticated queries.

BUILDING DATABASE APPLICATIONS

Topics in This Chapter

- Database design

- Creating applications

- Debugging DBI

Chapter 12

The last chapter introduced relational databases, including SQL and Perl's DBI module. In this chapter, we use these tools to create a suite of database applications.

Along the way, we look at database design, which (like software design) is a crucial but often neglected part of the programming process. In particular, we discuss *normalization*, which increases the database's efficiency and flexibility while reducing the possibility of error.

The applications that we write reinforce the techniques that we discussed in the previous chapter, while introducing new SQL data types of DBI methods. We will take a close look at the trace method, which allows us to debug SQL queries quickly and easily.

By the end of this chapter, you should understand the basic process of writing programs that work with a database, including how to design the tables and debug the resulting programs.

12.1   Database design

A bookstore has asked us to computerize its inventory. We will build the bookstore's database in PostgreSQL, and applications in Perl that allow us to manipulate the database.

The first step in writing a database application is always the construction of tables. This section demonstrates a simple design process, touching on issues that affect nearly every database application.

12.1.1   *The* Books *table*

Because our store will need to keep track of books, let's create a Books table, in which each row represents a single book:

```
CREATE TABLE Books
(
        book_id           SERIAL        NOT NULL,
        isbn              TEXT          NOT NULL,
        title             TEXT          NOT NULL,
        author            TEXT          NOT NULL,
        publisher         TEXT          NOT NULL,
        num_pages         NUMERIC(5,0)  NOT NULL,
        pub_date          DATE          NOT NULL,
        us_dollar_price   NUMERIC(6,2)  NOT NULL,

        PRIMARY KEY(book_id),
        UNIQUE(isbn)
)
;
```

Our Books table looks much like the tables we looked at in Chapter 11, with some data types and constraints that we have not seen before:

- pub_date is a column of type DATE, which is similar to TIMESTAMP but ignores the time of day.

- us_dollar_price is defined as NUMERIC(6,2), which means that it's a six-digit number with the final two digits that come after the decimal point. We can thus sell books with a price of up to $9,999.99.

- isbn, which contains a book's unique and unchanging ISBN (international standard book number), could have been our primary key. However, the ISBN is relatively long, and it is usually a good idea to keep primary keys as short as possible. To ensure that isbn is unique even if it isn't the primary key, we can add a UNIQUE constraint to our table definition. UNIQUE automatically creates an index for the named column.

Technically speaking, there is nothing wrong with the preceding definition of Books. However, there are a number of design issues that will become apparent when we begin to use the table.

For example, let's assume that the bookstore wants to print a catalog of Prentice-Hall books. The following query would retrieve the names of all books published by Prentice-Hall:

```
SELECT title
FROM Books
WHERE publisher = 'Prentice-Hall'
ORDER BY title
;
```

But what happens if one book has a publisher of Prentice Hall, rather than Prentice-Hall? This book will not match our query, and will be excluded from the catalog.

Similar problems will crop up when searching for books written by a particular author. If the typist accidentally misspells an author's name when entering a new book, then that book will not appear in a SELECT query on the author field.

12.1.2 *Normalizing* Books

The solution to these problems is *normalization*, which ensures that each piece of data appears only once in a database. Normalized databases have a lower risk of corrupt or unsynchronized data, and are more efficient than their non-normalized counterparts.

We can normalize Books by creating two new tables, Publishers and Authors. Those tables will allow us to enter each author's and publisher's name only once in our database, with foreign keys (see Section 11.3.6) pointing to those values:

```
CREATE TABLE Authors
(
    author_id    SERIAL    NOT NULL,
    author_name  TEXT      NOT NULL,

    PRIMARY KEY(author_id)
)
;


CREATE TABLE Publishers
(
    publisher_id    SERIAL    NOT NULL,
    publisher_name  TEXT      NOT NULL,

    PRIMARY KEY(publisher_id),
    UNIQUE(publisher_name)
)
;


CREATE TABLE Books
(
    book_id          SERIAL        NOT NULL,
    isbn             TEXT          NOT NULL,
    title            TEXT          NOT NULL,
    author_id        INTEGER       NOT NULL  REFERENCES Authors,
    publisher_id     INTEGER       NOT NULL  REFERENCES Publishers,
    num_pages        NUMERIC(5,0)  NOT NULL,
    pub_date         DATE          NOT NULL,
    us_dollar_price  NUMERIC(6,2)  NOT NULL,

    PRIMARY KEY(book_id),
    UNIQUE(isbn)
)
;
```

Notice how these tables enforce uniqueness on publisher names, but not on author names. After all, there might be more than one author named John Smith, but there shouldn't be more than one publisher named Prentice Hall.

Our normalized tables ensure that author and publisher names are spelled consistently throughout the database. Moreover, changing the name of a publishing house only requires updating a single row in Publishers, rather than many rows in Books. As if that weren't enough, our Books table has shrunk dramatically, replacing two TEXT columns with two INTEGER columns. Our normalized tables thus occupy less space on disk and in memory, which allows the database to run faster.

Our query for Prentice-Hall books now requires a join:

```
SELECT title
FROM   Books B, Publishers P
WHERE  P.publisher_name = 'Prentice-Hall'
  AND  P.publisher_id = B.publisher_id
ORDER BY title
;
```

Joining all three tables together, we can get a list of all books written by a particular author, such as Paul Krugman:

```
SELECT B.isbn, B.title, P.publisher_name,
       B.pub_date, B.us_dollar_price
FROM Books B, Publishers P, Authors A
WHERE A.author_name = 'Paul Krugman'
  AND B.author_id = A.author_id
  AND B.publisher_id = P.publisher_id
ORDER BY B.title
;
```

12.1.3 More normalization

The preceding version of Books is a step in the right direction. However, what happens when a book has more than one author? The existing table definitions do not allow for this.

One possible solution would require adding several new columns to Books. We could change author_id to author1_id, then add three NULL columns (author2_id, author3_id, and author4_id) for additional authors.

This solution artificially limits the number of authors a book can have and wastes disk space for each book with fewer than four authors. In addition, it means that our queries will become horribly complex—for example, consider how we could get a list of all books written by Paul Krugman:

```
SELECT B.isbn, B.title, P.publisher_name,
       B.pub_date, B.us_dollar_price
FROM Books B, Publishers P, Authors A
```

```
WHERE A.author_name = 'Paul Krugman'
   AND (   B.author1_id = A.author_id
        OR B.author2_id = A.author_id
        OR B.author3_id = A.author_id
        OR B.author4_id = A.author_id)
   AND B.publisher_id = P.publisher_id
ORDER BY B.title
;
```

A better approach is to remove author information from Books altogether. In its place, we will create a BookAuthors table with two columns—one foreign key to Books and another foreign key to Authors. Here is a revised definition of our Books table, along with a definition of BookAuthors:

```
CREATE TABLE Books
(
    book_id          SERIAL       NOT NULL,
    isbn             TEXT         NOT NULL,
    title            TEXT         NOT NULL,
    publisher_id     INTEGER      NOT NULL  REFERENCES Publishers,
    num_pages        NUMERIC(5,0) NOT NULL,
    pub_date         DATE         NOT NULL,
    us_dollar_price  NUMERIC(6,2) NOT NULL,

    PRIMARY KEY(book_id),
    UNIQUE(isbn)
)
;


CREATE TABLE BookAuthors
(
    book_id    INTEGER    NOT NULL  REFERENCES Books,
    author_id  INTEGER    NOT NULL  REFERENCES Authors,

    UNIQUE(book_id, author_id)
)
;
```

Although book_id and author_id may each appear more than once in the table, we want to ensure that each author appears only once per book. We do this by using UNIQUE with two columns, rather than just one.

With BookAuthors in place, our search for Paul Krugman's books now requires a four-way join:

```
SELECT B.isbn, B.title, P.publisher_name,
       B.pub_date, B.us_dollar_price
FROM Books B, Publishers P, Authors A, BookAuthors BA
WHERE A.author_name = 'Paul Krugman'
  AND A.author_id = BA.author_id
  AND BA.book_id = B.book_id
  AND B.publisher_id = P.publisher_id
ORDER BY B.title
;
```

Meanwhile, the following query tells us about the book with ISBN 123-456-789, returning one row for each book author:

```
SELECT B.title, P.publisher_name, B.num_pages,
       B.pub_date, B.us_dollar_price, A.author_name
FROM Books B, Publishers P, Authors A, BookAuthors BA
WHERE B.isbn = '123-456-789'
  AND B.book_id = BA.book_id
  AND BA.author_id = A.author_id
  AND B.publisher_id = P.publisher_id
ORDER BY B.title
;
```

As you can see, a properly designed database makes it possible for us to answer a wide variety of questions—even if we hadn't thought of those questions when we originally designed the database.

12.1.4 *Indexes*

As we saw in Section 11.6, we should add an index to each column that might be referenced in a **WHERE** clause. Primary keys and **UNIQUE** columns are automatically indexed, which saves us some work—but there are several other columns in our tables on which we might expect to perform queries.

```
CREATE INDEX author_name_index ON Authors (author_name);
CREATE INDEX publisher_name_index ON Publishers (publisher_name);

CREATE INDEX book_title_index ON Books (title);
CREATE INDEX book_publisher_id_index ON Books (publisher_id);
CREATE INDEX book_pub_date_index ON Books (pub_date);
CREATE INDEX book_us_dollar_price_index ON Books (us_dollar_price);

CREATE INDEX author_id_index ON BookAuthors (author_id);
```

Creating these indexes means that even when our bookstore has several million books, we will be able to execute speedy searches for books by title, author, publisher, publication date, or price.

12.1.5   *Referential integrity*

Our current table definitions forbid NULL values for book titles and ISBN numbers. However, we could accidentally enter the empty string into these and other columns.

Because the database is the central repository for information about our bookstore, data stored there must be as reliable as possible. PostgreSQL's CHECK keyword allows us to constrain a column such that all data must pass additional tests. For example, we can redefine our Books table as follows:

```
CREATE TABLE Books
(
    book_id         SERIAL       NOT NULL,
    isbn            TEXT         NOT NULL  CHECK (isbn <> ''),
    title           TEXT         NOT NULL  CHECK (title ~* '[A-Z0-9]'),
    publisher_id    INTEGER      NOT NULL  REFERENCES Publishers,
    num_pages       NUMERIC(5,0) NOT NULL  CHECK (num_pages > 0),
    pub_date        DATE         NOT NULL,
    us_dollar_price NUMERIC(6,2) NOT NULL  CHECK (us_dollar_price > 0),

    PRIMARY KEY(book_id),
    UNIQUE(isbn)
)
;
```

This revised definition of Books forbids us from entering the empty string for isbn, ensures that title contains at least one letter or number (using the PostgreSQL case-insensitive pattern-matching operator ¨*), and requires that num_pages and us_dollar_price be positive numbers.

PostgreSQL refuses to add a book that violates one or more of these constraints. For example, let's try to add a book without a title:

```
INSERT INTO Books
    (isbn, title, publisher_id, num_pages, pub_date, us_dollar_price)
VALUES
    ('12345-67890', '',  1, 500, '2001-Dec-01', 50)
;
```

PostgreSQL returns the following error:

```
ERROR:  ExecAppend: rejected due to CHECK constraint books_title
```

Such constraints might seem like a nuisance, but the opposite is true: Without them, we might accidentally enter invalid information into our database. Trying to repair a corrupt or inconsistent database is a big and difficult task, particularly when the database is required for day-to-day work. CHECK helps us to avoid this situation by ensuring that anything stored in the database is correct.

12.1.6 Book categories

We want to put each book in one or more categories. The simplest way to do this is to create a pair of tables similar to those we wrote for authors—a Categories table with category names, and a CategoryBooks table that will associate categories with books:

```
CREATE TABLE Categories
(
    category_id    SERIAL    NOT NULL,
    category_name  TEXT      NOT NULL,

    PRIMARY KEY(category_id),
    UNIQUE(category_name)
)
;


CREATE TABLE BookCategories
(
    book_id      INTEGER   NOT NULL   REFERENCES Publishers,
    category_id  INTEGER   NOT NULL   REFERENCES Categories,

    UNIQUE(book_id, category_id)
)
;


CREATE INDEX category_id ON BookCategories (category_id)
;
```

12.2 Writing the applications

Now that our database is in place, we can create some Perl programs that work with it. One set of programs will allow the bookstore's management to enter, update, and delete information about books, authors, and publishers. A separate set of programs is meant for the bookstore's customers, allowing them to search through the database for books.

12.2.1   Entering authors

It is tempting to begin with an application that lets us enter new books. However, the publisher_id column in Books is a foreign key from Publishers, meaning that we must populate Publishers before we populate Books.

The following program, `insert-author.pl`, connects to the PostgreSQL server, gets the name of an author from the user, and performs the INSERT. If something goes wrong, the program exits with a fatal error.

Notice how our program performs a simple, application-level form of integrity check, ensuring that the author's name contains at least one alphanumeric character. Most database applications check inputs at the table definition level (using CHECK), and again at the application level. The former ensures that the database cannot contain inconsistent or corrupt data, and the latter allows us to trap errors and produce useful error messages for the user.

```perl
#!/usr/bin/perl
# filename: insert-author.pl

use strict;
use warnings;
use DBI;

# Connect to the database
my $username = 'reuven';
my $password = '';
my $dbh = DBI->connect("DBI:Pg:dbname=coreperl", $username, $password,
                        {'AutoCommit' => 1, 'PrintError' => 1}) ||
    die "Error connecting: '$DBI::errstr' ";

# Get the new author's name from the user
print "Enter the new author name: ";
my $author_name = <>;
chomp $author_name;

# Author name must contain at least one printable character
if ($author_name !~ /\w/)
{
    print "Author names must contain at least one ";
```

```
    print "alphanumeric character.  Exiting.\n";
}

# If the author name is OK, insert it
else
{
    # Remove extra whitespace from the author's name
    $author_name =~ s/^\s+//g;
    $author_name =~ s/\s+$//g;

    # Create the query
    my $sql = "INSERT INTO Authors (author_name) VALUES (?) ";

    # Prepare the statement
    my $sth = $dbh->prepare($sql) ||
        die "Fatal error preparing the SQL '$sql': '$DBI::errstr' ";

    # Execute the statement
    my $success = $sth->execute($author_name);

    if ($success)
    {
        print "Successfully inserted the author '$author_name'.\n";
    }
    else
    {
        die "Fatal error executing the SQL '$sql': '$DBI::errstr' ";
    }

    # Finish with the staement
    $sth->finish;
}

# Disconnect from the database
$dbh->disconnect;
```

Notice our use of $dbh->do() in insert-author.pl. DBI's do method is designed for INSERT and UPDATE queries, for which we do not need to retrieve results via $sth. The first argument to $dbh->do() is a string containing SQL, the second argument is a hash reference containing attribute definitions (or undef), and the rest of the arguments are values that DBI should bind to placeholders in the SQL. $dbh->do() returns the number of rows affected in the table.

12.2.2   Entering categories

insert-category.pl, which inserts a new category into Categories is similar in many ways to insert-author.pl. However, there is a catch: The category_name column is defined as UNIQUE.

Our application could ignore this issue, of course, blindly trying to INSERT new category names into Categories. If PostgreSQL refuses to insert a new category, we can catch the error and report back to the user.

A more sophisticated approach involves checking the database to see if our new category name has already been entered. But this means performing a SELECT (to get the names of current categories) followed by an INSERT (to add the new category name). What happens if someone performs an INSERT between these two queries?

The solution, as we mentioned in Section 11.7.4, is to combine the SELECT and INSERT into a single transaction. In this way, we ensure that no one will modify the database between our two queries. We could accomplish this by setting the AutoCommit attribute to FALSE, but it is easier to turn off AutoCommit for a single transaction with $dbh->begin_work(), which disables AutoCommit until an explicit $dbh->commit() or $dbh->rollback().

Our code thus asks the user for the name of a new category, searches for that category name with SELECT, and exits with an error message if the category already exists—exiting from the transaction with $dbh->rollback(). (The rollback is not truly necessary in this case, because we have not modified the tables at all. However, I always prefer to abort a query with rollback, just to be on the safe side.) Once we have passed all of the application-level tests, we perform an INSERT and invoke $dbh->commit().

Note that insert-category.pl runs with RaiseError active. This means that we no longer need to check for return values when invoking prepare and execute, as our program will exit with a fatal error whenever there is a database error.

```perl
#!/usr/bin/perl
# filename: insert-category.pl

use strict;
use warnings;
use DBI;

# Connect to the database.
my $username = 'reuven';
my $password = '';
my $dbh = DBI->connect("DBI:Pg:dbname=coreperl", $username, $password,
```

```perl
                        { 'AutoCommit' => 1, 'RaiseError' => 1}) ||
    die "Error connecting: '$DBI::errstr' ";

# Get the new category's name from the user
print "Enter the new category name: ";
my $category_name = <>;
chomp $category_name;

# Category name must contain at least one printable character
if ($category_name !~ /\w/)
{
    print "Category names must contain at least one ";
    print "alphanumeric character.  Exiting.\n";
}

# If the category name is OK, try to insert it
else
{
    # Remove extra whitespace
    $category_name =~ s/^\s+//g;
    $category_name =~ s/\s+$//g;

    # Turn AutoCommit OFF for a single transaction.  AutoCommit will
    # remain off until $dbh->commit() or $dbh->rollback().

    $dbh->begin_work();

    # -----------------------------------------------------------
    # Does this category name already exist in the database?
    # If so, then rollback, tell the user that there's a problem, and exit.

    # Create the query
    my $select_sql = "SELECT COUNT(category_id) ";
    $select_sql .= "FROM Categories where category_name = ?";

    # Prepare the statement
    my $sth = $dbh->prepare($select_sql);

    # Execute the statement
    $sth->execute($category_name);

    # Retrieve the result
    my ($category_already_exists) = $sth->fetchrow_array;

    # Finish with this query
    $sth->finish;
```

```
    if ($category_already_exists)
    {
        print "The category '$category_name' already exists in the ";
        print "database.\nPlease try again with a different name.\n";

        # We're done with the transaction.
        $dbh->rollback();
    }

    else
    {
        # Create the INSERT query
        my $sql = "INSERT INTO Categories (category_name) VALUES (?) ";

        # Prepare the statement
        my $successfully_inserted = $dbh->do($sql, undef, $category_name);

        if ($successfully_inserted)
        {
            print "Successfully inserted the category '$category_name'.\n";
            $dbh->commit();
        }
        else
        {
            print "Error inserting: '$DBI::errstr'.\n";
            $dbh->rollback();
        }
    }
}

# Disconnect from the database
$dbh->disconnect;
```

You can imagine how `insert-publisher.pl` would look very similar to `insert-category.pl`.

12.2.3 Modifying values

`insert-category.pl` works just fine—but what happens if someone enters the wrong name? Our bookstore will need a mechanism for modifying existing category names. (The same is true for authors and publishers, but we only address categories here.)

`update-category.pl` requires two inputs from the user, which we will call $old_category_name and $new_category_name. But what happens if the user mistypes $old_category_name, such that no such category exists? Our SQL WHERE clause won't match any rows in the table.

Term::Complete, available from CPAN (see Section 1.6), can help by restricting the number of acceptable inputs. Term::Complete automatically exports the Complete subroutine into its caller's namespace.

Complete takes two inputs. The first is a text prompt that is presented to the user, and the second is a list or array reference containing acceptable responses to the prompt. At any time, the user may press CONTROL-D to list valid responses. If the user enters enough characters to uniquely identify one element of the response list, TAB will complete the rest.

update-category.pl gets a list of current categories (which will be passed to Complete) using SELECT, and then modifies the database with an UPDATE. We will keep these two queries in the same transaction, using $dbh->begin work as in insert-category.pl.

The list of categories is retrieved from Categories, but rather than place the category names in an array, we make them the keys to a hash (%categories). Checking for the existence of a hash key takes far less time than searching for an array element, so this technique improves our program's execution time.

Here is one possible implementation of **update-category.pl**:

```perl
#!/usr/bin/perl
# filename: update-category.pl

use strict;
use warnings;
use DBI;
use Term::Complete;

# Connect to the database.
my $username = 'reuven';
my $password = '';
my $dbh = DBI->connect("DBI:Pg:dbname=coreperl", $username, $password,
                       { 'AutoCommit' => 1, 'RaiseError' => 1}) ||
    die "Error connecting: '$DBI::errstr' ";

my %categories = ();

# -----------------------------------------------------------
# Start a transaction that will last until $dbh->commit() or
# $dbh->rollback()
$dbh->begin_work();

# Get the category names, and make them the keys of %categories
my $sql = "SELECT category_name from Categories";
my $sth = $dbh->prepare($sql);
$sth->execute;
```

```perl
while (my $rowref = $sth->fetchrow_arrayref)
{
    # Add a new key to %categories, with a value of 1
    $categories{$$rowref[0]} = 1;
}


# Finish with this statement
$sth->finish();

my $old_category_name = "";

# Get the existing category name, using Term::Complete.  When we break
# out of this loop, $old_category_name will contain the name of an
# existing category.
until (defined $categories{$old_category_name})
{
    $old_category_name =
        Complete("Enter an existing category: ", keys %categories);
}


# -------------------------------------------------------------
# Get the new category name

print "Change '$old_category_name' to: ";
my $new_category_name = <>;
chomp $new_category_name;

# Category name must contain at least one printable character
if ($new_category_name !~ /\w/)
{
    print "Error: The new category name cannot be blank!\n";
}

# If the category names are OK, check that the new category name isn't
# in the database
else
{
    # Remove extra whitespace from new name
    $new_category_name =~ s/^\s+//g;
    $new_category_name =~ s/\s+$//g;

    # If $new_category_name is in %categories, then we must stop
    # a potential uniqueness problem
    if (defined $categories{$new_category_name})
    {
        # Report an error to the user, and roll back the transaction
```

```
        print "Error: The category '$new_category_name' already exists!\n";
        $dbh->rollback();
        $dbh->disconnect();
        exit;
    }


    # Create the query
    my $sql = "UPDATE Categories ";
    $sql .= "SET category_name = ? ";
    $sql .= "WHERE category_name = ? ";

    # Prepare the statement
    my $number_of_affected_rows =
        $dbh->do($sql, undef, $new_category_name, $old_category_name);

    if ($number_of_affected_rows == 1)
    {
        # Report a result to the user, and commit the transaction
        print "Renamed '$old_category_name' to '$new_category_name'.\n";
        $dbh->commit();
    }
    else
    {
        # Report an error to the user, and roll back the transaction
        print "The category was not renamed.\n";
        $dbh->rollback();
    }
}

# Disconnect from the database
$dbh->disconnect();
```

12.2.4   *Adding new books*

Once we have some values in Authors, Publishers, and Categories, we can add
books to our store. Adding a new book means adding one row to Books, and
one or more rows to BookAuthors.

The following program, `insert-book.pl`, combines many of the techniques that we have already seen in this chapter: It queries the database
for the current author and publisher lists, it uses Term::Complete to allow
the user to complete the author and publisher names, and inserts rows into
Books and BookAuthors. Furthermore, it puts everything into a single transaction, such that the entire sequence of transactions will be handled in an
all-or-nothing manner.

Note also our use of the PostgreSQL-specific attribute pg_oid_status,
which returns the object ID (OID) of the most recently inserted row.

Object IDs are a PostgreSQL-specific feature; you can think of an OID as an invisible, global primary key on every row in the database. We can use the OID of our most recently entered row to retrieve the primary key from our most recent INSERT.

Finally, notice how we INSERT rows into BookAuthors using a single prepare, but multiple invocations of execute. This saves a bit of overhead from our Perl program, and can even give us a major speed boost when working with databases that cache queries.

insert-book.pl is by far the largest database program we have looked at in this book. However, each of its parts has appeared in a previous program in this chapter, and should be fairly easy to understand:

```perl
#!/usr/bin/perl
# filename: insert-book.pl

use strict;
use warnings;
use DBI;
use Term::Complete;

print "Welcome to the 'insert book' program.\n\n";

# Connect to the database.
my $username = 'reuven';
my $password = '';
my $dbh = DBI->connect("DBI:Pg:dbname=coreperl", $username, $password,
                        {
                            'AutoCommit' => 1, 'RaiseError' => 1}) ||
    die "Error connecting: '$DBI::errstr' ";

# Define some lexicals that we will use repeatedly
my ($sql, $sth);

# ------------------------------------------------------------
# Start a new transaction, which will end with the next $dbh->commit()
# or $dbh->rollback().
$dbh->begin_work();

# ------------------------------------------------------------
# Get the authors, and make them the keys to a hash
my %authors = ();

$sql  = "SELECT author_name, author_id ";
$sql .= "FROM Authors";

# Prepare the statement
$sth = $dbh->prepare($sql);
```

```perl
# Execute the statement
$sth->execute;

while (my $rowref = $sth->fetchrow_arrayref)
{
    my ($author_name, $author_id) = @{$rowref};
    $authors{$author_name} = $author_id;
}

# --------------------------------------------------------------
# Get the publishers, and make them the keys to a hash
my %publishers = ();

$sql  = "SELECT publisher_name, publisher_id ";
$sql .= "FROM Publishers";

# Prepare the statement
$sth = $dbh->prepare($sql);

# Execute the statement
$sth->execute;

while (my $rowref = $sth->fetchrow_arrayref)
{
    my ($publisher_name, $publisher_id) = @{$rowref};
    $publishers{$publisher_name} = $publisher_id;
}

# --------------------------------------------------------------
# Get a number of pieces of information from the user
my $isbn = get_info("ISBN");
my $title = get_info("title");

# Get multiple authors
my @authors;
while (my $author = get_info("author (or <enter> when done)", keys %authors))
{
    last unless $author;
    push @authors, $author;
}

my $publisher = get_info("publisher", keys %publishers);
my $pages = get_info("page count");
my $pub_date = get_info("publication date (YYYY-MM-DD)");
my $us_dollar_price = get_info("price in dollars");
```

```perl
# -------------------------------------------------------------
# Insert the book
$sql  = "INSERT INTO Books ";
$sql .= " (isbn, title, publisher_id, num_pages, ";
$sql .= "  pub_date, us_dollar_price) ";
$sql .= "VALUES (?, ?, ?, ?, ?, ?) ";

$sth = $dbh->prepare($sql);

$sth->execute($isbn, $title, $publishers{$publisher}, $pages,
              $pub_date, $us_dollar_price);

my $new_book_oid = $sth->{pg_oid_status};

$sth->finish();

# -------------------------------------------------------------
# Use the OID of the newly inserted book to retrieve the book_id

$sql  = "SELECT book_id ";
$sql .= "FROM Books ";
$sql .= "WHERE oid = ?";

# Prepare the statement
$sth = $dbh->prepare($sql);

# Execute the statement
$sth->execute($new_book_oid);

# Get book_id from the OID
my ($new_book_id) = $sth->fetchrow_array;

$sth->finish();

# -------------------------------------------------------------
# Insert the book-author connection
$sql  = "INSERT INTO BookAuthors (book_id, author_id) VALUES (?, ?) ";

$sth = $dbh->prepare($sql);

foreach my $author (@authors)
{
    $sth->execute($new_book_id, $authors{$author});
    print "Done.\n";
}

# We're done with this statement
$sth->finish();
```

```perl
# If we've made it this far, then we will commit the full transaction
$dbh->commit();

# Disconnect from the database
$dbh->disconnect();

# ------------------------------------------------------------
# Subroutine to get input from the user
sub get_info
{
    my $question = shift;
    my @completions = @_;
    my %completions_hash = map {($_, 1)} @completions;

    my $input = "";

    # Use Term::Complete if we have any completions
    if (@completions)
    {
        $input =
            Complete("Enter the book's $question: ", keys %completions_hash);
    }

    # If there are no completions, get standard impose
    else
    {
        print "Enter the book's $question: ";
        $input = <>;              # Get input from user
        chomp $input;             # Remove trailing newline

        $input =~ s/^\s+//g;      # Remove leading whitespace
        $input =~ s/\s+$//g;      # Remove trailing whitespace
    }

    return $input;
}
```

Although `insert-book.pl` does not handle categories, it is not difficult
to imagine how we could add that functionality.

12.2.5 Querying books

Now that the bookstore has been stocked, it is time to create a simple query
application that allows users to find information about particular books. As
an example, we will write a program that returns a list of books with titles
that contain the entered string.

Notice how we first read all of the book information into a hash (%book), and then print it out later. This is because PostgreSQL will return one row for each author of the book. If we were to simply display the results as they emerged from the database, two-author books would be printed twice, and five-author collaborations would be printed five times! We avoid this by reading all of the books into a hash of hashes, then sorting through them and printing everything out.

Because the results will eventually be re-ordered in the foreach loop, the order in which results are returned might not seem important. But this is not completely true: Authors are added to %book in the same order as rows are retrieved. The ORDER BY clause thus ensures that rows will be returned in order of author names.

To avoid missing some matches because of case issues, this query forces both the title and query string to lowercase with the SQL LOWER function:

```perl
#!/usr/bin/perl
# filename: query-title.pl

use strict;
use warnings;
use DBI;

print qq{Welcome to the "query title" program.\n\n};

# Connect to the database.
my $username = 'reuven';
my $password = '';
my $dbh = DBI->connect("DBI:Pg:dbname=coreperl", $username, $password,
                       { 'AutoCommit' => 1, 'RaiseError' => 1}) ||
    die "Error connecting: '$DBI::errstr' ";

# Get the user's title query
print "Enter a search string: ";
my $target = <>;
chomp $target;

# Quote SQL metacharacters
$target =~ s|%|\\\%|g;
$target =~ s|_|\\\_|g;

# Turn the target string into an SQL regexp
$target = "%$target%";

# Create the query
my $sql = "SELECT B.isbn, B.title, P.publisher_name, B.num_pages, ";
$sql .= "      B.pub_date, B.us_dollar_price, A.author_name ";
```

```perl
$sql .= "FROM Books B, Publishers P, Authors A, BookAuthors BA ";
$sql .= "WHERE LOWER(B.title) LIKE LOWER(?) ";
$sql .= "   AND BA.author_id = A.author_id ";
$sql .= "   AND B.book_id = BA.book_id ";
$sql .= "   AND B.publisher_id = P.publisher_id ";
$sql .= "ORDER BY A.author_name ";

# Prepare the statement
my $sth = $dbh->prepare($sql);

# Execute the statement
my $success = $sth->execute($target);

if ($success)
{
    my %book = ();

    while (my $rowref = $sth->fetchrow_arrayref)
    {
        my ($isbn, $title, $publisher, $pages,
            $date, $price, $author) = @$rowref;

        # Stick information about this book in %book
        $book{$isbn}->{title} = $title;
        $book{$isbn}->{publisher} = $publisher;
        $book{$isbn}->{pages} = $pages;
        $book{$isbn}->{date} = $date;
        $book{$isbn}->{price} = $price;

        # Deal with authors
        if ($book{$isbn}->{author})
        {
            $book{$isbn}->{author} .= ", $author";
        }
        else
        {
            $book{$isbn}->{author} = "$author";
        }
    }

    # Iterate through the books, and print information about them
    foreach my $isbn
        (sort {$book{$a}->{title} cmp $book{$b}->{title}} keys %book)
        {
            print "\n";
            print "$book{$isbn}->{title}\n";
            print "-" x length($book{$isbn}->{title}), "\n";
```

```
            print "by $book{$isbn}->{author}\n";
            print "ISBN: $isbn\tPublisher: $book{$isbn}->{publisher}\n";
            print "Publication date: $book{$isbn}->{date}\t";
            print "Price: \$$book{$isbn}->{price}\n";
            print "Pages: $book{$isbn}->{pages}\n";
        }

    if ($sth->rows == 0)
    {
        print "Sorry, no results found.\n";
    }


}
else
{
    print "Error preparing: $DBI::errstr";
}

$sth->finish();
$dbh->disconnect();
```

12.3   Debugging DBI

Perl is an easy programming language to debug; many programmers sprinkle print statements in their programs rather than using the built-in debugger (see Section 13.4.2). However, such techniques are not always sufficient when working with DBI.

For example, if your program exits with a database error after trying to INSERT a row into BookAuthors, you would like to know exactly what the final SQL query looked like before it was sent to the database. If you have used placeholders, then you will discover that it is very difficult to get such information.

The solution is $dbh->trace(), a method that helps us to debug DBI programs. $dbh->trace() takes one mandatory argument, an integer that ranges from 0 (no debugging) to 9 (more debugging information than you will probably ever need). A second optional argument names the disk file into which the trace information should be placed. By default, output from $dbh->trace() goes to STDERR.

Once activated, $dbh->trace() continues for the life of the program or until it is explicitly turned off. It is not uncommon to use $dbh->trace()

throughout the development process, only turning it off when a program goes into production.

If you prefer, you can also invoke trace as a class method, directly from the DBI module, as DBI->trace(). This lets you trace through DBI->connect(), which returns $dbh.

So that you can see what output $dbh->trace() produces, the following is the transcript of **insert-book.pl** when running with $dbh->trace() at level 1. Note that the only modification I made to **insert-book.pl** was the addition of the following line, immediately after the call to DBI->connect():

```
$dbh->trace(1, '/tmp/insert-book-trace.txt');
```

Here is a printout from inserting the book:

```
Welcome to the 'insert book' program.

Enter the book's ISBN: 123-456-789
Enter the book's title: I like Perl
Enter the book's author (or <enter> when done): Reuven M. Lerner
Enter the book's author (or <enter> when done):
Enter the book's publisher: Prentice-Hall
Enter the book's page count: 200
Enter the book's publication date (YYYY-MM-DD): 2001-01-01
Enter the book's price in dollars: 20
Done.
```

Behind the scenes, DBI traced the session as follows:

```
    DBI::db=HASH(0x8237fc0) trace level set to 1 in DBI 1.20-nothread
dbd_db_FETCH
2    <- FETCH= 1 at DBI.pm line 1051
dbd_db_STORE
2    <- STORE('AutoCommit' 0 ...)= 1 at DBI.pm line 1053
dbd_db_STORE
2    <- STORE('BegunWork' 1 ...)= 1 at DBI.pm line 1054
     <- begin_work= 1 at insert-book.pl line 27
dbd_st_prepare: statement = >SELECT author_name, author_id FROM Authors<
dbd_st_preparse: statement = >SELECT author_name, author_id FROM Authors<
     <- prepare('SELECT author_name, author_id FROM Authors' CODE)=
        DBI::st=HASH(0x8238140) at insert-book.pl line 37
dbd_st_execute
     <- execute(CODE)= 2 at insert-book.pl line 40
dbd_st_fetch
     <- fetchrow_arrayref= [ 'Foo Bar' '1' ] row1 at insert-book.pl line 42
dbd_st_fetch
dbd_st_fetch
     <- fetchrow_arrayref= undef row2 at insert-book.pl line 42
```

```
dbd_st_prepare: statement = >SELECT publisher_name, publisher_id FROM Publishers<
dbd_st_preparse: statement = >SELECT publisher_name, publisher_id FROM Publishers<
    <- prepare('SELECT publisher_name, publisher_id FROM Publishers'
       CODE)= DBI::st=HASH(0x82381dc) at insert-book.pl line 56
dbd_st_destroy
    <- DESTROY= undef at insert-book.pl line 59
dbd_st_execute
    <- execute(CODE)= 3 at insert-book.pl line 59
dbd_st_fetch
    <- fetchrow_arrayref= [ 'Prentice-Hall' '1' ] row1 at insert-book.pl line 61
dbd_st_fetch
dbd_st_fetch
dbd_st_fetch
    <- fetchrow_arrayref= undef row3 at insert-book.pl line 61
dbd_st_prepare: statement = >INSERT INTO Books
    (isbn, title, publisher_id, num_pages,   pub_date, us_dollar_price)
    VALUES (?, ?, ?, ?, ?, ?) <
dbd_st_preparse: statement = >INSERT INTO Books
    (isbn, title, publisher_id, num_pages,
     pub_date, us_dollar_price) VALUES (?, ?, ?, ?, ?, ?) <
    <- prepare('INSERT INTO Books
    (isbn, title, publisher_id, num_pages,
     pub_date, us_dollar_price) VALUES (?, ?, ?, ?, ?, ?) '
       CODE)= DBI::st=HASH(0x823f2e4) at insert-book.pl line 92
dbd_st_destroy
    <- DESTROY= undef at insert-book.pl line 94
dbd_bind_ph
dbd_st_rebind
dbd_bind_ph
dbd_st_rebind
dbd_bind_ph
dbd_st_rebind
dbd_bind_ph
dbd_st_rebind
dbd_bind_ph
dbd_st_rebind
dbd_bind_ph
dbd_st_rebind
dbd_st_execute
    <- execute('123-456-789' 'I like Perl' ...)= 1 at insert-book.pl line 94
dbd_st_FETCH
    <- FETCH= '121271' at insert-book.pl line 97
    <- finish= 1 at insert-book.pl line 99
dbd_st_prepare: statement = >SELECT book_id FROM Books WHERE oid = ?<
dbd_st_preparse: statement = >SELECT book_id FROM Books WHERE oid = ?<
    <- prepare('SELECT book_id FROM Books WHERE oid = ?'
       CODE)= DBI::st=HASH(0x818d458) at insert-book.pl line 109
dbd_st_destroy
    <- DESTROY= undef at insert-book.pl line 112
dbd_bind_ph
dbd_st_rebind
dbd_st_execute
    <- execute('121271' CODE)= 1 at insert-book.pl line 112
dbd_st_fetch
    <- fetchrow_array= ( '19' ) [1 items] row1 at insert-book.pl line 115
```

```
dbd_st_finish
    <- finish= 1 at insert-book.pl line 117
dbd_st_prepare: statement = >INSERT INTO BookAuthors
    (book_id, author_id) VALUES (?, ?) <
dbd_st_preparse: statement = >INSERT INTO BookAuthors
    (book_id, author_id) VALUES (?, ?) <
    <- prepare('INSERT INTO BookAuthors (book_id, author_id)
    VALUES (?, ?) ' CODE)= DBI::st=HASH(0x82381e8) at insert-book.pl line 123
dbd_st_destroy
    <- DESTROY= undef at insert-book.pl line 125
dbd_bind_ph
dbd_st_rebind
dbd_bind_ph
dbd_st_rebind
dbd_st_execute
    <- execute('19' '2' ...)= 1 at insert-book.pl line 127
    <- finish= 1 at insert-book.pl line 132
dbd_db_commit
    <- commit= 1 at insert-book.pl line 135
dbd_db_STORE
2   <- STORE('AutoCommit' 1 ...)= 1 at insert-book.pl line 135
dbd_db_disconnect
    <- disconnect= 1 at insert-book.pl line 138
dbd_st_destroy
    <- DESTROY= undef
dbd_db_destroy
    <- DESTROY= undef
```

As you can see, $dbh->trace(1) gives us a complete log of every time we changed or read an attribute, issued a **prepare**, issued an **execute**, or invoked $dbh->commit().

12.4   Conclusion

In this chapter, we went beyond the basic theory and syntax of databases, and looked at several design elements that come in handy when working on real-life applications. We examined one set of applications in detail, looking at how an online bookstore might wish to categorize its books. In particular, we saw:

- How normalization can make databases more efficient and easier to maintain,

- How to design a database for maximum flexibility and growth,

- How to use Term::Complete to restrict user choices, and

- How to use $dbh->trace() to debug our database applications.

MAINTENANCE AND SECURITY

Topics in This Chapter

- Identifying problems with strict and warnings
- Verbose error messages with diagnostics
- Writing good error messages
- Tainting
- Debugging
- Benchmarking and profiling

Chapter 13

Writing programs in Perl is quite easy. Indeed, Perl is popular in part because it removes much of the tedium of programming, allowing you to get to the heart of a matter and solve it quickly.

However, writing a working program is only half the battle. Most software contains bugs, which means that the ability to maintain that software becomes crucial. Moreover, the earlier in the development process that we find bugs, the easier they are to fix.

In this chapter, we look at how to write maintainable, secure programs in Perl. We will begin by looking at the strict and warnings modules, which identify potential problems in our code.

When things go wrong in our programs, it is important that we be able to provide as much information as possible to the person running it. We will look at the diagnostics module that comes with Perl, as well as how to write error messages that provide the maximum useful information.

Many Perl programmers find that they can usually do without a debugger, but even the toughest of programmers find themselves in need of one. We will look at the built-in Perl debugger as well as the ptkdb debugger from CPAN, demonstrating how they can help you fix your programs.

Good programming practice means checking your inputs as closely as possible. Perl's -T option forces you to check potential problems by marking all data gathered from external sources as suspect.

Once your program is working, you will undoubtedly want to squeeze the most performance out of it. The Benchmark and Devel::DProf modules, both available from CPAN, can help us to make our programs more efficient.

By the end of this chapter, you should understand what support Perl offers to programmers, and how to take advantage of that support in your programming efforts.

13.1   Identifying problems

Perl is a flexible, loosely typed language that allows for a variety of syntaxes and expressions. However, Perl also comes with a number of tools that can help you remove potential problems before they occur.

In this section, we look at several of the ways in which Perl programmers can identify problems before they occur.

13.1.1   warnings

Perl does not require us to declare variables before we use them. This means that we can find ourselves inadvertently working with new variables simply because of typographical errors:

```
#!/usr/bin/perl

my $name = <>;
chomp $name;

print "Your name is '$nmae'!\n";   # Misspelled variable name
```

As we know from Section 2.5.9, the preceding program is syntactically correct, even though it contains a misspelled variable name. Perl will happily treat $nmae as a new variable in the print statement whose value is undef.

We can avoid this and many other problems with the warnings module, which comes with Perl. Unless you have a very good reason for turning them off, you should use warnings in every Perl program you write. warnings will inform you of typographical errors, ambiguities, and other problems.

For example, warnings tells you when you have accidentally written to an unopened filehandle:

```
my $logfile = '/tmp/log';
open LOG, ">>$logfile"
    or die "Cannot append to '$logfile': $! ";
print LGO "hello\n";                # Misspelled filehandle
close LOG;
```

With warnings active, Perl will tell us that the filehandle LOG has not been opened, and that we have a potential typo in our program.

Earlier versions of Perl had a simple -w flag that turned warnings on. By moving this functionality into the warnings module, Perl has made it possible for us to turn on a number of optional warnings, to activate and deactivate individual classes of warnings.

You can, for example, turn on all of Perl's warnings:

```
use warnings qw(all);
```

You can also turn on only those warnings having to do with barewords and precedence:

```
use warnings qw(bareword precedence);
```

You can also turn off one or more types of warnings with the no keyword:

```
no warnings qw(syntax);
```

The use and no pragmas only have effect through the current lexical scope, meaning that their effects disappear when the smallest enclosing block disappears. You can thus do the following:

```
# Turn on all warnings, including optional ones
use warnings qw(all);
{
    # Don't warn be about deprecated features in this block
    no warnings qw(deprecated);
}
# All warnings are once again active
```

For a full list and description of the available warning categories, see perldoc perllexwarn.

13.1.2   strict

The strict module, as we saw in Section 6.1.3, tightens up the Perl compiler's standards for acceptable code. We have already seen how use strict forces us to declare each variable as lexical with my or as global with our, use vars, or an explicit package name.

But the strict module restricts our code in two additional ways, disallowing "barewords" (Perl's term for unquoted strings) and symbolic references (an advanced feature that we won't cover in this book, which often causes more harm than good). As with use warnings, you can activate one, two, or all three of these tests. You can also use no to turn off certain checks through the end of the current lexical scope.

By default, strict activates all tests. This means that a simple invocation of use strict is the same as:

```
use strict qw(vars subs refs);
```

use strict adds very little overhead to your programs, and increases their reliability. Unless you have a good reason for not doing so, you should include use strict in every program and module.

13.1.3   *Perl version information*

To find the version of your Perl installation, use the -v command-line switch:

```
perl -v
```

On my system, this produces the following output:

```
This is perl, v5.6.1 built for i686-linux

Copyright 1987-2001, Larry Wall

Perl may be copied only under the terms of either the Artistic License or the
GNU General Public License, which may be found in the Perl 5 source kit.

Complete documentation for Perl, including FAQ lists, should be found on
this system using 'man perl' or 'perldoc perl'.  If you have access to the
Internet, point your browser at http://www.perl.com/, the Perl Home Page.
```

From within a Perl program, you can get the current version with the $^V variable. However, the version is returned as a string, not as a number. This is done to prevent problems comparing version 5.10 (major version 5, minor version 10) with version 5.2 (major version 5, minor version 2). When working with version numbers, you must thus use eq, lt, and gt, rather than ==, =<, and =>.

A program can require a particular minimum version of Perl with use:

```
use 5.6.2;
```

On my system (running 5.6.1), this code results in a fatal compilation error:

```
Perl v5.6.2 required--this is only v5.6.1, stopped at - line 1.
BEGIN failed--compilation aborted at - line 1.
```

13.1.4 *Detailed configuration information*

The -V command-line switch returns a full listing of the configuration information used for Perl's compilation.

CORE Note

If Perl was installed from precompiled binaries, the version information will reflect the computer on which it was compiled, rather than the computer on which it was installed.

Configuration information is stored in a set of site-specific configuration files that are installed and maintained automatically. It is possible for the configuration information to be inaccurate or missing if these files are modified or deleted.

Here is the output from invoking perl -V on my system:

```
Summary of my perl5 (revision 5.0 version 6 subversion 1) configuration:
  Platform:
    osname=linux, osvers=2.2.17-14, archname=i686-linux
    uname='linux chaim-weizmann 2.2.17-14 #1 mon feb 5 17:53:36 est 2001 i686 unknown '
    config_args='-ds -e'
    hint=recommended, useposix=true, d_sigaction=define
    usethreads=undef use5005threads=undef useithreads=undef usemultiplicity=undef
    useperlio=undef d_sfio=undef uselargefiles=define usesocks=undef
    use64bitint=undef use64bitall=undef uselongdouble=undef
  Compiler:
    cc='cc', ccflags ='-fno-strict-aliasing
        -I/usr/local/include -D_LARGEFILE_SOURCE -D_FILE_OFFSET_BITS=64',
    optimize='-O2',
    cppflags='-fno-strict-aliasing -I/usr/local/include'
    ccversion='', gccversion='egcs-2.91.66 19990314/Linux
        (egcs-1.1.2 release)', gccosandvers=''
```

```
      intsize=4, longsize=4, ptrsize=4, doublesize=8, byteorder=1234
      d_longlong=define, longlongsize=8, d_longdbl=define, longdblsize=12
      ivtype='long', ivsize=4, nvtype='double', nvsize=8, Off_t='off_t', lseeksize=8
      alignbytes=4, usemymalloc=n, prototype=define
  Linker and Libraries:
      ld='cc', ldflags =' -L/usr/local/lib'
      libpth=/usr/local/lib /lib /usr/lib
      libs=-lnsl -lndbm -lgdbm -ldb -ldl -lm -lc -lposix -lcrypt -lutil
      perllibs=-lnsl -ldl -lm -lc -lposix -lcrypt -lutil
      libc=/lib/libc-2.1.3.so, so=so, useshrplib=false, libperl=libperl.a
  Dynamic Linking:
      dlsrc=dl_dlopen.xs, dlext=so, d_dlsymun=undef, ccdlflags='-rdynamic'
      cccdlflags='-fpic', lddlflags='-shared -L/usr/local/lib'


Characteristics of this binary (from libperl):
  Compile-time options: USE_LARGE_FILES
  Built under linux
  Compiled at Apr 17 2001 09:44:02
  @INC:
    /usr/local/lib/perl5/5.6.1/i686-linux
    /usr/local/lib/perl5/5.6.1
    /usr/local/lib/perl5/site_perl/5.6.1/i686-linux
    /usr/local/lib/perl5/site_perl/5.6.1
    /usr/local/lib/perl5/site_perl/5.6.0/i686-linux
    /usr/local/lib/perl5/site_perl/5.6.0
    /usr/local/lib/perl5/site_perl
    .
```

Each piece of information in this output is printed in a name–value pair, as in `osname=linux`. We can retrieve just one of these details by passing an argument to the -V switch:

```
perl -V:osname
```

Within a program, configuration information can be retrieved with the Config module. Config exports %Config, a hash whose keys are a superset of those listed by -V. Here is a short program that displays the full Perl configuration:

```
perl -e 'use Config;
        map { print "'$_' => '$Config{$_}'\n"; }
            sort keys %Config;'
```

13.2   When things go wrong

Try as we might, our programs will occasionally encounter problems. In such cases, the best thing that we can do is give the program's user and maintainer as much information as possible about what happened. This information can then be used to file a complete bug report, which can then help to improve the program.

In this section, we look at some of the tools and techniques that we can use to get a full picture of the situation when an error occurs.

13.2.1   diagnostics

The diagnostics module tells Perl that you would like error messages to be as complete as possible. In many cases, use diagnostics prints not only a description of the error, but also suggested fixes.

For example, consider the following program that declares $world as a lexical but fails to give it a value before passing it to print:

```perl
#!/usr/bin/perl

use strict;
use warnings;
use diagnostics;

my $world;
print "Hello, $world\n";
```

My computer produces the following output:

```
Use of uninitialized value in concatenation (.) or string at - line 8 (#1)
    (W uninitialized) An undefined value was used as if it were already
    defined.  It was interpreted as a "" or a 0, but maybe it was a mistake.
    To suppress this warning assign a defined value to your variables.

    To help you figure out what was undefined, perl tells you what operation
    you used the undefined value in.  Note, however, that perl optimizes your
    program and the operation displayed in the warning may not necessarily
    appear literally in your program.  For example, "that $foo" is
    usually optimized into "that " . $foo, and the warning will refer to
    the concatenation (.) operator, even though there is no . in your
    program.

Hello,
```

As you can see, use diagnostics displayed the warning (thanks to use warnings), followed by a verbose description of the problem and some possible solutions. Because the error message was nonfatal, the program continued to execute as usual.

use diagnostics is helpful during development. But because it slows down program execution dramatically, you should not use it in production code.

13.2.2   Writing good error messages

Good error messages make it relatively easy to pinpoint the source of a problem. Moreover, poor error messages can make it difficult to find a problem, let alone fix it.

However, many programmers ignore the significance of their error messages, writing code that looks like this:

```
open FILE, "foo.txt" or die;
```

The preceding code fails to provide any meaningful information to the user. If something goes wrong, the user and programmer will not know what has happened.

Here are some suggestions for improving this code:

- Calls to die that result from system failures should always pass the value of $!. open, for instance, may fail for a variety of reasons, ranging from permission problems to an illegal filename. By passing $! to die (as demonstrated in Section 3.10), the user will know why the program exited with a runtime error.

- String arguments to die should not end with NEWLINE. If the argument to die is anything but NEWLINE, Perl automatically appends the filename and the line number on which it stopped. If multiple programs contain identical error messages, this information helps to pinpoint the source of the problem.

- Error messages should indicate what was happening when the error occurred: Was the program trying to open a file for reading, or for writing? And what file was the program trying to open? If it was trying to rename a file, what were the old and new names? When giving such details, surround them with quotation marks ("). Without such delimiters, it is hard to see the difference between the empty string and a whitespace character.

- When invoking open, put the filename in a variable ($filename) rather than writing a constant value twice. This ensures that open and die receive the same argument, rather than slightly different values.

Taking all of these points into account, here is an improved version of the code:

```perl
my $filename = "foo.txt";
open FILE, $filename or
    die "Cannot open '$filename' for reading: $! ";
```

13.2.3 Special identifiers

You can make your error messages even more useful by indicating the package, file, and line number on which a problem occurred. These values are available using special identifiers whose values depend on context. These identifiers are not variables and thus do not get interpolated into double-quoted strings.

The two most popular identifiers are __LINE__ and __FILE__, which expand to the current line number and filename, respectively:

```perl
#!/usr/bin/perl
# filename: demonstrate-identifiers.pl

use strict;
use warnings;

print "Currently on line '", __LINE__, "'\n";
print "Currently running program '", __FILE__, "'\n";
print "Currently on line '", __LINE__, "'\n";
```

__PACKAGE__ similarly identifies the current default package (see Section 6.1). The default package, as we have seen, is main.

CORE Note

The special variable $0 contains the program name as invoked on the command line, whereas __FILE__ is the name of the file in which __FILE__ appeared. If all of the code is in a single file, then $0 and __FILE__ will be identical. If code is spread across several files, they will have different values.

13.3   Tainting

Programs often fail to test user input sufficiently to guard against security risks. Perl helps to avoid such problems with "tainting." Tainted programs suspect input from the outside world, requiring that such input be filtered before it can be used.

Tainting is automatically active when programs are run with suid or sgid permissions (see Section 9.7). A program can explicitly turn on tainting with the -T command-line flag.

With tainting active, data that originates outside the program—from a file, environment variable, outside program, or user input—is considered suspect. Data that depends on tainted data is also considered tainted.

Tainted data may not be used to affect anything outside of the program, with the exception of arguments to print, system, and exec. You may not send tainted information to a database server, use it when opening a file for writing, or use it when renaming a file. You may, however, use tainted input as the name of a read-only file.

Tainted programs also remove the current directory (.) from @INC, and require that the PATH environment variable be explicitly set before running other programs. This reduces the possibility of someone maliciously tricking poorly written suid programs into loading the wrong module or executing the wrong program.

The only way to untaint data is with m// (see Section 5.8), capturing the parts that interest us with parentheses (see Section 5.6.1), and retrieving these values from the variables $1, $2, and so forth.

Programs should filter by indicating which characters *will* be allowed, rather than which will not. It is far safer to list the characters we know to be good than to hope that we have remembered to list all of the dangerous characters.

The following program asks the user for a filename, then opens the file of that name and writes to it. In order to avoid potential problems, we only allow alphanumeric characters, hyphens, and underscores:

```
#!/usr/bin/perl -T
# filename: filter-bad-chars.pl

use strict;
use warnings;
```

```
# Give the user a prompt
print "Enter a filename: ";

# Get the filename
my $filename = <>;
chomp $filename;

# Check that we only used safe characters
if ($filename =~ m|^([-\w_]+)$|)
{
    my $safe_filename = $1;

    # Open the file
    open FILE, ">$safe_filename" or
        die "Cannot write to '$safe_filename': $! ";

    # Write to the file
    print FILE "Hello, world\n";

    # Close the file
    close FILE;
}
else
{
    die "Illegal characters in '$filename': Exiting ";
}
```

13.4   Debugging

Some time after you finish writing a program, you (or the people using it) will undoubtedly find that it fails under certain circumstances. This begins the well-known process of debugging.

13.4.1   *Using* print

Perhaps the most commonly used tool for debugging is print, the tried and true Perl function that sends information to a filehandle. Special identifiers (see Section 13.2.3) can help to improve these messages.

When debugging information might interfere with normal program output, use the STDERR filehandle instead of STDOUT. Alternatively, send output to an external logfile.

But such print statements can become a problem when the code goes into production. How can you remove them from production code and ensure that they are available for debugging?

One solution is to define a global $DEBUGGING variable, whose value is an integer reflecting how much logging you want the program to perform. When $DEBUGGING is 0, then the program displays no debugging information; when $DEBUGGING is 10, then the program displays lots of information. (This is similar to the strategy used by $dbi->trace(), described in Section 12.3.) Each statement and subroutine can then display information depending on the value of $DEBUGGING:

```
if ($DEBUGGING > 1)
{
    print STDERR "ENV{PATH} at start of sub 'foo'  is '$ENV{PATH}'\n";
}

if ($DEBUGGING > 5)
{
    print STDERR "ENV at start of sub 'foo' is:\n";

    foreach my $key (sort keys %ENV)
    {
        print STDERR "'$key' => '$ENV{$key}'\n";
    }
}
```

Notice how our debugging messages always indicate where they were invoked.

Conditional debugging code, using different levels of details, makes it easy to remove such messages when the program goes into production, while keeping them available when we need to find and fix problems.

13.4.2   The Perl debugger

print is an excellent tool, but there are times when it will not suffice. For these occasions, Perl comes with a built-in debugger, which is activated with the -d command-line switch. To debug a program, add -d to its list of switches:

```
#!/usr/bin/perl -d
```

Alternatively, type `perl -d` at the shell prompt, followed by the name of the program to debug:

```
perl -d program.pl
```

CORE Approach

This latter version is useful when debugging a production program, for which an active, working version must exist.

Perl's debugger allows you to run and halt programs, examine the current state of variables and subroutines, change variable values, and test code.

13.4.3 A simple program

We will use a simple program, `debugger-demo.pl`, to test our debugger. It defines three lexicals—a scalar, an array, and a hash—as well as one loop and one subroutine:

```perl
#!/usr/bin/perl -d
# filename: debugger-demo.pl

use strict;
use warnings;

# Define some lexicals
my $scalar = "hello";
my @array = qw(one two three);
my %hash = ("one" => 1,
            "two" => 2,
            "three" => 3);

# Handle a loop
foreach my $element (@array)
{
    print "Scalar: '$scalar'\n";
    print "Array element: '$element'\n";
    print "Hash: '$hash{$element}'\n\n";
}
```

```perl
# Handle subroutines
my $return_value;
$return_value = print_scalar_value($scalar);
$return_value = print_scalar_value(@array);
$return_value = print_scalar_value(%hash);

# Define our subroutine
sub print_scalar_value
{
    my @args = @_;
    my $value = scalar(@args);

    print "Subroutine returns '$value'\n";
    return $value;
}
```

13.4.4   Examining the simple program

Because `debugger-demo.pl` uses the -d flag, running it gives us the debugger prompt:

```
Default die handler restored.

Loading DB routines from perl5db.pl version 1.07
Editor support available.

Enter h or 'h h' for help, or 'man perldebug' for more help.

main::(/tmp/debugger-demo.pl:8):          my $scalar = "hello";
  DB<1>
```

This prompt indicates that the debugger has not yet executed line 8 of our program. We are now invited to enter a debugger command. Table 13.1 displays a list of the most common debugger commands; a full list is in `perldoc perldebug`, or by typing h at the debugger prompt.

In addition to the preceding one-letter commands, the debugger accepts Perl expressions, from simple arithmetic to variable assignments and subroutine definitions. You can exit from the debugger by typing exit.

Table 13.1	Common Debugger Commands

Command	Effect
l	List source code. This displays the line that you are currently examining, as well some lines of context before and after the current line. An optional numeric argument lets you examine the source code on a different line.
-	List the previous line (or lines) of source code.
.	List the current line of source code.
b	Set a breakpoint (see Section 13.4.7).
n	Step through the code (like s), treating subroutines as one-line commands (see Section 13.4.5).
p	Print the value of an expression, as if it were inside of a print statement.
r	Run the program, stopping at a breakpoint or when the program exits.
R	Restart the program.
s	Single-step through the code (see Section 13.4.5).
w	List around the current line.
x	Print the value of an expression, breaking out the elements of an array.

Debugger commands are recorded in a history that can be reviewed and edited using Emacs-style control keys. The most basic of these are CON-TROL-p (previous line), CONTROL-n (next line), CONTROL-b (back a character), CONTROL-f (forward a character), CONTROL-a (beginning of line), and CONTROL-e (end of line).

13.4.5 Stepping through the program

The two most common debugger commands are s and n, which move forward through the program. n goes to the next line of our program, executing subroutines as if they were built-in functions that cannot be debugged. s, by contrast, steps into subroutines as necessary, letting us enter and examine a subroutine's contents as it executes.

For example, assume that the debugger is at line 24 of debugger-demo.pl, where print_scalar_value is invoked:

```
main::(/tmp/debugger-demo.pl:24):
     $return_value = print_scalar_value($scalar);
```

Using n at this point would execute line 24 and move onto line 25. Using s would move us to the first line of print_scalar_value, on line 31.

13.4.6   Examining values

To examine values, use p (an alias for print) and x (for extended output). It is often best to use x when looking at nonscalars, given that p (like print) displays the value of an array or hash without any spaces between them:

```
onetwothree
```

x @array produces the following output:

```
0    'one'
1    'two'
2    'three'
```

If our array is too large to display entirely, we can view an array slice (see Section 2.6.3). For example, x @array[0..1] produces the following output:

```
0    'one'
1    'two'
```

x %hash displays the contents of %hash as if it were an array (see Section 2.7.3):

```
0    'three'
1    3
2    'two'
3    2
4    'one'
5    1
```

We can instead use a foreach loop to display a hash:

```
DB<37> foreach my $key (sort keys %hash) \
cont:   { print "$key => $hash{$key}\n"; }
```

Notice how we we were able to split our command across two lines by ending the first line with a backslash (\). The second line then begins with a special cont: prompt. The debugger treats the \-NEWLINE combination as whitespace.

13.4.7 Breakpoints

The Perl debugger allows for "breakpoints," lines of code at which execution halts. This means that we can use r to run a program until it hits a breakpoint, which is substantially easier than using n until we get there.

To set a breakpoint, use the b debugger command, naming the line at which execution should halt:

```
b 25
```

This command sets a breakpoint at line 25. After setting the breakpoint, restart the program with R, and run it with r:

```
Scalar: "hello"
Array element: "one"
Hash: "1"

Scalar: "hello"
Array element: "two"
Hash: "2"

Scalar: "hello"
Array element: "three"
Hash: "3"

Subroutine returns "1"
main::(./test-debugger.pl:25):
    $return_value = print_scalar_value(@array);
```

The debugger stopped at line 25, allowing us to inspect the program at that point with p and x. We can continue execution with r, delete the breakpoint with d, or quit with exit.

13.4.8 Debugging with Emacs

GNU Emacs and XEmacs support gud, the "grand unified debugger" mode. Recent versions of gud support the Perl debugger, as well as debuggers for C, Java, and Python.

The advantage of gud is that it provides a full-screen view of the Perl program, rather than the single-line view provided by the default Perl debugger. When an error occurs, gud makes it possible to jump to the offending line in the source code. You can also set and delete breakpoints, examine source code, and control the debugger using menus rather than typed commands.

To enter `gud`, type `M-x perldb RET`. Emacs will ask for the name of the program to debug, offering the current program as a default. Type the filename, or press ENTER to debug the current program.

At this point, the Emacs frame will be split into two windows. One looks like its command-line counterpart. The second displays the source code for the debugged program and an arrow on the current line in the source code.

More information about `gud` is available in the "Debuggers" section of the "Info" documentation that comes with Emacs.

13.4.9   Debugging with ptkdb

Although Emacs approaches the look and feel of a graphical debugger and is easily customizable in Emacs Lisp, many programmers have long wanted something more visually appealing. One answer to these requests is ptkdb, a graphical debugger based on the portable Tk graphics toolkit. Tk and ptkdb are both available from CPAN (see Section 1.6); whereas Tk is a large package that requires a fair amount of disk space, ptkdb (available as the module Devel::ptkdb) should take little time to download and install.

To debug a program with ptkdb, use the -d command switch, followed by a colon (:) and the string ptkdb. For example, here is the first line of `debugger-demo.pl`, rewritten to use ptkdb:

```
#!/usr/bin/perl -w -d:ptkdb
```

When `debugger-demo.pl` is invoked with ptkdb, a debugging window appears on the screen (see Figure 13.1). The main part of the window is split vertically, with the program's source code on the left and several tabs on the right. Above both of these sections is a set of buttons for the most commonly executed tasks, such as "step in," "step over," "return," and "run." And at the top of the window is a menu bar, with menus labeled "control," "data," "stack," and "bookmarks."

The source code window, taking up the bulk of the ptkdb window, highlights the current line of source code in blue. Each line of code is prefaced by a number, but lines of code that do not contain their own statements—and thus cannot have breakpoints set on them—are crossed out.

Pointing the mouse at a data structure brings up a help balloon containing a representation of that structure. Unlike the debugger's standard

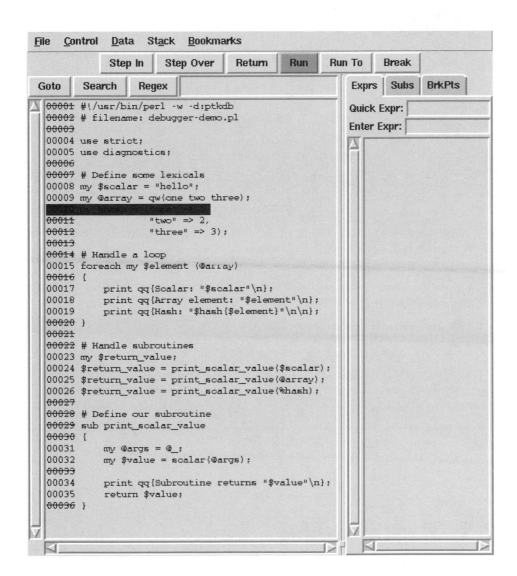

Figure 13.1 The initial window that ptkdb presents when debugging a program. Basic debugging functionality is available from the buttons at the top of the window.

p and x commands, ptkdb displays data in a readable format reminiscent of
Data::Dumper (see Section 6.4.4).

To set a breakpoint, click on the appropriate line of code with the mouse,
and click on the "break" button. The line number will then change to red.
A list of breakpoints is available on the "BrkPts" tab, on the right-hand side
of the screen. Under this tab, each breakpoint can be assigned a condition,
suspended, or deleted. Conditional breakpoints are useful when debugging
programs that only fail in certain situations.

To search through the code for a text string or regular expression, use the
search box at the top of the code frame. Repeatedly pressing the "Search"
or "Regex" button will move the cursor to successive instances of the search
term.

The two other tabs in the right-hand frame provide other utilities: The
"Exprs" tab is a wrapper around eval, making it possible to evaluate any Perl
expression, including one using variables or subroutines defined in the debugged code. The "Subs" tab produces a list of packages (see Section 6.1.1);
double-clicking on a package lists the subroutines in that namespace. Double-
clicking on a subroutine name moves the cursor to that subroutine.

CORE Approach

Because it does not interfere with output to STDOUT *and* STDERR,
ptkdb *is particularly useful when debugging CGI programs (see Chapter 14).
Used in conjunction with the* X *Window System, you can even display a
debugging window on one computer as the program executes on another.*

13.5   Benchmarking

Once you have found that your program works, you may want to optimize
it to run faster. But before you can do this, you must determine where your
program is wasting its time. After all, it would be foolish to optimize a
foreach loop if the program is spending all of its time waiting for an SQL
query to return, or reading data from a socket.

This section describes the Benchmark and Devel::DProf modules, which
are invaluable when trying to make such measurements.

13.5.1 Benchmark

The Benchmark module lets you test the speed of some Perl code. Benchmark will execute code one or more times, reporting how long it took to run. The code to be benchmarked is typically stored in a subroutine reference (see Section 4.5). By passing Benchmark several subroutine references, we can compare the relative speed of two different implementations.

For example, we can use the timethis subroutine, which Benchmark automatically exports, to execute some Perl code 100 times:

```
use Benchmark;

my @integers = ();
foreach (0 .. 1000)
{
    push @integers, int rand 10000;
}

timethis(100, 'my @output = sort  {$a <=> $b} @integers');
```

When I run this on my computer, I get the following output:

```
timethis 100:  0 secs ( 0.00 usr  0.00 sys =  0.00 cpu)
            (warning: too few iterations for a reliable count)
```

My computer performs 100 iterations too quickly to measure. We can remedy this by increasing the count to 1,000,000:

```
timethis 1000000:   2 wallclock secs
   ( 2.24 usr +  0.00 sys =  2.24 CPU) @ 446428.57/s (n=1000000)
```

To compare the relative speeds of two different approaches, we can use the timethese subroutine, whose second argument is a hash reference rather than a scalar. (The hash keys are labels used when displaying results.) For example, the following code sorts our integers 1 million times using both <=> and eq, to determine which is faster:

```
use Benchmark;

my @integers = ();
foreach (0 .. 1000)
```

```
{
    push @integers, int rand 10000;
}

timethese (1_000_000, {
            "<=>" => 'my @output = sort  {$a <=> $b} @integers',
            "cmp" => 'my @output = sort  {$a cmp $b} @integers'});
```

This program produces the following output:

```
Benchmark: timing 1000000 iterations of <=>, cmp...
      <=>:  2 wallclock secs ( 2.21 usr +  0.00 sys =
          2.21 CPU) @ 452488.69/s (n=1000000)
      cmp:  4 wallclock secs ( 2.30 usr +  0.00 sys =
          2.30 CPU) @ 434782.61/s (n=1000000)
```

As you can see, $<=>$ is slightly faster than cmp. Remember that the "wallclock" reading is less important than the "usr" and "CPU" readings, which reflect the actual amount of time the computer worked.

13.5.2   Devel::DProf

Benchmark is useful for considering different implementations, but does not let you profile an existing program. For that, you need Devel::DProf, a module available from CPAN (see Section 1.6) that tells you how much time a program is spending in each subroutine.

Executing our program with the -d:DProf flag creates a logfile named tmon.out, which keeps track of which subroutines are called and how long each call takes. tmon.out is not meant to be read by humans; instead, you will use a program named dprofpp to parse and display its contents. When run, dprofpp produces output that looks like the following:

```
Total Elapsed Time =  0.05986 Seconds
  User+System Time =  0.05986 Seconds
Exclusive Times
%Time ExclSec CumulS #Calls sec/call Csec/c  Name
 33.4   0.020  0.030     2   0.0100 0.0150  main::BEGIN
 16.7   0.010  0.010     1   0.0100 0.0100  warnings::BEGIN
 0.00   0.000 -0.000     1   0.0000     -   strict::import
 0.00   0.000 -0.000     1   0.0000     -   strict::bits
 0.00   0.000 -0.000     1   0.0000     -   Exporter::import
```

```
0.00   0.000 -0.000     1   0.0000     -   warnings::import
0.00   0.000 -0.000     1   0.0000     -   warnings::bits
0.00   0.000 -0.000     1   0.0000     -   main::foo
0.00   0.000 -0.000     1   0.0000     -   main::bar
```

By default, dprofpp displays the 15 subroutines whose execution took the greatest percentage of the program's execution time. We can change this with the -O flag, specifying a number (as in dprofpp -O 30 tmon.out).

The %Time column indicates the percentage of execution time spent in this subroutine, and the #Calls column shows how many times a particular subroutine was called. Using this information, you can easily determine which subroutines are the bottleneck in your program and focus your efforts on optimizing the most problematic code.

Some subroutines are obviously beyond our control: Although we can improve main::BEGIN (the body of our program), we cannot touch warnings::BEGIN or the various subroutines from strict.

CORE Note

Devel::DProff *only breaks out subroutine calls, not individual statements. A program without subroutines, or one in which a subroutine performs many tasks, is not a good candidate for profiling. It is sometimes worth moving functionality into subroutines just to be able to get accurate profiling information.*

13.6   Conclusion

Software maintenance and security are two of the most important issues facing modern programmers. In this chapter, we learned how to make our programs more robust, reducing the chance of errors before they occur and helping us to fix them when they do. In particular, we explored the following topics:

- How to tighten up Perl's notion of correct syntax with the strict and warnings modules,

- Improving Perl's error messages with diagnostics,

- How to write good error messages for when things go wrong,

- How to improve our program's security and robustness with Perl's "taint" mechanism,

- How to debug our programs using the built-in Perl debugger and the graphical `ptkdb` debugger, and

- Improving our program's performance with benchmarking and profiling.

CGI
PROGRAMMING

Topics in This Chapter

- HTTP, URLs, and HTML

- Dynamic Web content

- Configuring the server for CGI

- The CGI module

- Error messages and debugging

- Redirection

- Some useful methods

Chapter 14

Perl had been popular among Internet programmers before the World Wide Web appeared on the scene. But Perl's strengths quickly proved useful for Web developers as well.

This chapter introduces the Web from a technical perspective and demonstrates how we can write programs using the Common Gateway Interface, more often known as "CGI." We will use the standard Perl CGI module for much of this work, in order to dramatically reduce the amount of code that we must write.

By the end of this chapter, you should understand the CGI standard and how it works, and should feel comfortable writing basic CGI programs using Perl.

14.1 Dynamic Web content

This chapter describes how to create dynamic Web content. Creating such content requires a basic understanding of three standards: HTTP (Hypertext Transfer Protocol), URLs (Uniform Resource Locators), and HTML (Hypertext Markup Language).

14.1.1   HTTP

HTTP is the client–server protocol used for most Web traffic. Web browsers, such as Netscape Navigator and Internet Explorer, are the most obvious examples of HTTP clients. The most popular HTTP servers are the open-source Apache and Microsoft's IIS.

An HTTP transaction consists of a client-initiated request, followed by a response from the server, followed by the termination of the connection. Requests and responses are "stateless," neither inheriting information from previous transactions nor leaving hints for future ones.

HTTP supports a number of "request methods," which are sent as the first word of the request. GET is the simplest and most common method. The following request asks an HTTP server for the document /a/b/c/d.html using HTTP version 1.0:

```
GET /a/b/c/d.html HTTP/1.0
```

An HTTP request may contain one or more headers, name–value pairs that describe the user's browser or the request. For example, the following request includes the User-Agent header, which normally identifies the browser's name and version:

```
GET /a/b/c/d.html HTTP/1.0
User-Agent: Mozilla 10.0
```

GET requests pass arguments to the server by appending a question mark (?) to the URL, followed by one or more name–value pairs separated by ampersands (&):

```
GET /a/b/c/d.html?arg1=val1&arg2=val2 HTTP/1.0
```

The HTTP server's response consists of a response code, zero or more headers, a blank line, and a body:

```
HTTP/1.1 200 OK
Date: Fri, 28 Sep 2001 09:10:15 GMT
Content-Type: text/html

<HTML><Body>Foo</Body></HTML>
```

The server's response begins with the highest version of HTTP that it understands. This is followed by a "200" ("OK") response code, indicating success. Servers can choose from several dozen response codes, indicating a variety of possible conditions.

Headers provide additional information about the response. In this example, the Date header indicates when the requested file was last modified, and that it consists of HTML-formatted text. Other common content types are text/plain, image/jpeg, and image/png. This type/subtype format was borrowed from the MIME standard, which makes e-mail attachments possible.

The HEAD request method is identical to GET but indicates that the the client is only interested in the response headers:

```
HEAD /a/b/c/d.html HTTP/1.0
```

The POST request method overcomes the clumsiness associated with passing name–value pairs in the path and is also more reliable. In a POST request, the name–value pairs are passed after the initial request line, following a blank line:

```
POST /a/b/c/d.html HTTP/1.0

arg1=val1&arg2=val2
```

14.1.2 URLs

URLs uniquely identify documents on the Internet and serve as Web "addresses." A URL specifies a protocol, a server name, and path. ftp://ftp.example.com/foo.txt refers to the document foo.txt available via FTP on ftp.example.com. In the same way, http://www.example.com/foo.html refers to the document /foo.html via HTTP on www.example.com. Paths in a URL do not necessarily correlate to paths on the HTTP server's filesystem.

Some characters, such as SPACE and ?, cannot be transmitted safely in URLs. Such characters are replaced by %, followed by the hexadecimal ASCII code for the character in question. (This process is known as "URL-encoding.") SPACE (ASCII 0x20) thus becomes %20 inside of a URL and ? (ASCII 0x3F) becomes %3F.

14.1.3 HTML

HTML allows us to describe and design a text document with "tags." Each tag begins with a < and ends with a >, as in <hr> (which draws a horizontal rule).   Many tags come in pairs, describing the text between the start-ing and ending tag. Thus <p>Foo</p> turns Foo into a paragraph, and <title>Bar</title> makes Bar into a document title. HTML documents must begin with an <html> tag and end with an </html> tag. An HTML document is normally divided into a "head" (surrounded by <head> and </head>) and a "body" (marked off with <body> and </body>).

To insert a literal < or > in your HTML document, use < and >, respectively. These are just two of the many predefined "entities" that allow you to insert nearly any character into your HTML document.

Many tags take one or more "attributes," name–value pairs that modify the tag's operation. For example, the img tag inserts an image into a doc-ument, and its src attribute names the URL of the image to insert. So the HTML <img src="/image.jpeg"> inserts the image /image.jpeg into the current document.

HTML documents can contain links to other documents (thus the term "hypertext") with an <a> tag whose href attribute contains the URL of the destination document. In the following sentence, clicking on the words Mr. President takes the user to http://www.whitehouse.gov/:

```
<p>Hi, <a href="http://www.whitehouse.gov/">Mr. President</a>.</p>
```

14.1.4   HTML forms

An HTML form, created with the <form> tag, allows users to send name–value pairs to a URL using graphical elements inside of the browser. The browser determines the look and feel of these form elements.

Most HTML form elements are created with an <input> tag, where the name attribute determines the element's name ·and the type attribute indicates its appearance. (We can thus change a checkbox into a radio button, or a text field into a hidden field, simply by changing the value of the type attribute.)

Every form must have at least one "submit" button, created as follows:

```
<input type="submit" value="Enter your values">
```

The value attribute determines what text will be displayed inside of the button on the user's screen. When the user clicks on this button, the browser sends the contents of the form to the URL specified in the <form> tag's action attribute, using the request method (GET or POST) specified in the method attribute. For example, the following form will send its name–value pairs to http://www.example.com/cgi-bin/foo.pl using the POST method:

```
<html>
    <head>
        <title>Submit this form!</title>
    </head>

    <body>
    <form action="http://www.example.com/cgi-bin/foo.pl" method="POST">
        <input type="submit" value="Submit the form">
    </form>
    </body>
</html>
```

HTML forms support the following element types:

- Text fields allow users to enter a single line of text:

  ```
  <input type="text" name="myfield">
  ```

  The value attribute lets you give a text field a default value.

- Hidden fields are just like text fields, but do not appear in the user's browser:

  ```
  <input type="hidden" name="my-hidden-field" value="foo">
  ```

  They are useful for carrying state from one page to another, but they can be seen and modified with little difficulty by savvy users, so information that must remain secure should never be put in a hidden field.

- Radio buttons allow users to choose from several different options. Typically, you will have several radio buttons with the same name attribute but different value attributes. The browser ensures that only one radio button with a given name may be selected at a time. The selected attribute, which takes no value, indicates which radio button should be checked by default:

  ```
  <input type="radio" name="radio" value="1" selected>1
  <input type="radio" name="radio" value="2">2
  <input type="radio" name="radio" value="3">3
  ```

- Checkboxes let users make yes-or-no decisions. Each checkbox typically has a unique name, although it is permissible for multiple checkboxes to share one. The value parameter determines what value is sent to the HTTP server when the form is submitted; checkboxes without value parameters are set to on when active, and the empty string ("") otherwise. For example:

```
<input type="checkbox" name="checkbox-1" checked>1
<input type="checkbox" name="checkbox-2">2
<input type="checkbox" name="checkbox-3">3
```

- Selection lists work like radio buttons, but present a drop-down menu instead of a list of buttons. Each valid option has a value (named in the value parameter), as well as some displayed text:

```
<select name="selector">
    <option value="1">one
    <option value="2">two
    <option value="3">three
</select>
```

- To let users enter more than one line of text, you must use a <textarea> tag. The rows and cols attributes tell the browser how many rows and columns to display. Everything between <textarea> and </textarea> is displayed as the default text:

```
<textarea name="comments" rows="10" cols="60">
Enter your comments here.
</textarea>
```

14.2   CGI

HTTP clients cannot know if the HTTP response body comes from a disk file or was dynamically generated by a program. CGI, the "Common Gateway Interface," is a standard API that defines how a Web server passes information to an external program.

CGI can be summarized as follows:

- The program receives most information via environment variables (i.e., the %ENV hash).

- User input submitted via the POST method is sent to STDIN.

- Anything that the program writes to STDOUT is sent to the user's browser.

- Anything that the program writes to STDERR is sent to the server error log.

Because of the nature of HTTP, CGI programs have only one chance to read input from the user and can only send one output. Otherwise, CGI programs are just as powerful as their command-line counterparts.

14.2.1   Configuring Apache for CGI

Very few Web sites consist solely of CGI programs. This means that an HTTP server must be able to distinguish between CGI programs (which should be executed) and static files (which should be returned verbatim). The popular open-source Apache server offers a number of different ways to make this distinction.

The easiest method is to specify that all of the files in a particular directory should be treated as CGI programs with the ScriptAlias configuration directive. Putting such a line in the Apache configuration file `httpd.conf` indicates that any URL beginning with /cgi-bin/ will result in the execution of a program in `/usr/local/apache/cgi-bin/`:

```
ScriptAlias /cgi-bin/ /usr/local/apache/cgi-bin/
```

CORE Note

The default Apache installation normally defines one ScriptAlias *directory. Check* `httpd.conf` *on your system.*

For more information about downloading and configuring Apache, including the ScriptAlias directive, read the extensive documentation at http://www.apache.org/.

14.2.2   A simple CGI program

Writing CGI programs has never been particularly difficult. However, Lincoln Stein's CGI module, which is part of the Perl distribution, allows us to ignore many of the underlying details of the CGI standard, concentrating instead on writing our programs. This program demonstrates how to use the CGI module:

```perl
#!/usr/bin/perl -T
# filename: howdy.pl

use strict;
use warnings;

# Turn on autoflush
$| = 1;

# Bring in the CGI module
use CGI;

# Create an instance of CGI
my $query = new CGI;

# Send a Content-type header
print $query->header("text/html");

# Begin the HTML
print $query->start_html(-title => "Howdy!");

# Print some basic info
print "<p>Howdy!</p>\n";

# Print the current time
my $now = localtime;
print "<p>It is now '$now'.</p>\n";

print $query->end_html;
```

howdy.pl demonstrates most of the techniques that we will use when writing CGI programs:

- Always use strict, warnings, and the -T flag. The Internet is a nasty place, and it's hard to predict what sorts of inputs your program will receive from users.

- Turn on autoflush by setting $|. Buffered output may be more efficient, but means that users must wait longer to see results on their screen.

- howdy.pl creates an instance of CGI, and then invokes three common methods on it: header sends basic response headers (including a Content-type header), start_html returns the standard beginning of an HTML document, and end_html returns a standard ending to an HTML document.

  Forgetting to send a Content-type header is probably the most common mistake that beginning CGI programmers make. Avoid this problem by invoking header immediately after creating the instance of CGI.

- Because anything written to STDOUT is sent to the user's browser, we can create an HTML document dynamically with print.

If we place howdy.pl in the CGI directory on www.coreperl.com, we can see its output by requesting the URL http://www.coreperl.com/cgi-bin/howdy.pl. The Web server receives our request, executes howdy.pl, and returns the program's output to our HTTP client.

14.2.3 Retrieving parameters

As we have seen, an HTTP request may set one or more parameters, either in the query string (i.e., following a question mark in the URL), or in the body of the request (using the POST request method). The CGI module looks for name–value pairs in both places, translating URL-encoded characters as necessary.

To retrieve a parameter's value, pass the param method the parameter's name:

```
my $query = new CGI;
my $firstname = $query->param('firstname');
my $lastname = $query->param('lastname');
```

Invoked without any arguments, param returns a list of defined parameter names:

```perl
my $query = new CGI;
my @param_names = $query->param();

foreach my $name (@param_names)
{
    print "<p>'$name' => '",
        $query->param($name), "'</p>\n";
}
```

14.2.4 Sending a form as e-mail

A common use of CGI is to send the contents of an HTML form as e-mail. If we assume that the HTML form defines text fields named recipient, sender, and comments, we can send the e-mail by handing the values to the sendmail subroutine exported by Mail::Sendmail (see Section 10.3.4):

```perl
#!/usr/bin/perl -T
# filename: send-comments.pl

use strict;
use warnings;

use CGI;
use Mail::Sendmail;

# Turn on autoflush
$| = 1;

# Create a new instance of CGI
my $query = new CGI;

# Send a MIME header
print $query->header("text/html");

# Begin the HTML
print $query->start_html(-title => "Mail status");

# Create the message
my %message = ('To' => $query->param('recipient'),
                'From' => $query->param('sender'),
                'Subject' => 'Comments from the Web',
                'Message' => $query->param('comments'));
```

```
# Send the mail
if (sendmail %message)
{
    print "<p>The mail was sent successfully.</p>\n";
}
else
{
    print "<p>Error sending the mail: '$Mail::Sendmail::log'.</p>\n";
}

print $query->end_html();
```

The following HTML document could be used with this version of send-comments.pl to send e-mail via the Web:

```
<html>
    <head><title>Send mail</title></head>

    <body>
    <form method="POST" action="/cgi-bin/send-comments.pl">
        <p>Sender: <input type="text" name="sender"></p>
        <p>Recipient: <input type="text" name="recipient"></p>
        <p>Comments: <input type="text" name="comments"></p>

        <p><input type="submit" value="Send mail"></p>
    </form>
    </body>
</html>
```

When the HTML form is submitted, the comments are sent to the e-mail address named in recipient.

14.3   Error messages and debugging

It can often be more difficult (and frustrating) to debug a CGI program than a similar standalone program. This is because you invoke a standalone program directly, whereas a CGI program is invoked for you by a Web server, in response to an HTTP request that the Web browser has submitted.

The first place to look for clues is the HTTP server's error log. Apache's error log is installed by default in **/usr/local/apache/log/error-log**, and will contain any errors or warnings that your program might have generated. If you aren't sure where or why something has gone wrong, consider using the diagnostics module, which often has useful suggestions.

Most problems with CGI programs can be debugged by examining the error log and liberally sprinkling print and warn statements into your program.

This tips in this section complement those in Sections 13.4.2 and 13.4.9, which describe the built-in and graphical ptkdb debuggers, respectively.

14.3.1   Command-line execution

CGI programs that use the CGI module will execute normally when invoked from the command line. You can even pass name–value pairs to the program:

```
./mycgi.pl foo=bar arg1=val1
```

mycgi.pl will act as if the foo and arg1 parameters had been set in an HTML form.

You can turn on additional debugging features, such as the ability to read arguments from STDIN, by importing -debug:

```
use CGI qw(-debug);
```

You can similarly turn off all command-line debugging features with -no-debug:

```
use CGI qw(-no-debug);
```

14.3.2   CGI::Carp

Carp, which comes with the Perl distribution, makes Perl's standard error messages more verbose. CGI::Carp, which also comes with Perl, extends this functionality to the CGI domain, ensuring that messages sent to the HTTP server's error log include a full, valid timestamp.

Moreover, importing the subroutine fatalsToBrowser from CGI::Carp sends fatal error messages (but not warnings and nonfatal errors) to the user's browser, in addition to the error log:

```
use CGI::Carp qw(fatalsToBrowser);
```

fatalsToBrowser can be a terrific help while developing Web applications. However, be sure to remove it when your application goes into production—otherwise, your users may see your error messages, which can be quite embarrassing.

14.3.3   Dump

Another common problem is the accidental misspelling of one or more HTML form parameters. use warnings and use strict prevent a program from using undeclared variables, but cannot check the arguments to param.

The CGI module's Dump method (note the capitalization) can help us discover such problems by listing all of the name–value pairs that were passed to the program. Not only does it identify such misspellings, but it lets us find out exactly what the user's browser is submitting.

Dump returns a string containing an HTML-formatted list of name–value pairs, which you can then include in your CGI program:

```perl
#!/usr/bin/perl -T
# filename: demo-dump.pl

use strict;
use warnings;

use CGI;

# Turn on autoflush
$| = 1;

# Create a new instance of CGI
my $query = new CGI;

# Send a MIME header
print $query->header("text/html");

# Begin the HTML
print $query->start_html(-title => "Mail status");

# Display the name-value pairs we received
print $query->Dump();

print $query->end_html();
```

14.4   Redirection

So far, we have only considered HTTP response codes as a means of indicating success or failure. But response codes can do much more than that. For example, the 302 ("redirect") status code tells the HTTP client to issue a second request. A 302 HTTP response will normally include a Location header whose value is the URL to which the client should direct a new request.

14.4.1   redirect()

To generate a 302 response, use the CGI module's redirect method:

```
# Get the new URL
my $new_url = 'http://www.coreperl.com/';

# Create an instance of CGI
my $query = new CGI;

# Send the user's browser to $new_url
print $query->redirect($new_url);
```

The preceding code produces the following output:

```
Status: 302 Moved
Location: http://www.coreperl.com/
```

As you can see, the response consists of a 302 status code, followed by a Location header with the target URL.

CORE Note

Because Location *is a header, it must be sent along with other HTTP headers, and not following the blank line that separates headers from content. For this reason, you should not invoke* $query->header() *before* $query->redirect().

14.4.2   A "thank you" page

Many CGI programs display a "thank you" page after processing a user's inputs. We could create and send such a document from within a program, but this means that the site's editors and designers must modify the program—or ask a programmer to modify it—every time they want to change the text or style of the "thank you" page. Keeping the "thank you" page in a static HTML file allows such non-programmers to modify the file whenever they want.

The following program demonstrates this technique, sending a 302 response after writing the values of two HTML form elements (name and email) to disk:

```perl
#!/usr/bin/perl -T
# filename: write-and-redirect.pl

use strict;
use warnings;
use CGI;
use Fcntl qw(:flock);

# Turn on autoflush
$| = 1;

# Create an instance of CGI
my $query = new CGI;

# Get the form elements
my $name = $query->param("name") || "";
my $email = $query->param("email") || "";

my $logfile = "/tmp/write-log";

# Save the form elements to disk
if (open LOG, ">>$logfile")
{
    # Lock the filehandle
    my $status = flock LOG, LOCK_EX;
    die "Cannot lock '$logfile': $! " unless $status;

    # Print $name, $email separated by a tab
    print LOG "$name\t$email\n";
```

```
    # Unlock the filehandle
    flock LOG, LOCK_UN;

    # Close the log
    close LOG;

    # Send them to the thank-you page
    print $query->redirect("/thanks.html");
}


# If we could not open the logfile, print an error message
else
{
    print $query->header;
    print $query->start_html(-title => "Error!");
    print "<p>Could not open logfile for writing: '$!'</p>";
    print $query->end_html;
}
```

14.4.3 Advertising referrals

Web sites often record information each time a user clicks on an advertising banner. You can easily accomplish this with a CGI program: The banners all link to this CGI program, rather than directly to the advertisers' sites. The CGI program is invoked with a **target** parameter whose value is the URL of the advertiser's site. Once the CGI program has recorded all necessary information, it redirects the user's browser to the content of the **target** parameter:

```
#!/usr/bin/perl -T
# filename: redirect-url.pl

use strict;
use warnings;
use CGI;
use Fcntl qw(:flock);

# Turn on autoflush
$| = 1;

# Set the logfile
my $logfile = "/web/redirect-log.txt";
```

```perl
# Create an instance of CGI
my $query = new CGI;

# Get the URL to which the user should be redirected
my $target = $query->param("target") || "";

# Log the target to disk
if (open LOG, ">>$logfile")
{
    # Lock the file
    flock LOG, LOCK_EX;

    # Get the current date and time
    my $now = localtime(time);

    # Log the current time, the URL, and the user's remote address
    print LOG "$now\t$target\t", $query->remoto_addr, "\n";

    # Unlock the file
    flock LOG, LOCK_UN;

    close LOG;
}
# If the logfile could not be opened, die elegantly
else
{
    # Send a warning to the HTTP server's error log
    warn("Error opening '$logfile': $!");

    # Send something to the user's browser
    print $query->header("text/html");
    print $query->start_html(-title => "Error");

    print "<p>There was an error opening the logfile '$logfile'.
            Please contact the webmaster.</p>";

    print $query->end_html;

    die "Could not open $logfile: $! ";
}

# Now redirect to the target
print $query->redirect($target);
```

14.5   More CGI methods

This section describes some other popular methods that the CGI module provides. Complete documentation is available from `perldoc CGI`.

14.5.1   remote_host

This method returns the name of the computer that send the HTTP request. If the hostname is unavailable, the IP address is returned. For example, if an HTTP request from the-tech.mit.edu invoked a CGI program, that program can include the following code:

```
my $remote = $query->remote_host;
```

$remote will contain either the-tech.mit.edu or 18.187.1.156, which refer to the same computer. HTTP servers are often configured to track IP addresses, rather than hostnames, because of the additional load such hostname lookups cause.

If the user connects through another computer (known as a "proxy"), then remote_host will reflect the proxy's address rather than the HTTP client's address.

14.5.2   script_name

The script_name method returns the URL of the currently executing CGI program. It does not include any information about the program's state.

CORE Note

script_name *is different from* $0, *the built-in variable that returns the name of the current program.* $0 *contains the name of the program, whereas* script_name *returns its URL.*

For example:

```
#!/usr/bin/perl -T
# filename: whoami.pl

use strict;
use warnings;
use CGI;
```

```perl
# Turn on autoflush
$| = 1;

my $query = new CGI;
print $query->header("text/html");

# Get the current script's name
my $script_name = $query->script_name();

# Start the HTML output
print $query->start_html(-title => "Who am I?");

# Print both variables
print "<p>'\$0' = '$0'</p>\n";
print "<p>'\$script_name' = '$script_name'</p>\n";

print $query->end_html;
```

CORE Approach

Use script_name *and* self_url, *rather than a program's name. This avoids problems if the program is ever renamed.*

14.5.3   referer

HTTP requests often include a **Referer** header—misspelled since the standards were first written—naming the URL from which the user arrived on your site. If the page foo.com contains a link to bar.com, clicking on the link to bar.com will send a header that looks like this:

```
Referer: foo.com
```

By checking a site's "referer logs," companies can know whether their advertising on nytimes.com gave more responses than on cnn.com. Some referer logs are integrated into the main HTTP server logfile, whereas others place it into another file.

14.6   Conclusion

In this chapter, we looked at one of the most popular uses for Perl, writing CGI programs. In particular, we discussed:

- The standards for HTTP, URL, and HTML,

- How CGI programs work,

- Using the CGI module,

- How to configure Apache to execute CGI programs,

- Debugging CGI programs, and

- Redirection.

In the next chapter, we will build on what we have seen so far, creating more advanced CGI programs.

ADVANCED CGI PROGRAMMING

Topics in This Chapter

- Registration
- Cookies
- Personalization
- Graphic output
- Templates

Chapter 15

In the last chapter, we wrote some CGI programs that produce simple dynamic content for the Web. This chapter takes things one step further, demonstrating more sophisticated CGI programs, as well as the techniques that professional programmers need.

We begin with a look at a simple application-level registration mechanism. Many Web sites want to restrict content to users, and this is one common way to accomplish that.

Next, we look at HTTP cookies, variables that an HTTP server can set in the user's browser. Cookies are a vital part of any sophisticated Web application, particularly when we want to personalize content for individual users. We then touch on personalization, which uses cookies to track a user's identity and preferences.

Many programmers forget that CGI programs can create graphics, as well as HTML files. We look at the GD module, which lets us draw graphics from within our programs, and at the PNGgraph module, which makes it trivial to create sophisticated charts.

Finally, we look at templates, which allow us to mix Perl code with static HTML. This allows us to create dynamically generated pages, without forcing designers to read and modify our code.

By the end of this chapter, you should understand how CGI programs can be integrated into your Web site, performing a variety of tasks that static files could not accomplish on their own.

15.1   User registration

Many Web sites restrict some or all of their content to registered users. While this can become a complicated affair, such functionality can be implemented using two simple CGI programs: One which captures registration information, and another which displays content to authenticated users.

15.1.1   The registration program

Our registration program, `register.pl`, expects three parameters from an HTML form—username, email, and password. If these parameters are defined, and if no other user has chosen this user name, `register.pl` saves the user's information in a DBM file (see Section 8.3.1). DBM is not as popular or portable as XML, but it is far faster than a TAB-delimited file, particularly as the number of records grows.

So that we can store a hash of hashes, we will use MLDBM. MLDBM requires an underlying DBM library in order to store and retrieve information; in this case, we use Tie::DB_Lock, which takes care of locking issues for us. We also use the Storable back-end storage mechanism, rather than the default of Data::Dumper.

It is almost always a bad idea to store unencrypted passwords on a filesystem. We will thus use the Digest::MD5 module from CPAN (see Section 1.6) to encrypt the password with a one-way hash function. Programs will always be able to tell if the user has entered the correct password by encrypting the user's input with MD5 and comparing it with the stored results. However, there is no realistic way to retrieve the original password once it has been encrypted.

Finally, `register.pl` imports the :standard tag group from CGI, which defines a large number of subroutines that define HTML tags. For example, the p subroutine surrounds its arguments with <p> and </p>, while the h1 subroutine turns its argument into an <h1> headline. These subroutines can often make the code more legible and make it less likely that you will forget to close a tag if you're entering them manually:

```
#!/usr/bin/perl -T
# filename: register.pl
```

```perl
use strict;
use warnings;
use CGI qw(:standard);                # import HTML subroutines
use MLDBM qw(Tie::DB_Lock Storable);  # MLDBM with locking
use Digest::MD5 qw(md5_hex);          # Use MD5 to encrypt passwords

# Turn on autoflush
$| = 1;

# Give each parameter a long name, for error messages
my %parameters = ("username" => "Your username",
                  "email" => "Your e-mail address",
                  "password" => "Your password");

# Where will the user info file be?
my $userinfo = "/web/users.dbm";

# Create an instance of CGI
my $query = new CGI;

# Send a MIME header
print $query->header("text/html");

# ------------------------------------------------------------
# Check to ensure that each parameter has a value
# ------------------------------------------------------------
my $error_message;
foreach my $parameter_name (sort keys %parameters)
{
    $error_message .= li($parameters{$parameter_name})
        unless $query->param($parameter_name);
}

# If $error_message is defined, tell the user what was missing
if ($error_message)
{
    print $query->start_html(-title => "Missing information!");
    print h1("Missing information");
    print p("You were missing the following required fields",
            "from your form:");
    print ol($error_message);
    print $query->end_html;
    exit;
}

# ------------------------------------------------------------
```

```perl
# Write information to the DBM file, if this is a new user
# ------------------------------------------------------------
my %users;
tie %users, "MLDBM", $userinfo, 'rw' or die "Error tying \%user: $! ";

my $username = $query->param('username');

# If there is already a user by this name, then exit
if (exists $users{$username})
{
    print $query->start_html(-title => "Username is taken!");
    print h1("Username is taken");
    print p("Sorry, but someone else has already taken the user name ",
            "'$username'.  Please try again.");
    print $query->end_html;

    untie %users;

    exit;
}

# Encrypt the password with MD5, and then save it
$users{$username}->{password} = md5_hex($query->param('password'));

# Save the e-mail address as plaintext
$users{$username}->{email} = $query->param('email');

untie %users;

# ------------------------------------------------------------
# If everything went well, send some feedback to the user
# ------------------------------------------------------------

print $query->start_html(-title => "Successful registration!");
print h1("Success");
print p("You have successfully been registered.");
print $query->end_html;
```

The following HTML form allows users to register on our Web site:

```html
<html>
    <head>
        <title>Register with our site</title>
    </head>

    <body>
```

```
<h1>Register with our site</h1>

<p>Please fill out the following information:</p>

<form method="POST" action="/cgi-bin/register.pl">

<table>
    <tr>
        <td>Requested user name</td>
        <td><input type="text" name="username"></td>
    </tr>

    <tr>
        <td>E-mail address</td>
        <td><input type="text" name="email"></td>
    </tr>

    <tr>
        <td>Password</td>
        <td><input type="text" name="password"></td>
    </tr>
</table>

<input type="submit" value="Register">

</form>
    </body>
</html>
```

15.1.2　The downloading program

Once users have registered, we will let them view or download restricted content using a second HTML form and CGI program.

CORE Note

The only difference between viewing and downloading is the Content-type *header. A browser normally tries to display any content that it can, saving to disk only those documents for which it has no viewer. To force a browser to download a document, set a* Content-type *of* `application/octet-stream`.

This HTML form asks people for their user name, password, and the name of the file they would like to retrieve:

```html
<html>
    <head>
        <title>Download software</title>
    </head>

    <body>

        <h1>Download software</h1>

        <form method="POST" action="/cgi-bin/download.pl">
            <table>
                <tr>
                    <td>Your username:</td>
                    <td><input type="text" name="username"></td>
                </tr>
                <tr>
                    <td>Your password:</td>
                    <td><input type="text" name="password"></td>
                </tr>
                <tr>
                    <td>File to download</td>
                    <td>
                        <select name="file">
                            <option value="file1.gz">File #1
                            <option value="file2.gz">File #2
                        </select>
                    </td>
                </tr>
            </table>
            <input type="submit">
        </form>
    </body>
</html>
```

download.pl is the CGI program that this form invokes, sending username, password, and file parameters. It opens the registration file with MLDBM in read-only mode and compares an encrypted version of the user's password with the stored value. If they match, download.pl returns the contents of the file.

CORE Security

Notice how download.pl *strips leading* . *and* / *characters from the filename to ensure that malicious users do not try to download files from elsewhere on the disk.*

```perl
#!/usr/bin/perl -T
# filename: download.pl

use strict;
use warnings;
use CGI qw(:standard);                 # import HTML subroutines
use CGI::Carp qw(fatalsToBrowser);     # show errors on the browser
use MLDBM qw(Tie::DB_Lock Storable);   # Use MLDBM with locking
use Digest::MD5 qw(md5_hex);           # Use MD5 to encrypt passwords

$ENV{PATH} = '';

# Turn on autoflush
$| = 1;

# Create an instance of CGI
my $query = new CGI;

# Where will the user info file be?
my $userinfo = "/web/users.dbm";

# ----------------------------------------------------------------
# Check user authentication
# ----------------------------------------------------------------

my %users;
tie %users, "MLDBM", $userinfo, 'rw' or die "Error tying \%user: $! ";

my $username = $query->param('username');
my $password = $query->param('password');

# ----------------------------------------------------------------
# If there is already a user by this name, then exit
# ----------------------------------------------------------------
if ((exists $users{$username}) and
    ($users{$username}->{password} eq md5_hex($password))) {
    # Get the filename
    my $form_file = $query->param('file');

    # Remove leading / and . characters
    $form_file =~ s|^[/.]+||g;

    # Open the file
    open FILE, "/downloads/$form_file" or
        die "Cannot open '$form_file' for reading: $! ";
```

```
    # Send a header indicating binary data
    print $query->header("application/octet-stream");

    # Now send the file
    print while (<FILE>);

    # Close the file, and exit
    close FILE;
}


# --------------------------------------------------------------
# If the username isn't registered, or if the password doesn't match,
# then give the user an error message.
# --------------------------------------------------------------
else
{
    print $query->header("text/html");

    print $query->start_html(-title => "Bad user name/password combination");
    print h1("Bad user name/password combination");
    print p("Sorry, but this user name/password combination does not exist. ");
    print $query->end_html;
}

untie %users;
```

15.2   Cookies

HTTP is a stateless protocol, meaning that every transaction exists in a contextual vacuum. While this reduces the protocol's complexity, it means that sites cannot keep track of specific users for more than a single transaction. One common solution to this problem is HTTP cookies, which allow servers to store state information on the user's computer.

15.2.1   Cookies provide state

When a server returns an HTTP response, it can send one or more Set-Cookie headers along with it. Each Set-Cookie header sets a single name–value pair on the user's computer, known as a "cookie." For example, the response to an HTTP request to www.lerner.co.il includes the following header:

```
Set-Cookie: AF_SID=8cc93b183ff002c325526c76c64c4eaf; path=/
```

The Web browser associates this name–value pair with the site that sent it. The next time it sends an HTTP request to www.lerner.co.il—and cookies are only returned to the domain that set them—it includes a Cookie header, reminding the server of the cookie value:

```
Cookie: AF_SID=8cc93b183ff002c325526c76c64c4eaf
```

Cookies would appear to turn HTTP into a stateful protocol and seem like a programmer's panacea. However, there are reasons to be cautious when using cookies:

- HTTP connections are normally unencrypted, allowing eavesdroppers to read your cookie values. If a Web application uses a cookie as the sole identifying characteristic, a hijacked cookie is at least as good as a user's password.

- Cookies are often stored in a text file on the user's filesystem. Users can edit and delete cookies without a browser.

- Browsers may drop cookies without warning.

- Cookies trace the activity from a browser, not from a user. If a user browses from another computer, cookies from the first computer may not be available.

Despite these failings, cookies have become an essential part of most Web applications because they are so convenient.

15.2.2   Reading and writing cookies

To retrieve a cookie from within a CGI program, use the CGI object's cookie method:

```
my $value = $query->cookie('cookie_name');
```

While we retrieve cookies and parameters in similar ways, there is no overlap between the two namespaces. We can thus have a username parameter and a wholly unrelated username cookie.

To set a cookie on the user's browser, we create a new cookie object with the cookie method. We then insert the cookie object into the HTTP response headers with the header method. Until now, we have only used header to send a Content-type header; as this example demonstrates, it is sending a Set-Cookie header along with the Content-type:

```
# Create the cookie
my $cookie = $query->cookie(-name => "cookie_name",
                            -value => "cookie_value",
                            -expires => "+1y");

# Send the HTTP response headers (Content-Type and Set-Cookie)
print $query->header(-type => "text/html",
                     -cookie => $cookie);
```

This cookie has a name of cookie_name, a value of cookie_value, and
an expiration date one year after it is set. (perldoc CGI lists the symbols
used in setting relative expiration dates.)

To set multiple cookies in the same HTTP response, use an anonymous
array reference:

```
# Create the first cookie
my $cookie1 = $query->cookie(-name => "cookie_name_1",
                             -value => "cookie_value_1",
                             -expires => "+1y");

# Create the second cookie
my $cookie2 = $query->cookie(-name => "cookie_name_2",
                             -value => "cookie_value_2",
                             -expires => "+1y");

# Send the HTTP response headers (Content-Type and Set-Cookie)
print $query->header(-type => 'text/html',
                     -cookie => [$cookie1, $cookie2]);
```

The following CGI program uses a cookie as a counter. Each invocation
of the CGI program increments the counter for that particular browser:

```
#!/usr/bin/perl -T
# filename: increment.pl

use strict;
use warnings;
use CGI qw(:standard);
use CGI::Carp qw(fatalsToBrowser);
```

```perl
# Create an instance of CGI
my $query = new CGI;

# Grab the existing cookie value
my $counter = $query->cookie(-name => "counter");

# Create a new cookie with the updated value
my $cookie = $query->cookie(-name => "counter",
                            -value => $counter + 1,
                            -expires => "+1y");


# Send the cookie with the header
print $query->header(-type => "text/html",
                     -cookie => $cookie);

# Now print some HTML
print $query->start_html(-title => "Cookie counter");
print p("The counter is now $counter");
print $query->end_html;
```

The following program, cookie-input.pl, sets two cookies (name and color) based on user input. Notice how we use || to let parameters override cookies. You can also see how the CGI module's subroutines for creating HTML allow us to set attributes, passing a hash reference as the initial argument:

```perl
#!/usr/bin/perl -T
# filename: cookie-input.pl

use strict;
use warnings;
use CGI qw(:standard);
use CGI::Carp qw(fatalsToBrowser);

# Create an instance of CGI
my $query = new CGI;

# -------------------------------------------------------------
# Get user input
# -------------------------------------------------------------
```

```perl
# Get the user's name
my $name = $query->param("name") ||
    $query->cookie(-name => "name") || "";

# Get the user's favorite color
my $color = $query->param("color") ||
    $query->cookie(-name => "color") || "";

# -------------------------------------------------------------
# Create cookies
# -------------------------------------------------------------

# Create a new cookie with the name
my $name_cookie = $query->cookie(-name => "name",
                                 -value => $name,
                                 -expires => "+10m");

# Create a new cookie with the color
my $color_cookie = $query->cookie(-name => "color",
                                  -value => $color,
                                  -expires => "+10m");

# -------------------------------------------------------------
# Send headers and HTML
# -------------------------------------------------------------

# Send the cookie with the header
print $query->header(-type => "text/html",
                     -cookie => [$name_cookie, $color_cookie]);

# Now print some HTML
print $query->start_html(-title => "Cookies!");
print p("Enter a new value to change the cookie.");

my $script_name = $query->script_name();
print qq{<form method="POST" action="$script_name">\n};

# Insert the name in this text field
print p("Your name:", textfield({name => "name", value => $name}));

# Insert the color in this text field
print p("Your favorite color:", textfield({name => "color",
                                            value => $color}));
```

```perl
# Create a "submit" button
print qq{<p><input type="submit"></p>\n};

# Finish the HTML form and page
print "</form>\n";
print $query->end_html;
```

15.2.3   *Personalization*

One of the chief uses for cookies is in personalization, or creating a Web site that caters specifically to the needs of each user. For instance, we can allow the user to register his or her name and preferred background color. If every page on our site uses CGI, then we can insert the user's name and background color on every page:

```perl
#!/usr/bin/perl -T
# filename: personalized-homepage.pl

use strict;
use warnings;
use CGI qw(:standard);
use CGI::Pretty;
use CGI::Carp qw(fatalsToBrowser);

# Create an instance of CGI
my $query = new CGI;

# Get the user's name, or use a generic "you"
my $name = $query->cookie(-name => "name") || "you";

# Get the user's favorite color
my $color = $query->cookie(-name => "color") || "white";

# Send the cookie with the header
print $query->header(-type => "text/html");

# Now print some HTML
print $query->start_html(-title => "Home page for $name",
                         -bgcolor => $color);
```

```
print p("Welcome to your home page, $name!");
print $query->end_html;
```

While the preceding program works, it does not scale well: Using each cookie for a value, a site that stores 100 pieces of information about its users would need to exchange 100 cookies with each HTTP transaction. Section 16.3 demonstrates how we can get around this problem by storing user information in a relational database, and keeping the user's ID number (i.e., primary key) in a cookie.

15.3   Graphic output

Most CGIs return their content in HTML-formatted text. But CGI programs can produce any sort of content, including graphics. Using modules from CPAN, we can easily create on-the-fly graphics.

15.3.1   Dynamic graphics

The simplest way to produce dynamic graphics is with the GD library. GD (available from CPAN, described in Section 1.6) is written by Lincoln Stein, and is based on the gd library in C, written by Thomas Boutell. (More information on gd is available on the Web at http://www.boutell.com/gd/.) GD produces images in PNG, a non-proprietary format that all modern browsers support.

To produce an image, a program creates an instance of GD::Image, and invokes methods on that object to change colors, draw arcs, draw and fill shapes, and finally render the image. GD describes colors in terms of the primary colors (red, green, and blue), each of which can be given a strength between 0 and 255, such that white is (255,255,255) and black is (0,0,0). The png method returns a PNG-formatted image based on whatever drawing you have done.

The following CGI program demonstrates GD's abilities, producing a circle of random diameter, with a randomly generated outline color and a randomly generated fill color:

```
#!/usr/bin/perl -T
# filename: graphics-output.pl

use strict;
use warnings;
```

```perl
use CGI;
use CGI::Carp qw(fatalsToBrowser);
use GD;

# Create an instance of CGI
my $query = new CGI;

# Send a MIME header indicating that we will send a PNG
print $query->header(-type => "image/png",
                     -expires => "-1h");

# Create a new image object
my $image = new GD::Image(100,100);

# ---------------------------------------------------------------
# Set colors and sizes
# ---------------------------------------------------------------
my $white = $image->colorAllocate(255,255,255);

my $outline_color = $image->colorAllocate(int rand 255,
                                          int rand 255, int rand 255);

my $fill_color = $image->colorAllocate(int rand 255,
                                      int rand 255, int rand 255);

my $size = int rand 100;

# Set the background to white
$image->transparent($white);

# ---------------------------------------------------------------
# Draw a circle of color $outline_color
$image->arc(50,50,$size,$size,0,360, $outline_color);

# Fill the circle with $fill_color
$image->fill(50,50, $fill_color);

# Convert the image to a PNG, and send it to
# the user's browser
print $image->png;
```

Because the output of the preceding program is a graphic, it can be used instead of a static image filename in an HTML <img> tag. For example, if this program is in /cgi-bin/graphics-output.pl, we can display it in a page of HTML as follows:

```
<html>
    <head><title>Displaying graphic</title></head>

    <body>
        <h1>Displaying graphic</h1>
        <p>This is a dynamically included graphic:</p>
        <img src="/cgi-bin/graphics-output.pl">
        <p>The above was a dynamically included graphic.</p>
    </body>
</html>
```

15.3.2   Creating graphs

While GD is an extremely useful tool, it is too low-level for many applications. The PNGgraph module (available on CPAN; see Section 1.6), written by Steve Bonds and based on an earlier module written by Martien Verbruggen, makes it easy to graph data in a variety of formats, including pie charts and bar graphs.

PNGgraph defines a number of similar object classes, each of which defines a different type of graph. To draw a simple graph that connects the data points with a line, create an instance of PNGgraph::linespoints and invoke its plot method. plot expects an array of array references describing the data. Each array reference should be of the same length; the first contains the x-axis labels, and the others describe the data points.

You can change the default graphing parameters by invoking the set method before plot. There are dozens of different parameters that let you customize the graphs; see `perldoc PNGgraph` for a full list.

The following program draws a simple chart describing high and low temperatures for a given city:

```perl
#!/usr/bin/perl -T
# filename: create-graph.pl

use strict;
use warnings;
use CGI;
use CGI::Carp qw(fatalsToBrowser);
use PNGgraph::linespoints;

# Create a new instance of CGI
my $query = new CGI;
```

```perl
# Send an appropriate header, for a PNG image
# that should never be cached
print $query->header(-type => "image/png",
                     -expires => "-1d");


# Create a new instance of PNGgraph::bars
my $graph = new PNGgraph::linespoints(500,500);

# Define our data points
my @data = ([qw(Sunday Monday Tuesday Wednesday
              Thursday Friday Saturday)],
          [20, 21, 23, 25, 29, 32, 20],
          [15, 18, 16, 22, 25, 28, 16]);

# Set some parameters for our graph
$graph->set(x_label => 'Day',
            y_label => 'Temperature (in Celsius)',
            title => 'Local Temperature',
            y_tick_number    => 10,
            y_label_skip     => 2);


# Create a legend
$graph->set_legend(qw(High Low));

# Plot the chart, and send it to the user's browser
print $graph->plot(\@data);
```

The following variation on **create-graph.pl** allows users to set the values via an HTML form. Because we allow the user to choose the type of graph that will be drawn, we must import all three classes with **use**, invoking the appropriate **new** method:

```perl
#!/usr/bin/perl -T
# filename: choose-graph.pl

use strict;
use warnings;
use CGI;
use PNGgraph::linespoints;
use PNGgraph::pie;
use PNGgraph::bars;
```

```perl
# Create a new instance of CGI
my $query = new CGI;

# ------------------------------------------------------------
# Create the graph
# ------------------------------------------------------------

# What kind of graph do we want?
my $graph;
my $graph_type = $query->param("type") || "";

if ($graph_type eq "linespoints")
  {
    $graph = new PNGgraph::linespoints(500,500);
  }
elsif ($graph_type eq "bars")
  {
    $graph = new PNGgraph::bars(500,500);
  }
elsif ($graph_type eq "pie")
  {
    $graph = new PNGgraph::pie(500,500);
  }
else
  {
    print $query->header;
    print $query->dump;
    die "I don't know what a '$graph_type'! chart is: $! ";
}

# Turn each of the seven parameters into a value, with a default
# value of 0
my @points = map { $query->param("point-$_") or 0}  (1 .. 7);

# Define our legend and data points
my @data = ([(1 .. 7)],
            \@points);

my $image = $graph->plot(\@data);

# ------------------------------------------------------------
# Now send output to the user's browser
# ------------------------------------------------------------
```

```
# Send an appropriate header, for a PNG image
# that should never be cached
print $query->header(-type => "image/png",
                     -length => length($image));

# Plot the chart, and send it to the user's browser
print $image;
```

Here is an HTML form that allows users to send input values to the preceding CGI program:

```
<html>
<head><title>Choose a graph</title></head>

<body>
    <h1>Choose a graph</h1>

    <form method="GET" action="/cgi-bin/choose-graph.pl">
        <p>Type of graph:
            <input type="radio" name="type"
                value="linespoints" checked> Linespoints
            <input type="radio" name="type" value="bars"> Bars
            <input type="radio" name="type" value="pie"> Pie
        </p>

        <p>Data points:
            <input type="text" size="3" name="data-1">
            <input type="text" size="3" name="data-2">
            <input type="text" size="3" name="data-3">
            <input type="text" size="3" name="data-4">
            <input type="text" size="3" name="data-5">
            <input type="text" size="3" name="data-6">
            <input type="text" size="3" name="data-7">
        </p>

        <input type="submit" value="Create graph">
    </form>
</body>
</html>
```

15.4   Templates

As we have seen, CGI programs can create HTML documents without much trouble at all. However, putting the content inside of a program can cause problems. Even the smallest design detail can only be changed by modifying the CGI program, which frustrates everyone involved in a project. One of the most popular techniques for avoiding this problem is the "template," in which Perl code and HTML coexist.

Most templates work on the same principle: Code inside of the template is marked off with special characters. Anything inside of those characters is passed to Perl, which replaces the code with the result of its evaluation. The rest of the template is kept verbatim. This section describes how you can use templates on your Web site, mixing HTML and Perl in the same document.

15.4.1   *Working with* Text::Template

The Text::Template module, written by Mark-Jason Dominus and available on CPAN (see Section 1.6), is one of the most popular Perl templating systems. Text::Template takes a text file as input, and produces a text string as output.

The following template contains one Perl fragment, which begins with [[and ends with]]. The rest of the document is HTML:

```
<html>
    <head>
        <title>Templates in action</title>
    </head>

    <body>
        <p>The result of 2+2 is: [[ 2+2; ]]</p>
    </body>
</html>
```

Text::Template evaluates the expression 2+2 inside of the brackets and replaces them with the result of evaluating the expression (i.e., 4). What's left is a static HTML document that can be sent to the user's browser:

```
<html>
    <head>
        <title>Templates in action</title>
    </head>

    <body>
        <p>The result of 2+2 is: 4</p>
    </body>
</html>
```

The constructor for Text::Template takes several parameters, each of which affects the way in which input or evaluation is handled. We will set the TYPE parameter to FILE, indicating that the template resides in a file. We will then set the SOURCE parameter to the template's filename, and the DELIMITERS parameter to [[and]]. Following this, all that's left is to evaluate the template with the fill_in method, specifying that its output should be sent to STDOUT:

```perl
#!/usr/bin/perl

# template.pl, a CGI program that expects to receive the name
# of the template file in the 'filename' parameter

use strict;
use warnings;
use CGI;
use Text::Template;

# Create an instance of CGI
my $query = new CGI;

# Send an appropriate MIME header
print $query->header("text/html");

# Get the filename
my $filename = $query->param("filename");

# Remove any attempts to move up a directory
$filename =~ s|../||g;

# Get the name of the template
my $file = "/usr/local/apache/templates/$filename";
```

```
# Create an instance of template
my $template = new Text::Template(TYPE => "FILE", SOURCE => $file,
                                  DELIMITERS => [ '[[', ']]']);

# Perform the evaluation, and send the results
# to the user's browser
print $template->fill_in();
```

CORE Security

Because Text::Template *evaluates the template with* eval *(see Section 3.15), a program invoking* fill_in *cannot use the* -T *flag (see Section 13.3). For maximum security,* Text::Template *supports Perl's* Safe *module; see* perldoc Text::Template *and* perldoc Safe *for more information.*

15.4.2   Scopes and templates

A template may contain more than one Perl fragment. Lexicals only exist within a single Perl block, but global variables assigned in one fragment may be accessed in another. For example, consider the following template, in which each fragment is replaced with a text string:

```
<html>
    <head>
        <title>Multiple fragments</title>
    </head>

    <body>
        <h1>Multiple fragments</h1>

        [[
            my $x = 5;
            "x is '$x'.\n";
        ]]

        <hr>
```

```
[[
     "x is '$x'.\n";
]]

    </body>
</html>
```

The first fragment declares the lexical **$x**, and prints its value. The second fragment retrieves the value of **$x**, but since there is neither a lexical nor a global named **$x**, the resulting HTML looks as follows:

```
<html>
    <head>
        <title>Multiple fragments</title>
    </head>

    <body>
        <h1>Multiple fragments</h1>

        x is '5'.


        <hr>

        x is ''.



    </body>
</html>
```

15.4.3   print *and* $OUT

Beginning template writers often use print inside of Perl fragments. It is almost always a mistake to do this: As we saw in Section 3.1.1, print returns TRUE or FALSE, and not the string that it sent to the specified filehandle. Text::Template replaces a block of Perl with the value of its last line, ignoring your calls to print. If print happens to be the final line of your template, your block will be replaced with 1 or 0.

Luckily, there is a better way: Text::Template defines $OUT, which is automatically reset at the top of each block. By assigning or appending to $OUT, we can modify the output of our template:

```
{
    $OUT .= qq{<a href="$url">$title</a>};
}
```

15.5   Conclusion

In this chapter, we took a closer look at CGI programs, which allow us to add dynamic content to the Web with a minimum of effort. In this chapter, we built on what we learned in the previous chapter, building a number of sample Web applications that would be impossible with CGI. In particular, we examined:

- How to require that users register in order to retrieve a file via HTTP or FTP,

- How to use cookies to get around the Web's inherent statelessness,

- How to create simple personalized sites based on cookies,

- How to create images and graphs on the fly, and

- How templates make life easier for designers and programmers.

WEB/DATABASE
APPLICATIONS

Topics in This Chapter

- Retrieving and displaying stock values
- Sending and receiving postcards
- Personalization with databases

Chapter 16

Web/database applications are the latest and most important trend on today's Internet. Whether your applications are meant to be accessed directly by end users, or if they are "Web services" that interact with other programs, modern programmers must know how to create such programs.

This chapter introduces Web/database applications, which use relational databases to create dynamic Web content. Our examples are all CGI programs, but the principles easily extend to other technologies such as mod_perl (see Chapter 17), as well as the open-source PHP language, Java Server Pages and servlets, and Microsoft's Active Server Pages.

We begin by producing a stock monitor, including an on-the-fly chart of a user's holdings. We then look at a postcard-sending application that allows users to send personalized greetings to friends and relatives. Finally, we expand our discussion of personalization from Section 15.2.3, looking at ways in which databases can help.

16.1 Stock updates

Our first set of Web/database applications will let us look at the performance of one stock in a variety of ways.

All of these examples assume that another program, perhaps invoked on a regular basis by the Unix `cron` utility, inserts stock information into two tables: StockSymbols, which associates a stock symbol with an artificial primary key, and StockValues, which describes a stock's value at a particular moment in time. StockSymbols changes only when a new company is listed on the stock exchange, merges with another company, or changes its symbol. StockValues, by contrast, is continuously updated, with one new row added each minute for every symbol in StockSymbols. Here is how we can define the tables in PostgreSQL:

```
CREATE TABLE StockSymbols (
    symbol_id   SERIAL   NOT NULL,
    symbol      TEXT     NOT NULL  CHECK (symbol <> ''),
    PRIMARY KEY(symbol_id),
    UNIQUE(symbol)
);
```

```
CREATE TABLE StockValues (
    symbol_id       INT4        NOT NULL  REFERENCES StockSymbols,
    value_timestamp TIMESTAMP   NOT NULL  DEFAULT NOW(),
    stock_value     NUMERIC(6,2) NOT NULL  CHECK (stock_value > 0),
    UNIQUE(symbol_id, value_timestamp)
);
```

```
CREATE INDEX stock_timestamp_index ON StockValues (value_timestamp);
CREATE INDEX stock_value_index ON StockValues (stock_value);
```

Let's now create some stock symbols:

```
INSERT INTO StockSymbols (symbol) VALUES ('ABC');
INSERT INTO StockSymbols (symbol) VALUES ('DEF');
```

And now we'll insert some rows into StockValues. I'm assuming here that the values of symbol_id are 1 and 2, corresponding to the symbols we entered:

```
INSERT INTO StockValues
    (symbol_id, value_timestamp, stock_value)
VALUES (1, '2001-Oct-01', 100);

INSERT INTO StockValues
    (symbol_id, value_timestamp, stock_value)
VALUES (1, '2001-Oct-02', 110);

INSERT INTO StockValues
    (symbol_id, value_timestamp, stock_value)
VALUES (1, '2001-Oct-03', 120);

INSERT INTO StockValues
    (symbol_id, value_timestamp, stock_value)
VALUES (1, '2001-Oct-04', 130);

INSERT INTO StockValues
    (symbol_id, value_timestamp, stock_value)
VALUES (1, '2001-Oct-05', 75);

INSERT INTO StockValues
    (symbol_id, value_timestamp, stock_value)
VALUES (2, '2001-Oct-01', 30.5);

INSERT INTO StockValues
    (symbol_id, value_timestamp, stock_value)
VALUES (2, '2001-Oct-02', 50.5);

INSERT INTO StockValues
    (symbol_id, value_timestamp, stock_value)
VALUES (2, '2001-Oct-02', 123);
```

Now that we have populated these tables with some data, we can write Web applications that draw on these values.

16.1.1   Retrieving simple values

Our first example CGI program is quite simple: It takes the value of the symbol parameter and uses that to retrieve the latest value of that symbol from StockValues. To retrieve just the latest value, we request the results in chronological order (ORDER BY value_timestamp), and then use SQL's LIMIT modifier to request only the first row from the result set:

```perl
#!/usr/bin/perl -T
# filename: lookup.pl

use strict;
use warnings;
use CGI qw(:standard);
use CGI::Carp qw(fatalsToBrowser);
use DBI;

# Create a new instance of CGI
my $query = new CGI;

# Connect to the database.
my $username = 'reuven';
my $password = '';
my $dbh = DBI->connect("DBI:Pg:dbname=coreperl", $username, $password,
                       { 'AutoCommit' => 1, 'RaiseError' => 1}) ||
    die "Error connecting: '$DBI::errstr' ";

# Get the symbol the user wants
my $symbol = $query->param("symbol") ||
    die "No symbol provided; try again.";

# All symbols are uppercase, so let's translate it
$symbol = "\U$symbol";

# Retrieve the current value of that symbol from the
# database
my $sql =  "SELECT V.stock_value, V.value_timestamp ";
   $sql .= " FROM StockSymbols S, StockValues V ";
   $sql .= "WHERE S.symbol = ? ";
   $sql .= "  AND S.symbol_id = V.symbol_id ";
   $sql .= "ORDER BY V.value_timestamp DESC ";
   $sql .= "LIMIT 1";

# Prepare the query
my $sth = $dbh->prepare($sql);

# Execute the query
$sth->execute($symbol);
```

```perl
# We only expect one row, so we don't need a while loop
my ($value, $timestamp) = $sth->fetchrow_array();

# Now produce some output
print $query->header("text/html");

# Indicate success
if ($value and $timestamp)
{
print $query->start_html(-title => "Value for '$symbol'");
print h1("Value for '$symbol'"),
    p("The value is $value (last updated at $timestamp).");
}

# Indicate failure
else
{
    print $query->start_html(-title => "No value for '$symbol'");
    print h1("No value for '$symbol'"),
        p("No value was available for the stock with",
          "a value of $symbol.  Perhaps you spelled it wrong?");
}

print $query->end_html;

# We're done with this statement
$sth->finish;

# Disconnect from the database
$dbh->disconnect;
```

As this example demonstrates, a Web/database application does not have to be very different from its command-line counterpart. Indeed, the only real differences here are the way in which the symbol parameter is passed and the fact that the result is sent in HTML.

16.1.2 Stock history

For many investors, a stock's current price is less important than the context of that price. We can modify lookup.pl such that it retrieves a range of values, specified by the parameters start_date and end_date.

This program contains the most dynamically built SQL query to date, since it has to take into account the possibility that both start_date and

end_date are optional. If start_date is present, we include a check for the
beginning date, using SQL's >= operator, which works with dates as well
as with numbers. By the same token, the presence of end_date forces a
check with the SQL <= operator. Here is one possible implementation of
lookup-range.pl:

```perl
#!/usr/bin/perl -T
# filename: lookup-range.pl

use strict;
use warnings;
use CGI qw(:standard);
use CGI::Carp qw(fatalsToBrowser);
use DBI;

# Create a new instance of CGI
my $query = new CGI;

# Connect to the database.
my $username = 'reuven';
my $password = '';
my $dbh = DBI->connect("DBI:Pg:dbname=coreperl", $username, $password,
                       { 'AutoCommit' => 1, 'RaiseError' => 1}) ||
    die "Error connecting: '$DBI::errstr' ";

# Get the symbol the user wants
my $symbol = $query->param("symbol") ||
    die "No symbol provided; try again.";

# All symbols are uppercase, so let's translate it
$symbol = "\U$symbol";

# Get the starting and ending dates
my $start_date = $query->param("start_date");
my $end_date = $query->param("end_date");

# Create the query
my $sql =  "SELECT V.stock_value, V.value_timestamp ";
$sql .= "  FROM StockSymbols S, StockValues V ";
$sql .= "  WHERE S.symbol = ? ";
$sql .= "    AND S.symbol_id = V.symbol_id ";

my @placeholders = ();
if ($start_date)
```

```perl
{
    $sql .= "AND V.value_timestamp >= ? ";
    push @placeholders, $start_date;
}

if ($end_date)
{
    $sql .= "AND V.value_timestamp <= ? ";
    push @placeholders, $end_date;
}

$sql .= "ORDER BY V.value_timestamp";

# Prepare the query
my $sth = $dbh->prepare($sql);

# Execute the query
$sth->execute($symbol, @placeholders);

# Send results to the user's browser
print $query->header("text/html");
print $query->start_html(-title => "Values for $symbol");

print h1("Values for $symbol");

print '<table border="1">';
print th(['Date', 'Value']);

# Get the results from the row
while (my $rowref = $sth->fetchrow_arrayref)
{
    my ($value,$date) = @$rowref;
    print Tr(td([$date, $value]));
}

print "</table>\n";

# No results?  Something is wrong!
if (! $sth->rows())
{
    print p("No results were available.  Either no data has been",
            "entered for", b($symbol), "during this period, ",
            "or the symbol was misspelled.");
}
```

```
print $query->end_html();

# Finish the statement
$sth->finish;

# Disconnect from the database
$dbh->disconnect;
```

Notice how the preceding program uses the subroutines Tr, th, and td from the CGI module to create a table without having to use explicit HTML tags. (Tr is capitalized so as not to conflict with the built-in tr function, as described in Section 5.13.) As the program demonstrates, we can pass an array reference to th or td, such that each value is placed in its own cell. See perldoc cgi for more information about the HTML-generating subroutines in the :standard tag group.

16.1.3   Stock history with graph

Although lookup-range.pl returns useful information, the format is rather ugly. However, we can use PNGgraph to create charts of the user's requested symbol and range. As we retrieve information from $sth->fetchrow_arrayref, we stuff the information into @dates and @values. We then create the array @data using references to @dates and @values, and pass this to PNGgraph's plot method:

```
#!/usr/bin/perl -T
# filename: graph-range.pl

use strict;
use warnings;
use CGI qw(:standard);
use CGI::Carp qw(fatalsToBrowser);
use DBI;
use PNGgraph::linespoints;

# Declare our arrays of values and dates
my (@values, @dates);

# Create a new instance of CGI
my $query = new CGI;

# Connect to the database
my $username = 'reuven';
```

```perl
my $password = '';
my $dbh = DBI->connect("DBI:Pg:dbname=coreperl", $username, $password,
                       { 'AutoCommit' => 1, 'RaiseError' => 1}) ||
    die "Error connecting: '$DBI::errstr' ";

# Get the symbol the user wants
my $symbol = $query->param("symbol") ||
    die "No symbol provided; try again.";

# All symbols are uppercase, so let's translate it
$symbol = "\U$symbol";

# Get the starting and ending dates
my $start_date = $query->param("start_date");
my $end_date = $query->param("end_date");

# Create the query
my $sql =   "SELECT V.stock_value, V.value_timestamp ";
$sql .= "  FROM StockSymbols S, StockValues V ";
$sql .= "  WHERE S.symbol = ? ";
$sql .= "    AND S.symbol_id = V.symbol_id ";

my @placeholders = ();
if ($start_date)
{
    $sql .= "AND V.value_timestamp >= ? ";
    push @placeholders, $start_date;
}

if ($end_date)
{
    $sql .= "AND V.value_timestamp <= ? ";
    push @placeholders, $end_date;
}

$sql .= "ORDER BY V.value_timestamp";

# Prepare the query
my $sth = $dbh->prepare($sql);

# Execute the query
$sth->execute($symbol, @placeholders);

# Create an instance of PNGgraph::linespoints
my $graph = new PNGgraph::linespoints(500,500);
```

```
# Get the results from the row
while (my $rowref = $sth->fetchrow_arrayref)
{
    # Get the value from the row
    my ($value,$date) = @$rowref;

    # Add this new value, date pair to the arrays
    push @values, $value;
    push @dates, $date;
}

# If nothing was returned, create an error message
if ($sth->rows() == 0)
{
    print $query->header("text/html");
    print $query->start_html(-title => "No data available");
    print h1("No data available"),
        p("Sorry, but no data is available for $symbol",
          "during this period.");
    print $query->end_html;
    exit;
}

# Define our data points
my @data = (\@dates, \@values);

# Set some parameters for our graph
$graph->set(x_label => 'Dates',
            y_label => 'Stock prices',
            title => "Stock prices for $symbol");

# Send an appropriate MIME header
print $query->header("image/png");

# Plot the chart, and send it to the user's browser
print $graph->plot(\@data);

# Finish with this statement
$sth->finish;

# Disconnect from the database
$dbh->disconnect;
```

16.1.4   Comparing stock performance

Finally, we can further modify graph-range.pl such that it retrieves the
values of two symbols—named in parameters symbol1 and symbol2—and

graphs both of them. This program demonstrates how easily we can compare not only two stocks, but also the performance of a stock against an index such as the Dow Jones Industrial Average:

```perl
#!/usr/bin/perl -T
# filename: graph2-range.pl

use strict;
use warnings;
use CGI qw(:standard);
use CGI::Carp qw(fatalsToBrowser);
use DBI;
use PNGgraph::linespoints;

# Declare our arrays of values and dates
my (@values1, @values2, @dates);

# Create a new instance of CGI
my $query = new CGI;

# Connect to the database
my $username = 'reuven';
my $password = '';
my $dbh = DBI->connect("DBI:Pg:dbname=coreperl", $username, $password,
                       { 'AutoCommit' => 1, 'RaiseError' => 1}) ||
    die "Error connecting: '$DBI::errstr' ";

# Get the symbols the user wants
my $symbol1 = $query->param("symbol1") ||
    die "No symbol1 provided; try again.";

my $symbol2 = $query->param("symbol2") ||
    die "No symbol2 provided; try again.";

# All symbols are uppercase, so let's change them
$symbol1 = "\U$symbol1";
$symbol2 = "\U$symbol2";

# Get the starting and ending dates
my $start_date = $query->param("start_date");
my $end_date = $query->param("end_date");

# Create the query
my $sql =  "SELECT S.symbol, V.stock_value, V.value_timestamp ";
```

```perl
$sql .= "  FROM StockSymbols S, StockValues V ";
$sql .= "  WHERE (S.symbol = ? OR S.symbol = ?)";
$sql .= "    AND S.symbol_id = V.symbol_id ";

my @placeholders = ();
if ($start_date)
{
    $sql .= "AND V.value_timestamp >= ? ";
    push @placeholders, $start_date;
}

if ($end_date)
{
    $sql .= "AND V.value_timestamp <= ? ";
    push @placeholders, $end_date;
}

$sql .= "ORDER BY V.value_timestamp";

# Prepare the query
my $sth = $dbh->prepare($sql);

# Execute the query
$sth->execute($symbol1, $symbol2, @placeholders);

# Create an instance of PNGgraph::linespoints
my $graph = new PNGgraph::linespoints(500,500);

# Get the results from the row
while (my $rowref = $sth->fetchrow_arrayref)
{
    my ($symbol, $value, $date) = @$rowref;

    # Add this new value, date pair to the arrays
    push @values1, ($symbol eq $symbol1 ? $value : "");
    push @values2, ($symbol eq $symbol2 ? $value : "");
    push @dates, $date;
}

# If nothing was returned, create an error message
if ($sth->rows() == 0)
{
    print $query->header("text/html");
    print $query->start_html(-title => "No data available");
```

```
    print h1("No data available"),
        p("Sorry, but no data is available for $symbol1 or",
          "$symbol2 during this period.");
    print $query->end_html;
    exit;
}


# Define our data points
my @data = (\@dates, \@values1, \@values2);

# Set some parameters for our graph
$graph->set(x_label => 'Dates',
            y_label => 'Stock prices',
            title => "Price of $symbol1 vs. $symbol2");

# Send an appropriate MIME header
print $query->header("image/png");

# Plot the chart, and send it to the user's browser
print $graph->plot(\@data);

# Finish with this query statement
$sth->finish;

# Disconnect from the database
$dbh->disconnect;
```

16.2   Postcards

Many sites offer users the opportunity to send each other postcards via the
Internet. We can write our own postcard-sending application with two CGI
programs. The first program creates a postcard, storing data in a table and
sending the recipient an e-mail notification. Another CGI program reads the
postcard, using a unique identifier that helps to ensure privacy.

16.2.1   Creating the table

Before we can write the applications, we must define the database in which
the information is stored. Luckily, our application can be handled with a
single Postcards table and an index to speed up searches:

```
CREATE TABLE Postcards (
    id               SERIAL    NOT NULL,
    oid_md5          CHAR(32)  NOT NULL,
    sender_name      TEXT      NOT NULL  CHECK (sender_name <> ''),
    sender_email     TEXT      NOT NULL  CHECK (sender_email ~ '@'),
    recipient_name   TEXT      NOT NULL  CHECK (recipient_name <> ''),
    recipient_email  TEXT      NOT NULL  CHECK (recipient_email ~ '@'),
    message          TEXT      NOT NULL  CHECK (message <> ''),
    message_datetime TIMESTAMP NOT NULL  DEFAULT NOW(),
    UNIQUE(sender_email, recipient_email, message_datetime),
    UNIQUE(oid_md5),
    PRIMARY KEY(id)
);

CREATE INDEX postcard_oid_md5_index ON Postcards (oid_md5);
```

The only unusual-looking column is oid_md5, which we will use to retrieve
postcards. Although we could simply pass an id parameter to a retrieval CGI
program, this would allow users to view other people's postcards simply by
changing a numeric argument. We can give our users a bit more privacy
by computing the MD5 digest on the oid (which is not guaranteed to be
unique within a PostgreSQL installation, but which is close enough for most
medium-size systems), plus a hidden string. We will store this value in
Postcards and index it, allowing users to retrieve their postcards quickly,
easily, and securely. MD5 sums are not guaranteed to be unique, but are
close enough that we can impose a UNIQUE restriction without concern.

16.2.2   Sending postcards

Now we can create a program to send postcards. After checking its inputs,
send-postcard.pl performs an INSERT to add a new postcard, performs
an UPDATE to set the MD5 value for that postcard, and sends e-mail to the
recipient's address with retrieval instructions. The INSERT and UPDATE are
placed within a single transaction, so as to avoid the potential for problems:

```
#!/usr/bin/perl -T
# filename: send-postcard.pl

use strict;
use warnings;
use CGI qw(:standard);
use CGI::Carp qw(fatalsToBrowser);
use DBI;
use Mail::Sendmail;
use Digest::MD5 qw(md5_hex);
```

```perl
# We will compute the MD5 of our phrase (which is secret) with the ID,
# making it hard for someone to retrieve another user's postcard.
my $secret_md5_phrase = 'coreperl-postcards';

# Create a new instance of CGI
my $query = new CGI;

# Connect to the database
my $username = 'reuven';
my $password = '';
my $dbh = DBI->connect("DBI:Pg:dbname=coreperl", $username, $password,
                       { 'AutoCommit' => 1, 'RaiseError' => 1}) ||
    die "Error connecting: '$DBI::errstr' ";

# Get the user's input
my $oid_md5 = 'dummy data';
my $sender_name = $query->param("sender_name");
my $sender_email = $query->param("sender_email");
my $recipient_name = $query->param("recipient_name");
my $recipient_email = $query->param("recipient_email");
my $message = $query->param("message");

# Start a transaction
$dbh->begin_work();

# Create the query
my $sql = "INSERT INTO Postcards ";
$sql   .= "(oid_md5, sender_name, sender_email, ";
$sql   .= " recipient_name, recipient_email, message) ";
$sql   .= "VALUES (?, ?, ?, ?, ?, ?) ";

# Prepare the query
my $sth = $dbh->prepare($sql);

# Execute the query
$sth->execute($oid_md5, $sender_name, $sender_email, $recipient_name,
              $recipient_email, $message);

# Now get the OID of the row we just inserted
my $new_row_oid = $sth->{pg_oid_status};

# Generate a hard-to-crack value from the new row's OID and our phrase
$oid_md5 = md5_hex($new_row_oid . $secret_md5_phrase);

# Now UPDATE the value in the database
my $update_sql = "UPDATE Postcards ";
$update_sql .= "  SET oid_md5 = ? ";
$update_sql .= "  WHERE oid = ? ";

my $rows_modified =
    $dbh->do($update_sql, undef, $oid_md5, $new_row_oid);

# Commit the transaction if our row was affected
if ($rows_modified)
```

```
{
    $dbh->commit();
}
else
{
    $dbh->rollback();
}

# Now send e-mail to the recipient, using Mail::Sendmail
my $mail_message = "You have received an electronic postcard.  To \n";
$mail_message   .= "retrieve it, go to \n\n";
$mail_message   .= "http://www.coreperl.com/cgi-bin/read-postcard.pl?id=$oid_md5\n";

my %mail = (To => $recipient_email,
            From => $sender_email,
            Message => $mail_message);

sendmail (%mail);

# Send an appropriate MIME header
print $query->header("text/html");

print $query->start_html(-title => "Postcard was sent successfully");

print h1("Successfully sent"),
    p("Your postcard was sent successfully.",
      "The recipient has been sent an e-mail message with",
      "directions for retrieving it. You can look at the card",
      a({href => "/cgi-bin/read-postcard.pl?id=$oid_md5"},  "here."));

print $query->end_html;

# Finish with this statement handle
$sth->finish;

# Disconnect from the database
$dbh->disconnect;
```

Here is an HTML form that submits its inputs to send-postcard.pl,
making it easier to create a postcard:

```
<html>
    <head>
        <title>Send a postcard</title>
    </head>

    <body>
        <h1>Send a postcard</h1>

        <form method="POST" action="/cgi-bin/send-postcard.pl">
```

```
<table>
<tr>
    <td><p>Sender's name:</p></td>
    <td><input type="text" name="sender_name"></td>
</tr>

<tr>
    <td><p>Sender's e-mail address:</p></td>
    <td><input type="text" name="sender_email"></td>
</tr>

<tr>
    <td><p>Recipient's name:</p></td>
    <td><input type="text" name="recipient_name"></td>
</tr>

<tr>
    <td><p>Recipient's e-mail address:</p></td>
    <td><input type="text" name="recipient_email"></td>
</tr>

<tr>
    <td><p>Message:</p></td>
    <td><textarea name="message"
        rows="10" cols="50"></textarea></td>
</tr>
</table>

<input type="submit" value="Send postcard">

</form>
</body>
</html>
```

16.2.3   Reading postcards

Our postcard-reading program takes a single parameter (id) and uses it to perform a SELECT into our table on the oid_md5 column. This lookup is

fast, because declaring it UNIQUE implicitly created an index on it. Once
we retrieve the appropriate row, we display it for the user to see:

```perl
#!/usr/bin/perl -T
# filename: read-postcard.pl

use strict;
use warnings;
use CGI qw(:standard);
use CGI::Carp qw(fatalsToBrowser);
use DBI;

# Create a new instance of CGI
my $query = new CGI;

# Connect to the database
my $username = 'reuven';
my $password = '';
my $dbh = DBI->connect("DBI:Pg:dbname=coreperl", $username, $password,
                       { 'AutoCommit' => 1, 'RaiseError' => 1}) ||
    die "Error connecting: '$DBI::errstr' ";

# Get the symbol the user wants
my $id = $query->param("id") || die "You must provide an ID!";

# Create the query
my $sql = "SELECT sender_name, sender_email, ";
$sql .= "recipient_name, recipient_email, message ";
$sql .= "FROM Postcards ";
$sql .= "WHERE oid_md5 = ?";

# Prepare the query
my $sth = $dbh->prepare($sql);

# Execute the query
$sth->execute($id);

# Send an appropriate MIME header
print $query->header("text/html");

# Get the results from the row
while (my $rowref = $sth->fetchrow_arrayref)
{
    # Get the value from the row
    my ($sender_name, $sender_email, $recipient_name,
        $recipient_email, $message) = @$rowref;
```

```
    print $query->start_html(-title =>
                              "Postcard from $sender_name ($sender_email)");
    print h1("Postcard from $sender_name ($sender_email)"),
        p("You have a postcard, $recipient_name ($recipient_email)",
          pre($message));
}

if ($sth->rows == 0)
{
    print $query->start_html(-title => "No postcard found");
    print h1("No postcard found"),
        p("No postcard was found with id '$id'.  Please try again.");
}

print $query->end_html;

# Finish with this statement
$sth->finish;

# Disconnect from the database
$dbh->disconnect;
```

16.3   Personalization with databases

In Section 15.2.3, we saw how Web sites can create personalized pages by saving user information in cookies. However, each cookie can only store one value. A common solution is to store user information in a relational database, storing unique identifiers in the user's cookie.

The easiest and most obvious solution would be to store the user's primary key in a cookie. However, this leads to significant privacy and security issues. A user could pretend to be someone else simply by changing the cookie. One solution is to use the MD5 digest of the primary key along with a secret phrase, as we saw in `send-postcard.pl`.

It might be tempting to use the MD5 sum itself as a primary key. But this would make our tables much larger than necessary—on disk and when joining them in memory—since MD5 returns results that are between 16 and 32 bytes long. It is a better idea to use an integer (such as PostgreSQL's SERIAL type) for the primary key, but an MD5 sum as a unique identifier.

So there will be a one-to-one correspondence between the (small) primary key and the (large, hard to forge or crack, and unique) MD5 signature. The former will be used in all internal database operations, and the latter will be stored in a cookie on the user's browser.

16.3.1   The user table

Now that we know how the user's ID will be passed to the server, we can begin to define one or more tables of user information. For the purposes of our examples, we will store everything in the following **UserInfo** table:

```
CREATE TABLE UserInfo (
    id              SERIAL    NOT NULL,
    oid_md5         CHAR(32)  NOT NULL,
    first_name      TEXT      NOT NULL   CHECK (first_name <> ''),
    last_name       TEXT      NOT NULL   CHECK (last_name <> ''),
    birthday        DATE      NOT NULL,
    bgcolor         CHAR(7)   NOT NULL   DEFAULT '#000000',
    email           TEXT      NOT NULL   CHECK (email ~ '@'),
    password        TEXT      NOT NULL   CHECK (password <> ''),

    PRIMARY KEY(id),
    UNIQUE(oid_md5),
    UNIQUE(email)
);
CREATE INDEX first_name_index ON UserInfo (first_name);
CREATE INDEX last_name_index ON UserInfo (last_name);
CREATE INDEX password_index ON UserInfo (password);
```

CORE Note

Colors in HTML are specified using the pound character (#) followed by six hex digits (two for red, two for blue, and two for green). We thus define bgcolor *as a seven-character, fixed-width column.*

16.3.2   Preferences registration

With our **UserInfo** table defined, we can write a registration program:

```
#!/usr/bin/perl -T
# filename: save-personalization.pl

use strict;
use warnings;
use CGI qw(:standard);
use CGI::Carp qw(fatalsToBrowser);
```

```perl
use DBI;
use Digest::MD5 qw(md5_hex);

# Create a new instance of CGI
my $query = new CGI;

# Connect to the database
my $dbusername = 'reuven';
my $dbpassword = '';
my $dbh = DBI->connect("DBI:Pg:dbname=coreperl", $dbusername, $dbpassword,
                       {
                         'AutoCommit' => 1, 'RaiseError' => 1}) ||
    die "Error connecting: '$DBI::errstr' ";

$dbh->trace(3, "/tmp/dbi-trace.txt");

# We will compute the MD5 of our phrase (which is secret) with the ID,
# making it hard for someone to retrieve another user's postcard.
my $secret_md5_phrase = 'coreperl-personalization';

# ------------------------------------------------------------
# Get the user's inputs, or die trying
# ------------------------------------------------------------

my $first_name = $query->param("first_name") ||
    die "No first name provided.";
my $last_name = $query->param("last_name") ||
    die "No last name provided.";
my $background_color = $query->param("background_color") ||
    die "No background color provided.";
($background_color =~ /^\#[a-z0-9]{6}$/i) ||
    die qq{Background color "$background_color" has non-hex digits!};
my $email = $query->param("email") ||
    die "No e-mail address provided.";
my $password = $query->param("password") ||
    die "No password provided.";
my $birthday = $query->param("birthday") ||
    die "No birthday provided.";

my $oid_md5 = 'dummy md5 value';

# ------------------------------------------------------------
# Insert a new row, first checking that the e-mail address is new.
# ------------------------------------------------------------

# Start a new transaction, which ends with commit() or rollback()
$dbh->begin_work();
```

```perl
my $sql = "SELECT id FROM UserInfo ";
$sql .= "  WHERE email = ? ";

my $sth = $dbh->prepare($sql);
$sth->execute($email);

# If there is even a single matching row, then we exit with an error.
die "This e-mail address has already been taken! "
    if ($sth->fetchrow_arrayref);

# Finish with this statement
$sth->finish;

# Insert the new row
$sql = "INSERT INTO UserInfo ";
$sql    .= "(oid_md5, first_name, last_name, email, ";
$sql    .= " bgcolor, birthday, password) ";
$sql    .= "VALUES (?, ?, ?, ?, ?, ?, ?) ";

my $insert_sth = $dbh->prepare($sql);
$insert_sth->execute($oid_md5, $first_name, $last_name, $email,
                     $background_color, $birthday, $password);

# Get the ID that was inserted
my $new_row_oid = $insert_sth->{pg_oid_status};

# We're done with this sth
$insert_sth->finish();

# -------------------------------------------------------------
# Generate a hard-to-crack value from the new row's OID and our phrase
# -------------------------------------------------------------
$oid_md5 = md5_hex($new_row_oid . $secret_md5_phrase);

# Now set our MD5 ID
$sql  = "UPDATE UserInfo ";
$sql .= "SET oid_md5 = ? ";
$sql .= "WHERE oid = ? ";

# Prepare the query
my $rows_modified = $dbh->do($sql, undef, $oid_md5, $new_row_oid);

# If no rows were affected, then we have to indicate an error to the user
if ($rows_modified eq "0E0")
{
    $dbh->rollback();
```

```
    # Send an appropriate MIME header, with the cookie
    print $query->header(-type => "text/html");

    # Now print a failure message
    print $query->start_html(-title => "Personalization failed!");
    print h1('Personalization failed!');
    print p('Sorry, but we could not register you.  Please try again.');
    print $query->end_html;
}

# Commit the transaction, set a cookie on the user's browser, and
# send a "success" response
else
{
    $dbh->commit();

    # -----------------------------------------------------------
    # Set a cookie on the user's browser with the MD5 signature
    # -----------------------------------------------------------
    my $cookie = $query->cookie(-name => "userid",
                                -value => $oid_md5,
                                -expires => "+1y");

    # Send an appropriate MIME header, with the cookie
    print $query->header(-type => "text/html",
                         -cookie => $cookie);

    # -----------------------------------------------------------
    # Now we can send the HTML response
    # -----------------------------------------------------------
    print $query->start_html(-title => "Personalization complete!",
                             -bgcolor => $background_color);
    print h1("Personalization complete!");
    print p("Welcome to our site, $first_name $last_name!");
    print $query->end_html;
}

# Disconnect from the database
$dbh->disconnect;
```

16.3.3 Using the cookie

Now that the user's browser contains a cookie with the MD5 value, any number of Web/database applications can use the cookie to retrieve information about the user. The following program, personal-db-homepage.pl, creates a simple home page for the user with information from the UserInfo table.

The personalized home page has a background color of the user's choosing and displays a special message on the user's birthday. Because the birthday field includes a year, we cannot simply compare birthday with NOW(). Rather, we must extract the month and date from birthday and the built-in CURRENT_DATE value with PostgreSQL's to_char function, comparing the results of those strings:

```perl
#!/usr/bin/perl -T
# filename: personal-db-homepage.pl

use strict;
use warnings;
use CGI qw(:standard);
use CGI::Carp qw(fatalsToBrowser);
use DBI;

# Declare some variables that we will use later
my $first_name;
my $last_name;
my $bgcolor;
my $today_is_birthday;

# Create a new instance of CGI
my $query = new CGI;

# Connect to the database
my $username = 'reuven';
my $password = '';
my $dbh = DBI->connect("DBI:Pg:dbname=coreperl", $username, $password,
                        { 'AutoCommit' => 1, 'RaiseError' => 1}) ||
    die "Error connecting: '$DBI::errstr' ";

# Get the user's MD5 cookie
my $oid_md5 = $query->cookie(-name => "userid");

# Send an appropriate MIME header
print $query->header(-type => "text/html");

# If the user has an ID, then grab personalization information
# from the database
if ($oid_md5)
{
    # Create the query
    my $sql = "SELECT first_name, last_name, bgcolor, ";
    $sql    .= "( to_char(birthday, 'Day Mon D') = ";
    $sql    .= "  to_char(CURRENT_DATE, 'Day Mon D')) as today_is_birthday ";
    $sql    .= "FROM UserInfo ";
    $sql    .= "WHERE oid_md5 = ?";
```

```perl
    # Prepare the query
    my $sth = $dbh->prepare($sql);

    # Execute the query
    $sth->execute($oid_md5);

    # Grab data about this user
    while (my @row = $sth->fetchrow)
    {
        ($first_name, $last_name,
         $bgcolor, $today_is_birthday) = @row;
    }

    # Print a "welcome back" page for this user
    print $query->start_html(-title => "Welcome back!",
                             -bgcolor => $bgcolor);
    print h1("Welcome back!"),
        p("You are: $first_name $last_name");

    # Congratulate the user if today is the birthday
    if ($today_is_birthday)
    {
        print p(b("Happy birthday!"));
    }

    # Finish this SQL statement
    $sth->finish;
}

# Otherwise, welcome people to the site, and point them toward
# personalization
else
{
    print $query->start_html(-title => "Welcome!");
    print h1("Welcome!"),
        p("You can personalize the site by going to",
          a({href => "/personalize-form.html"}, "this page"), "."),
            p("Enjoy!");
}
print $query->end_html;

# Disconnect from the database
$dbh->disconnect;
```

16.3.4   Restoring cookies

When a user buys a new computer or installs a new browser, the cookie that we set will effectively disappear. Web sites that use cookies for personalization must therefore provide a way for users to restore lost cookies.

The simplest approach is to let the user enter his or her e-mail address and password into an HTML form. (The e-mail address was declared UNIQUE in the definition of UserInfo, so there is no danger of mistakenly restoring the wrong user's cookie.) For example:

```perl
#!/usr/bin/perl -T
# filename: restore-cookie.pl

use strict;
use warnings;
use CGI qw(:standard);
use CGI::Carp qw(fatalsToBrowser);
use DBI;

# Declare a variable for the user's ID
my $oid_md5;

# Create a new instance of CGI
my $query = new CGI;

# Connect to the database
my $dbusername = 'reuven';
my $dbpassword = '';
my $dbh = DBI->connect("DBI:Pg:dbname=coreperl", $dbusername, $dbpassword,
                       { 'AutoCommit' => 1, 'RaiseError' => 1}) ||
    die "Error connecting: '$DBI::errstr' ";

$dbh->trace(3, "/tmp/dbi-trace.txt");

# Get the email and password that were entered
my $email = $query->param("email");
my $password = $query->param("password");

# Make sure that both were entered
unless ($email and $password)
{
    print $query->header("text/html");
    print $query->start_html(-title => "Missing information");

    print h1("Missing information"),
        p("Your e-mail address and password are required",
          "in order to restore the cookie.  Please try again.");
```

```perl
    print $query->end_html;
    exit;
}

# Create the query
my $sql = "SELECT oid_md5 ";
$sql   .= "FROM UserInfo ";
$sql   .= "WHERE email = ? ";
$sql   .= "AND password = ?";

# Prepare the query
my $sth = $dbh->prepare($sql);

# Execute the query
$sth->execute($email, $password);

# Get the returned row, if there was one
($oid_md5) = $sth->fetchrow_array;
warn "oid_md5 = '$oid_md5'";


$sth->finish();

# If there is an ID, then restore the user's cookie
if ($oid_md5)
{
    # Create a cookie
    my $cookie = $query->cookie(-name => "userid",
                                -value => $oid_md5,
                                -path => "/cgi-bin",
                                -expires => "+1y");

    # Send an appropriate MIME header, with the cookie
    print $query->header(-type => "text/html",
                         -cookie => $cookie);

    print $query->start_html(-title => "Success!");

    print h1("Success!"),
        p("We were able to restore your registration cookie."),
            p("Go to your",
                a({href => "/cgi-bin/personal-db-homepage.pl"},
                    "personal home page"));
}
else
{
    print $query->header(-type => "text/html");
    print $query->start_html(-title => "Bad email or password");
```

```
      print h1("Bad email or password"),
          p("Sorry, but the entered email address and password",
            "were not in our records."),
                p("Try again, or",
                  a({href => "/personalize-form.html"},
                    "register."));
}


# End everything
print $query->end_html;

# Disconnect from the database
$dbh->disconnect;
```

16.3.5   Editing the profile

The preceding applications demonstrate how to add personalization to a Web site. But if we want to let them modify the information in the database, we must write a "profile editor."

The simple profile editor in this section takes advantage of the difference between GET and POST requests. Invoked using GET, our program displays the user's current profile inside of an HTML form. This form can then be modified and submitted—using POST—to the Web server. The program updates the database with the user's information, and then displays the HTML form again, such that users can make their modifications.

edit-profile.pl makes heavy use of the HTML-formatting functions provided by the CGI module, including the popup_menu and table-related functions. See perldoc CGI for a full explanation of these functions:

```
#!/usr/bin/perl -T
# filename: edit-profile.pl

use strict;
use warnings;
use CGI qw(:standard);
use CGI::Carp qw(fatalsToBrowser);
use DBI;


# -------------------------------------------------------------
# Set up some useful variables
# -------------------------------------------------------------
my ($first_name, $last_name, $bgcolor, $birthday, $email, $password);
```

```perl
my %months = (1 => "January", 2 => "February", 3 => "March",
              4 => "April",   5 => "May",       6 => "June",
              7 => "July",    8 => "August",    9 => "September",
              10 => "October", 11 => "November", 12 => "December");

my %colors = ("#000000" => "Black", "#0000FF" => "Blue",
              "#00FF00" => "Green", "#FF0000" => "Red",
              "#FFFFFF" => "White");

# Create a new instance of CGI
my $query = new CGI;

# Send an appropriate MIME header
print $query->header(-type => "text/html");

# Connect to the database
my $dbusername = 'reuven';
my $dbpassword = '';
my $dbh = DBI->connect("DBI:Pg:dbname=coreperl", $dbusername, $dbpassword,
                       {
                           'AutoCommit' => 1, 'RaiseError' => 1}) ||
    die "Error connecting: '$DBI::errstr' ";

# Get the user's ID from the cookie
my $oid_md5 = $query->cookie(-name => "userid");

# Make sure that the user has a cookie
die "You do not have a user ID! Register or restore your cookie."
    unless $oid_md5;

# -------------------------------------------------------------
# If we were invoked with POST, then UPDATE the user's row
# with the values they provided
# -------------------------------------------------------------

if ($query->request_method eq "POST")
{
    my @pairs;

    my $sql = "UPDATE UserInfo ";
    $sql   .= "    SET first_name = ?,        last_name = ?, ";
    $sql   .= "        bgcolor = ?, birthday = ?, ";
    $sql   .= "        email = ? ,            password = ? ";
    $sql   .= "WHERE  oid_md5 = ?";

    # Prepare the query
    my $sth = $dbh->prepare($sql);
```

```
    # Execute the query
    $sth->execute($query->param("first_name"),
                  $query->param("last_name"),
                  $query->param("bgcolor"),
                  $query->param("birthday"),
                  $query->param("email"),
                  $query->param("password"),
                  $oid_md5);
}

# ------------------------------------------------------------
# Regardless of whether we were invoked with POST or GET,
# we need to retrieve the user's information from the database
# with a SELECT.
# ------------------------------------------------------------

# Create the query
my $sql = "SELECT first_name, last_name, ";
$sql   .= " bgcolor, birthday, email, password ";
$sql   .= "FROM UserInfo ";
$sql   .= "WHERE oid_md5 = ?";

# Prepare the query
my $sth = $dbh->prepare($sql);

# Execute the query
$sth->execute($oid_md5);

# Grab data about this user
while (my @row = $sth->fetchrow)
{
    ($first_name, $last_name, $bgcolor,
     $birthday, $email, $password) = @row;
}

$sth->finish;

# Display an HTML form
print $query->start_html(-title => "Edit your profile");
print h1("Edit your profile");

# Point the form to ourselves
print '<Form method="POST" action="', $query->script_name, '">', "\n\n";

print "<Table>\n";
```

```
# Print some basic text fields using CGI.pm's helpful functions
print
    TR(td(p("First name")),
        td(textfield({name => "first_name", value => $first_name}))),
    TR(td(p("Last name")),
        td(textfield({name => "last_name", value => $last_name}))),
    TR(td(p("E-mail address")),
        td(textfield({name => "email", value => $email}))),
    TR(td(p("Birthday")),
        td(textfield({name => "birthday", value => $birthday}))),
    TR(td(p("Password")),
        td(textfield({name => "password", value => $password})));

# Print a list of background colors
print TR(td(p("Background color")),
        td(popup_menu({-name => "bgcolor",
                        -values => [keys %colors],
                        -default => $bgcolor,
                        -labels => \%colors})));

print "</Table>\n";

# Create a "submit" button
print '<P><input type="submit" value="Save settings"></P>', "\n";
print "</Form>\n";

print $query->end_html;

# Disconnect from the database
$dbh->disconnect;
```

16.4 Conclusion

This chapter introduced the idea of Web/database applications, which combine server-side Web applications with relational databases. As we saw, Perl's CGI and DBI modules make it easy and straightforward to create sophisticated applications in a short amount of time. The programs in this chapter demonstrated:

- How to read information from a database into a CGI program,

- How to write a CGI program that produces graphic output, based on information in a database,

- How to create a simple postcard system, and

- How to create a personalized Web site, in which users' preferences are stored in a database.

MOD_PERL

Topics in This Chapter

- mod_perl installation and configuration

- Writing handlers

- Apache::Registry

- Apache::DBI

- Apache::Session

Chapter 17

The last few chapters demonstrated how easily we can create dynamic Web content and Web/database applications with CGI programs. But anyone who has written CGI programs can attest, there's one major problem with CGI: It is terribly slow.

Luckily, users of the Apache HTTP server have the option of using mod_perl, which places a complete copy of Perl inside of Apache. This makes it possible to use Perl modules to create Web/database applications without creating any additional processes.

After discussing the mod_perl installation process, we look at a variety of Perl modules for creating custom content. We also look at the Perl modules Apache::DBI (which keeps database connections open for an additional performance gain), Apache::Session (which allows us to keep track of a single user's session information), and Apache::Registry (which speeds up legacy CGI programs).

By the end of this chapter, you should understand how mod_perl can help you to write Web applications, how to write such applications, and how to integrate it into a Web site that creates dynamic content from a database.

17.1   Installing and configuring mod_perl

mod_perl (written by Doug MacEachern) places a copy of Perl inside of your Apache HTTP server. Once installed, mod_perl makes it possible for you to change Apache's default behavior using Perl modules, rather than compiled modules written in C. Perl modules written for mod_perl are executed within the Apache process, saving the overhead of starting a new process for each invocation of a CGI program.

17.1.1   *Advantages of* mod_perl

Compiling mod_perl into your Apache server gives you the following benefits:

- An object-oriented Perl interface to Apache's internals,

- The ability to write Perl modules that customize Apache's behavior, including generating dynamic Web content, and

- Setting configuration directives in Perl, rather than Apache's traditional name–value pairs.

The main cost associated with mod_perl is memory: An Apache server compiled with mod_perl uses significantly more memory than its non-mod_perl counterpart, and each loaded Perl module adds to its footprint. In addition, working with mod_perl restricts you to using Apache rather than sticking with a common standard such as CGI.

17.1.2   *Handlers*

When Apache receives an HTTP request, it invokes a series of subroutines known as "handlers" to parse the request and generate a response. Normally, a handler is written in C, written as part of an Apache module, and compiled into the server when it is installed. mod_perl allows us to write handler subroutines in Perl, customizing anything from authentication to content production to error logging.

Each handler type has a different name in the mod_perl world. A subroutine that generates content—dynamically or from the filesystem—is simply known as a PerlHandler, one that denies access based on IP address is known as a PerlAccessHandler, and one that modifies the way in which Apache translates URLs to filenames is known as a PerlTransHandler. A complete list of handlers is available in Stas Bekman's mod_perl guide at http://perl.apache.org/guide/.

Handlers are normally written as subroutines named handler inside of a Perl module. So when we say that a PerlHandler is Apache::Foo, we really mean that Apache::Foo::handler will be invoked every time Apache needs to produce content.

17.1.3   Installation

Installing mod_perl almost always means recompiling Apache, using source code from both http://www.apache.org and http://perl.apache.org. Detailed instructions for how to compile mod_perl are in the file named INSTALL.apaci when you unpack the mod_perl source code. Be sure to set EVERYTHING=1 during compilation if you want to use mod_perl for more than just custom content creation.

CORE Note

It is now possible to install mod_perl *without recompiling Apache, using a system known as Dynamic Shared Objects (DSO). Unfortunately, many people have experienced problems with* mod_perl *as a DSO. It is probably best to avoid this combination for the time being.*

Once mod_perl is installed, Apache returns a signature in the Server HTTP header. For example, my server (at www.lerner.co.il) returns the following Server header:

```
Server: Apache/1.3.20 (Unix) mod_perl/1.26
```

As you can see, I'm running Apache 1.3.20 on a Unix system, with mod_perl version 1.26 installed. Checking the Server header is a quick and easy way to determine if you installed or upgraded mod_perl successfully.

17.1.4   Configuration

To designate a Perl module—actually a module's handler subroutine—as a handler, we must use a combination of Apache's SetHandler directive and one of the directives defined by mod_perl. Both directives go in httpd.conf, the Apache configuration file that is placed in /usr/local/apache/conf/ by default.

For example, the following configuration gives Apache::Foo control over all dynamic content on the Web site:

```
SetHandler perl-script
PerlHandler Apache::Foo
```

The following configuration attaches Apache::Throttle to the PerlTrans Handler:

```
SetHandler perl-script
PerlTransHandler Apache::Throttle
```

We can restrict our configuration directives by enclosing them in <Directory>, <Location>, or <File> sections, described in the Apache manual (see http://httpd.apache.org/). For example, the following makes Apache::Bar responsible for access to the headerfooter directory, but nowhere else:

```
<Directory /usr/local/apache/htdocs/headerfooter>
    SetHandler perl-script
    PerlAccessHandler Apache::Bar
</Directory>
```

We can similarly restrict the effects to a single URL with a <Location> directive. The following configuration tells Apache that any URL beginning with /perl-status should be handled by Apache::Status:

```
<Location /perl-status>
    SetHandler perl-script
    PerlHandler Apache::Status
</Location>
```

17.2   Configuration directives

mod_perl defines a number of configuration directives that we can place inside of httpd.conf. This section lists several of them; a full list can be found in perldoc Apache.

17.2.1   PerlModule

Before a Perl module can be associated with a handler, we must first load it into memory with the PerlModule directive. This directive can take

```
PerlModule Apache::Foo
PerlModule Apache::Bar
```

This loads the module into memory before Apache splits into numerous child processes. In many cases, this means that the module will be shared across the various Apache processes, which can lead to significant memory savings. You should thus use PerlModule not only for every handler module, but also for every module that a handler might load with use.

Normally, PerlModule only loads modules when Apache first starts up. But by activating the Apache::StatINC module, which comes with mod_perl, you can tell Apache to compare a module's modification timestamp with the last time that it was loaded. This is a terrific help during development, saving you from having to restart Apache every time you modify a Perl module. To activate this functionality, insert the following into your `httpd.conf`:

```
PerlModule Apache::StatINC
PerlInitHandler Apache::StatINC
```

17.2.2 PerlRequire

You can define variables and otherwise execute Perl code when Apache starts up with the PerlRequire directive. This directive, which takes a filename as an argument, evaluates the contents of the file during initialization. The named file must return TRUE, or Apache will report an error:

```
PerlRequire filename.pl
```

17.2.3 *Tainting and warnings*

To activate tainting under mod_perl, you must use the PerlTaintCheck directive with a value of On. mod_perl will issue a warning if it encounters a -T flag in a module, reminding you to use PerlTaintCheck instead.

The warnings module continues to work as usual within mod_perl. However, mod_perl can activate warnings even in modules that lack a use warnings statement by giving PerlWarn a value of On.

17.2.4 PerlSetVar

The PerlSetVar directive allows us to set variables in `httpd.conf` that can be read from within our handler. For example, the following sets the variable Foo the value Bar:

```
PerlSetVar Foo Bar
```

17.3   Three simple handlers

Writing a Perl handler module is relatively straightforward:

- It is traditional to put mod_perl-related modules under the Apache:: namespace hierarchy.

- Always include use strict in a mod_perl handler to avoid accidentally defining globals. mod_perl caches global values across HTTP requests, whereas lexicals go out of scope after each request. (Globals are cached within a particular Apache process, which makes debugging such problems particularly difficult.) use strict ensures that we cannot use globals by mistake, thus avoiding memory leaks and unexpected results.

- Its handler subroutine should expect to be invoked with a single argument, the Apache request object traditionally called $r. Your module can use this object to set the Content-type response header (with $r->content_type()), send the HTTP response headers (with $r->send_http_header()), write a message to the error log ($r->log_error()), and send data to the user's browser (with $r->print()), among other things. See perldoc Apache for a full list.

- Perform whatever computation is necessary, including opening files, reading parameters sent in the user's HTTP request, and communicating with relational databases.

- Return a constant (defined in Apache::Constants) telling Apache whether the handler successfully handled its assignment (OK), will allow another handler the opportunity to produce a response (DECLINED), or could not find the named file (FORBIDDEN). A Perl handler does not directly return an HTTP response code, but rather passes a result to Apache, which in turn sends a response to the user's browser.

- Do not invoke exit from within your handler unless you want to kill off the entire Apache process in which it is executing. If you must invoke exit and cannot return a simple value, use Apache::exit.

The next three sections demonstrate how easily you can change Apache's default behavior using mod_perl with some simple Perl modules.

17.3.1   Apache::HelloWorld

Here is a simple "Hello, world" handler module:

```perl
package Apache::HelloWorld;
# filename HelloWorld.pm

use strict;

# Import constants for mod_perl
use Apache::Constants qw(OK);

sub handler
{
    # Get the Apache request object
    my $r = shift;

    # Set the Content-type
    $r->content_type('text/html');

    # Send the HTTP response headers
    $r->send_http_header();

    # Send some HTML
$r->print('<html><head><title>Hello, world!</title>
</head>
<body>
<p>Hello, world!</p>
</body>
</html>');

    return OK;
}

1;
```

To install Apache::HelloWorld as the default handler for all URLs beginning with /hello-world, put the following in your `httpd.conf` and restart your Apache server:

```
PerlModule Apache::HelloWorld
<Location /hello-world>
    SetHandler perl-script
    PerlHandler Apache::HelloWorld
</Location>
```

17.3.2   Apache::HeaderFooter

We can also write handlers that interpret or modify the contents of disk files before returning them to a user's browser. For example, Apache::HeaderFooter silently inserts a header and footer at the top and bottom of all HTML files.

The handler retrieves the requested filename with $r->filename(), and determines whether it's an HTML file by invoking $r->content_type() without any arguments. To read the contents of a file, we use Apache::File, which works similarly to IO::File (see Section 9.3.6) but is faster and includes several methods that make server-side file handling relatively easy.

Also notice how the header and footer texts are set within `httpd.conf` with PerlSetVar and retrieved in our handler subroutine with the $r->dir_config() method:

```
package Apache::HeaderFooter;
# filename: HeaderFooter.pm

use strict;
use Apache::File;

# Import constants for mod_perl
use Apache::Constants qw(OK DECLINED NOT_FOUND);

sub handler
{
    # Get the Apache request object
    my $r = shift;

    # Only handle text/html files
    return DECLINED unless ($r->content_type eq "text/html");

    # Send an appropriate MIME header
    $r->send_http_header;
```

```perl
    # Send the file

my $FILE;
if (my $FILE = Apache::File->new($r->filename))
{
    # Slurp up files at once
    undef $/;

    # Grab the file's contents
    my ($contents) = (<$FILE>);

    # Set the header and footer
    my $header = $r->dir_config("header-text") ||
        "<!-- Default header -->\n";
    my $footer = $r->dir_config("footer-text") ||
        "<!-- Default footer -->\n";

    # Add a header to the top
    $contents =~ s|(<Body.*?>)|$1\n$header|i;

    # Add a footer to the bottom
    $contents =~ s|</Body>|$footer\n</Body>|i;

    # Print the contents
    $r->print($contents);

    # Close the filehandle
    $FILE->close;

    # Indicate that all went well
    return OK;
}
# produce an appropriate error message
else
{
    return NOT_FOUND;
}
}

1;
```

Once we have installed Apache::HeaderFooter, we can activate it for all of the HTML files on our server by placing the following configuration in `httpd.conf`:

```
PerlModule Apache::HeaderFooter

<Directory /usr/local/apache/htdocs>
    PerlSetVar header-text "<P>This is the header</P>"
    PerlSetVar footer-text "<P>This is the footer</P>"
    SetHandler perl-script
    PerlHandler Apache::HeaderFooter
</Directory>
```

17.3.3 Apache::IgnoreCaps

This handler, Apache::IgnoreCaps, retrieves files even when the capitalization is wrong. With Apache::IgnoreCaps installed, a user can make a capitalization error, and the server will still return the correct file.

Apache::IgnoreCaps first tests for a file's existence with -e. If -e returns FALSE, Apache::IgnoreCaps searches through the file's directory for a close match, combining **grep** with **readdir** to find files whose names are identical to the requested filename except for their capitalization.

If it finds a match, **handler** sends the file's contents to the user's browser, returning OK to Apache. Otherwise, it returns NOT_FOUND, which sends an appropriate response code and message to the user's browser.

```
package Apache::IgnoreCaps;
# filename: IgnoreCaps.pm

use strict;
use Apache::File;
use File::Basename;

# Import constants for mod\_perl
use Apache::Constants qw(OK NOT_FOUND);

sub handler
{
    # Get the Apache request object
    my $r = shift;
```

```perl
# Get the name of the file
my $filename = $r->filename;

# If no file exists by that name, iterate through
# the others in that directory, looking for one
# with different capitalization.  If the file
# exists, then no more work is necessary

if (! -e $filename)
{
    my $dirname = dirname($filename);

    if (opendir DIR, $dirname)
    {
        # Search for files in that directory
        # whose names match when ignoring case
        my @matches =
            grep { lc(basename($filename)) eq lc($_) }
                readdir(DIR);

        # Give up unless we found something
        unless (@matches)
        {
            $r->log_error("[Apache::IgnoreCaps]",
                        "No matches for $filename");
            return NOT_FOUND;
        }

        # Take the first match we got
        $filename = $dirname . "/" . $matches[0];

        # Finish with this directory
        closedir DIR;
    }

    # If we cannot open the directory, then give up
    # trying to open that directory, logging
```

```
        # an error in the process
        else
        {
            $r->log_error("Apache::IgnoreCaps cannot",
                         qq{open dir "$dirname": $! });
            return NOT_FOUND;
        }
    }

    # Send an appropriate MIME header
    $r->send_http_header;

    # Send the file
    my $FILE;
    if ($FILE = Apache::File->new($filename))
    {
        # Print the file contents
        $r->print($_) while (<$FILE>);

        # Close the file handle
        $FILE->close;

        return OK;
    }
    # produce an appropriate error message
    else
    {
        $r->log_error("[Apache::IgnoreCaps] ");
        $r->log_error(qq{Error opening file "$filename": $! });
        return NOT_FOUND;
    }

    return OK;
}

1;
```

17.4   Apache::Registry

Many Web sites have invested heavily in CGI programs over the years. The authors of mod_perl recognized that it would be difficult for such sites to switch entirely to mod_perl, and thus developed Apache::Registry. Apache::Registry is a PerlHandler that largely emulates a CGI execution environment. At the same time, it provides many of the advantages of mod_perl, including caching of programs so that they need only be compiled a single time. This means that a CGI program run under Apache::Registry will be faster than the same program run under CGI.

We configure Apache::Registry just like any other PerlHandler, giving it authority over an entire set of URLs with a Location section. Notice how we use Alias to connect the /perl-bin URL to a physical directory on the disk. We also specify the ExecCGI option, which makes it possible to execute programs in this directory:

```
<Directory /usr/local/apache/perl-bin>
    SetHandler perl-script
    PerlHandler Apache::Registry
    Options ExecCGI
</Location>
```

This configuration turns perl-bin into a directory similar to cgi-bin However, programs run under Apache::Registry are still executing via mod_perl. As a result, the -T flag is ignored, and globals are persistent across program invocations.

17.5   Useful modules

mod_perl comes with about two dozen modules, and many more are available from CPAN (see Section 1.6). This section describes four of these modules that will make it easier to work with mod_perl.

17.5.1   Apache::Request

Apache::Request is a subclass of Apache that makes it easy to handle user input. In particular, it implements a param method that works much the same as the CGI module's param method. The following module displays the values of its foo and bar parameters, which may be passed with the GET or POST method:

```
package Apache::Params;
# filename: Params.pm

use Apache::Request;

sub handler
{
    my $r = shift;
    my $request = new Apache::Request($r);

    $r->content_type("text/html");
    $r->send_http_header();

    my $foo = $request->param('foo');
    my $bar = $request->param('bar');

    # Send some HTML
    $r->print("<html><head><title>Parameters</title>
</head>
<body>
<p>Foo = '$foo'</p>
<p>Bar = '$bar'</p>
</body>
</html>");

    return OK;
}

1;
```

You can install Apache::Params on your Apache server by inserting the following into your httpd.conf:

```
PerlModule Apache::Params
<Location /params>
    SetHandler perl-script
    PerlHandler Apache::Params
</Location>
```

17.5.2   Apache::Cookie

The Apache::Cookie module makes it relatively easy to work with HTTP cookies, without having to manually read Cookie and write Set-Cookie headers. Apache::Cookie has a similar interface to CGI::Cookie, a module that provides an object-oriented interface to cookie reading and writing.

To read a cookie value, invoke fetch on the Apache::Cookie class. This returns a hash whose keys are the cookie names and whose values are cookie objects. You can get the value of an individual cookie object by invoking the value method on it.

You can similarly create a cookie (and send an appropriate Set-Cookie header to the user's browser) by invoking the new constructor, specifying the Apache object ($r), the cookie's name and value, and a number of optional parameters. To send the cookie as part of the HTTP response, you must then invoke the bake method.

The following Apache::CookieStuff module uses these methods to retrieve a cookie and reset its value with each HTTP request. The module records its progress in the Apache error log and displays the most recently received cookie value in the displayed document:

```perl
package Apache::CookieStuff;
# filename: CookieStuff.pm

use strict;
use Apache::Cookie;
use Apache::File;

# Import constants for mod_perl
use Apache::Constants qw(OK DECLINED NOT_FOUND);

sub handler
{
    # Get the Apache request object
    my $r = shift;

    # Only handle text/html files
    return DECLINED unless ($r->content_type eq "text/html");

    # ------------------------------------------------------------
    # Get the existing last_visited cookie, if it exists

    my %cookies = fetch Apache::Cookie;

    my $last_visited;
```

```perl
if (exists $cookies{'last_visited'})
{
    $last_visited = $cookies{'last_visited'}->value;
    $r->log_error("Got 'last_visited' cookie => '$last_visited'");
}
else
{
    $r->log_error("No 'last_visited' cookie");
}

# ----------------------------------------------------------
# Send a new last_visited cookie

my $current_time = localtime;

my $cookie = Apache::Cookie->new($r,
                                 -name => 'last_visited',
                                 -value => $current_time);

$r->log_error("Setting last_visited to '$current_time'");

$cookie->bake();

# ----------------------------------------------------------
# Send an appropriate MIME header
$r->send_http_header();

# Send the file
my $FILE;
if (my $FILE = Apache::File->new($r->filename))
{
    # Slurp up files at once
    undef $/;

    # Grab the file's contents
    my ($contents) = (<$FILE>);

    my $footer = "<hr>\n<p>Last visited: '$last_visited'</p>\n"
        if $last_visited;

    # Add a footer to the bottom
    $contents =~ s|</body>|$footer\n</body>|i;
```

```
        # Print the contents
        $r->print($contents);

        # Close the filehandle
        $FILE->close;

        # Indicate that all went well
        return OK;
    }
    # produce an appropriate error message
    else
    {
        return NOT_FOUND;
    }
}

1;
```

I installed Apache::CookieStuff on my system's main HTML directory with the following directives in `httpd.conf`:

```
PerlModule Apache::CookieStuff
<Directory /usr/local/apache/htdocs>
    SetHandler perl-script
    PerlHandler Apache::CookieStuff
</Directory>
```

17.5.3 Apache::DBI

A PerlHandler is significantly faster than a CGI program with the same functionality. However, one additional bottleneck stands in the way of higher performance: database access.

Connecting to a relational database is a relatively time-consuming task, because databases were not designed to handle short-term connections. Rather, they were designed to handle a small number of long-term connections, handling many queries in each connection. Because CGI programs run as independent processes from the HTTP server, there is no way for them to keep a database connection open for more than one invocation.

Apache::DBI avoids this by connecting to a database once and storing the resulting $dbh in a global variable. Because globals are cached across HTTP transactions, this means that your mod_perl handler only needs to connect to the database the first time it is executed. Better yet, Apache::DBI keeps the same interface as DBI, making its use transparent. Simply include the following line in `httpd.conf`:

```
PerlModule Apache::DBI
```

Even if $dbh is a lexical variable, Apache::DBI takes care of the connection, creating a new connection or returning a cached one as necessary.

In order to stop careless programmers from disconnecting from the database (and thus forcing a new connection), Apache::DBI also modifies DBI::disconnect, such that it only disconnects when absolutely necessary. Programs can thus continue to use connect and disconnect, without any loss of functionality or speed.

CORE Note

Apache::DBI *cannot keep a single* $dbh *for all of Apache. Rather, there is one instance of* $dbh *for each Apache child process. A Web server with five Apache child processes will thus have five database connections at a time.*

17.5.4 Apache::Session

Apache::Session makes it possible to associate one or more pieces of information with a particular user. The information is stored in a persistent back end, which can range from a relational database to a disk file. The user's session is uniquely identified with an HTTP cookie.

To store session information on the filesystem, you must tie the %session hash to Apache::Session::File, indicating where you want session information to be stored:

```
tie %session, 'Apache::Session::File', $id, {
    Directory => '/tmp/sessions',
    LockDirectory  => '/var/lock/sessions',
};
```

Once that tie is in place, you can store and retrieve an arbitrary number of scalars, including array and hash references, inside of %session. %session is created and handled independently for each user, meaning that $session{name} is guaranteed to contain the name value for the current user (if it has been set), and not for any other user.

The following module demonstrates how to use Apache::Session to store and retrieve user-specific information. Notice how we use Apache::Request to retrieve parameters, and Apache::Cookie to handle the session cookie:

```
package Apache::RememberMe;
# filename: RememberMe.pm

use strict;
use Apache::Request;
use Apache::Cookie;

# Import OK constant
use Apache::Constants qw(OK DECLINED);

sub handler
{
    # --------------------------------------------------------------
    # Get the Apache request object
    my $r = shift;

    # Create a pseudo-CGI object
    my $request = new Apache::Request($r);

    # What is my URL?
    my $self = $r->uri;

    # --------------------------------------------------------------
    # Get the existing ID cookie, if one exists

    my %cookies = fetch Apache::Cookie;

    my $id;

    if (exists $cookies{'SESSION_ID'})
    {
        $id = $cookies{'SESSION_ID'}->value;
    }

    # --------------------------------------------------------------
    # Get the user's session, if it exists, based on $id
    my %session;

    tie %session, 'Apache::Session::File', $id,
    {
     Directory => '/tmp/sessions',
     LockDirectory  => '/var/lock/sessions',
    };
```

```perl
# ------------------------------------------------------------
# Send a new last_visited cookie

my $cookie = Apache::Cookie->new($r,
                                 -name => 'SESSION_ID',
                                 -value => $session{_session_id});

$cookie->bake();

# ------------------------------------------------------------
# Set the Content-type header
$r->content_type("text/html");

# If invoked with GET, then print a form
if ($r->method eq "GET")
{
    # Now send the response headers
    $r->send_http_header;

    # Retrieve the user's e-mail address from the session database
    my $email = $session{email};

    # Now produce the HTML form
    $r->print("<html>\n");
    $r->print("<head><title>Your e-mail address</title></head>\n");
    $r->print("<body>\n");

    $r->print(qq{<form method="POST" action="$self">\n});

    # Create a text input element, displaying the
    # user's address as necessary
    $r->print("<p>Enter your e-mail address: \n");
    $r->print(qq{<input type="text" name="email" value="$email"></p>\n});
    $r->print(qq{<input type="submit">\n});

    $r->print("</body>\n");
    $r->print("</html>\n");

    # Indicate that all went well
    return OK;
}

# Handle POST, in which case someone is submitting a new value
elsif ($r->method eq "POST")
{
    # Send the HTTP response headers
    $r->send_http_header;
```

```
        # Grab the e-mail address
        my $email = $request->param("email");

        # Store the address in the user's session
        $session{email} = $email;

        # Now produce the HTML form
        $r->print("<html>\n");
        $r->print("<head><title>Updated.</title></head>\n");
        $r->print("<body>\n");
        $r->print(qq{<p>Your address was stored as "$email".</p>\n});
        $r->print("</body>\n");
        $r->print("</html>\n");

        # Indicate that all went well
        return OK;
    }

    else
    {
        # Indicate that we don't want to handle this
        return DECLINED;
    }
}

# Return "true" to the caller
1;
```

The preceding PerlHandler can be installed on its own URL with a
<Location> section:

```
PerlModule Apache::RememberMe
<Location /remember-me>
    SetHandler perl-script
    PerlHandler Apache::RememberMe
</Location>
```

Once installed, the URL /remember-me will display the user's e-mail
address as it was last entered.

17.6   Conclusion

In this chapter, we saw how to use mod_perl to create dynamic content with much higher performance than CGI. All of our standard Web/database techniques apply when writing mod_perl handlers, but we have greater access to the underlying Apache API, with much faster execution. Among other things, we looked at:

- How to configure mod_perl,

- How to write and configure Perl handlers for a variety of tasks,

- How to use the modules Apache::Request and Apache::Cookie for an easier development API,

- Using Apache::Registry to speed up legacy CGI programs, and

- How Apache::DBI improves the performance of database applications.

MASON

Topics in This Chapter

- Installing and configuring Mason

- Components

- Arguments

- Mason sections

- autohandler **and** dhandler

- Session management

Chapter 18

As we saw in the last chapter, mod_perl makes it relatively easy to create high-performance server-side Web applications. While mod_perl provides us with a rich interface to Apache and HTTP, it requires that we implement many popular features, such as Perl/HTML templates, on our own.

Many authors have tried to fill this void, and dozens of Perl/HTML templates are now available for download from CPAN. Mason is one of the most popular such systems, having been developed by Jonathan Swartz for CMP, a publisher of computer magazines.

This chapter introduces Mason and demonstrates some of the many things that you can do with it. As you will see by the end of this chapter, Mason makes it easy to create a full-featured Web site in a short time.

18.1 Mason

Mason is a set of Perl modules and mod_perl handlers that make it easy to create dynamically generated Web content and server-side Web applications. Mason divides a Web site into files known as "components," where each component consists of a Perl/HTML template or a portion thereof.

Mason translates each component into a Perl subroutine, which is then compiled, cached, and executed by mod_perl. Mason thus combines the ease of templates (see Section 15.4) with the speed of mod_perl.

18.1.1   Installing and configuring Mason

To use Mason, you must download and install the HTML::Mason package from CPAN (see Section 1.6). Next, create a configuration file—traditionally called `handler.pl`—which creates the three central Mason objects when Apache is started:

$parser The Mason parser object, which turns components into Perl subroutines.

$interp The interpreter object, which executes the component subroutines that were created by $parser. In order to perform its job, $interp must know where the Mason components reside, in a directory known as the "component root." $interp must also know the location of the Mason "data directory," into which the parsed subroutines and Mason's debugging output are placed.

$ah The ApacheHandler object, which defines the PerlHandler that routes Apache requests to the appropriate Mason component.

Here is a simple `handler.pl` file:

```perl
#!/usr/bin/perl

package HTML::Mason;

use HTML::Mason;
use strict;

# Create the parser
my $parser = new HTML::Mason::Parser;

# Create the interpreter, specifying the component root and data
# directory
my $interp = new HTML::Mason::Interp
        (parser=>$parser,
         comp_root=>'/usr/local/apache/mason/',
         data_dir=>'/usr/local/apache/masondata/');
```

```
# Create the ApacheHandler object
my $ah = new HTML::Mason::ApacheHandler (interp=>$interp);

# Our mod_perl handler asks the ApacheRequest to handle the request,
# returning the value it receives.
sub handler
{
    my $r = shift;
    return $ah->handle_request($r);
}

1;
```

To execute the contents of **handler.pl** every time Apache is started, place a line similar to the following in **httpd.conf**:

```
PerlRequire /usr/local/apache/conf/handler.pl
```

Finally, tell Apache that HTML::Mason is responsible for handling all HTTP requests to **/usr/local/apache/mason/**, the "component root" named in **handler.pl**:

```
<Directory /usr/local/apache/htdocs/mason>
    SetHandler perl-script
    PerlHandler HTML::Mason
</Directory>
```

18.1.2   Basic Mason syntax

Each Mason component consists of HTML, Perl code, or both. The simplest components consist exclusively of HTML, without any embedded Perl code. However, most components contain at least some Perl, which can be added in three ways:

- Lines beginning with a % character are considered Perl code, rather than HTML. This is typically used for control structures and conditional insertion of HTML:

  ```
  % if ($logged_in)
  <P>You are logged in.</P>
  % } else {
  <P>You are not logged in.</P>
  % }
  ```

- The pseudo-HTML tags <% and %> contain Perl code. This is normally used for variable and value interpolation inside of otherwise static HTML pages:

```
<P>The time is <% localtime time %>.</P>
<P>2 + 2 is <% 2 + 2 %>.</P>
```

- Longer sections of Perl can be placed inside of <%perl> sections. These sections are useful for performing calculations, but any return value is ignored. This means that <%perl> sections cannot be used to interpolate values into a component. However, they are often used in conjunction with the other types of Perl sections:

```
<%perl>
my $login_name = get_login_name();
</%perl>

% if ($login_name) {
<P>Hi, <% $login_name %>!</P>
% } else {
<P>Hi there!</P>
% }
```

As the preceding code demonstrates, lexical variables defined in a <%perl> section are available from anywhere within a component.

18.1.3 $r *and* $m

Every Mason component has access to $r, the Apache request object. A component may thus make use of $r to retrieve or set values having to do with Apache. Such uses of $r range from checking the HTTP request method to testing the Content-type of the returned document.

The second object, $m, is the Mason request object, and makes it possible to execute a variety of component-related tasks. For example, the $m->current_comp method returns an object corresponding to the current component, $m->scomp retrieves the HTML produced by a component, and $m->fetch_comp retrieves an object corresponding to the named component. (Component objects are of type HTML::Mason::Request, and support a wide variety of methods.)

18.1.4   <%once> *and* <%init>

In addition to regular <%perl> sections, each component may have one <%once> and one <%init> section. These work like <%perl> sections, with a few minor differences.

<%init> sections are evaluated before any <%perl> section, but following <%once>. <%init> sections are traditionally placed toward the end of a component, so that the topmost part of the component can appear as similar to standard HTML as possible. The following <%init> section assigns the $username variable a constant value:

```
<%init>
# Get the user's name
my $username = get\_user\_name();
</%init>
```

The advantage of <%init> over <%perl> is aesthetic. There is no difference between putting code in an <%perl> section at the top of a document, and in an <%init> section at its end.

A <%once> section is evaluated before <%init>, but only when the component is first loaded into Mason. This is particularly useful for defining constant variables:

```
<%once>
my @months = qw(Jan Feb Mar Apr May Jun
                Jul Aug Sep Oct Nov Dec);
</%once>
```

<%once> can also be used to initialize more complex data structures and objects. However, some objects, such as database handles, should not be defined inside of a <%once> section, because they cannot be passed to new child processes. If we have installed and configured Apache::DBI, then we can define our database-related variables in a <%once> section, connecting to the database in the <%init> section:

```
<%once>
my $dbh;    # Declare, but don't assign

# Define all of our database-related variables,
# but don't connect to the database itself
my $dbuser = 'reuven';
my $dbpassword = 'reuvenpass';
```

```
my $dsn = "DBI:Pg:dbname=coreperl";
</%once>

<%init>
$dbh = DBI->connect($dsn, $dbuser, $dbpassword,
         {'AutoCommit' => 1, 'RaiseError' => 1, 'PrintError' => 1}) ||
      die "Cannot connect: $DBI::errstr";
</%init>
```

18.1.5 Invoking components

One Mason component can invoke another component, just as one subroutine can call another. The syntax for doing so is:

```
<& other-component.comp &>
```

If this appears in a Mason component, it is replaced with the contents of `other-component.comp`. (The `.comp` suffix is my personal convention for indicating that a component is meant to be imported into another, and is not designed for public consumption.) The following component demonstrates how to insert a header (`header.comp`) and footer (`footer.comp`) into a document:

```
<html>
<head><title>Test page</title></head>

<body>
    <& header.comp &>
    <h1>Test page</h1>
    <& footer.comp &>
</body>
</html>
```

Here is a sample definition of `header.comp`:

```
<!-- beginning of header.comp -->
<hr>
<p>Test Web site for Mason</p>
<hr>
<!-- end of header.comp -->
```

To the end user, it appears as though the contents of `header.comp` were always part of the test page, rather than separate components. The HTML comments, while not necessary, make it easier to debug problems when they occur.

18.1.6   Arguments

Like CGI programs, Mason components can receive name–value pairs passed in a GET or POST request. In Mason, however, such arguments become full-fledged Perl variables, removing the need to invoke $query->param() for each value we wish to retrieve. Arguments are normally declared within an <%args> section. Such sections are traditionally placed at the bottom of a component. For example:

```
<html>
<head><title>Your name is <% $firstname %></title></head>

<body>
<p>Your first name is <% $firstname %></p>
</body>

</html>

<%args>
$firstname
</%args>
```

Invoking the preceding component with a firstname name–value pair will assign the appropriate value to the lexical $firstname variable:

```
argsdemo.html?firstname=Reuven&lastname=Lerner
```

If no firstname name–value pair is passed to the component, Mason will exit with an error, displaying a stack trace and complaining that no firstname parameter was passed. In this way, Mason tightens Perl's normally lax system for passing parameters.

To make an argument optional, place an arrow (=>) between its name and a default value:

```
<%args>
$firstname => '(No first name)'
</%args>
```

CORE Note

Placing a semicolon after the default value results in a syntax error.

When one component invokes another, it can pass one or more parameters in a list following the invoked component's name:

```
<& footer.comp, email => 'webmaster@coreperl.com' &>
```

The following version of footer.comp produces a footer that can be incorporated into another Mason component. If the caller passes an email parameter (as in the preceding example), that value will be printed in the footer:

```
<p><i>Our company's Web site</i></p>
<!-- beginning of footer.comp -->
<hr>
% if ($email) {
<address><a href="mailto:<% $email %>"><% $email %></a></address>
% }
<!-- end of footer.comp -->

<%args>
$email => undef
</%args>
```

Components can also invoke each other with the $->comp method. The following line of code is functionally equivalent to the <& &> section preceding:

```
<%perl>
$m->comp('footer.comp', email => 'webmaster@coreperl.com');
</%perl>
```

18.1.7   HTML Components

The simplest Mason components produce HTML output, much like header.comp and footer.comp. However, components can be more sophisticated than that. For example, a site might want to produce an HTML menu consisting of the latest news items that were inserted into a database. The following component produces an HTML-formatted listing of the latest entries in an Articles table:

```
<!-- beginning of show-stories.comp -->
% if (@articles) {

% foreach my $story (@articles) {
<H2><% $story->{headline} %></H2>
<P><% $story->{body} %></P>
% }

% } else {

<P>No news items.</P>

% }

<%once>
my $dbh;
</%once>

<%init>
# Connect to the database
my $user = 'news';
my $password = 'newspw';
my $dsn = "DBI:Pg:dbname=coreperl";

$dbh = DBI->connect($dsn, $user, $password,
        {'AutoCommit' => 1, 'RaiseError' => 1, 'PrintError' => 1}) ||
    die "Cannot connect: $DBI::errstr";

# Get the news items
my $sql = "SELECT headline, body, posting_date ";
  $sql .= "FROM Articles ";
  $sql .= "ORDER BY posting_date DESC ";

my $sth = $dbh->prepare($sql);
$sth->execute();

my @articles;
my $row_ref;

# Put the list of articles into @articles
while ($row_ref = $sth->fetchrow_arrayref)
{
```

```
    my ($headline, $body, $posting_date) = @$row_ref;

    push @articles, {headline => $headline,
                     body => $body,
                     posting_date => $posting_date};
}
</%init>
<!-- end of show-stories.comp -->
```

Once this component is in place, any component on the site can incorporate a "latest news items" section by including the following:

```
<& show-stories.comp &>
```

18.1.8 Value components

Because Mason components are actually Perl subroutines, they can return values rather than produce HTML. (Theoretically, a component can both return a value and produce HTML. However, this is a bad idea, and generally means that the component should be split into two separate subcomponents.) Common functionality, such as connecting to a database, can be put in one component and then invoked by other components.

A component that returns a value may do so by invoking **return** within a <%perl> section. As with a normal subroutine, the returned value may be a scalar or a list.

Although <& &> and the $m->comp() method call are equivalent when a component produces HTML, you may only use the latter syntax to retrieve a value from another component:

```
my $dbh = $m->comp("database-connect.comp");
```

You can pass arguments to an invoked component by adding name–value pairs:

```
my $dbh = $m->comp("database-connect.comp",
                   name1 => 'value1',
                   name2 => 'value2');
```

Here is one version of `database-connect.comp`, which connects to a database server and returns a database handle:

```
<%perl>
# Connect to the database
my $user = 'atfnews';
my $password = 'atfpass';
my $dsn = "DBI:Pg:dbname=coreperl";

$dbh = DBI->connect($dsn, $user, $password,
        {'AutoCommit' => 1, 'RaiseError' => 1, 'PrintError' => 1}) ||
    die "Cannot connect: $DBI::errstr";

# Now return the database handle
return $dbh;
</%perl>

<%once>
my $dbh;
</%once>
```

18.2   autohandler **and** dhandler

Mason defines two special components, autohandler and dhandler. autohandler is invoked automatically before every component, and dhandler is invoked when no component of the requested name exists.

18.3   autohandler

If a component named `autohandler` exists in a directory, Mason will invoke it instead of other components in that directory. This might not sound like a feature, but it allows sites to set common variables, create uniform designs, and conditionally invoke other components from one central location. The autohandler may invoke the originally requested component with the $m->call_next() method.

For example, here is a simple autohandler that gives each page a uniform title and footer:

```
<html>
<head>
<title>Our site </title>
```

```
</head>

<body>
    <% $m->call_next(); %>
</body>
</html>
```

The contents of other components in this directory will be inserted between the <body> and </body> tags. This means that these components only need to contain text and images:

```
<h1>This is a page</h1>

<p>Welcome to our page!</p>
```

If the user requests the preceding component, Mason will invoke the autohandler, which will in turn invoke our content component, generating a page of HTML that is sent to the user's browser. If and when we decide to change the design of our site, we only need to modify the autohandler; all of the other components can remain intact.

18.3.1   Attributes and methods

Unfortunately, the autohandler guarantees that every page on the site will have an identical <title>. Given how useful the title can be for users, it would be nice to let each component determine its own title.

We can do that by defining an "attribute" in our component. Attributes are name–value pairs designed to be retrieved by an autohandler component, defined in an <%attr> section:

```
<h1>This is a page</h1>

<p>Welcome to our page!</p>

<%attr>
title => 'Our page'
</%attr>
```

As we have seen, $m->call_next() invokes the component that was requested in the URL. We can similarly use $m->fetch_next() to retrieve a copy of an object representing the to-be-invoked component, invoking the attr method to retrieve the title attribute:

```
<html>
<head>
<title><% $m->fetch_next->attr('title') %> </title>
</head>

<body>
    <% $m->call_next(); %>
</body>
</html>
```

Because attributes can only contain static values, they are very efficient. But components sometimes need to calculate values that they will return to an autohandler. Mason components can thus define methods, minisubroutines that can be invoked from the autohandler or elsewhere:

```
<%method current_time>
return scalar localtime;
</%method>
```

Just as we can retrieve an attribute value with $m->attr(), we can invoke a method with $m->call_method(), passing the method name as a parameter.

18.3.2   dhandler

Another special component is the dhandler, which is invoked as a default when no other document matches the requested URL. dhandler can thus be used to create better error messages. This dhandler is invoked only when no other component matches the requested filename, using $r->filename() to display the missing file:

```
<HTML>
<Head><Title>Error: No such page</Title></Head>

<Body BGCOLOR="#FFFFFF">
    <P>Sorry, but the page <i><% $r->filename() %></i> does not exist.</P>
</Body>

</HTML>
```

A dhandler can also be used to provide top-level functionality without having to name a component, much as `index.html` is commonly displayed when a user requests a URL that matches a directory name. A directory with only a dhandler effectively gives control over that URL to the dhandler.

18.4   Session management

We can modify our `handler.pl` such that it uses Apache::Session (see Section 17.5.4) to create a global %session hash whose values are available within every component on our site. Once %session is in place, we can quickly and easily create applications that depend on session information, such as shopping carts and stock portfolios.

Here is a modified version of `handler.pl` that imports Apache::Session and defines %session. Notice how we use eval to test for the existence of a user's session ID; if none exists, then we create one:

```perl
package HTML::Mason;
use HTML::Mason;
use HTML::Mason::ApacheHandler;

use strict;
use vars qw(%session);

# use Apache::DBI;

# Import some modules for use in components
{
    package HTML::Mason::Commands;

    use vars qw(%session);
    use Apache::Cookie;
    use Apache::Session::File;
}

# Create the parser
my $parser = new HTML::Mason::Parser;

# Create the interpreter, specifying the component root and data
# directory
my $interp = new HTML::Mason::Interp
        (parser=>$parser,
         comp_root=>'/usr/local/apache/mason/',
         data_dir=>'/usr/local/apache/masondata/');

# Create the ApacheHandler object
my $ah = new HTML::Mason::ApacheHandler (interp=>$interp);

# Make sure that things are done as nobody, and not root!
chown ( [getpwnam('nobody')]->[2], [getgrnam('nobody')]->[2],
        $interp->files_written );

# -----------------------------------------------------------
# Create our content handler.
```

```
sub handler
{
    # Get the Apache request object
    my $r = shift;

    my $cookies = fetch Apache::Cookie;

    # Does this user have a session?  If so, then define %session
    eval {
        tie %HTML::Mason::Commands::session, 'Apache::Session::File',
            ( $cookies->{'AF_SID'} ? $cookies->{'AF_SID'}->value() : undef );
    };

    # If the user has an invalid session, then remove it.
    if ( $@ ) {
        if ( $@ =~ m#^Object does not exist in the data store# ) {
            tie %HTML::Mason::Commands::session, 'Apache::Session::File', undef;
            undef $cookies->{'AF_SID'};
        }
    }

    # If the user lacks a session cookie, then  create a new session.
    if ( !$cookies->{'AF_SID'} ) {
        my $cookie = new
            Apache::Cookie($r, -name=> 'AF_SID',
                               -value=>
                               $HTML::Mason::Commands::session{_session_id},
                               -path => '/');
        $cookie->bake;
    }

    # Handle the request
    my $status = $ah->handle_request($r);

    # Now that we have handled the request, we can untie %session
    untie %HTML::Mason::Commands::session;

    return $status;
}

1;
```

Defined in the preceding way, %session is available in all Mason components. For example, the following component expects to receive three HTML
form elements (name, address, and email), and stores then in %session:

```
<html>
<head><title>Stored!</title></head>

<body>
<h1>Stored!</h1>
```

```
<p>The session information has been stored.</p>

</body>
</html>

<%init>
# Store the inputs in %session
$session{name} = $name;
$session{address} = $address;
$session{email} = $email;
</%init>

<%args>
$name => ''
$address => ''
$email => ''
</%args>
```

18.4.1   Registration using %session

Although it is tempting to put all of the persistently stored information
about a user in %session, we would be better off storing such information in
a relational database. This ensures that a user can remove the cookie file,
or change to a different computer, without having to worry about deleting
personal information.

We will now look at a simple Mason-based user registration system that
solves these problems similarly to Section 16.3.1: Actual user information
will be stored in a relational database table with a numeric primary key.
The user's %session hash will contain the user's primary key (user_id), which
we can then use to retrieve information about the user.

18.4.2   The registration component

Our first task is to create a component that registers new users in a database
table. The component expects to receive four parameters (username, password, password_hint, and email_address). Notice how we define all of these
parameters to have a default value of undef; this allows us to catch the error
when one or more is missing. We assign $dbh by using using database-
connect.comp, as seen in Section 18.1.8:

```
% # Check to see if all of the required arguments arrived.
% unless ($username and $password and $password_hint and $email_address)
% {
<head><title>Missing information</title></head>
<body>
<h1>Missing information</h1>

<p>Sorry, but your registration information could not be saved because
it was missing the following:</p>

<ul>
% unless ($username) {
<li> Username
% }

% unless ($password) {
<li> Password
% }

% unless ($password_hint) {
<li> Password hint
% }

% unless ($email_address) {
<li> E-mail address
% }
</ul>

<p>Please go <a href="register-form.html">back</a>, and fill in the
missing information.</p>

</body>

% # ------------------------------------------------------------
% # If the inputs were valid, then add this user to the database
% # ------------------------------------------------------------
% } else {

<%perl>
# Begin a transaction that ends with $dbh->commit() or $dbh->rollback()
$dbh->begin_work();

# Let's see if this username is already taken
$sql = "SELECT user_id ";
$sql .= "FROM Users ";
$sql .= "WHERE username = ?";
```

```
$sth = $dbh->prepare($sql);
$result = $sth->execute($username);

my ($user_name_taken) = $sth->fetchrow_array;
$sth->finish;
</%perl>

% if ($user_name_taken) {

<Head><Title>Username already taken</Title></Head>
<Body>
<H1>Username already taken </H1>

<P>Sorry, but the username <b><% $username %></b> has already been
taken by someone else. Please try to <a
href="register-form.html">register</a> with a different username.</P>

# Roll back this transaction
% $dbh->rollback();

% } else {

<%perl>
# Since this username is unique, we can
# store this user's information in the database

 $sql = "INSERT INTO Users ";
$sql .= " (username, password, password_hint, email)";
$sql .= " VALUES ";
$sql .= " (?, ?, ?, ?)";

$sth = $dbh->prepare($sql);
$result = $sth->execute($username, $password, $password_hint, $email_address);
$sth->finish;
</%perl>

% # ----------------------------------------------------------
% # Indicate whether the INSERT was successful
% # ----------------------------------------------------------

% if ($result) {
% my $new_row_oid = $insert_sth->{pg_oid_status};
% $session{user_id} = $user_id;

<Head><Title>Registration inserted</Title></Head>
<Body>
<H1>Registration inserted</H1>
```

```
<P>Your registration was successful.</P>

<P>Welcome, <b><% $username %></b>!</P>

% $dbh->commit();

% } else {

<Head><Title>Error registering</Title></Head>
<Body>
<H1>Error registering</H1>
<P>Sorry, but your registration was unsuccessful.</P>

% $dbh->rollback();

% } # Checking $result

% } # Checking $user_name_taken

% } # Ending top-level if/else

<%once>
my ($dbh, $sql, $sth, $result, $user_id);
</%once>

<%init>
$dbh = $m->comp("database-connect.comp");
</%init>

<%args>
$username => undef
$password => undef
$password_hint => undef
$email_address => undef
</%args>
```

18.4.3   *Logging in*

Once users have registered, we need to let them log in. The following component compares the **username** and **password** arguments with the database. If there is a match, then we put the user's ID in **%session**, where it will be available for the duration of the session.

```
<Head>

% if ($user_id) {
<Title>You have been logged in.</Title></Head>
```

```
<Body>
<H1>You have been logged in.</H1>

<P>Welcome back, <b><% $user_info->{username} %></b>!</P>
% } else {

<Title>Invalid login.</Title></Head>

<Body>
<H1>Invalid login.</H1>

<P>Either your password was wrong, or no such user exists.</P>

% }

<%once>
my ($dbh, $sql, $sth, $result, $user_id, $user_info);
</%once>

<%init>
$dbh = $m->comp("database-connect.comp");

 $sql = "SELECT user_id ";
$sql .= "FROM Users ";
$sql .= "WHERE username = ? ";
$sql .= "AND password = ? ";

$sth = $dbh->prepare($sql);
$result = $sth->execute($username, $password);

# Get the user ID
($user_id) = $sth->fetchrow_array;

# Set the user ID for this session
$session{user_id} = $user_id;

# Now get information about the user
$user_info = $m->comp("get-user-info.comp", user_id => $user_id);
</%init>

<%args>
$username
$password
</%args>
```

18.4.4 Logging out

Web sites that offer users the chance to log in should also offer them the chance to log out. We can do this quite easily, by removing the user_id key from %session:

```
<Head><Title>You have been logged out.</Title></Head>

<Body>
<H1>You have been logged out.</H1>

<P>That's it -- you're no longer logged in!</P>

<%init>
delete $session{user_id};
</%init>
```

18.5 Conclusion

In this chapter, we saw how useful it could be to incorporate a complete version of Perl inside of our Apache server. In particular, we saw:

- How to install and configure Mason,

- How to write components that return HTML and values,

- Component arguments,

- Different ways to insert Perl into a Mason template,

- The special autohandler and dhandler components,

- Connecting to databases from within Mason, and

- Managing user information and sessions.

BIBLIOGRAPHY AND RECOMMENDED READING

Topics in This Chapter

- Books

- Periodicals

- Web sites

Appendix A

The computer industry is growing rapidly, and Perl is growing along with it. Since I began to program in Perl, the number of books describing it and related technologies has grown by leaps and bounds.

This bibliography lists some of the resources I recommend you consult as you begin to program in Perl and related technologies.

A.1   Perl books

In this age of the World Wide Web, it might seem odd to recommend one or more printed books about Perl. But there are some excellent Perl books on the market, each of which has a slightly different focus.

A.1.1   *Programming Perl, 3rd edition*

This is the definitive guide to Perl, written by Perl's inventor Larry Wall and some of the best-known programmers and advocates: Tom Christiansen, Jon Orwant, and Randal L. Schwartz. *Programming Perl* is based on the free documentation that comes with the Perl distribution. It is a complete reference to the Perl language, including all of its functions, object-oriented programming constructs, and many command-line options. (O'Reilly and Associates, ISBN 1-596-00027-8)

A.1.2   *Advanced Perl Programming*

Advanced Perl Programming, written by Sriram Srinivasan, describes Perl's underlying implementation and goes into detail about complex issues. For example, it discusses typeglobs, ways in which to connect your Perl programs to C and C++ using XS, object-oriented programming, extending Perl, and creating user interfaces with Tk. Inexperienced Perl programmers might be confused by it. (O'Reilly and Associates, ISBN 1-56592-220-4)

A.1.3   *Effective Perl Programming*

Effective Perl Programming, written by Joseph N. Hall, concentrates instead on improving a programmer's appreciation for Perl. The book contains many short lessons on important topics related to object-oriented programming, exporting functions, writing new modules, and operators and variables that are often confused. All programmers will benefit greatly from this book. (Addison-Wesley, ISBN 0-201-41975-0)

A.1.4   *The Perl Cookbook*

This book, written by Tom Christiansen and Nathan Torkington, demonstrates nearly every major aspect of Perl, using programs and program fragments. If you are looking for large hunks of example code that can help you wrap your mind around some new ideas, this is a good book to turn to. (O'Reilly and Associates, ISBN 1-56592-243-3)

A.1.5   *Perl: The Programmer's Companion*

This book, written by Nigel Chapman, is similar to *Effective Perl Programming* in that it takes a long, deep look at the basics of Perl programming. It discusses many of the mistakes that beginning and intermediate programmers make. (John Wiley & Sons, ISBN 0-47197-563-X)

A.1.6   *Mastering Regular Expressions*

This book, by Jeffrey E. F. Friedl, takes a long and detailed look at regular expressions, including Perl's patterns. The treatment is very thorough and probably includes more than the casual programmer will ever need to know. (O'Reilly and Associates, ISBN 1-56592-257-3)

A.2 Periodicals

A.2.1 *The Perl Journal*

The Perl Journal, published quarterly as an independent magazine for several years, is now a quarterly supplement to *SysAdmin* magazine, published by CMP. *TPJ* articles discuss Perl techniques, modules, advances, and cross-platform issues. All serious Perl programmers should read *TPJ* on a regular basis. Back issues are available online at http://www.tpj.com/.

A.2.2 *Linux Journal*

Much Perl development is happening on Linux, so keeping up with the world of Perl often means keeping up with Linux. At least one article each month includes Perl code and updates, often including my columns about Web/database applications. Information about *Linux Journal*, as well as the text from back issues, are available at http://www.linuxjournal.com/.

A.3 World Wide Web

A.3.1 *Philip and Alex's Guide to Web Publishing*

Philip Greenspun's classic book about Web/database applications is a must-read for anyone working on Web sites. It is informative and funny, and gives many excellent pieces of advice regarding software development. You can also read it online at http://www.arsdigita.com/books/panda/. (Morgan Kaufmann Publishers, ISBN 1-55860-534-7)

A.3.2 *Writing Apache Modules with Perl and C*

This book, written by Lincoln Stein and Doug MacEachern, is indispensable for anyone writing Perl handlers or working with mod_perl. The book is full of examples and reference documentation. (O'Reilly, ISBN 1-56592-567-X)

A.3.3 *Apache: The Definitive Guide, 2nd edition*

This book is a comprehensive introduction to the Apache Web server, including all of its runtime directives. The authors, Ben Laurie and Peter Laurie, describe the server's architecture. They then offer complete descriptions of how to compile, install, and configure it for your needs. (O'Reilly and Associates, ISBN 1-56592-529-9)

A.4   Databases

A.4.1   *LAN Times Guide to SQL*

In this book, James R. Groff and Paul N. Weinberg describe the theory and practice of relational databases in a way that is broad enough to apply to most database servers, without ignoring all databases in favor of one particular brand. Numerous diagrams and examples make it easy to learn from this book. Database programmers of all levels can benefit from this book. (McGraw-Hill, ISBN 0-07-882026-X)

A.4.2   *SQL for Web Nerds*

Philip Greenspun, whose book about databases and the Web I recommended earlier, has produced an online book introducing SQL and relational databases. If you are looking to learn SQL, and particularly if you plan to use Oracle, strongly consider reading Greenspun's book on the Web. You can read it at http://www.arsdigita.com/books/sql/.

A.4.3   *SQL for Smarties*

Joe Celko's book reviews a large number of SQL functions with which programmers might not be familiar, as well as some tips and tricks for how to use them. He describes how to use SQL in many real-life programming assignments. If you are looking to stretch your knowledge of SQL, no other printed reference compares. (Morgan Kaufmann, ISBN 1-55860-323-9)

A.5   Useful Web sites

A.5.1   http://www.perl.com

Publisher O'Reilly and Associates runs this Web site, with frequent articles and updates about the Perl language.

A.5.2   http://www.perldoc.com

This site is an online collection of all Perl documentation, including documentation for most modules.

A.5.3   http://www.apache.org

This is the home page of the Apache Software Foundation, which sponsors development of the Apache HTTP server. All Apache source code, mailing lists, and documentation is available from this URL.

A.5.4   http://perl.apache.org

This is the home page for mod_perl described in Chapter 17.

A.5.5   http://dbi.symbolstone.org/

The DBI home page contains pointers to DBDs for many relational database products, as well as documentation and hints related to DBI.

A.5.6   http://www.postgresql.org

The PostgreSQL home page, with downloadable source and binaries, documentation, links to mailing lists and archives, and code samples for your own use.

INDEX